Edward J. Steptoe
and the Indian Wars

ALSO BY RON MCFARLAND
AND FROM THIS PUBLISHER

Appropriating Hemingway: Using Him as a Fictional Character (2015)

The Long Life of Evangeline: *A History of the Longfellow Poem in Print, in Adaptation and in Popular Culture* (2010)

The Rockies in First Person: A Critical Study of Recent American Memoirs from the Region (2008)

Edward J. Steptoe and the Indian Wars

Life on the Frontier, 1815–1865

RON McFARLAND

McFarland & Company, Inc., Publishers
Jefferson, North Carolina

LIBRARY OF CONGRESS CATALOGUING-IN-PUBLICATION DATA

Names: McFarland, Ronald E., author.
Title: Edward J. Steptoe and the Indian wars : life on the frontier, 1815–1865 / Ron McFarland.
Description: Jefferson, North Carolina : McFarland & Company, Inc., Publishers, 2016. | Includes bibliographical references and index.
Identifiers: LCCN 2016000089 | ISBN 9781476662329 (softcover : acid free paper) ∞
Subjects: LCSH: Steptoe, Edward Jenner, 1815–1865. | Soldiers—United States—Biography. | Pacific Coast Indians, Wars with, 1847–1865. | Mexican War, 1846–1848—Biography. | Seminole War, 2nd, 1835–1842. | United States. Army—Biography.
Classification: LCC E83.84 M34 2016 | DDC 973.5/7092—dc23
LC record available at http://lccn.loc.gov/2016000089

BRITISH LIBRARY CATALOGUING DATA ARE AVAILABLE

ISBN (print) 978-1-4766-6232-9
ISBN (ebook) 978-1-4766-2388-7

© 2016 Ron McFarland. All rights reserved

No part of this book may be reproduced or transmitted in any form or by any means, electronic or mechanical, including photocopying or recording, or by any information storage and retrieval system, without permission in writing from the publisher.

Front cover image of Edward J. Steptoe, painting on wooden board, ca. 1860, Edward R. Morgan & Co, Photograph Rooms (courtesy the Segar family of "Woodfarm," Middlesex County, Virginia)

Printed in the United States of America

McFarland & Company, Inc., Publishers
 Box 611, Jefferson, North Carolina 28640
 www.mcfarlandpub.com

For Georgia

And for my father
Earl A. McFarland (1914–2015)
Captain, U.S. Army Air Force, 1942–1945

Contents

Preface	1
ONE. Privileged Boyhood	7
TWO. At West Point	20
THREE. In Florida: The Second Seminole War	39
FOUR. In Mexico	64
FIVE. The Gunnison Affair	92
SIX. In the Washington Territory: Building Forts at Walla Walla	120
SEVEN. "Chapter of Accidents"	146
EIGHT. Last Years	179
Epilogue: Legacy	189
Chapter Notes	201
Bibliography	225
Index	235

Preface

THE LIFE AND MILITARY CAREER of Edward J. Steptoe (1815–1865) is intertwined with the antebellum history of the United States, the era of Manifest Destiny. He grew up near the western Virginia tobacco city of Lynchburg, graduated from West Point, was involved in the pursuit and capture of Seminole leader Coacoochee, was brevetted for gallantry under fire during the Mexican War, investigated the Gunnison Massacre in Utah and dealt with the powerful Mormon leader Brigham Young, built forts at Walla Walla in the newly defined Washington Territory. His battle with the Northern Plateau Indian tribes in 1858 constituted the high-water mark of his military service. Because of ill health, Steptoe resigned his commission in 1861 and with that the probability he would become a general during the Civil War.

In this book I have attempted to make a case for what was gained from some of Steptoe's un-successes, most notably in Utah and in his defeat at the Battle of To-hots-nim-me in the Washington Territory. In the process I've corrected some errors that have haunted his biography over the decades, including some fairly obvious ones: he was born in 1815, not 1816; his middle name was Jenner, not Jevnor. And I have investigated some issues pertaining to his controversial sojourn in Salt Lake City and to his defeat near present-day Rosalia, Washington.

What did Steptoe accomplish in the Utah Territory (1854–1855) and why did he decide not to accept the governorship of that territory offered by his friend and former comrade-in-arms, President Franklin Pierce? How "disastrous," really, was his defeat in the Washington Territory, especially considering the consequences thereof? Why did he risk moving into potentially hostile Palouse country in his march toward the Colville gold mines? To what extent was he responsible for the size of his command and its equipment? That is, was he somehow negligent? How *did* his heavily outnumbered command escape annihilation that mid–May afternoon and evening in 1858? Did his defeat in the Washington Territory destroy his health, leaving him, as some have suggested, a broken man?

Known to some family and friends as "Ned," Edward J. Steptoe was connected with a prominent family in western Virginia. His maternal grandfather was an esteemed veteran of the Revolutionary War and a prosperous farmer and businessman near the flourishing city of Lynchburg. His paternal grandfather, clerk of what was then a huge county, was a particular friend and classmate at William and Mary of Thomas Jefferson. His father served as personal physician to Jefferson when he resided in his nearby estate at Poplar Forest.

Edward's 1837 graduating class at West Point placed him in the company of such Civil War generals-to-be as fellow Virginian Jubal A. Early, Braxton Bragg, and Joseph Hooker. Ranking second in the class a year behind him, P.G.T. Beauregard would command Confederate forces that opened fire on Fort Sumter; Irvin McDowell from Ohio and William J. Hardee of Georgia also graduated in that class. Such coincidences whereby classmates became adversaries proved all too common between 1861 and 1865. Isaac Ingalls Stevens stood at the head of the class two years behind Cadet Steptoe and served as territorial governor of Washington during the years Colonel Steptoe was building forts at Walla Walla. As a young lieutenant serving in Florida during the Second Seminole War, Edward would meet an even younger lieutenant, William T. Sherman, and on the western frontier in 1856 then Brevet Lieutenant Colonel Steptoe would commend young Lieutenant Philip Sheridan for his part in the Battle of the Cascades.

When possible I have let Steptoe speak for himself by quoting from the personal letters archived at the University of Washington Library and elsewhere. This correspondence begins with a letter to his father concerning his visit to Washington, D.C., on the eve of his appointment to West Point in 1833, and ends with a letter to former president Pierce sent from Lynchburg and dated June 18, 1860. So far as I have been able to determine, these 38 letters are the only ones extant, but their contents indicate they represent only a fraction of the total number he composed, and I have found some degree of conjecture based upon their contents to be irresistible. He addressed most of them to his father, usually with salutations to his mother (actually his stepmother), and to his half-sister Nannie. Literate, but not literary, in nature, these letters reflect just enough of the character and personality of the writer to be intriguing but also a bit frustrating. One wishes he'd say more on life at West Point and about his classmates, on his pursuit of the Seminoles from Fort Pierce, on his engagements at Cerro Gordo and Chapultepec that won him brevet ranks in Mexico, on his first impressions of Brigham Young, on his interactions with Indians in the Washington Territory.

Preface

The correspondence reveals a modest, self-consciously low-key man, understated and not inclined to boast. Apparently he lacked the aggressive character that would mark the most successful military leaders, the Stonewall Jacksons and William T. Shermans. This may owe something to the fact that throughout his life he was plagued by ill health. He shows himself to have been solicitous of the welfare of the men serving under him, and he appears generally to have been a capable and respected if not a "spectacular" officer. He did not marry until 1860, while on what would now be called convalescent leave, and their one child, a daughter, died before she was three years old. Commentators during his day refer to him as notably religious (he was a lifelong Episcopalian), but perhaps no more so than most of that time. He died at age 49, a few days before Lee surrendered at Appomattox. Throughout his career, news writers attached to his name the epithet "gallant officer." From what I can tell, that seems appropriate.

Thanks to his communications with the Office of the Adjutant General, which I examined in the National Archives, we have a fairly extensive collection of official correspondence that dates from Steptoe's posting to Fort Payne in Alabama in September of 1838, where he was involved with Indian relocation, what history has called the "Trail of Tears," to his letter of resignation dated October 10, 1861, in which he indicates he has lost his power of speech and has only partially regained the use of his right side (the registered date of his resignation is November 1). The official documents include his after action report from the Battle of Pine Creek or To-hots-nim-me (also spelled Tohotonimme), as the engagement in eastern Washington is properly called, and his lengthy letter to President Pierce concerning the proffered governorship of the Utah Territory. These and other pertinent documents are available in the House and Senate documents, and are accessible in B.F. Manring's *The Conquest of the Coeur d'Alenes, Spokanes and Palouses* (1912).

Relying on extensive secondary sources, I have attempted to represent the full range of opinions on various controversial issues pertaining to the climactic battle, an excellent recent account of which is available in Mahlon E. Kriebel's ably researched monograph, *Battle of To-hots-nim-me* (2012), a revised edition of the piece as it appeared in *Bunchgrass Historian* 34:2&3, a periodical publication of the Whitman County Historical Society, in 2008.

What I wish I *knew*, for certain, about Edward J. Steptoe: Did he attend school at nearby New London Academy, where his grandfathers served on the board? School records were destroyed during the Civil War. Did he enjoy liaisons (*dangereuse* or otherwise), amours, high romance in Lynchburg, New York, St. Augustine, or Baltimore? Did he dally with señoritas in Veracruz or Mexico City, conduct clandestine intrigues with Mormon ladies in Salt

Lake City? Did he drink excessively as so many officers did at such distant outposts as Walla Walla? Was his "deranged liver," as I have speculated, some form of hepatitis, or was it connected with alcoholism? Did he in fact visit Europe, presumably to observe the Austro-Sardinian War, as the New York papers reported and as other evidence appears to corroborate? Was he able to enjoy much at all of his brief family life as husband and father? As he lay suffering from a stroke while the Battle of Lynchburg raged in June of 1864, did his old comrades-in-arms, Confederate generals Jubal Early and D.H. Hill, stop by to pay their respects?

* * *

My debts to others begin with Lieutenant Lawrence Kip (1836–1899) and B.F. Manring (1866–1946) and with such historians as Robert Ignatius Burns, S.J., Robert M. Utley, Waldo E. Rosebush, David Henry Miller, Robert Kent Fielding, Kurt R. Nelson, Mahlon Kriebel, and Greg Partch. I hope I've credited them appropriately in the following pages.

Two generous grants from the University of Idaho's history department, under the chairmanship of Professor Rick Spence, enabled me to visit the National Archives in Washington, D.C., Lynchburg and West Point, Fort Pierce, Florida, Salt Lake City and Fillmore, Utah, and Vancouver and Walla Walla, Washington. These grants were provided through the John Calhoun Smith Memorial Fund.

Growing up in Florida, I fought the Seminoles many times in my boyish imagination. When it came to the chapter concerning Steptoe's involvement in the Second Seminole War, I made a special trip to impose on my Florida relatives, notably my brother Tom and his wife George, who chauffeured me and my wife Georgia down to Fort Pierce. A retired academic librarian who worked for many years at the Florida Institute of Technology and who has sat on the editorial board of the Florida Historical Society, Tom has served me in other ways throughout my research and writing, not least of which has been the onerous office of initial reader of the manuscript.

My father, Earl A. McFarland, a proud centenarian, was also roped into early readings of this book, and to him I owe my fascination with history. In fact, it was with my father and brother in mind that I embarked on this project, which proved to be more challenging than I had imagined. After years of writing poems, stories, essays, and literary criticism, which my siblings and parents, including my late mother, Mary Maxine Stullenburger McFarland, always dutifully read, I thought I might write a book they would actually *enjoy*. I hope this is it.

I am profoundly grateful to my wife Georgia Tiffany Toppe, who has served as my research assistant and editorial overseer along the way, more than four years now, and whose close reading of the drafts has proved invaluable. We've seen a lot of the United States in the process of assembling this biography. At Jones Memorial Library in Lynchburg I was ably assisted by Chuck Bradner, among others, and for information on New London, Forest, and the Steptoe home, Melvin Lester and Randy Lichtenberger of the Friends of New London came to my rescue. Suzanne Christoff answered my questions and helped me gain access to the archives at the U.S. Military Academy at West Point. At Whitman College I was ably guided through the Fort Walla Walla Collection by Michael J. Paulus, Jr., and at the Fort Walla Walla Museum it was James Payne. When we visited Utah and the archives at the Latter Day Saints Church History Library in Salt Lake City, we imposed on my former University of Idaho colleague and Brigham Young University professor emeritus in English, Stephen Tanner, and his wife Madlyn, who treated us nobly. Here at the University of Idaho Library I was ably assisted by Theresa Dahmen and Jesse Thomas, master of interlibrary loans, and at neighboring Washington State University's Special Collections, Greg Matthews proved most helpful.

Among many others, I wish particularly to thank Anne Leyden and Robert Steptoe, both great-great grandchildren of Edward J. Steptoe's half-brother Thomas for their kind assistance. Thanks to Mrs. Leyden, I was able to contact Mrs. Hildie Bottom of Richmond, Virginia, who owns the only original painting of E.J. Steptoe as well as his artillery officer's sword. She has kindly provided me with images of both items. Our family friend Bill Rember, a paleontologist and long-time resident of the Palouse country, drove me along Steptoe's route from the Snake River toward his climactic battle, describing the geology and botany along the way. My wife's sister's husband, Colonel Robert Enquist, U.S. Army, retired, an internist at Joint Base Lewis-McChord in western Washington, helped me understand Steptoe's physical maladies, and his son Jeff provided some inside information on contemporary life at West Point. Through all of this, the chair of the English department here at the University of Idaho, J. Gary Williams, offered his support in every way for this project.

CHAPTER ONE

Privileged Boyhood

Place a dime on a highway map of Virginia between Lynchburg and the hamlet of Forest (formerly New London) to the southwest and you will have pretty much covered the world Edward Jenner Steptoe knew as a boy. That world would encompass not only Lynchburg and New London, but also his parents' home of Cedar Grove, his paternal grandfather's mansion Federal Hill, his maternal grandfather's plantation Ivy Cliff, and Thomas Jefferson's estate, Poplar Forest, which served after 1806 as his retreat from Monticello. The New London area grew up around crossroads, had been settled around 1750 and would serve as the seat of Bedford County for more than thirty years. At its height the town numbered around three hundred citizens, but by 1834 the population had dwindled to about a hundred: 25 homes, two mercantile stores, two inns with taverns (one of which still stands), two saddlers, and one each Methodist meeting house, blacksmith shop, wheelwright, tannery, and ropewalk (rope factory).[1] The New London Academy, founded in 1795, became the oldest continually operating secondary school in the state (it now operates as a public elementary school). Both Edward's paternal grandfather, James Steptoe, and his maternal grandfather, Captain Henry Brown, served on the Board of Trustees. But the moving of the county seat to Liberty (now Bedford) in 1782, about 14 miles to the west, and the evolution of the town of Lynchburg, about 11 miles to the northeast, after 1786, ended the town's dreams of prosperity.[2]

Edward's father, William, a respected physician with an office in New London, was the son of the renowned James or "Jemmy" Steptoe, who lived a half mile north at Federal Hill and served as county clerk, an office he held for more than fifty years until his death in 1826, when Edward was ten years old. James Steptoe had met Thomas Jefferson when both were students at William and Mary College, and as early as 1770, when he worked in the Secretary's Office at what was then the colonial capital in Williamsburg, he was employed as Jefferson's agent. Jefferson was at the time a 27-year-old member

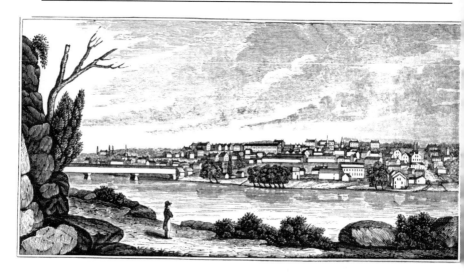

Panoramic view of Lynchburg, Virginia, in 1845 from Henry Howe's *Historical Collections of Virginia* (1852), facing page 212. The original caption reads, "The above shows Lynchburg as it appears from the northern banks of James River. On the left is shown the bridge across the river and in front of the town, which is finely situated on rising ground, in the midst of bold and romantic scenery."

of the Virginia House of Burgesses. A succinct note recorded in the first volume of *Jefferson's Memorandum Books* reads, "Pd. James Steptoe £15 as my agent."[3] By 1772 Steptoe had moved west to the frontier county of Bedford to serve as county clerk, where his duties as agent included acting as a middle man between George Rogers Clark, later famous for Revolutionary War success in the Illinois country, and Jefferson for the procurement of "big bones," elk antlers and fossils (the correspondence is dated November 26, 1782).[4]

"A courteous and kindly gentleman," begins a passage describing James Steptoe when his portrait was presented to the circuit court of Bedford County in 1953, "scrupulously neat in his attire, not large of stature but graceful and with a quick, firm step which he retained to his death." Perhaps his grandson Edward inherited something of that grace and courtesy. His letters imply as much, and the single extant portrait suggests he, too, was "not large of stature."[5] James is further described as a man whose "affection for the members of his family was unbounded. [...] His character was impeccable, and he was uncompromising in his ideas of rectitude." As it happens, we know considerably more about Edward's grandfather than we do about his father, the "eminent physician" who looked after Jefferson when he was in the vicinity and who was occasionally called upon to take care of his slaves.[6]

Ann Smart Martin offers a black-and-white illustration of the painting

One. Privileged Boyhood

of James Steptoe in her 2008 study of consumers in backcountry Virginia in the Early American Economy and Society series.[7] In a feature article that appeared in the *Bedford Bulletin* (February 6, 2008) local appraiser Elizabeth Gladwell notes that the chair in which Jemmy Steptoe is sitting, facing the viewer straight on, is still in existence and was made in the Monticello joinery.[8] The article in the Bedford newspaper appeared on the occasion of the restored portrait's return to the Bedford County Courthouse. Gladwell also indicates the painting was completed just before James Steptoe's death in 1826, so the image we might view would show Edward's socially prominent grandfather as he would have appeared to the boy at about age ten. Ann Smart Martin provides several interpretive comments: "The map intimates the sitter's worldliness; the portrait of Jefferson alludes to his ties to the well-known statesman. Steptoe's pen is at the ready, and a book—not an account book, he is no mere merchant—is in his hand."[9] The Bedford County clerk, more than fifty years into this important office of public trust, wears a light-colored frock coat, unbuttoned to reveal a dark vest and white shirt and cravat. Steptoe's face is long, his nose rather prominent, chin firm, lips pursed, eyes focused straight ahead. His glasses are propped on his broad forehead. It is the image of a serious, although not necessarily severe, no-nonsense gentleman in his mid-fifties.

James Steptoe may have been an "intimate friend" of Jefferson, as local historians have suggested, or merely a good neighbor during Jefferson's visits to Poplar Forest and a quondam business agent. "Mr. Steptoe was beloved by everyone, and especially so by his slaves," the family historian asserts, because he taught them "different trades that they might support themselves after his death when by his will, they were all set free." Coincidentally, James died in 1826, the same year as Jefferson, and his son James Callaway Steptoe (1781–1827) succeeded him, briefly, as Clerk of the Court of Bedford County. James Steptoe left four daughters and four additional sons, including twins William (1785–1862), Edward's father, and George (1785–1858), whose son John also became court clerk for Bedford County. If the Steptoe family was noted for producing county clerks, it was perhaps equally so for producing physicians, as two of William's four sons, John and Patrick, became doctors, as did one of George's 11 children, and William's daughter Nannie married a doctor. Edward's great-grandfather, Colonel James Steptoe (ca. 1710–1778) of Hominy Hall (also spelled "Nominy" and "Homany") in Westmoreland County, Virginia, was also a physician.[10]

Edward Jenner Steptoe, the only child of Dr. William Steptoe's first marriage, to Ann "Nancy" Brown (1795–1817), was born on November 7, 1815, and was almost certainly named after British physician and scientist Edward Jenner who created the vaccination against smallpox in 1796 and was still living at the time (he died in 1823).[11] Dr. Steptoe received his medical degree from the University of Pennsylvania in 1807, having submitted a thesis "On animal sympathy,"[12] or animal consciousness, as we might phrase it today. If the naming of their son signaled some hope he might follow the medical profession, his father would be disappointed, and there is some evidence in the correspondence he might have had such hopes. Edward's boyhood home, now privately owned, is located between the town of New London and the Academy. Built as a wedding gift from Captain Henry Brown for his daughter, Cedar Grove was modeled after James Steptoe's Federal Hill.[13] An early photograph shows a solid two-story structure featuring an ample porch and carriage port. A simple pediment surmounts the front entrance.[14] Edward's mother died on April 5, 1817, before he turned two. His father married Mary Dillon (ca. 1797–185?) in 1822, when Edward was seven. They were to have seven children, three sons and four daughters, one of whom (Mary Catherine) died young, so Edward would grow up in a fairly large family, typical of his time, and he would be the oldest child by several years. In his correspondence Edward refers to his stepmother as "Ma," and he clearly regards his half-siblings as actual brothers and sisters. His letters reveal him as a responsible, conscientious big brother, and he mentions various relatives, at least in passing, including his cousin Edward Dillon Steptoe (1811–1854), his Uncle James Callaway (or Calloway) Steptoe's son.

Edward's maternal grandfather, Captain Henry Brown (1760–1841), maintained the large plantation (some 3,400 acres) of Ivy Cliff (or Hill) just a few miles from New London. Serving under General Nathaniel Greene, Brown was wounded at the Battle of Guilford Courthouse on March 15, 1781; he was made captain some years after the Revolutionary War. The single extant letter from Edward to his grandfather, sent from West Point in April of 1834, suggests they were fairly close, and his references to Uncle Sam and Uncle John in various letters apparently concern his mother's brothers, Samuel Thompson Brown (1810–1856) and John Thompson Brown (1802–1836), who graduated from Princeton, read law, and was elected to the Virginia House of Delegates, where he spoke out on slavery and states' rights issues. It was through his Uncle John that Edward would acquire his appointment to West Point.[15] At Ivy Cliff the prosperous Captain Brown raised the signature crop of that part of Virginia, the crop that made Lynchburg a commercial hub—tobacco. And axiomatically, at that time, tobacco depended on the "peculiar institution" of slavery. Uncle John's third and last son, John Thompson Brown II (1835–1864), born while Edward Steptoe was a cadet at West Point, was serving as a colonel in the 1st Virginia Artillery when a sharpshooter killed him at the Battle of the Wilderness.

But all of that lay years ahead. The world in which Edward Jenner Steptoe grew up must have been rather comfortable, although a letter from his father to Edward's half-brother William dated February 22, 1850, indicates some concern over debt: "Interest on money is a very serious thing, William & without a profession I could not have stood it as well as I did."[16] Moreover, although Dr. Steptoe warns his son in that letter never to "share or buy Negroes," only two years earlier, according to a document dated December 7, 1848, the doctor made a Deed of Trust to his son Edward, then serving in Mexico, offering four slaves (Isaac, Nancy, Lucy, and Leah) as collateral on a debt of a thousand dollars owed to him.[17] In his letter to William, Doctor Steptoe also praises Henry Clay's recently speech in the Senate, suggesting it was worth "a thousand such resolves [state sovereignty]" of the sort made in the Nashville Convention in June of that year when it came to settling "the difficulty with the North."

Most likely young Edward had the opportunity, through his Grandfather James, to meet Thomas Jefferson at Poplar Forest, where the former president had built what was probably the first octagonal home in America and cultivated at least 14 species of trees.[18] A letter he sent to his father just before confirmation of his appointment to the Academy depicts 17-year-old Edward very much at ease in the District of Columbia among the movers and shakers of the moment: President Andrew Jackson and the great triumvirate of senators, Webster, Clay, and Calhoun. Apparently, he met both President Jackson and Senator Calhoun on that occasion. Edward's family lived within a mile of his grandfather's manor Federal Hill in the rolling hills and amid the hardwood trees that today still provide a scenic landscape, between Lynchburg and Bedford. A dozen or so miles away as the crow flies, the Blue Ridge Mountains, "a scenery which has been universally admired for its beauty and boldness," rise up over the Big Otter River watershed.[19]

The old Bedford Alum Springs Tavern, now a private residence, built before the Revolutionary War, is one of the few certifiably original buildings still standing from former New London (Forest). The tavern where Thomas Jefferson and Patrick Henry once imbibed stood on the old stagecoach road across from the Bedford County courthouse that later burned down. Henry argued a precedent-setting case there to the effect that a purchaser would have at least three days after the sale of the merchandise to regain his cost should that merchandise prove defective, the merchandise in this case being a mule. In a 1781 case involving Johnny Hook, "a Scotchman, a man of wealth, and suspected of being unfriendly to the American cause," and a commissary of the Continental army, Patrick Henry is said to have argued so vehemently at the New London courthouse that "the whole audience were convulsed," and James Steptoe, the clerk of the court, "unable to command himself, and unwilling to commit any breach of decorum in his place, rushed out of the court-house, and threw himself on the grass, in the most violent paroxysm of laughter, where he was rolling, when Hook, with very different feelings, came out for relief into the yard also. 'Jemmy Steptoe,' he said to the clerk 'what the devil ails ye, mon?' Mr. Steptoe was only able to say, that *he could not help it.*"[20]

Jefferson's octagonal home, Poplar Forest, is located within five miles of New London. He acquired the estate of some 4,800 acres from his father-in-law John Wayles in 1773. Jefferson first arrived there in 1781, escaping a British raid near Charlottesville and Monticello, but work on the estate had started as early as 1768. He found there a double plantation with 16 slaves working on each one, raising mostly wheat and tobacco. In the midst of his second term as president Jefferson directed much of the building of Poplar Forest through detailed letters. The foundation was laid in 1806, the same year Lewis and Clark journeyed back from their expedition to the Northwest, but he did not stay there for the first time until 1809. Eventually the plantation housed seven families, numbering between sixty and a hundred people.

Captain Brown's Ivy Cliff, a few miles south along the New London Road, is no doubt considerably altered from its appearance when he began building it in 1790. The property includes an unusual two-story log slave cabin about a hundred yards down the hill.[21] Because it is somewhat farther away from a major highway, Ivy Cliff offers a greater sense of what life might have been like in that area during Edward Steptoe's day. Some architectural historians believe Thomas Jefferson designed the triple hung windows.

The nature of Steptoe's boyhood invites more speculation than certainty, but it would not likely have included farm work or other drudgery, inasmuch as his father, like both of his grandparents and other relatives, kept slaves for such tasks. If he was like most boys, he probably played at marbles, indulged in an occasional ballgame of one sort or another.[22] He most likely enjoyed exploring the area, hiking, messing around, as kids today might say, and later he would ride horseback, hunt, and fish. Nearby Big Otter River remains a good fly-fishing stream, and he would possibly have tried some of the creeks that feed into it as well. Letters he sent home from Fort Walla Walla in the Washington Territory decades later attest to his enthusiasm for hunting and fishing. A fellow officer who served with him in Florida during the Second Seminole War mentions riding with the young lieutenant and a lady friend. Again, if he was like most boys, Edward would have played at war, defending his home against marauding Indians and perhaps refighting the Battle of New Orleans, which happened the year he was born. Or maybe he was bookish. Maybe he favored a certain beech or walnut where he could climb just high enough to make his stepmother nervous and then lean back and dream and listen to the song of the cardinal or the mockingbird.

One. Privileged Boyhood

In the biographical sketch appended to his account of Colonel Steptoe's battle with the "Northern Indians" in 1858, B[enjamin] F[ranklin] Manring offers only the hasty, stereotypical observation that Edward's boyhood "was no more eventful than that of other Virginia boys who learned the precepts of Christian religion and good citizenship in homes where such things were revered and taught."[23] Perhaps he is correct in this brief summation, as far as it goes. Certainly Edward's letters substantiate Manring's premise as to his religious interests, and his choice of a career in the military indicates his "good citizenship," but his boyhood and coming to manhood invite further investigation and speculation.

A note from Thomas Jefferson to Dr. Steptoe archived in the Jones Memorial Library in Lynchburg and dated September 18, 1815, indicates a pair of visitors, the Abbé Joseph Correa de Serra (1750–1823), a Portuguese philosopher, diplomat, and botanist, and Francis Walker Gilmer (1790–1826), a lawyer and botanist, intended to spend a few days "in Botanising the circumjacent country." "Will you do us the favor to come and breakfast with us tomorrow," Jefferson requested, "as they will set out on their peregrinations after an early breakfast. On Sunday we all depart for the peaks of Otter & Natural bridge."[24] The three Peaks of Otter in the Blue Ridge Mountains overlook the city of Bedford (then called Liberty) and Natural Bridge, then regarded as one of the nation's most significant natural wonders, is located about 35 miles northwest of Lynchburg. Jefferson purchased land including Natural Bridge in 1774 and built a log cabin and guest house there.[25]

James Monroe promulgated what would become the Monroe Doctrine in an address to Congress on December 2, 1823, when Edward was eight years old. He would not likely have been told of it, and if he had been, it probably would not have registered, but it would touch his life significantly a couple of decades later when war with Mexico loomed. Independence movements against Spain erupted in Latin America between 1810 and 1825, and after 1821 the newly independent Mexico struggled to maintain control over its vast territory, what had once been known as the Viceroyalty of New Spain. The area encompassed nearly all of the Trans-Mississippi West, minus the lands obtained by the Louisiana Purchase in 1803 and what would later be known as the Oregon Territory.

In addition to his young siblings, Edward would have ready access to a good number of nearby cousins closer to his own age. His Uncle George served as a magistrate in Lynchburg, the nearest city of consequence, numbering more than five thousand, and his son George was the same age as Edward. Although New London and Lynchburg were both founded the same year, 1757, the latter had outstripped the former by the time Edward was a boy, and a visit to the city would mean a visit to Lynchburg, the "city set on seven hills" overlooking the James River.[26] In 1845 Henry Howe described Lynchburg as "finely situated on rising ground, in the midst of bold and romantic scenery."[27] The busy city that had evolved from John Lynch's ferry landing in the late 1750s had exchanged its Quaker roots for more conventional Methodist, Presbyterian, Baptist, and Episcopalian denominations by the 1820s. Edward's family remained mostly staunch Episcopalians, according to Stella Hardy Pickett's *Colonial Families of the Southern States of America* (1911).[28] Although Edward Steptoe is buried in the Presbyterian Cemetery in Lynchburg, neither he nor his wife appears to have been members of that congregation.

John Lynch's brother, Colonel Charles Lynch, a quondam Quaker, had set up what was known as "Lynch's Law" in 1780, a series of impromptu judgments against Tories in the area that led to whippings (but apparently not lynching, although those actions gave rise to that word in the language).[29] In 1786 a township was established, by 1798 Lynchburg had its first newspaper, and by January of 1813 the town had acquired its first courthouse. In 1817 Thomas Jefferson called it "the most interesting spot in the state." Noted for the lottery, horse racing and other forms of gambling, evangelist Lorenzo Dow dubbed the town "The Seat of Satan's Kingdom" in 1804. Nevertheless, it boasted at least half a dozen churches by 1830.[30] Based on its tobacco industry (thirty factories were located there by 1850), Lynchburg achieved city status in 1852 and by 1855 was known as the "second wealthiest city per capita in the United States, surpassed only by New Bedford, Massachusetts."[31]

Quintessentially a tobacco city, the Lynchburg of Edward's boyhood featured a vibrant downtown and a rough-and-tumble waterfront where the tobacco warehouses were located, but during the 1820s and 1830s it was not renowned as a hub of education. "Until the 1870s," Clifton and Dorothy Potter note, "education, even the barest rudiments, was the privilege of those who could afford it."[32] The town "has no incorporated [public] seminary of learning," Joseph Martin lamented in 1835. "The business of education is left entirely to individual enterprise [tutors or private schools]."[33] Consider this item from a Lynchburg newspaper, *The Virginian*, dated December 21, 1826: "EDUCATION.—ROBERT S. SHELTON intends opening a School in the Brick Office, nearly spossite [sic] the Presbyterian Church, and respectfully solicits a share of the public patronage. He will teach Orthography, Reading, Writing, Arithmetic, Geography, and English Grammar, for $12; the Latin language and Mathematics, for $15 per session [school term]. Satisfactory testimonials of competency and conduct can be exhibited."[34] Such items appeared frequently in the newspapers of that era, essentially offering the services of itinerant teachers or tutors. At some point Dr. William Steptoe might well have obtained the services of such a pedagogue for his children.

One. Privileged Boyhood

New London might boast of its Academy; Lynchburg would draw attention to its tobacco factories, retail businesses, banks, and newspapers, which dated back to the *Union Gazette* of 1793. By 1830, when Edward turned fifteen, the city could boast 41 grocery stores, 18 dry-goods stores, six tailor shops, five millenary shops, three apothecaries, three shoe stores, three confectionary shops, two semi-weekly newspapers, and two book shops, among numerous other establishments.[35] If he were to have visited his cousin George in Lynchburg around 1827, at age 11, Edward and his father may have taken the stagecoach. The 11- or 12-mile trip would likely have taken just a couple of hours. Young Steptoe may or may not have known about the chartering of the first railroad in the U.S. intended to carry passengers, the Baltimore & Ohio in 1827. Apparently Edward was not an avid reader, but he might have encountered James Fenimore Cooper's *The Prairie*, which appeared that year, following the great popular success of *The Last of the Mohicans*, published the year before. Cooper's Leatherstocking Tales would contribute significantly to romanticized and idealized literary portraits of American Indians. Eventually Edward's life would be intimately connected with the lives and destinies of real, non-literary Native Americans.

In April with the dogwoods in bloom young Edward and his father might have strolled along the busy waterfront where he could watch the narrow, flat-bottomed bateaux load up with hogsheads of tobacco, and then make their way up the steep hill toward the courthouse at the top of Water Street. "The river in front of town is about 200 yards wide, and flows to the S.E., giving the same direction to the principal streets. The navigation is difficult," wrote Joseph Martin in *A New and Comprehensive Gazetteer of Virginia* (1835), "the river being obstructed by shoals, rocks, and rapids, throughout a considerable part of its course above tide-water, and admitting only the use of batteaux [sic] carrying about 5 tons. Their form is peculiar and excellent."[36] The ten streets which then comprised the town ran parallel to the river with Second Street, the major thoroughfare, occupying "a bench on the river bank, at an elevation of about 125 feet; while 4th st. is nearly 100 feet higher"; Water Street runs uphill through the middle and during the 1820s and 1830s was "too precipitous for carriages of any kind."[37]

Edward and his father might have dined at the Franklin Hotel on Second Street before calling on Uncle George, and afterward his father would perhaps point out the finest home in town, Dr. George Cabell's mansion named "Point of Honor."[38] Duels were said to have been fought on the expansive lawn some years earlier.

At his uncle's house Edward could perhaps scan a copy of a Lynchburg newspaper, *The Virginian*. Published twice a week, it ran just four pages, six columns per page, in very small font, the left two columns dominated by ads of the sort that might have interested his father: Thomas J. Duval's pharmacy at the "Sign of the Golden Mortar" on Main Street, where "Dr. Rush's Anti-Dyspeptic or Sour Stomach Pills" were the featured item.[39] *The Virginian* mostly dealt with news of national or international interest, including such items as General Jackson's candidacy for the presidency and how Lynchburg favored him over the incumbent, John Quincy Adams.

In nearly every issue of *The Virginian* published during his boyhood, Edward would have had the opportunity to read such items as this: "NOTICE.—Runaway from the subscriber about the middle of last month (Feb.) my negro man Anderson, he is about 23 or 24 years old, something under six feet high, stout made and strong, tolerably handsome featured, has rather a down look. It is presumable he will endeavor to make off, as he has procured a spade, and crossed Dan river at Maj. Irvin's Ferry, in the name of one of William Bird's laborers who is a coloured man and well known ditcher. I will give ten dollars rewards for his delivery to me at my residence in Halifax county, Va. South of Dan river at or near Claybourne's Ferry, formerly Chappell's. WILEY JAMES."[40] Edward may have reflected on the economics implicit in the following ad: "FORTY DOLLARS REWARD.—Stolen from the stable of the subscriber living on the Forest Road, five miles from Lynchburg, on Wednesday night last, a large sorrel horse, four years old come spring, about 6 feet 2 inches high, and lengthy in the body, carries a lofty head, and paces very well[...]. I will give the above reward for the apprehension of the thief and horse, or ten dollars for any information of the horse, so that I get him again. BEVERLY R. SCOTT."[41]

More likely, however, the 11-year-old boy would have been drawn to the following announcement, which reads in part:

THEATRE.
For Charitable Purposes.
On Wednesday Evening, 4th inst.
The Lynchburg Dramatic Society will perform
The Grand Tragic Play of
PIZARRO:
Or; The Death of Rolla.

This would refer to British dramatist Richard Brinsley Sheridan's 1800 adaptation of German playwright August von Kotzebue's *Die Spanier in Peru*. The five-act tragedy was to be followed by a "burlesque tragic opera" or farce by British playwright William Barnes Rhodes entitled *Bombastes Furioso* (1810). Between the tragedy and the farce, the players would entertain the audience with a couple of songs and the "GRAND MARCH of General Lafayette, gotten up expressly for this night." Tickets for one dollar, box or pit, or fifty cents for gallery seats could be obtained at either of Lynchburg's two bookstores or at the offices of *The Virginian*. Such were the attractions of the city for Edward Steptoe when he was coming of age.

Whether he visited Lynchburg eagerly and often, we can only surmise, but the city was home to a good number of physicians with whom his father might wish to consult, and he might have had some patients there as well as in New London, where he kept his office.[42] Apparently Lynchburg had no hospital until the 1840s, when the "Pest House" or "House of Pestilence" was put into use for those to be quarantined with such contagious diseases as small pox and cholera. The white frame structure is now located in the Old City Cemetery and serves as the city's medical museum. During the Civil War, when several tobacco warehouses and buildings of Lynchburg College accommodated the wounded, the city served as an important medical center for the Confederacy.

In 1830, the year Edward turned 15, Joseph Smith, Jr., founded the Latter Day Saint movement in upstate New York, a historical event that would have an important impact on his life in coming years. By the time Edward was serving in the Second Seminole War in Florida, the Mormons would be establishing themselves in Nauvoo, Illinois, and in 1847 Brigham Young would lead them into what would become the Utah Territory. Edward would likely have been aware of a momentous event that occurred in 1831—the slave revolt known as Nat Turner's Rebellion in eastern Virginia. More than fifty white men, women and children were killed, and by the time it was put down, as many as two hundred African Americans, both slave and free, were also killed.[43] Nat Turner's trial and conviction on November 5 nearly coincided with Edward's sixteenth birthday just two days later (Turner was executed on the 11th of November).

Exactly when Edward Steptoe left Bedford County, both New London and Lynchburg, is difficult to determine. In his biographical essay B.F. Manring indicates he "graduated from Chapel Hill university, North Carolina" at age 17 and proceeded "immediately thereafter" to the U.S. Military Academy at West Point in June of 1833.[44] He did not graduate from what was to become the University of North Carolina, however, as alumni records at the school indicate he enrolled for just a single academic year (1832–1833). The University of North Carolina received its first students on January 15, 1795, and is regarded as the first state-supported public university in the nation.[45] Steptoe is listed in the "Catalog of the Philanthropic Society," one of the two debating societies, at Chapel Hill along with 17 other students in 1832, but as a "Non-Graduate."[46] Curiously, his hometown is listed as Liberty, Virginia (now Bedford), about 14 miles west of New London, but letters he sent to his father, beginning with those mailed from West Point in 1833, are addressed to him in New London. Most likely Edward's year at Chapel Hill served as a prep school for him prior to his entering West Point.

According to William S. Powell, the natural sciences "were given equal place" in the curriculum at Chapel Hill along with traditional studies in the Classics during the 1820s, and in 1832 the university acquired its first observatory. Edward would join a small body of students, just 107 in 1831, less than half the size of the Corps of Cadets at West Point in the fall of 1833.[47] The freshman class at Chapel Hill in the fall 1833 numbered just 28 students; the freshman class at the Military Academy that year numbered 85, about three times as large. Erika Lindermann observes some considered the university "too Presbyterian."[48] Steptoe would have been required to prove himself in Latin and Greek prior to admittance, unless, as apparently was the case, he enrolled among the seven or eight "irregular students," who did not plan to seek a degree. His first year of studies would have included additional work in those languages, arithmetic, algebra, and geometry, English grammar and composition, and declamation. As at West Point and other universities, classes revolved around recitation.

The faculty at the time numbered just five professors and a couple of tutors. In 1833 tuition cost $15 per session with room and board running about $120 per year. All of Steptoe's classmates would have hailed from southern states, about ninety per cent of them from North Carolina, a very different composition from what he would find at West Point. He most likely did not attend the 1832 commencement in which trustee and North Carolina Supreme Court justice, William Gaston (1778–1844), delivered a "memorable" address to the cheers of the student body in which he "advocated the ultimate abolition of slavery."[49]

In a letter to his half-sister Nannie sent from Fort Walla Walla in the Washington Territory and dated August 20, 1858, nearly three months after his defeat at the hands of Northern Plateau tribes, Edward claims his religion "has always been too much of a spasm," and he blames "a wayward, faulty youth."[50] He does not elaborate here or elsewhere, but with the exception of an episode during his senior year at West Point, no other occasion for such waywardness appears to have offered itself other than his brief stay at Chapel Hill. Maybe the 16-year-old on his first prolonged stay away from home indulged in drinking and gambling, in wine and women. In his letter penned 26 years later, however, Brevet Lieutenant Colonel Steptoe, his command having escaped annihilation at the hands of a vastly superior force, commends his sister's decision to embrace the Christian faith. Nothing would give him greater pleasure, he writes, than to see her become "a bright, & *even brighter* example of Christian life."

Edward would have returned to New London during the month-long

Christmas break, and he apparently visited Washington, D.C., during the second session of the 22nd Congress (December 3, 1832–March 3, 1833) to learn of his admission into the fourth-year (freshman) class at West Point starting with the summer encampment, which began in June. The first of his extant letters sent from the Academy to his father in New London is dated August 30, 1833, by which time the encampment had ended. He would return to western Virginia for a couple of months after his graduation in 1837 before being deployed to Florida during the Second Seminole War. After his 21 years of active service, which included a distinguished record during the Mexican War and important action during the Indian wars in the Washington Territory, Steptoe returned to Lynchburg, where he married in 1860. The vicinity of New London and Lynchburg would be his home town until his death on April 1, 1865, 11 days before General Robert E. Lee's surrender at Appomattox Court House, about 26 miles to the east.

Chapter Two

At West Point

Whenhe crossed the slow-moving Potomac probably in mid–January 1833, 17-year-old Edward Steptoe would have found Washington swarming in the few weeks before Andrew Jackson's second inauguration (March 4, 1833): "It is vain to seek a separate room at the hotels, or a seat in the senate chamber after 10 o'clock," he wrote his father in New London, Virginia. Young Steptoe was visiting the capital to inquire into the progress of his bid for admission into West Point, as may be inferred from that undated letter.[1] His Uncle John Thompson Brown would procure the appointment for him. Steptoe's crowded Washington, however, would not have resembled ours. Only about thirty thousand then lived in the federal district. South of the capital, the city of Alexandria, Virginia, totaled about eight thousand inhabitants.

Up the broad mall stood the magnificent new Capitol, not even twenty years old then, having been rebuilt right after the British burned it in 1814, a catastrophe his father and uncles would likely have told him about. Much of the flourishing, bustling city was under construction. Pennsylvania Avenue: The North Portico of the White House had been added just four years earlier, and down the street stood a magnificent hotel, the best in Washington, the splendid Indian Queen, or Jess Brown's Indian Queen, built in 1820 and the haunt of the most powerful and influential men in the country.[2] To picture E.J. Steptoe's Washington in February of 1833 we would need to subtract the familiar monuments and memorials, along with the Smithsonian Institution. Andrew Jackson became the first U.S. president to ride a railroad train on June 6 of that year, taking a 12-mile ride on the B&O near Baltimore, but Steptoe most likely did not see his first locomotive on this visit.

In this January or February letter to his father, written during the second session of the 22nd Congress (December 3, 1832–March 3, 1833), Edward reflects on his stay in Washington, where he met with Representative Nathaniel H. Claiborne of Virginia and in his company was "most graciously received" by President Andrew Jackson, who was about to begin his second term in office, having soundly defeated Senator Henry Clay of Kentucky. Jackson would face a divided legislature, the House majority being Jacksonian and the Senate majority being Anti-Jacksonian. Clay had worked out an important compromise to resolve the Nullification Crisis in 1832 over the controversial Tariff of Abominations introduced under President John Quincy Adams in 1828 and the Tariff of 1832, which was seen in the South as an insufficient remedy. At issue was whether a state (namely, Senator John C. Calhoun's South Carolina) had the right to "nullify" or reject a law passed by Congress. But the stakes ran high during the 1830s—in a word, slavery. South Carolina was already flirting with secession, but Steptoe reports President Jackson saying that South Carolina "cannot & shall not secede, if he can prevent it."

The current congressional session was not the first to have begun with talk of the abolition of slavery and of states' rights, and the two topics often led to talk of secession. "I have seen the great men of the day," Edward writes. He planned to attend a session of the Senate the next day, where he hoped to hear the great triumvirate of Daniel Webster, "a low, thick, chunky man," as Steptoe describes him, with "a dark, keen eye," the senior senator from Massachusetts; Henry Clay ("Mr. Clay you have seen," Steptoe notes in passing), and Calhoun himself.

In 1830 Webster, the Yankee Whig, had uttered the words that would forever be associated with his name: "Liberty and union, now and forever, one and inseparable!" Famous for his Missouri Compromise of 1820, that entered Maine into the Union as a free and Missouri as a slave state, Clay had lost his bid for the presidency partly over his support of the national bank, an issue that would come to the fore again following the Panic of 1837, the year Edward graduated from West Point. The greatest of Clay's efforts lay nearly twenty years ahead: the Compromise of 1850, which would temporarily stave off the Civil War.

But it was Calhoun, the senator at whom Webster's famous words were aimed, that Steptoe most admired, and he offers his father a description: He is "a straight small man & very gracefull [sic]—has a calm, dignified, resolute look—but of all the eyes you ever saw in the heads of men, I reckon you never looked on such as his—its glance is quick but irresistible." "I am told," Edward continued, that Calhoun "receives daily letters informing him that the hemp is growing or twisting for his halter." Most likely the noose being prepared for Calhoun would have been connected with the Force Bill, the "Bloody Bill" as some Southerners called it, which would empower the president to use force to collect federal tariffs. While the Compromise Tariff constituted the olive branch or carrot, easing up on tariff rates for the Southern states, the Force Bill amounted to the sword or stick.[3] In his letter Steptoe mentions how Senator George M. Bibb of Kentucky "held the floor for several days" to denounce the bill (apparently two days[4]). "I wish you could have seen him [Calhoun] the other day when Wilkins was on the floor," Steptoe continues, referring to Senator William Wilkins of Pennsylvania, who had introduced the Force Bill on January 22, 1833: "For three hours he [Calhoun] did not move a muscle & no change could be seen only now & then he was a little pale." Contemporary accounts describe Calhoun as "careworn" and "haggard."[5]

Which meetings of the Senate Steptoe attended is impossible to tell from his letter, but after offering his father a few "imperfect caricatures" of two other senators, he says he has "promised to wait on Mr. Calhoun today—at his request." Steptoe also mentions having "seen the secretary," presumably Secretary of War Lewis Cass, but "he told me no information could be given me till the regular time arrived for selections." He indicates his plans to return home in another couple of weeks. How much Steptoe understood of the political turmoil he witnessed may only be conjectured, but he appears to have been observant and very much engaged with the personalities and issues of the age, as subsequent letters demonstrate.

* * *

The acknowledged "father" of the United States Military Academy, Sylvanus Thayer, shaped the school as its superintendent between 1817 and July 1, 1833, but he was departing as Cadet Steptoe arrived in June. A friend of former Secretary of War Calhoun, long-time adversary of President Jackson, Thayer had submitted his formal letter of resignation on January 19 of that year, around the time Steptoe arrived in Washington to find out whether he had been selected. The Academy's first class had started in the spring of 1802. Historians consider it ironic that Thomas Jefferson, who had opposed the concept of a military academy when he served as Secretary of State, would as president "smuggle his national scientific school into the nation under the guise of a military academy."[6] Until Thayer took over, the college had been very much a work-in-progress. He saw to it that West Point became a full four-year institution, initiating a general system of examinations for all cadets and establishing strict discipline, which had gone lax under the previous indulgent administration.[7] Thayer served creditably during the War of 1812, then returned to France to study fortifications and military schools and to acquire up-to-date textbooks, maps, and equipment.

The Academy would provide a curriculum in civil engineering; unlike other American colleges of the day, it would evolve into a school of empiricists and pragmatists. In the essay "Literature and Science," originally delivered as a lecture in his tour of the United States in 1883, British poet and intellectual

Matthew Arnold wrote, "for the majority of mankind a little of mathematics, even, goes a long way."[8] This sentiment decidedly did not prevail at West Point, but then the cadets decidedly did not represent "the majority of mankind." All other subjects at the academy were subordinated to or dependent upon the discipline of mathematics, while virtually every other university in the young nation cleaved to the tradition of a curriculum firmly grounded in the Classics: Latin and Greek.

The corps of cadets during Steptoe's four years typically numbered no more than 250, so a certain degree of camaraderie among the cadets might be predictable, despite (or perhaps because of) Thayer's inclination to embrace the role of stern disciplinarian. Stephen Ambrose and others agree that another of Thayer's important contributions was the "merit roll," which rated each cadet's standing within his class, the top cadets being destined for service in the Corps of Engineers.[9] He also attempted to end the harassment of new cadets known as hazing. Above all else, Ambrose notes, Thayer was "scrupulously fair."[10] In any event, if the young cadet from Virginia would have viewed Colonel Thayer only briefly, for Major René DeRussy had assumed the position of commandant and superintendent by the time the summer encampment ended.

Thomas J. Fleming describes the new superintendent, Major DeRussy, who had distinguished himself in the War of 1812 at the Battle of Plattsburg (New York), as an "urbane man of polished manners." DeRussy "attempted to remove the aura of aloof dignity" that stamped Thayer's years, and one feature of the new and more sociable atmosphere was the ball held at the end of the summer encampment.[11] At the end of his first extant letter home from West Point, dated August 30, 1833, fourth classman Steptoe mentions being distracted by "a great noise in the hall occasioned by a *great* dance of the cadets—I think you would be amused at the preparations & decorations for a military Ball."[12] While DeRussy commanded at West Point throughout Steptoe's undergraduate years, his efforts at leniency failed, in part, Fleming indicates, because he lacked faculty support, and Thayer had vested the true identity of the Academy in its faculty.

Indeed, the nucleus of Thayer's professoriate remained not only during Steptoe's stay but for many years afterward, starting with the noted mathematician and Professor of Civil and Military Engineering (1833–1871), Dennis Hart Mahan (first in the Class of 1824) whose tenure ran more than forty years beginning with the two years following his graduation. By 1830 Mahan was an assistant professor and most likely Cadet Steptoe's instructor in mathematics and engineering throughout his years at the Academy. James L. Morrison, Jr., describes Mahan as "aloof and relentlessly demanding […] a man to be respected and perhaps feared, but not loved."[13]

"The Plain at West Point" (1828) by George Catlin. Created five years before he entered the U.S. Military Academy, this painting depicts artillery practice, which Cadet Steptoe complained gave him headaches. Cadets are depicted in full dress uniforms. The images of two ladies and children in the foreground reflect the increasing public acceptance of the academy. Courtesy West Point Museum Collection, United States Military Academy.

Cadet life, however, depended on factors other than the administration or the faculty of the Academy. The campus itself created an imposing and impressive sight to the cadets, many of whom came in literally "off the farm" from such then frontier territories as Michigan and Arkansas. Cadet Abner Hetzel, a fourth classman from Pennsylvania writing to his father in 1823, reported "it far exceeds the most Sanguine expectations I had formed of it." He found not just "a few old Buildings used as habitations for the Cadets," but "7 or 8 large brick buildings occupied by professors & officers. Two very large Stone Buildings 2 Story High, one used as the Hotel & mess-hall for the cadets, the other as Library, Chapel & Examination hall, & two very large Stone buildings one 3 & the other 4 Story high, used as Barracks for the Cadets."[14] Ten years later, Steptoe would see the newly constructed West Point Hotel, and if he were inclined to slip off campus for illicit refreshment, the infamous tavern run by Benny Havens and frequented by Cadet Edgar Allen Poe, who left the Academy without graduating just two years before Steptoe arrived. During Steptoe's second class year, 1836, a new chapel was constructed (today located at the post cemetery).[15] The aura of mystery and suspicion surrounding the Academy began to dissolve to the point that during the summer it was becoming "a favorite spot for tourists," particularly during Fourth of July festivities.[16]

Steptoe, some six months short of 18, would not have been the youngest plebe officially admitted on the first of July in 1833; that distinction among the 85 fourth class cadets listed in the Academy's register for 1833–1834 belonged to Daniel A. Thatcher of Connecticut, age 15 years, 9 months. No fewer than 29 of those fourth classmen, slightly more than a third of the total, were under the age of 17. Just half a dozen of those who entered the Academy in 1833 were more than twenty years old. For the most part, then, the steamer that took Steptoe up the Hudson would likely have been loaded with an array of boys now regarded as high-school age. A diverse group, they represented twenty of the then 24 states of the union along with representatives from the District of Columbia and the territories of Michigan and Florida.[17] If James L. Morrison, Jr.'s statistics for occupations and financial status apply, despite the fact that they are drawn between a decade and two decades later (1842–1854), about 25 percent of these young men came from farm families, not counting planters, with another 12 percent each, roughly, from the families of merchants and lawyers. Only about four percent would have been regarded as the products of affluent families; some 12 percent would have come from indigent or reduced economic circumstances; the remaining 80-plus percent would have been judged as being of moderate means.[18]

Steptoe may well have been as awed by what he saw standing on the wharf at West Point after the sixty-mile steamboat ride from New York as was Abner Hetzel ten years earlier. Here, not much more than fifty years earlier, a memory within the grasp of men like Edward's maternal grandfather, Captain Brown, who had served during the Revolutionary War, General Benedict Arnold had betrayed his country. There the Great Chain was linked across the Hudson to halt British naval incursions, and about two hundred feet up from the dock, on the parade ground, stood Fort Arnold, renamed Fort Clinton, and some four hundred feet above it Fort Putnam. Across the river on Constitution Island stood the fort from which fields of fire would control the river against a British invasion from the north. From where Steptoe stood, the Hudson is about six hundred yards across, about three times the width of the James at Lynchburg. He most likely watched numerous sloops and schooners sailing among the steamships on the Hudson, a great working river. The James featured mostly small bateaux and canal boats.

Conditions inside the cadet barracks remained primitive during Steptoe's time. Fleming writes, "The would-be lieutenants still slept two to a narrow room on mattresses thrown on bare floors. The only heat came from small fireplaces, and reminiscences of those days tell of studying on winter nights wrapped in blankets, numb feet pressed against the fender around the fire."[19] In fact, the reminiscence of Cadet William Dutton dated June 19, 1842, five years after Steptoe graduated, begins, "we have five in our room, which you know is but 10 by 12." If Dutton is to be credited, even the mattresses were gone: "We have no mattresses & only 2 blankets to lay on the floor and cover ourselves with, & when we all five spread ourselves out we just cover the floor."[20] Cadet Steptoe would experience no luxuries during his four years at West Point, nor would the food surpass the rating of "atrocious" universally agreed upon by all who left memoirs, diaries, or letters. Thus, opines Fleming and others, the special appeal of Benny Havens' off-limits tavern.[21]

The beginning of every cadet's life at West Point was the summer encampment begun in June of his fourth class year. "We are now instructing the Plebes in firing cannon which affords us no small quantity of amusement," reported George Washington Cullum in a letter dated July 30, 1832, the summer before Steptoe's first year at the Academy. "Never being accustomed to hear so many pieces discharged at once so near them they make as much fuss as though they had an arm or two shot off."[22] The jocular Cullum, a first classman, would graduate third in the Class of 1833, serving as an instructor of engineering at West Point (1848–1855) and later as superintendent (1864–1866) after being promoted to the rank of brigadier general early in the Civil War.[23] Ironically, given his posting to an artillery regiment upon graduation, Steptoe's first letter home concerns his stay at the infirmary during his first summer encampment: "I am certain that my sickness was occasioned by the storming of the cannon. We had been firing large pieces the greater part of the day & at night I scarcely knew where I was." He reports he has been "entirely recovered" for the past two or three weeks.

Summer encampment would jolt nearly any cadet out of his complacency. "I marched off guard more like a drowned rat this morning than any thing else," William D. Fraser (Class of 1834) wrote to his brother on June 21, 1833: "I stood post 8 hours out of the 24 I stood last night from 12 to 2 and I never knew it to rain harder in my life."[24] Future major general John Pope (Class of 1842) wrote to his mother in Kaskaskia, Illinois, on July 7, 1838, that he had "been obliged to stand Guard 4 hours in the Day & 4 hours in the night. I tell you about 3 o'clock at night walking Post both Cold & Dark and raining I thought of my Dear Mother & home & wished that I were with them but as the old saying is [quoting from Alexander Pope's poem "An Essay on Man," 1733], Whatever is, is right, and with that I console myself, although it is but poor Consolation." In his post script he comments on a change in the weather: "The skin is coming off my face up to my nose on account of standing Guard yesterday for four hours during the most intense heat and we are obliged to wear those tall bell crowned leather Caps which with the brass trimmings weight about 5 pounds and hurt my head extremely and the rim also coming just to the nose."[25]

In another letter from the 1832 summer encampment Cullum reports having "some rare sport" with the plebes that included wrapping themselves in sheets and running across their sentry posts on hands and knees "muttering some undiscovered language, which they, poor simpletons, take to be ghosts or the devil himself."[26] If Edward experienced such hazing or deviltry, or of such hardships as Fraser and Pope complain, his letter shows no resentment: "The military term [his first summer encampment] has closed & what in it has been irksome I cannot see—I always thought this great terror to our young men was mostly imaginary & now I have proof positive of it. Certainly I have at times been tempted to believe some particular duty probably superfluous, but never have once suffered myself to think it hardship." He notes his father was "of opinion the novelty of the thing would bear me up for a short time, but I can assure you it has long since worn off—I came here with the firm resolution to stay here at all events & the resolution is strengthened every day. Here I see all manner of men and very many risk their all on a single chance—many who get their fill of Demerit in 1 or 2 months but I am certain I can stay four years & not get one eighth of the required number." Steptoe's letter also reveals he was dealing not only with his father's uncertainty as to the wisdom of his decision to attend the Academy, but also with his mother's concerns: "Tell Ma that could she see me now doff my cap to a lady or officer or perform any other part of a soldier's gallantry I think it would tend somewhat to conquer her prejudices against W.P."

The second of Steptoe's letters from West Point, dated April 3, 1834, is directed to his maternal grandfather, Captain Henry Brown, informing him of his success on having passed his probationary exams. He reflects that his initial examination was "an unfortunate one & it really was, but I flatter myself I have retrieved my lost ground already—if so I am content." In his previous letter, Edward recalls, his grandfather may have perceived "that my usual tone respecting this place was somewhat altered [...], but you may well know how apt a little unexpected adversity is to alter ones notions of things. I thought my Professor rather partial & I said so—Now, though I cannot retract all, I am willing to acknowledge I was a little hasty, for in fact I am better pleased with the Institution at this time."[27] The next month, he continues, will complete his first year at West Point, and he has been told "every year brings with it new inducements to remain—it is true my time here has not afforded me much leisure, but I can truly say it has not been passed disagreeably." Edward adds, "it was a good reflection of an old sage 'I might have done *better*; but it is certain I might have done *worse*.'" After complaining of not having heard from his father for five weeks despite having written to him "regularly," Edward writes, "I believe when I came on here the prevailing opinion was that I would not stay two months. [...] I trust another year will enable me to prove, in person, its fallacy." Curiously, although he addresses the letter "My D. Grandfather," he signs himself as follows: "My D. Grandfather your most attached Nephew Edward."[28]

By the end of his first year Steptoe ranked 32nd in his class of 85, half a dozen of whom were to be "turned back" for academic deficiencies and a couple of whom had not been examined due to illness. At the end of his second year he ranked 37th in a class that had shrunk to 73, including a dozen who were "turned back" for academic deficiencies and four who were not examined. Along with 14 fellow cadets, he was awarded the rank of corporal. In his third year Steptoe ranked 34th in the ever dwindling class of 58, six of whom were held back, including Henry H. Sibley of Louisiana, who was to graduate with the Class of 1838 and serve as a brigadier general for the Confederacy, being defeated at the Battle of Glorieta Pass, the so-called "Gettysburg of the West." Cadet Steptoe achieved the rank of sergeant during his third year along with 16 others.

On June 15, 1836, at the conclusion of his second class year, Steptoe was appointed cadet lieutenant of A Company along with Joseph Hooker, who would go on to acquire brief fame as organizer and commander of the Army of the Potomac in 1863. Such ranks at West Point, from corporals through cadet captains, typically applied to anywhere from 12 to 16 for any class year, so Steptoe's promotion to cadet lieutenant indicates his overall solid standing in his class, taking into account both academic and military achievements. On February 17, 1837, however, more than halfway through his first class year, Steptoe joined other cadet officers resigning their commissions in protest over a decision made by Superintendent DeRussy, the details of which are sketchy at best. Those resigning included John Gunnison, who graduated second in his class that June and whose path Steptoe would cross nearly twenty years later. The cadets promoted to fill those positions included Braxton Bragg, who would command the Army of Tennessee for the Confederacy, and John Sedgwick, who was serving in the Union army as a major general at Spotsylvania Court House when a Confederate sharpshooter killed him shortly after he insisted to his cowering troops that "they couldn't hit an elephant at this distance."[29]

One feature of the Thayer System was small class sizes and the sectioning of classes with respect to academic capability, typically three sections per course. While it is not certain who Steptoe's classmates may have been in any given course for any given term, the class standings suggest he probably would not have taken courses with the likes of John Gunnison or Braxton Bragg. However, he might very well have taken classes with Sedgwick (24th in his class) or fellow Virginian Jubal A. Early, who would command an infantry corps in the Army of Northern Virginia, or Joseph Hooker (29th in his class). A note to Early, dated September 27, 1838, testifies to Edward's continued association with that former classmate, but no additional extant letters indicate ongoing connections with others from the Class of 1837.

The issue of demerit, which accompanied Thayer's Code of Integrity (later known as the Honor Code) rankled Cadet William Fraser, who wrote his brother on June 21, 1833, that President Jackson was "not a going to have the cadets treated like a parcel of dogs, by those lazy drunken officers, which has been the case too long," noting demerit would no longer count on class standing. Demerit had once counted "as much as engineering," Fraser complains, "but any fool can have the luck to get a few reports, but any fool can not get along in the studies." The *Register of Officers and Cadets* for 1835, his third class year, shows Steptoe had accumulated only 21 demerits, placing him a commendable 38th out of 240. In 1836, however, among 216 cadets ranked by order of demerits Edward placed 104th with 86, just 14 notches above Cadet Sibley. Future Confederate general P.G.T. Beauregard, then a third classman, received only three demerits and ranked second in his class. When he graduated in 1837, Steptoe ranked 34th in a class of fifty, but he accumulated no fewer than 152 demerits, placing him 161st among 211 cadets ranked. The anomaly may well have been connected with his opposition to the superintendent's policies that occasioned his resignation of his rank as cadet lieutenant. Perhaps he followed in the footsteps of former Cadet Poe and became a regular at the establishment of Mr. Benjamin J. Havens.

Cadet Fraser sometimes lashes out in his rambling, run-on syntax against the restrictive nature of life at West Point, as in this passage from a letter to his brother written on November 12th of that year: "We are here shut up as in a jail, we know very little that is going on, and every thing goes on here just like clock work, so that there is nothing for us to write about, we study, go to bed, then to the section room and recite, and so on every day from one years end to another."

Yet in that same letter Fraser describes West Point as a transformative experience, observing "there is assembled here young men from every portion of the union, and you may say almost all tempers and classes, and never have I seen a set of young men, act more gentlemanly or honorably in my life." On October 28 he wrote, "I feel indeed like a different being from what I was two short years ago, I perceive the change in myself and in every thing connected with me, in fact from the very moment I got my appointment as Cadet, I felt a care on my mind which I never had before, I know that from that moment commenced my buffeting with the world and that every thing depended upon my own exertions." Whether Steptoe experienced such a transformation may only be surmised, but Fraser's comments are of additional interest because he subsequently tempers his self-analysis: "How often do I long again for those times when I had nothing to care for, and was as happy as the day is long, but they are never to return in this world, to be sure I feel very happy and contented but still there is a great deal of anxiety, and no one knows the competion [sic] there is amongst us until he comes here himself."

Nothing in Steptoe's letters indicates he relished such competition, as did Cadet Robert E. Lee, second in the Class of 1829 (without a single demerit in his four years). Nor did he delight in accumulating demerits for various forms of mischief, as did William T. Sherman, Class of 1840, who owned up to about 150 of them per year, or Philip Sheridan, who coincidentally, like Steptoe, ranked 34th in his class (1853). Perhaps Cadet Steptoe more nearly resembled his Virginia neighbor and classmate Jubal Early, who discovered he "had very little taste for scrubbing brass, and cared very little for the advancement to be obtained by the exercise of that most useful art."[30]

But there were some pleasures. In his journal Cadet Samuel Peter Heintzelman (Class of 1826), a Pennsylvanian who would rise to the rank of major general during the Civil War, writes of skating, chess, and playing some form of "Foot-Ball."[31] Cadet Jeremiah Mason Scarritt of Illinois (Class of 1838) writes to his sister on February 23, 1836, of the "plaisir" snow brings to a man and of having his "reflections" sometimes "interrupted by the tinkling of sound of sleigh bells."[32] He also notes the entertainment the band provided every Saturday night: "You cannot well conceive the delight a good band can occasion—the excitement of feeling—the enthusiasm music can call forth— To know that you are listening to the same strains that once sounded in the gay salons of Paris and has been listened to by the great Napoleon and that corps of Generals who held Europe in awe." He adds that he likes West Point, "more than I expected and some of the happiest moments of my life have been spent here. The scenery is delightful—the com[p]any is pleasant—the Academic exercises are useful and necessary and I like them on that account. The military duties I love." One might conjecture that Edward's experiences were closer to those of Jeremiah Scarritt than to those of William Fraser.

Steptoe's letter to his father dated November 1, 1835, typically mentions little of his academic life, but he appears amenable to the proposal of his father and Uncle John that he go into engineering.[33] Significantly, he does not appear to be anticipating a career in the military even though he reflects that in just a year and a half he will launch out into the "wide world to struggle for myself." He expresses concern with his health, his "sickness," which he attempts to shrug off casually, even though it is "true my head hurt me sometimes considerably." Edward may well be referring to migraines here, but he claims he "did not trouble the Phisician very much about it, asking only for some medicine occasionally. [...] I do not think at all I have to fear that disease of which you are so apprehensive." One would very much like to know just what disease so concerned Dr. William Steptoe. But Edward observes at the Academy their "manner of living is regular & systematic," and he assures his father any slight "injury to the health" is "easily counteracted" by a little medicine and "wholesome exercise." Three letters sent from mineral springs in western Virginia shortly after his graduation indicate efforts to restore his health, so one tends to doubt his claim in this letter to a "habitually strong constitution."

Of greater interest, however, is Edward's response to his father's request for his "ideas about the great topic of the day—Abolition." He asserts his conviction that practically speaking it cannot be achieved without "a humane *sacrifice* of those who are interested": "No policy, no measures of state or federal government under existing circumstances can possibly rid us of this most unwelcome burden." Nearly all members of both his father's and his mother's families kept slaves, and many of the eligible males served with the Confederacy in the years ahead. Most immediately this included his half-brother William, Jr. (Captain, CSA) and his sister Nannie's husband, John Wesley Eldridge (Major, CSA); the number of cousins or husbands of cousins who enlisted in the Confederate forces runs into the dozens.

But if Cadet Steptoe did indeed lament the burden of slavery, that did not equate with approval of the cause of the Abolitionists, which he describes as "inexpedient, inefficient, uncalled for & treasonable—it is inexpedient because you and every one acquainted with southern character, in the east, know that a man or set of men had as well try to stop the Atlantic as to persuade the South to give up its slave population without an equivalent—it is uncalled for since the domestic concerns of a people must be arranged & altered *only* by themselves to have any permanency—and it is treasonable from the simple fact that its tendency is total ruin of the white portion of the community—indeed I look upon it as worse if possible than treason for it is that insinuation & terrible treason which is not amenable to The Law." Nevertheless, Edward advised his father, the cause of Abolition "is exercising a fearful & *increasing* influence" in the northern states: "The time will come, is coming, when this subject will shake and convulse our nation through." Cadet Steptoe, nearing his twentieth birthday, was surely no more prophetic in this "*ineloquent* essay," as he calls it, than other young men might have been at the time, and like many Southerners, he concludes, "How much soever I may grieve that slavery exists, [...] I must cling to those interests which have ever been identified with mine. I think Slavery an evil & wish it could be eradicated—but it *cannot* be. I must therefore make a virtue of necessity—and when Northern incendiaries in their holy & deadly enthusiasm attempt to interfere in the shape of Abolition pamphlets, I for one, in defense, will go to any lengths to stop them."

In closing, Steptoe refers to the upcoming presidential election, asserting Van Buren "is used up in Pennsylvania essentially," and perhaps even in New York; however, Martin Van Buren signed Steptoe's commission as second lieutenant in 1837, and Van Buren also prosecuted the conflict known as "The Florida War" or the Second Seminole War, which erupted with the massacre of more than a hundred of Major Francis L. Dade's troops on December 28, 1835. Most historians agree the evolution of that war had much to do with slavery: "By 1820 it was recognized throughout the slave-holding states that a Seminole enclave in Florida was a threat to slavery. The conflict that followed was the only Indian war that the United States fought not for land but rather to defend the institution of slavery."[34]

Abstracts of wills and deeds from Bedford County show that on December 7, 1848, Dr. William Steptoe consigned four slaves (named Isaac, Nancy, Lucy, and Leah) to his son Edward, then serving in Mexico, as "collateral on a debt of $1000 owed to Edward J. Steptoe," to be "held in trust" until "the debt was discharged or, in the case of default, to be sold to pay the debt." Edward's grandfather, Captain Henry Brown, in his will names 14 slaves.[35] As noted earlier, Edward's paternal grandfather James Steptoe, like his friend Thomas Jefferson, also kept slaves; both were regarded as benevolent masters. Additional transactions between the late 1840s and the late 1850s show Edward's half-brothers John R. and William, Jr., also owned slaves. So the "evil" of slavery had indeed, as Edward suggested, made "a virtue of necessity." This harsh paradox was widely recognized and in many cases lamented throughout the antebellum South.

Steptoe's next extant letter home is dated February 17, 1836, just a week before the siege of the Alamo began in Texas, the eventual annexation of which would also involve the "unwelcome burden" of slavery. This letter, however, mostly deals with more personal matters: "It is true I was pretty well affrightened on the Examination & as I assured you reaped the bitter fruits of it—but—that's a 'matter of moon-light.' I have regained the lost ground already."[36] Now in the middle of his second class year, he was taking chemistry, natural philosophy (acoustics, optics, astronomy), and drawing (topography).[37] His instruction in tactics that year would include studies in artillery and infantry, but significantly not in cavalry or "equitation," which did not become a regular part of the curriculum until the fall of 1839.[38] In response to his father's apparent suggestion that he should return home, he replies "with perfect sang froid not till next June *twelve* months." He claims to be doing better now in his academics than "a majority of my class," and he optimistically declares he will improve his standing from the middle of his class: "If I do not rise within the first 20—an humble calculation—if I do not I say, then it will be a sad mistake in me—."

He then shifts the topic to a resolution before the House "to effectually break up this Institution," but while he discounts the likelihood of any success, Cadet Steptoe suspects they will "probably correct some flagrant abuses practiced with reference to this place," and while he does not specify the abuses, he goes on to suggest "a strict inquiry would disclose many irregularities in the operation of the Institution which cannot be too soon made publick." It seems likely his eventual reaction to these unspecified "abuses," in consort with other cadet officers, led to his resignation as cadet lieutenant during his senior year.

E.J., as he had signed his letters since arriving at West Point,[39] then responds to his father's questions about church, attendance at chapel being mandatory for all cadets: "We have an Episcopalian minister, who, with all his pomp & circumstance, his high church notions & aristocracy, is nevertheless accounted a learned Divine & devout man." Morrison claims religious training at the Academy was ineffective: "[T]he records suggest that it was usually insignificant or negative. Most references to the spiritual atmosphere in cadet letters are derogatory in some way or other."[40] That was apparently not the case, however, with Cadet Steptoe, who writes that although he does not know the chaplain "personally," he supposes "his character, his principles are calculated to correct the unsteady habits & direct the wild & giddy brain of young men subject to all the variations & changes of a soldier's life."

At the end of this letter Steptoe turns his attention to the railroads, mentioning a journal published in New York and "said to be a valuable work"; he offers to obtain it for his father. The first railroad in the state of New York, the Mohawk and Hudson, operating on a sixteen-mile between Albany and Schenectady, began its run in August of 1831. Train travel between Albany and New York City did not begin until 1851. In his next extant letter, dated September 6, 1836, the day after Sam Houston was elected first president of the Republic of Texas, E.J. pursues the subject of railroading: "My Professor in Drawing says he is authorised to procure the services of ten assistants on a contemplated Rail Road in Virginia with outlay of one thousand dollars—so it is continually here—every year there is demand for Engineers from different parts of the union."[41] The horse- or mule-drawn Chesterfield Railroad in Virginia had experienced commercial success mostly hauling coal since its inception in 1831, and by 1836 was considered the most profitable railroad in the world.[42] But the steam locomotives of the Baltimore & Ohio would not reach Harper's Ferry until the end of 1834, and although surveying was underway toward Wheeling on the Ohio River (then in Virginia) by 1836, the first train would not arrive there until January 1, 1853. The B&O Railroad was using the improved Lafayette engine by 1837, but the financial Panic of 1837 stalled the rapid expansion of rails westward.[43]

The high pay offered for working with the emergent railroads, however, fueled the ongoing controversy over West Point as an institution of privilege. As Thomas J. Fleming observes, state and local governments as well as private corporations "were bidding fiercely for [the cadets'] services, dangling salaries that ranged from five to sixteen thousand dollars a year—startling sums in an era when the annual pay for second lieutenant in the elite Engineers was $700. West Pointers resigned from the Army by the dozen."[44] E.J. also informs his father that now, at the start of his first class year, he is finding Military Engineering "an easy & pleasant study" and is looking forward to Civil Engineering, "with which I design making myself perfectly familiar." Having been told the course "is remarkably simple & short but *sufficiently* comprehensive," he adds, "It is practice that perfects the Engineer as all other artists." That Steptoe was not to find the engineering courses to be as "easy" or "simple" as he imagined and that he was not to rank among the "artists" is implicit in his class ranking on the subject in October of that year—43rd out of fifty.

Judging from the circulation records for his years at the Point, Steptoe did not often visit the library. Only the three volumes of Walter Scott's *Napoleon*, which he checked out during the second semester of his fourth class year (1834), attracted Cadet Steptoe's interest, although others among his classmates, including Jubal Early, Joseph Hooker, and John Gunnison, were frequent patrons, borrowing such volumes as Edward Gibbon's *Decline and Fall of the Roman Empire*, David Hume's *History of England*, and David Ramsay's *History of the United States*. Of course one cannot necessarily conclude from such evidence that E.J. was not a reader. He may well have borrowed books from his classmates, or he may have had books of his own.

Indeed, a survey of the circulation records of those years reveals that many cadets did not allow their shadows to cross the threshold of the library's collection, which as of 1830, according to Morrison, numbered "123 works on military engineering, 308 on civil engineering, 366 on mathematics, 187 on natural philosophy [science—mostly biology], 182 on chemistry, mineralogy, and geology, 273 on strategy and tactics, and 235 on military history, compared to 317 which were classified as 'miscellaneous literature.'"[45] Morrison notes the library also subscribed to a number of literary journals, including *The Edinburgh Review* and *The North American Review*, and a cadet might well have read stories, essays, or poems on site from such periodicals. In one of his letters from Florida, Steptoe mentions having read an item in *The Southern Literary Messenger*, of which former Cadet Poe was quondam editor and frequent contributor. Morrison adds, "Since classroom recitations were based on material from textbooks, there was no necessity and little incentive for cadets to use the library."[46]

E.J. may have been distracted by such other events as the "Annual Ball" and an excursion to Boston, to which he also refers in this letter. "A beautiful thing it was," he writes of the ball, "People of all countries, and all creeds—don't fancy it a drunken frolic of two hundred mad-cap Cadets—not at all—it differs in this respect from the usual sports of that kind—Not a breath of intoxication was allowed to be breathed there." Drinking alcohol, after all, was at least in theory a "dismissal offense."[47] E.J. describes the ball as "a mixing of soldiers and citizens" in friendship, and "the holiest Christians, the purest moralists unite with us in the innocent amusements of the evening." Although we have no reason to doubt his candor both here and elsewhere in his letters, one does wonder to what extent Steptoe reported to his family what he knew they wanted to hear.

Boston he found to be "a lovely place & the most interesting city I ever saw, decidedly—there is more *true* hospitality & kindness in this calumniated city than in N. York or any of its immediate neighbors." Although he discovered the streets were "unaccountably crooked," he finds the buildings "generally beautiful & many of them most splendid." Moreover, "what pleases preeminently in Boston is the air of peace & evening calmness"; "in short, there is a *moral* beauty in Boston I have never met in any other city." Watching the building of the Bunker Hill monument one evening he encountered an old man who had witnessed the action there and who pointed out to him the lines of battle. "I felt the full force of [Edward] Everett's glowing reflections," E.J. reports, referring to Everett's 1824 oration on the Bunker Hill monument: "who indeed can stand on such ground and have not his piety & patriotism increased!"[48]

By mid–April of 1837, within two months of his graduation from West Point and only a month away from the start of the economic crisis known as the Panic of 1837 that haunted Van Buren's administration, Steptoe professed to be "perplexed by various little matters" and in search of advice.[49] "It is not here as at other schools," he writes his father. There, the graduate "has but to prove himself—with funds sufficient to bear him home—here, he is constantly oscillating between a number of pursuits & objects," chief among these being the corps from which he must choose, each of which essentially differs "in pay, promotion & kinds of duty." Although he proposes the possibility of the dragoons, where he would be deployed "on the Western Frontier" and be paid "$30 more than equal rank in other corps," E.J. seems to have had some presentiment as to his eventual posting (certainly his grades were not high enough to qualify him for the elite Corps of Engineers): "I might get into the

Artillery corps; well perhaps then I should be ordered to Maine or any intermediate Fort—from there to Florida."

But then the 21-year-old cadet cuts to the chase: "Now you may suppose from the nature of our Institution, that we have few debts of importance to discharge. But let me undeceive you. It is true we have none of great magnitude, but such a number of small ones, that it amounts to the same. [...] Could you not, Pa, borrow me $80 or $100 from some friend?" He proposes to acquire a "situation" during the time of his furlough, perhaps surveying, and once he receives his officer's pay he promises to repay the loan. That he requests money not directly from his father but from "some friend" may suggest his awareness of his father's limited financial resources. While E.J. frequently sends best wishes to his mother, calling her "Ma," this appears to be the only place among the 19 extant letters addressed to his father where he refers to him as "Pa." In a note to his father dated five days later, E.J. bumps his loan request to $150, adding that he is not as indebted as the majority of his class by a hundred dollars or more. Stephen Ambrose indicates Steptoe's impecunious circumstances followed the rule rather than the exception: "They never saw their pay of $28.00 a month [...]; they could only draw on it at the commissaries, and the only items available there were clothes, mirrors, razors, and other essentials. The monthly pay was never high enough to keep the cadets out of debt at the commissaries, and they could not deposit money to escape their debt."[50]

Part of his furlough that summer before shipping out to Florida, Second Lieutenant E.J. Steptoe spent convalescing at White Sulphur Springs and Red Sweet Springs not far from Lynchburg in what is now West Virginia, but his days at West Point had not ended. In January 1843 E.J. would write from the Academy, where he was then serving as an instructor in infantry tactics, to his half-brother William, Jr., about "the profession of arms," which he commended as "honourable." But William's military service was deferred for twenty years, and that service would be as a captain in the Confederate army serving with the 2nd Virginia Cavalry.[51] The June 1843 *Register of Officers and Cadets* lists First Lieutenant Edward J. Steptoe as Instructor of Tactics, and in a letter dated February 18th of that year Cadet William Dutton (Class of 1846) tells his cousin the details of an Order posted by Steptoe concerning the proper disposition of a cadet's room signed, "By order of Lieut. E.J. Steptoe—1st Lieut. 1st Art. & commd't A compy."[52]

* * *

What kind of cadet was Edward J. Steptoe during his four years at West Point? The extant letters leave only a partial record to enhance the impression we might get from the numerical statistics that show him graduating near the bottom of the third quartile of his class and with demerits that rank him 161st among the 211 cadets at the academy in 1837. Jubal Early ranked 18th in their class but accumulated an impressive 189 demerits, which placed him 195th overall. No evidence suggests E.J. was a hell-raiser, a frequenter of Benny Haven's tavern, a malcontent, or a bon vivant. He seems not to have been among those cadets who might have rebelled against mandatory attendance at chapel, even though he apparently found high church Episcopalian views unappealing. His one letter from Washington, D.C., and the letter in which he speaks out on Abolitionism indicate his political sentiments: predictably pro-Southern, but relatively moderate, notably on the painful issue of slavery. He appears not to have joined the Dialectic Society, although he had joined a debating organization during his year at Chapel Hill, or to have had significant literary, artistic, or musical interests.

The seven extant letters from West Point clearly represent only a fraction of the total he sent from the Academy, but there is no way of knowing how small or large a fraction. They describe a determined and earnest student who apparently believed he had little parental support for his decision to go to West Point. He mentions no other cadet by name in those letters, not even the one in which he describes his pleasant visit to Boston. Perhaps he was something of a loner, but his correspondence from these years reveals no sense of melancholy. Moreover, he never mentions being lonely or having a nostalgic longing for New London, Lynchburg, or the bosom of his family, although his first letter home asks to be remembered to his "old companions," and he frequently inquires after the well-being of various relatives and friends. At the end of the letter he sent on April 13, prior to his graduation in June, E.J. asks about his cousin Edward Dillon Steptoe and whether he has married, and he asks after his half-brothers John and William, Jr., whether they are "progressing yet in the classicks since they *are* to devote so much of their lives to them. I am anxious they should learn the French & design teaching them practically as much as possible of that language—if they will *study & improve* enough, I will bring them most *certainly* this time something handsome—by the way, do you think a monkey would occupy too much of their time?"[53]

Surely, we may be inclined to speculate, he is jesting, but perhaps not. "I could get one for a trifle & bring it easily," E.J. writes. "This was a present my poor Uncle John once promised me under similar circumstances & has occasioned my suggesting it." Here and elsewhere in his letters, albeit subdued, we may detect an element of playfulness. On the brink of his first assignment, which would send him to Florida and action in the Second Seminole War for the next four years, we see a thoughtful young man who exhibits no airs, no sense of self-importance. He was 21 years old in the summer of

1837, and a letter sent from New London to his half-brother William, dated July 8, 1837, expresses concern about his personal finances and his own present inability to pay his share of their younger sister Nannie's tuition: "I have squandered so much money all my life & have so much immediate need of the little I possess at present, that I must be content to unite with you in defraying her late expenses."[54] But despite what he says here, we have little evidence E.J. was a wastrel. We have ample evidence, however, that he cared very much about his family. Four subsequent letters from the summer of 1837 are addressed to his father and to his sisters Kate (Mary Catherine) and Nannie, all from mineral springs to the north of New London which E.J. visited for unspecified health reasons.

The single known portrait of Edward J. Steptoe, as well as his sword, in possession of Mrs. Hildie Bottom of Richmond, Virginia, shows a dark-haired, rather slightly built man with a high forehead, full mustache, straight nose, and large blue eyes.[55] He wears civilian dress, black coat and high white collar. Numerous black-and-white photographic images of varying clarity and sharpness have been made of this painting, or it may be that the painting was based on the single extant photograph, a copy of which appears in B.F. Manring's *Conquest of the Coeur d'Alenes, Spokanes & Palouses*, first printed in 1912. Both the photograph and the portrait may have been occasioned by Edward's marriage in January of 1860, when he was 44 years old. If one were to attempt some interpretation, one might be inclined to say the features are those of a handsome, sincere, and serious man, but lacking a stern military expression, serene rather than intense in disposition, thoughtful, given perhaps to reflection or meditation.

Edward J. Steptoe, photograph by A.H. Plecker of Lynchburg, Virginia, ca. 1860. This photograph may have been made on the occasion of Edward's marriage in January 1860 to Mary Rosanna Claytor. A.H. Plecker also photographed General Robert E. Lee in 1866. The photograph was provided to B.F. Manring, author of *The Conquest of the Coeur d'Alenes, Spokanes and Palouses* (1912), most likely by Edward's sister Nannie Steptoe Eldridge. Courtesy Greg Partch.

Chapter Three

In Florida: The Second Seminole War

Suspecting he could be posted to Florida upon graduation from West Point, Cadet Edward Jenner Steptoe, a second classman (junior), surely lingered over newspaper accounts of the Dade Massacre when he read them sometime in January of 1836, about a month after the event. On December 28, 1835, Major Francis L. Dade had departed Fort Brooke on the Hillsborough River (present day Tampa) heading north and east toward Fort King (present day Ocala), a distance of about a hundred miles over what historian John K. Mahon has described as "a perfectly plain gash in the otherwise heavy wilderness."[1] Nearly two hundred Seminole Indians struck the column, which was divided into an advance unit, main body, and rear guard, without flankers. Overconfidence on Dade's part may explain his failure to deploy flankers, but the area features heavy palmetto growth, which is hard going and can offer good cover for an ambush. Three soldiers survived, but only one, Ransom Clark, lived long enough to tell the story. Among the 107 killed Steptoe would likely have been acquainted with at least four junior officers: Brevet Second Lieutenants Richard Henderson and John L. Keais, both graduated from the West Point Class of 1835 (their commissions had not yet been finalized); Second Lieutenant Robert R. Mudge, Class of 1833, had served as an Assistant Instructor of Infantry Tactics during Steptoe's second year; First Lieutenant William E. Basinger, Class of 1830, had served in a similar capacity during Steptoe's first semester at the Academy.

Cadet Jeremiah Mason Scarritt, who graduated a year after Steptoe, wrote to his sister of "the Florida war" on February 23, 1836, noting, "It has been almost the only topic of conversation here."[2] As to the massacre, "the slaughter of 108 men and 8 officers," he writes, "if you are the girl (excuse me if I am wrong) I hope you are—the particulars of the fate of gallant soldiers cannot be noninteresting. [...] As some of them were well known at the Point you may well conceive that their bloody though glorious death excited our sympathies as well as our admiration." Scarritt describes Lieutenants Mudge, Keais, and Henderson as "intimate" acquaintances. Steptoe probably knew them even better than he did.

Eastern publishers typically reprinted extracts from Captain Francis S. Belton's account, as reported in newspapers from such cities as St. Augustine, New Orleans, Mobile, and Charleston. An officer who had distinguished himself at the defense of Fort Erie during the War of 1812, Belton commanded the garrison at Fort Brooke and had dispatched Major Dade on his ill-fated march under the orders of General Duncan L. Clinch. The *New York Spectator*'s italicized header for January 27, 1836, drew attention to "*the disastrous defeat of the detachment of the U.S. troops, under the gallant Major Dade, of the 5th* [4th] *Regiment of Infantry.*"

"Now it becomes my melancholy duty," Cadet Steptoe might have read, "to proceed to the catastrophe of this fated band, an elite of energy, patriotism, military skill and constant courage." One mortally wounded survivor, John Thomas, had shown up at the fort on the 29th, followed by Ransom Clark "with four wounds, very severe." Major Dade and his horse "were both killed at the onset."[3] "Lt. Keaye's, 3rd Artillery, had both arms broken the first shot, was unable to act; and was tomahaw[k]ed, the latter part of the second attack, by a negro." Most of the artillerymen participated as "red-leg infantry" (red being the trim or piping for artillery service) during the battle, although they also manned the six-pounder cannon.

The dramatic rendition continued: "Muskets were clubbed, knives and bayonets used, and parties clinched. In the second attack, our own men's muskets, from the dead and wounded, were used against them; a cross fire cut down in succession of artillerists at the fence, from which 19 rounds were fired—the gun-carriages were burnt, and the guns sunk in a pond [the troops had brought only a single 6-pounder]. A war-dance was held on the ground; many negroes were in the field, but no scalps were taken by the Indians, but the negroes, with hellish cruelty, pierced the throats of all, whose loud cries and groans showed the power of life to be yet strong."[4] From the second floor library Steptoe may have looked out on the icy Hudson and speculated on the exotic territory of Florida and the tribe known as Seminoles, a hodgepodge of Creeks (Miccosukees) and runaway slaves. He had not likely conversed with anyone who had visited the newly acquired territory, ceded by Spain in 1821.

Cadet Steptoe was about three years old in 1818 when General Andrew Jackson defeated the Seminoles after entering then Spanish Florida in what historians call the First Seminole War. Negro slaves had been fleeing plantations in Georgia and Alabama, and their renegade existence on the border threatened the "peculiar institution." The Indians themselves kept slaves, but

Three. In Florida: The Second Seminole War

historian Joe Knetsch describes the Indians' practice to have been "of a rather benign form." He concludes, "The relationship and existence of the combined Seminoles, Miccosukees, and escaped slaves would be the most important cause of the Seminole Wars."[5] "Whether slave or free," Mahon emphasizes, "the Negroes among the Seminoles constituted a threat to the institution of slavery north of the Spanish border."[6] A year before the outbreak of the First Seminole War in 1817, under orders from General Andrew Jackson, Lieutenant Colonel Duncan L. Clinch crossed into Spanish Florida and destroyed the so-called Negro Fort on the Apalachicola River, sixty-plus miles southwest of present-day Tallahassee, resulting in the loss of some three hundred lives, both escaped slaves and Seminoles.

How much the cadet from Bedford County, Virginia, may have known of the backstory associated with Dade's debacle is open to conjecture, but he most likely knew of the thirty year-old Osceola, a mixed-blood (Muscogee or Lower Creek and either Scottish or English), who would die in prison at Fort Moultrie (Charleston) in late January 1838, by which time Edward had already deployed to Florida. He might have heard the apparently unfounded rumor, still credited by some, that at the inking of the Treaty of Payne's Landing in May of 1832 Osceola plunged his knife into the document and declared, "This is the only way I will sign." Seminole leaders Micanopy, Halpatter ("Alligator"), and Hote Emathla ("Jumper"), however, led the ambush of Dade's troops. The army's main adversary during Lieutenant Steptoe's years in the Florida territory would be Coacoochee ("Wild Cat").

If Steptoe had read such

Coacoochee (Wild Cat), primary Seminole leader during Lieutenant Steptoe's deployment to the Florida Territory (1837–1841). Coacoochee was captured and detained near Fort Pierce while Steptoe was serving there in early June 1841. Drawing by George Catlin (1838). Courtesy State Archives of Floria.

accounts as the botanist William Bartram's *Travels through North & South Carolina, Georgia, East & West Florida*, published with relatively little fanfare in Philadelphia in 1791, he may have pictured a subtropical region with humidity that could rust a musket in minutes, muck that could bog down even ox-drawn cannon, rank swamps filled with roaring alligators and devastating rattlesnakes as long as a man is tall, huge clouds of mosquitoes, terrible hurricanes, and a plethora of exotic diseases. The sparsely populated territory (around 35,000 in 1830), was ill-mapped, as he and other officers would discover. Although the Spanish had owned the colony for three hundred years, they had neglected their garrisons, and they exhibited rather slight reluctance to part with it. Army surgeon Jacob Rhett Motte, who served at Fort Mellon (today's Sanford), where Steptoe would be posted in January of 1838, described Florida in a passage historians have been fond of citing as "the poorest country two people ever quarreled over," calling it "a most hideous region to live in, a perfect paradise for Indians, alligators, serpents, frogs, and every other kind of loathsome reptile."[7]

On the other hand, if Steptoe did happen to come across Bartram's *Travels*, his inclination to embrace harsh stereotypes of the Florida Territory might have been countered by the naturalist's ebullience over the rich variety of flora and fauna and of the native inhabitants he discovered in his travels, primarily in 1774. Consider, for instance, Bartram's one-paragraph depiction of the Seminoles:

> How happily situated is this retired spot of earth! What an Elysium it is! where the wandering Siminole, the naked red warrior, roams at large, and after the vigorous chase retires from the scorching heat of the meridian sun. Here he reclines, and reposes under the odoriferous shades of Zanthoxylon [prickly-ash], his verdant couch guarded by the Deity; Liberty, and the Muses, inspiring him with wisdom and valour, whilst the balmy zephyrs fan him to sleep.[8]

The Seminoles who had destroyed Dade's column and who Steptoe would confront in another two years would not greatly resemble the generically wise and valorous Noble Savage described above. If he did encounter the *Travels*, Steptoe may well have assumed the territory was blanketed with orange groves and the waters teeming with fish, but also with a superabundance of menacing alligators.

True Florida evaded the grasp of those attempting to find words to express what they were witnessing. Surgeon Motte's description of the territory, cited above as "a most hideous region to live in," follows by only half a dozen pages a passage concerning the St. Johns River in which he indicates that nothing

> can be imagined more lovely and picturesque than the thousand little isolated spots, scattered in all directions over the surface of this immense sheet of water, which seemed like a placid inland sea shining under a bright sun. Every possible variety of shape, colour, contour, and size were exhibited in the arrangement of

trees and moss upon these islets, which reflected from the limpid and sunny depths of the transparent water overshadowed by them, brought home to the imagination all the enchanting visions of oriental description.[9]

In that same large paragraph, however, Motte presents the countryside outside Fort Pierce as "one unbroken extent of swamp and morass" and as a realm of "more venomous '*critters*' than one can shake a stick at." Nevertheless he concludes, after noting "the characteristics of wildest desolation," that "a landscape painter would delight to dwell" upon what he has seen and that "we felt the most intense admiration, and gazed with a mingled emotion of delight and awe." Florida constituted something of a paradox, then, even for the poetic soul of Jacob Motte.

Cadet Augustus Porter Allen, who graduated from West Point the year before Steptoe, departed Florida by sea, and in his journal entry dated May 10, 1836, he appears not in the least ambivalent about what he is leaving behind: "Here am I upon the sea—'The open open sea.' I have at last thank God shaken the dust of Florida from my feet—and exchanged its noxious atmosphere for the invigorating breezes of the Gulf—And now a long-long-farewell to thee Florida! thou land of flowers & frogs."[10]

If he had indeed read an account of the Dade Massacre in late December 1835 or early January 1836, Cadet Steptoe may have forgotten much about it by the time he graduated in June 1837, an undistinguished 34th in a class of fifty that would produce 17 generals, ten for the Union and seven for the Confederacy. That war lay two dozen years ahead. Most of Steptoe's fellow graduates were commissioned in one of the four active artillery regiments, and many were sent to Florida. Commissioned second lieutenant on July 1, 1837, Steptoe was assigned to the Third Artillery Regiment, a good number of whose officers served in Florida and came to prominence during the Civil War: George Meade (Class of 1835—he left Florida in 1836, before Steptoe arrived), Braxton Bragg and Jubal A. Early (both Class of 1837), Edward Ord (Class of 1839), and George Thomas and William T. Sherman (both Class of 1840). Steptoe may not have served alongside all of these junior officers from the Third Artillery who were posted to Florida, but he certainly connected with several of them, notably with William T. Sherman.

Of course a graduate of the Academy in 1837 would not have been sure he would be posted to Florida. One might be assigned to the Canadian border, for example, as the provinces were teetering on the brink of revolt, both Upper Canada (Ontario) and Lower Canada (Quebec), which would break out in earnest by the fall of that year, the year in which young Victoria would begin her long reign. Or one might be posted to the western frontier. The Alamo had fallen on March 6, 1836, and less than two months later, at the Battle of San Jacinto, Sam Houston had routed the Mexican troops and taken

General and President Santa Anna captive. In October 1836 American settlers brashly declared their independence as the Republic of Texas and raised their Lone Star flag. Certainly Mexico had not recognized the republic, and there were the Comanche to contend with as well. One might be posted to the newly minted state of Arkansas (June 15, 1836) bordering the Indian Territory, the Great American Desert that would one day become such states as Kansas, Nebraska, and Oklahoma.

"What think you of the Dragoons?" Cadet Steptoe wrote to his father on April 13, 1837, just a couple of months before his scheduled date of graduation.[11] After 11 years of neglect, Congress in 1833 had recognized the need for cavalry and approved a single regiment (some six hundred men) of dragoons. If he were to be assigned to the western frontier, Edward noted, he could make $30 more than he would earn as a second lieutenant serving elsewhere. And apparently young Steptoe needed the money. As a cadet he was paid $28 a month, but most of that went to cover expenses. Although he reflected on his 21st year with satisfaction, feeling himself more "like a man" than ever, Steptoe had to request a loan from his father.

But if Edward was experiencing some fiscal distress personally, that was nothing relative to the national economic disaster, the Panic of 1837, which struck a month later, on May 10, 1837, when the bubble burst on land speculation that involved Indian removal and payments in scrip or paper money issued by local banks and not backed by silver or gold. Amidst a culture of surging prosperity, blithe confidence in the idea of Progress, and manic speculation, nearly half of the nation's banks collapsed, and the resulting inflation, record unemployment, and depression lasted for the next five years. Martin Van Buren, who took the oath of office as president on the fourth of March as Andrew Jackson's Democratic successor, had no apparent inkling of what lay two months ahead. His would be one of the shortest presidential honeymoons in U.S. history.

During the summer of 1837, however, by the early part of July the newly fledged second lieutenant was ill. Or "ill again," perhaps, if one recalls his first extant letter home from West Point in April 1833. In a letter dated July 8, Edward asks his brother William Jr., to cover his share of their sister Nannie's tuition, promising to reimburse him in the fall, so his financial issues obviously remained unresolved. About two weeks later, in a fragment of a letter to Nannie, Edward reports on his convalescence at White Sulphur Springs, a popular resort throughout the century, just across the Alleghenies in present-day West Virginia, then simply western Virginia. He claims sadly to have discovered no ladies "remarkable for beauty. Some of the Southern *married* Ladies appear well, but the Virginians so-so-ish."[12]

Although he informs his sister he has "not made the acquaintance of a single lady at the Springs," he reminds her he has come for "improvement, not pleasure; and besides, to meet new faces has ceased to be a desire with me." He claims to have "only peeped into" the ballroom once, and then detected "no animation—no polka-ing." In a letter to his half-sister Kate dated July 28 he repeats his lack of "acquaintance of a single Lady" and his lone "glance into the Ball room," although he does mention having watched a quadrille and finding the girls "generally pretty & graceful."[13] Near the end of that letter, however, he tells Kate he has seen a woman from North Carolina and her brother "whom I know very well," perhaps from his year spent at Chapel Hill before entering West Point, but he notes, "I did not speak to them—probably shall not." He does not elaborate.

The tone of the three letters from the springs suggests at times that Steptoe was inclined to be standoffish or even antisocial, but that tone could also reflect his ill health—he refers to weight loss and concerns about his appetite, and in a letter dated August 11 he mentions being "not at all well today—nervous & weary."[14] His playfulness with word choice ("so-so-ish" and "polka-ing"), however, indicates the sort of humor we encounter fairly often in his letters home. Referring to his brother John, he writes, "Tell Jack if he comes here for health, this is good as any time;—if to see the '*Lions*,' two weeks hence will be better, for they are not here yet." Presumably, he refers here to the upcoming visit of President Van Buren, which he also mentions in this letter. Van Buren would then have been entering his sixth month in the presidency, but he may well have been in need of a relaxing visit to the spa, as he was already facing a double-barreled dilemma: the financial Panic of 1837, which erupted in early May, and the appeal of the Texas Republic for annexation, to which he was opposed.

The sulfur springs were developed as early as 1778 because of their supposed curative value, and in the first half of the 19th century they hosted both Martin Van Buren and Henry Clay, who was a frequent visitor throughout the 1830s.[15] In his August 11 letter to Nannie, Steptoe mentions his plans to visit White Sulphur Springs "to see the president." The resort is located about 120 miles north and west of Lynchburg.

In his July 28th letter to Kate, Edward tells of his admiration for a sermon he attended on a text that he found directed at himself: "Come to me all ye that are weary." His letter to Nannie dated August 11, 1837, finds Edward at nearby Red Sweet Springs, stricken by the beauty of the scenery, but still unwell. In correspondence to his father from the Sweet Springs sent after his return from Florida five years later, on August 31, 1842, Edward complained of "biliousness," a catch-all term popular throughout the century for any number of liver-related diseases, which he "endeavoured to remove by starving," but also by taking "blue mass & oil," a mercury compound (mercuric chloride, like calomel) taken later by President Lincoln to combat depression or "melancholy" as it was then called.[16]

* * *

By fall of 1837 the Second Seminole War was entering its third year and was bidding well to become a graveyard of generals. Much had happened since Cadet Steptoe read of the Dade Massacre in January 1836, but little had been resolved. General Clinch had failed in his attack on the Seminoles in the Cove of the Withlacoochee River north of the Dade battlefield on December 29, 1835, one day after the massacre, and by the middle of September 1836 he had resigned his commission after having been superseded by General Edmund Gaines and by General Winfield Scott who, despite his successes against the Cherokees in Georgia, failed in his grandly designed campaign, "a marvel of precise strategy," one historian has noted, doomed to failure because of imprecise knowledge of the terrain and flawed logistics.[17] Enter then, albeit briefly, the newly elected territorial governor, Richard Call who, as a major general of the Florida militia, was relieved of command on December 9, 1836. His replacement was Major General Thomas Sidney Jesup, who would still be running operations when Steptoe arrived at Fort Mellon in January 1838.[18] Jesup, however, requested to be relieved of his command in April of that year, to be replaced by Zachary Taylor, who had been brevetted to major general during the Black Hawk War in the Illinois and Michigan territories in 1832 and who would last two years in charge of operations in Florida, longer than any other commanding general.

That hurried summary accounts only loosely for what had been going on during the past two years in the Florida peninsula. General Jesup, a veteran of the War of 1812 and of successful campaigns against the Creeks in Alabama and Georgia, proved considerably more effective than others in the field, although he, too, was dogged by the "logistical nightmare that was Florida."[19] After Seminole leaders Jumper and Alligator signed a ceasefire on March 6, 1837, Jesup believed he had arranged for most of the Seminoles to migrate to the West. Sam Jones (Arpeika), Osceola, King Philip, and his son Coacoochee encamped at Fort Mellon, "where relations were so friendly that Osceola slept in the tent of Lieutenant Colonel William S. Harney," and this even though Harney was later described as being "heartless toward Indians."[20] Apparently, however, distrust over Jesup's commitment to permitting African American allies of the Seminoles to migrate with them ended any hopes of peace. Osceola and Sam Jones left Fort Mellon, traveled to where another body of Indians was meeting near Fort Brooke, and seized the leaders, leaving only the aged Micanopy behind.

On September 8, 1837, a detachment of the East Florida Militia under General Joseph M. Hernandez operating about thirty miles south of St.

Three. In Florida: The Second Seminole War

Aerial view of Fort Marion (Castillo de San Marcos) in St. Augustine, Florida, which Lieutenant Steptoe visited on several occasions when he was deployed to the Florida Territory during the Second Seminole War (1837–1841). He was stationed at St. Augustine between the Second and Third Seminole Wars (1845–1846). The Castillo is the oldest masonry fort in the continental United States (construction began in 1672). Library of Congress.

Augustine captured King Philip and shortly after that, his son Coacoochee (Wild Cat) and Yuchi Billy. General Jesup also approved the seizure under a white flag of Osceola and Coa Hadjo, who were then imprisoned in Fort Marion (formerly the Castillo de San Marcos, as it is known today). Coacoochee and 19 others managed to escape, but in December Micanopy, Osceola, Coa-Hadjo, King Philip and nearly two hundred other Indians were shipped to Fort Moultrie where Osceola died of chronic malaria on January 31, 1838.

By late fall of 1837 Lieutenant Steptoe had evidently arrived at Fort Marion in St. Augustine. It seems likely he was billeted there while Osceola was being held, but we have no conclusive evidence. Steptoe stayed there briefly on his way to Fort Mellon on the St. Johns River (Lake Monroe), about ninety miles to the south, but he returned to St. Augustine from time to time and was stationed there when the Second Seminole War ended. Built by the Spanish as the Castillo de San Marcos, the massive coquina-walled fort, the construction of which began in 1672, remains the largest masonry fortification in the United States and the only existing 17th-century fort in North America. At one time, as Steptoe may have been informed, no fewer than 77 cannon and mortars were mounted. By the 1830s just twenty or so cannon were positioned, 18- and 24-pounders that could hold their own against any invasion, not that the Seminoles would have been inclined to float their cypress dugouts down the salty estuary known as the Matanzas River, which flows to the east.[21]

Officers and enlisted men considered St. Augustine a good post with a vivid social life. Then the largest city in the territory, it boasted a population of nearly 2,500 in 1840, including 863 slaves. By comparison, Steptoe's hometown of Lynchburg, Virginia, numbered nearly 6,400 residents, of whom some 2,730 were slaves. Most officers and personnel were billeted at the St. Francis Barracks, formerly a Franciscan monastery. Army Surgeon Jacob Motte records attending "several parties" there during his stay in late July of 1837:

> I found the society of St. Augustine, composed of American, Spanish, and Minorcan families, to be characterized by refined intelligence, and polished manners; and their elegant hospitalities I shall always bear in mind with grateful feelings. [...] The St. Augustine ladies certainly danced more gracefully, and kept better time, than any of my fair country women I ever saw in our more northern cities [112].

Stricken by their "dark and fawn-like eyes" that "shed a pure radiance of glad light with their kindling beams" and taken with "the rich black tresses and olive complexion" that attested to their Spanish descent, Motte found himself "in Elysium." One may recall Steptoe's less ebullient response to the unremarkable beauties of White Sulphur Springs, Virginia, at about that time.

The exact movements and postings of junior officers are difficult to ascertain, but Arthur E. Francke, Jr.'s *Fort Mellon, 1837–1842* lists Steptoe among the officers serving with "two companies of recruits" (115 troops) in January 1838.[22] The fort was named for Captain Charles Mellon, killed in action on February 8, 1837, by "six hundred blood-thirsty Micasukies led on by *King Philip* and his son *Coa-coo-ché*, or *Wild-Cat*," as Motte phrases it, overestimating the Indian force by about three times the plausible number.[23] The hastily erected log breastworks were later replaced by a stockade typical in design to the one used for many of the two hundred forts constructed in Florida during the war. Abandoned because of its "unhealthy" location in mid–June of 1837, Seminoles burned it down, but the army rebuilt in early November to use it as a supply depot and staging area after General Jesup instituted his plan to compress the Indians into the southern half of the territory.

Steptoe would descend the St. Johns River about a hundred miles by steamboat from the garrison town of Picolata, about twenty miles west of St. Augustine, to Fort Mellon. The lazy St. Johns, the longest river in the state, inches northward some 310 miles at a rate of about a third of a mile per hour. The river widens frequently to form basins or lakes, and it remains a popular haunt of waterfowl hunters and largemouth bass anglers. When he made his way south on the river in June of 1837, Surgeon Motte was dazzled:

> In what bright contrast [to Black Creek] did the broad bosom of the St. John's river first burst upon my sight! Never shall I forget my sensations at that rare and beauteous sight. [...] From orange groves, whose golden fruit and snowy blossom stood in beautiful contrast with their dark foliage, we'd pass on to long rows of tall and slim palmettos [sabal or cabbage palms]; their graceful trunks shooting up along the river banks for miles. Then a change would come over the beauty of the scenery; and in place of orange and palm trees, would appear the spreading oak, the bay, the beautiful cedar, and stately magnolia; their pendant branches casting mysterious shadows on the St. Johns, as they hang over its placid bosom in every variety of form and beauty.[24]

Steptoe possessed little of Motte's literary pretensions, so we may only speculate as to how he may have reacted to his journey on the St. Johns. We know from letters he wrote years later that he enjoyed bird hunting and fishing, so it appears likely he would have found Fort Mellon on the banks of Lake Monroe an amenable site.

About his posting to Fort Mellon, Steptoe has left no impressions, but we know that by February 1838 he was visiting St. Augustine, because a West Point classmate named William Warren Chapman (also Class of 1837), serving with the First Artillery, mentions going riding with him on February 26 in a letter to his fiancée Helen Blair in Massachusetts. Chapman graduated seventh in the class from which Steptoe graduated 34th, and his letters are much lengthier and considerably more detailed than Edward's, owing partly to the nature of his audience. Usually posted to Fort Foster, about twenty miles up the Hillsborough River from Fort Brooke, on the west coast, Chapman writes, "How agreeable to be once more in the society of intelligent ladies, after being for many months in the swamps of Florida, enduring all the hardships and privations of an Indian campaign."[25] He notes that on his ride with Lieutenant Steptoe he was accompanied by "a young lady from Philadelphia and the reputed belle of St. Augustine," but he is quick to add he would prefer it had been Helen. Perhaps Steptoe was drawn to this "belle."

On Christmas day of 1837, which Steptoe may likely spent in St. Augustine, Zachary Taylor met the Seminoles in the largest engagement of the war, the Battle of Lake Okeechobee. By the end of 1837 General Jesup had nearly nine thousand troops at his command, including no fewer than 4,636 regulars. The total authorized strength of the army at this time of general disapprobation of standing armies in the United States was only 7,130.[26] Popular support lay not with professional soldiers or the ostensibly pampered graduates of West Point, but with state or territorial militias. Mahon describes the Indian forces numbering more than four hundred, led by Sam Jones, Alligator, and Coacoochee, as "crazy for revenge" and lying in wait in their hammock having carefully prepared a field of fire. Although the Seminoles lost only 11 killed and 14 wounded to Taylor's loss of 26 killed and 112 wounded, the Indians dispersed (as they most often did after an initial encounter) and the battle was declared a victory. "Wild Cat [Coacoochee], the *detenu* [prisoner], who escaped from St. Augustine was the fiercest in the battle," reported St. Augustine's weekly, the *Florida Herald*, and he remained at large.

Nevertheless, writers for the newspaper were jubilant: "This is keeping with Christmas and New-Year *à la Seminole*. [...] Most of the aristocracy of the nation are now in Gen. Jesup's possession."[27] Colonel B[enjamin] K[endrick] Pierce was reported to have moved his troops south to establish a port at the mouth of the St. Lucie River, present day Fort Pierce, where Steptoe was to be stationed by February 1839 through the fall of 1841. In a lengthy letter written two weeks *before* the Battle of Lake Okeechobee, William Chapman confidently tells his fiancée "there is not the possibility of a doubt that the war is over."[28] Talk in the newspapers of imminent "unconditional surrender" of the Indians proved to be overly optimistic; nevertheless, Colonel Taylor was promoted to brigadier general for his pyrrhic victory.

Mahon and others have observed the major body of "Negro warriors" was not present at the Battle of Lake Okeechobee, and by the spring of 1838 "inducements" to split the African Americans from the Indians had worked so well that "they had ceased to be an important factor in Seminole resistance" and instead "worked for negotiated removal" to the West.[29] In his journal Army Surgeon John T. Sprague wrote, "It was not until the negroes capitulated, that the Seminoles ever thought of emigrating."[30]

General Jesup's command in Florida, however, was coming to an end. In 18 months his troops had captured about 2,900 Indians, and it was their uncertain fate to be shipped to the West, usually from Fort Brooke and on to New Orleans.[31] Some impression of the trials they would face may be gotten from reading a few pages of Edwin C. McReynolds' *The Seminoles*, where he observes that Lieutenant Joseph W. Harris (West Point Class of 1825) reported 55 of the 512 Indians he was taking to Fort Brooke died before they reached Tampa Bay. More moving are McReynolds' quotations from the journal of Lieutenant Jefferson Van Horne (West Point Class of 1827), who accompanied a group of 78 sick Seminoles on May 14, 1836, for its last hundred miles from Arkansas into the Indian Territory. This band included the chief Holata Emathla, who died en route.[32] Jumper died at Fort Pike, near New Orleans, in April 1838, and old King Philip also died before reaching the Indian Territory.[33] Lieutenant Steptoe may have encountered some of these chiefs, as he was to play a small role in this portion of the Trail of Tears.

Sent to Fort Payne, Alabama, apparently in the spring or summer of 1838, Steptoe assisted with the emigration to the future state of Oklahoma. In what appears to be his first letter to Adjutant General Roger Jones, a veteran of the War of 1812 who was then in the midst of his long term in office (1825–1852), Steptoe accepts his appointment "by the President of the U. States, of Assistant Commissary of Subsistence."[34] The letter from Fort Payne is dated September 17, 1838. Edward's single extant personal letter sent from Fort Payne is dated ten days later and addressed to his West Point classmate and fellow Virginian, Jubal A. Early, who had participated in the Battle of Lockahatchee (Loxahatchee) on January 24, 1838. In his memoirs Early, who had been posted to Fort Pierce in the spring of 1838, claims never to have seen an Indian during that skirmish.[35] After serving briefly in the Indian removal early that summer, Lieutenant Early resigned his commission on July 31 to pursue a career in law and perhaps to seek the company of a young lady he had met at White Sulphur Springs.[36]

Steptoe's brief letter to Early encapsulates the tedium of garrison life that his classmate had opted to escape: "We […] do nothing under the sun but eat, sleep & drink, or under the *moon* but drink, sleep and _____ etc."[37] Motte also mentions the monotony of camp life, "nothing doing, nothing done."[38] Steptoe's letter mentions fellow officers Poole and Wall, most likely Benjamin Poole (West Point Class of 1830) and William Wall (West Point Class of 1832). Poole died a year later, apparently from non-combat causes; Wall died of illness in Mexico in August 1847. Steptoe continues, "I am the general staff officer of the Post and my duties are *general* with a vengeance." He concludes by sending his regards to Early's parents and encouraging him to stop by his father's place when he reaches Lynchburg.

By February 1839 Steptoe had been posted to Fort Pierce, where his life was apparently more interesting. He would have taken an ocean steamer most of the way, sailing on a smaller vessel across the Indian River Lagoon to Fort Pierce, which is located about 126 miles south of Fort Mellon. The lagoon is shallow, typically just three feet in depth, except where a channel has been dredged, but it ranges in width from half a mile to five miles.[39] It flows, more or less, 156 miles from Ponce de Leon Inlet near New Smyrna Beach in the north to Jupiter Inlet in the south and includes both the Mosquito Lagoon and the Banana River. Lieutenant Steptoe would have observed a more primitive and natural version of an ecosystem that today boasts more than two thousand animal and two thousand plant species. Redfish, saltwater trout, and whiting would have been common catches during Steptoe's sojourn, and contemporary accounts refer to oysters being harvested by the bushels. As Motte put it, "A whole Army might be subsisted here upon the produce of this river, if fish diet agreed with them, and not fear an exhaustion of supplies."[40] Serving as commissary officer, Steptoe found ample seafood to supplement the troops' diet.

Motte describes the building of Fort Pierce out of palm logs in January 1838 on a bluff ten to 15 feet above the Indian River. The surgeon pitched his tent just a few feet from the water's edge. "Here was luxury!" he exults, "To lie upon my blanket, and have the water constantly in view, and almost within reach of my hand."[41] Motte had left Florida by the time Steptoe arrived in Fort Pierce about a year after its construction was complete. Despite his celebration of the luxurious billet on the riverbank, Motte summons up his relief at leaving the territory and the war against the Seminoles thus: "The criminal under the gallows, who, when just about to be swung off, receives a reprieve, could not have experienced more enviable sensations than I did at that moment."[42]

Knetsch describes the "drudgery" of garrison life, which often included "the brutality of the officers and the occasional violence, frequently caused by bad whiskey," and he observes that in Florida "the insects, vermin, alternate cold and hot and the nearly constant dampness caused untold miseries."[43] He describes Fort Pierce as "relatively open," featuring "officers' quarters measuring 124' × 18' covered with boards, etc., with three 30' × 15' tarpaulin covered log enclosures for the enlisted men and a hospital 28' × 16'."[44] Such a layout usually featured a blockhouse for the artillery with lower rooms used for storage. The detachment at Fort Pierce between January 1839 and January 1842 varied from around 80 to 140 officers and men with typically no more than four to six commissioned officers on the post.[45]

By the time he arrived at Fort Pierce, Steptoe had been promoted to first lieutenant (July 9, 1838) and Brigadier General Zachary Taylor was running the show in Florida with a much smaller force than Jesup had commanded (about 2,300, mostly regulars). The Commanding General of the Army, Alexander Macomb, arrived in the territory in March 1839 and by the end of May had contracted a treaty with the Seminoles to withdraw south of Pease Creek (Peace River), which runs northward from Charlotte Harbor on the Gulf coast, present day Port Charlotte. This was intended to confine them to the region of Lake Okeechobee and the Everglades; Fort Pierce roughly marked the northern terminus on the Atlantic coast. This treaty failed, however, for the usual reason, that the leaders who signed it did not represent a majority of the Seminole people. Coacoochee, for example, was not a signatory, and Sprague refers to him as "by far the most dangerous chieftain in the field."[46] Taylor's effort to establish a trading post on the Caloosahatchee River, about thirty miles south of Pease Creek met with disaster. "In all quar-

Three. In Florida: The Second Seminole War   53

ters," Mahon writes, including middle Florida and the Tallahassee vicinity, "murder and rapine blazed up."[47]

In a March 10 letter to his father Steptoe claims never to have been in better health, except for having been shot in the foot. He does not elaborate. Overhead the sky might have reflected the bland blue of his troops' uniforms on those rare days when they stood to for formal review. White fatigues were more common daily wear. Rather than go on about his health or the wound, Edward's letter moves into a teasing vein as he claims to be "falling in love & making love a little, wherever I go—never fear, however, for me; I intend to astound you all some of these days—and no jest about it—don't care a pin for your Va. girls, poor & proud!—too much like 'love in a Cottage,' by half—this, between us—I would not wish to be known as that object so horrible to ladies—called a '*fortune hunter*.'"[48] So goes Edward's playful take on the almost universally proverbial, romantic premise of the day that love in a cottage is better than misery (or boredom) in a palace.

Edward also tells of the death of Captain Samuel L. Russell of the Second Infantry Regiment killed by the Seminoles on the Miami River, February 28, 1839, and of "another classmate of mine & a most particular friend" who was wounded by Coacoochee's men.[49] Buffalo, New York, native Captain Russell was, Lieutenant Steptoe writes, "one of the gentlest, most amiable men of my army acquaintance." He also notes one of his own teamsters was shot at Palatka (about twenty miles southeast of St. Augustine) "at a spot across which I have repeatedly ridden with one soldier, or else, alone, on my way to the Ocklawha [Ocklawaha]," and "since I have returned here [to Fort Pierce] I have strolled away gathering shells, etc.—perhaps ten miles from the fort—when two Indians could have cut me off easily. I tell you these things to show how rash this continued & tiresome war rending enemy are." The war was farther from being over than many back home realized: That was his message. Still struggling with the fiscal aftereffects of the Panic of 1837, Congress continued to grumble over the expense. When the war would end, Edward writes, "no imagination can conceive."

He mentions he's now serving as quartermaster. Presumably that would reassure the folks back in Virginia he wouldn't be in the field quite so often: He wouldn't be in harm's way. "We live well here," he writes, "the finest fish & oysters you ever saw, & very abundant. I have boats & horses to sail or ride—guns & dogs—books," a good assortment, he says. His office has become the "evening rendezvous," and then there are sermons on Sundays. At the conclusion of this letter, recalling "the winning eloquence of my old schoolmaster," Edward indulges himself in a rare flight of fancy: "Memory rakes up painful reminiscences oft, but how pleasant when it steals on us, as on me today, far away, & recalls the features and occupations of those we love! 'I slept & a dream came o'er me.'" The sentiment rings reminiscent of Keats's blends of sleeping and dreaming, but Steptoe does not pursue the thought. After returning from special duty in St. Augustine in April, Lieutenant Steptoe added to his role as assistant quartermaster the task of acting ordinance officer and later commanding officer of Company F, 3rd Artillery.

On July 23, 1839, a band of Seminoles on the Caloosahatchee, a hundred or so miles to the southwest of Fort Pierce, overwhelmed Lieutenant Colonel Harney's detachment of the Second Dragoons, killing or capturing 18 men, torturing some of the captives before they died.[50] Now in command of more than three thousand regulars, General Taylor launched an offensive against Indian bands east of the Suwanee in the northern part of the territory; Mahon describes the results as "solid" but "by no means decisive."[51] The failure of the strategy of pushing southward into the Everglades any Indians who resisted emigration is implicit in the fact that raids into north-central Florida continued into the spring of 1840, including one in which Coacoochee attacked a theatrical troupe outside of St. Augustine, killing three actors and plundering their trunks of costumes.[52]

Taylor's creation of "squares" twenty miles on a side and posting an officer and twenty men at the center proved somewhat effective in middle Florida. But he had had enough: "On February 26, 1840, Taylor, worn out and discouraged by his lack of success and ill health, asked for relief from the Florida assignment."[53] On the eleventh of May yet another general stepped into the line of fire with Brevet Brigadier General Walker K. Armistead, who had served previously as second in command to Jesup. Although he would eventually draw on a force of some 4,500 regulars and 2,000 militia, Armistead accomplished little during his year at the helm, perhaps because he did not enjoy full support of Secretary of War Joel Poinsett. Knetsch employs the term "micro-management" to describe Poinsett's dealings with Armistead.[54]

In October 1840 Steptoe welcomed recent West Point graduate and freshly minted second lieutenant William T. Sherman to Fort Pierce. In the spring of 1839 E.J. would have become acquainted with "the other Sherman," Thomas W., who was also posted briefly to Fort Pierce.[55] In his memoirs William T. Sherman (not related to Thomas) offers a good description of the primitive living conditions there:

> Pulling across the lagoon […] we approached the lights of Fort Pierce. Reaching a small wharf, we landed, and were met by the officers of the post, Lieutenants George Taylor [like Steptoe, West Point Class of 1837] and Edward J. Steptoe, and Assistant Surgeon James Simons.[56] Taking the mail-bag, we walked up a steep sand-bluff on which the fort was situated, and across the parade ground to the officers' quarters. These were six or seven log-houses, thatched with palmetto leaves, built on high posts, with a porch in front, facing the water.[57]

We have no record of further interaction between Steptoe and Sherman, but Sherman offers some vivid accounts of life at Fort Pierce, which his biographer, John F. Marszalek, describes as "a languid life, pleasantly different from the rigidity of West Point."[58] Sherman mentions fishing and catching green turtles for the mess table.

It may be that Lieutenant Sherman, who went by "Cump" and was an avid reader, brought with him, in addition to some recent newspapers from St. Augustine, one of Sir Walter Scott's novels, or something by the new British sensation Charles Dickens. *Oliver Twist* and *Nicholas Nickleby* both appeared in 1839, and former West Point cadet Edgar Allen Poe's macabre stories, aptly titled *Tales of the Grotesque and Arabesque*, drew some attention late that year. His first year at the Academy Steptoe may have heard some cadets had pooled their money to help Poe have a volume of his poetry published after he was dismissed in 1831. It has been said Colonel Thayer himself suggested this idea to Cadet Poe.[59] While there is no evidence Steptoe was a great reader of fiction and poetry, he did apparently read whatever copies of *The Southern Literary Messenger* came to hand.[60] Other pastimes would have included checkers or chess, maybe whist or some other card game. Perhaps he engaged in conversation or debate over the upcoming presidential election that placed the Whig, "Old Tippecanoe," William Henry Harrison, in the White House. It proved a historically short term (March 4–April 4, 1841); John Tyler, from eastern Virginia, was in office when the Second Seminole War finally ended.

Sherman mentions several expeditions made by boat during the winter of 1840 to round up Indians on streams and lagoons running from Fort Ann at the Haulover Canal on Merritt Island, about two hundred miles to the north, to Jupiter Inlet about fifty miles to the south.

He also tells of a ship's pilot named Ashlock who "initiated" him "into the mysteries of shark-spearing, trolling for red-fish, and taking the sheep's-head and mullet." When Ashlock returned from escorting an unnamed soldier to St. Augustine for trial, he was accompanied by his newly acquired, attractive young wife and her sister, "a very pretty little Minorcan girl of about fourteen years of age." Ashlock left his bride and her sister at the pilot's hut and went out to ferry several soldiers from the steamer across the bar, but a strong wave upset the boat and nearly all were drowned. Sherman returned to the scene to find "poor Mrs. Ashlock on her chest of clothes, a weeping widow, who had seen her husband perish amid sharks and waves." The ship's pilot could not swim. The next day Sherman, accompanied by Lieutenant Edward O.C. Ord, who was to have a distinguished career fighting Indians in the West during the latter half of the 1850s and commanding Union troops during the Civil War, found a couple of bodies washed ashore "torn all to pieces by the sharks, which literally swarmed the inlet at every new tide."[61]

Three letters Lieutenant Steptoe, commanding Company F of the Third Artillery, sent from Fort Pierce to the Adjutant General between mid-February and early September of 1841 suggest something of the dull routine of barracks life even on the border of hostilities and near shark-infested waters. One letter indicates a soldier in his command was working as a tailor in Savannah two months previous; another concerns possible back pay due a noncom in his company; the third denies clothing allotment for a private until such time as his enlistment is up, "he having been a *Deserter*."[62]

On the first of May 1841, however, Coacoochee, the most important Seminole leader still in Florida, showed up at Fort Pierce demanding "food and liquor."[63] We have no account of how Steptoe responded to that noteworthy event, but he very likely was at the fort then, as he filed a routine report on a personnel matter dated May 31. Mahon notes that Coacoochee "freely came and went" from Fort Pierce for some thirty days before he was made prisoner on June 4 and sent to Tampa for relocation to the Indian territory. General Armistead had by then been relieved of command per his request, and Colonel William Jenkins Worth, a respected officer and veteran of the War of 1812 took over. Worth was placed in command of the new Eighth Infantry Regiment, and it was he who would see the war through to its official conclusion on August 14, 1842, and be brevetted to brigadier general in recognition of his feat. By that date Steptoe had been gone from Florida for at least six months.[64]

Something of the nature of the Second Seminole War is indicated by the fact that Worth's summer campaign of 1841 was aimed at the Cove of the Withlacoochee, in the vicinity of the Dade Massacre that had set off the war in December of 1835; in fact, the Miccosukee chief Halleck Tustenuggee attacked a settlement just 35 miles from St. Augustine on December 20, 1841. In short, efforts to confine the marauding bands of Seminoles to the vicinity of Lake Okeechobee had not succeeded. When Coacoochee surrendered at Fort Pierce, the commander was Major Thomas Childs, West Point Class of 1814, whom Knetsch describes as "another gritty veteran of the War of 1812."[65] Childs was brevetted to lieutenant colonel for his achievements in the war against the Seminoles, and for his action during the Mexican War he would be brevetted to brigadier general. In a hasty letter to his father dated June 11, 1841, which begins as usual with assurances as to his "continued good health," Steptoe indicates he has received orders "to lay fast hold of Coacoochee & warriors." He opines, "Once in the fort, if they get out alive it will be quite a miracle."[66] Presumably, Coacoochee had slipped away after his capture a week earlier.

Although Sherman offers a portrait of Coacoochee as he appeared a few miles outside of Fort Pierce on May 1, John T. Sprague's description has been cited most often:

Coacoochee is about thirty-two years of age, five feet eight inches in height, well-proportioned, with limbs of the most perfect symmetry. His eye is dark, full, and expressive, and his countenance extremely youthful and pleasing. [...] With mind active and ingenuous, clear and comprehensive, he carried into all his measures, spirit and influence; governing his band in a firm, but politic manner.[67]

Sherman describes Coacoochee as "a very handsome young Indian warrior," but he appears to have been unimpressed.[68] After the parley, the young lieutenant observes with evident contempt, "Coacoochee and his envoys proceeded to get regularly drunk."

His few extant personal letters from Florida do not indicate where Steptoe was during the capture of Coacoochee, although the date of the letter cited above (postmarked June 12 from St. Augustine) suggests it was written before rather than after he was captured, or perhaps retaken. In any event, he was mistaken in his supposition the Seminole leader would not leave the fort alive. In fact, Coacoochee was later released in order to bring in other members of his band for emigration. Sprague's observations on the Seminoles as Coacoochee was about to disembark from Fort Brooke on October 12, 1841, reflect the paradoxical attitude of the day: the Indians are "degraded and treacherous," "barbarous" in their manner of warfare, and given to "atrocious acts," but "they have been wronged." On the other hand, Sprague asserts, they have been treated with "much generosity, kindness, and forbearance" by both civil and military authorities.[69] Perhaps Sprague's best tribute comes in quoting the chief's laconic response to a question put to him while he stood on deck just before sailing: "I am looking at the last pine tree on my land."[70] Coacoochee accompanied more than two hundred Seminoles to Arkansas.[71]

Steptoe's primary concern in June 1841, in the midst of a summer that Knetsch describes succinctly as "hot and brutal," appears to have been neither with the weather nor with Coacoochee, but with his promotion to the rank of captain.[72] Counting his four years at the Academy, he could claim eight years of service, and hearing that Congress would soon establish additional regiments, he requested that his father use his influence to secure the promotion. Edward indicates he has written to the Whig senator from Virginia, William S. Archer, with his request because he is aware "political influence" often figures in such decisions. The ambitious young officer adds they are having "fine weather so far, which promises good health to us," but he promptly alters his upbeat spirit: "if forced to live in Florida through another summer."

And he was so "forced." In a letter dated September 27, 1841, Edward complains his father has not answered three prior communications, none of which appear to be extant, and he refers in passing to the "new administration," John Tyler having taken office on the death of William Henry Harrison in April. Steptoe writes "despite the fierce heat of summer," he has "crossed the Everglades twice, or been, in other words fourteen days in boats in a vast expanse of water, *not a foot* of dry land in view day after day."[73] This expedition is the one Joe Knetsch mentions, in which Steptoe, along with First Lieutenant George Taylor, commanded fifty men in eight boats sent to "explore the branches of the 'Alleatsokee' River" [probably the south fork of the St. Lucie River, formerly called the Halpatiokee].[74] Colonel Worth launched the action as part of an unusual summer campaign out of Fort Pierce on September 6, late fall and early spring being generally preferred as cooler and dryer. Although "Navy & Army cooperated," Steptoe writes, no significant results were achieved. By this time they were likely chasing remnants totaling no more than three or four hundred Indians. "Since that expedition," he continues, "I have been on two others—saw a few Indians but could not catch them—destroyed thirty or forty acres of Indian cultivation, corn, potatoes, rice, sugar cane, etc., etc. From these facts you will perceive that exposure to a Florida summer is not so fatal as many believe—at least to those living on or near the seacoast." By some accounts, notably those of Major Childs, the destruction of crops dealt "a heavy blow to the Indian's supply base."[75]

Lieutenant Steptoe also took the opportunity in this letter to tease his father about "His Accidency," the president: "I suppose you good Whigs are highly exasperated against Mr. Tyler for his second veto, and think the country lost beyond redemption." The veto almost certainly was the second one aimed at the national banking act, which was intended to repair the ravages of the Panic of 1837 and which Senator Henry Clay had concocted. In response to the veto, all of Tyler's cabinet but Secretary of State Daniel Webster resigned and the Whigs kicked Tyler, their own president, out of the party. By the end of his term the Whigs had become the party of the North and the Democrats that of the South. Edward takes "a very different opinion," expressing pride in a president, a native Virginian, "who dares to be honest & carries out his principles independent of all parties." Edward declares himself quite boldly, and disputatiously, on this point: "You are the sovereign people 'tis true, and may continue to be so, but why stick up a man to rule over you, with no more character than a weathercock. I am proud of a ruler who defies a fickle people and dares to do right. The Whigs want a Bank, one half of them, I truly believe, principally from a spirit of retaliation—a feeling of revenge on their opponents, and it behooves someone to stand between them & the inevitable consequences of vindictiveness." He adds, however, "Pray show not this hasty letter to any but the family circle."

Rumor had it that elements of the Third Artillery would be ordered back to Old Point Comfort (Fort Monroe at Hampton, Virginia) in October, Steptoe wrote hopefully. One of the more curious moments in his September letter occurs when he asks his father whether he thinks England would declare war on the United States, noting "the poor savages are speculating vainly on the probability & consequences of a rupture." Such an event was unlikely, despite the ongoing dispute over the border between the U.S. and Canada in Maine and the tension over the Oregon Territory that would help Democratic candidate James K. Polk into office over Henry Clay in 1845 with the slogan "Fifty-four Forty or Fight!" But the point Steptoe makes at the end of that paragraph is telling: "Captivity—even to the British—would almost be preferable to a longer sojourn here."

In a letter to the Adjutant General dated March 20, 1842, and posted from Washington, D.C., Lieutenant Steptoe requests a six-month extension of his leave of absence, pointing out he did not receive the customary three-month leave upon graduation from West Point, "And since joining the Florida army in the winter of '37, I have continued on active service up to the 4th inst." He adds he would like to travel to Europe "for improvement & general information," and he appends a letter from Colonel Worth granting him a two-month leave and a note from Major General Scott approving his plans. His request was granted on March 22nd, but we have no record of his having undertaken what Englishmen of the day knew as the "Grand Tour." Instead, as indicated above, with respect to his letter to his father from Red Sweet Springs dated August 31, 1842, Edward spent some weeks at the spa attempting to recuperate from the rigors of his years in the Florida Territory.

"The society was very select & the people for the most part wealthy," he writes his father. "Had both been less so, I might have enjoyed myself better." But he claims to have "thrown" himself on the "haughtiest" of the aristocrats from both North and South, acquaintance with whom "may do me much good in after life for aught that I know. [...] My reason for visiting the mountains, you may be sure, was not entirely to restore my health." What ambitions the young lieutenant may have nurtured that summer following nearly four years on the nation's southern frontier we may only speculate. Obviously he was seeking connections. Perhaps he was considering a career outside the military. Edward's next move, he informs his father in his letter of August 31, will be to accompany some of his new friends on a visit to Philadelphia, where he will attend a wedding, and "rapidly" on to New York, where he will look into his military "interests." According to one passage in that letter, Edward anticipated a posting to the Carolina coast, "where the Singleton family may be of much service & certainly of great convenience as I shall often be in Charleston." The connection here would have been with prominent cotton planter Richard Singleton, whose son Matthew was two years younger than Edward. Family correspondence archived at the University of North Carolina in Chapel Hill mentions Richard Singleton occasionally visited White Sulphur Springs.[76]

The exact nature of Steptoe's experience during his deployment to Florida in the Second Seminole War may only be surmised. In his list of 25 officers recommended for promotion via brevet dated April 25, 1842, General Worth wrote: "First-Lieutenant E.J. Steptoe, 3d artillery, distinguished for intelligence and capacity for service; has served uninterrmittingly since leaving the academy (three years); and has been constantly in the field, and often in combat: recommended for captain by brevet."[77] This promotion, however, was not granted. Why that was the case is impossible to ascertain, but it appears such brevet promotions were not often granted unless specifically qualified by the phrase "for gallantry and good conduct," as in the case of George H. Thomas, brevetted to first lieutenant, or for "meritorious and successful conduct," as with John T. Sprague, Colonel Worth's aide-de-camp and son-in-law to be, brevetted to captain. Steptoe was not to find himself a captain for another five years, in March of 1847, by which time he was about to lead his battery at the Siege of Vera Cruz. His unit during the Seminole War and later in Mexico was the Third Artillery Regiment, which was deployed to Florida from 1836 until March of 1842. Its death toll reflects that of other units engaged in that conflict (note the ratio of losses to disease as opposed to those in combat): "lost 8 officers to disease, 3 in battle, 125 enlisted men to disease, 33 in battle."[78]

In a letter almost certainly misdated tenth of January 1842 (it should be 1843) Steptoe wrote to his half-brother William from West Point, where he would serve for a year beginning that fall as an Assistant Instructor of Infantry Tactics. Steptoe praises the "profession of arms" as "honorable," but he cautions that he makes his observations away from "Pa's eye," as he suspects their father regards him as not "much better than a rational murderer."[79] Perhaps from a physician's point of view such an attitude is understandable, but if Edward's feelings about his father's disapprobation are accurate, we may detect here and elsewhere in his letters and life decisions, an urgent need for his father's approval. Dr. William Steptoe was the grandson of a physician, and two of his sons by second marriage (John and Patrick) would also become physicians. Edward's appointment to West Point, after all, came through connections with his mother's family. The striking passage to the effect that his father might regard him as no more than a "rational murderer" recalls early letters to his father in defense of his decision to stay at West Point; it also suggests some degree of estrangement existed, and that may account for his occasional complaints, throughout his correspondence, about not having his letters answered. Edward also offers a relatively rare self-appraisal in this letter: "My nature is silent for the most part, and when my course is plain before me, active."

Surely, however, the most notable observations in Edward's letter to his brother William, who did not matriculate at West Point, concern the officer's responsibilities:

Three. In Florida: The Second Seminole War

> If the Government declares a war however unjust, its citizens are as much bound, individually, to help its preservation, as to continue allegiance to that government after it passes iniquitous laws, exterminating the Indians or sanctioning slavery, or partitioning Poland, or any laws on record that are condemned by mankind. Governments are responsible, not we [soldiers]—if they do injustice they must answer, not we.

It may be argued that Steptoe offers here the standard officer's disclaimer, "I was just following orders," or that he simply echoes the boast of the purblind patriot, "my country, right or wrong."

What should draw our attention most forcefully, however, is Steptoe's reference to "iniquitous laws" pertaining to extermination of the Indians and the sanction of slavery. In a letter to his father dated November 1, 1835, Steptoe refers to slavery as "this most unwelcome burden," but he expresses little sympathy for the abolitionists. That he regarded treatment of the Indians to be possibly the result of an "iniquitous" law comparable to the partitioning of Poland late in the 18th century by Russia, Prussia, and Austria also reveals something of Edward's character at age 26. Then into his fifth year as a commissioned officer, Lieutenant Steptoe was telling it straight as he saw it, speaking for citizens generally as well as military officers, and quite possibly with an eye to the approaching maelstrom of the Civil War.

For Steptoe, despite his awareness of the government's mistreatment of the Indians and of the evils of slavery, the citizen, the soldier, and especially the officer, owes his allegiance to the government. One could object that his effort to justify his participation in what he has come to see as an unjust and iniquitous war amounts to little more than a form of rationalization. But, particularly for an officer, to think otherwise could have calamitous consequences. The government's "preservation" is at issue here, as Lieutenant Steptoe constructs the circumstances of this moral dilemma. It will be incumbent upon that government, subsequent to its survival, to answer to any "injustice" done.

In a note directed to the Adjutant General dated September 17, 1842, Steptoe asks whether his "services for West Point are accepted."[80] He lists his return address as the Astor House in New York City. The answer was affirmative, and on September 30 he began his year as Assistant Instructor of Infantry Tactics. Such employment of young West Point graduates after field service was fairly common. He would stay at the Academy until graduation of the class on July 5, 1843, after which he would serve a year in garrison at star-shaped Fort McHenry, the site of Francis Scott Key's "The Star Spangled Banner," in Baltimore harbor. Major improvements had been made to the fort in the past few years, so posting there was considered favorable duty.

After his service at West Point and his garrison posting to Fort McHenry, Steptoe spent a year at Savannah, Georgia, before returning to Florida in

August 1845. In a passing reference in a letter to his father dated January 12, 1845 (probably 1846) and mailed from St. Augustine, E.J. outlines plans to speculate in the Florida turpentine industry.[81] He adds, with respect to "*the affair so long discussed between us*, I can only repeat what has been said over and over. It is impossible that I should remain in the army *married*. I cannot do so, and to resign without ample support would be a living death to me." The subject of matrimony emerges periodically in his correspondence, but he did not marry until 1860, while on convalescent leave.

Lieutenant Steptoe posted several letters to the Adjutant General from Fort Marion in St. Augustine between August 21, 1845, and June 20, 1846, all of a routine nature pertaining to personnel or financial matters. In his letter dated August 21, E.J. indicates he arrived the day before with Company H of the Third Artillery and was quartered at St. Francis Barracks. He would surely have been aware that remains of soldiers killed in the 1835 Dade Massacre, including young officers he had almost certainly known at West Point (see above), had been buried on the site in 1842. Steptoe's first letters concern the sending of troops to Tampa Bay, from which post (Fort Brooke) some would be sent on to Texas, in anticipation of the outbreak of the war with Mexico in April 1846.

St. Augustine was a familiar and probably welcome post, but Lieutenant Steptoe turned thirty in November of 1845, and he was doubtless pondering his future, as may be inferred from his reference to speculation in the turpentine industry. In a letter dated May 10, 1846, he applied for promotion to the rank of captain in a Regiment of Mounted Riflemen, "should it be raised."[82] The promotion was not forthcoming. By July of that year he was stationed at Fort Moultrie, where he wrote to the Adjutant General concerning muskets and "accoutrements" which he had examined and found "unserviceable."[83] Considering that what must be regarded as the definitive episode of his military career, in the Washington Territory in the spring of 1858, would also involve "unserviceable" firearms (the much maligned musketoon), this letter rings prophetic. The specific problem in this case was the need for percussion caps as the army continued to change over from flintlock muskets. By his next birthday, on November 7, 1846, Lieutenant Steptoe would be in a ship off Brazos Santiago (Brazos Island) on the border with Mexico commanding Companies G and H of the Third Artillery that had sailed from Fort Moultrie on the 27th of October. The following year, 1847, would be the most rewarding in his career as an officer engaged in combat.

* * *

So far as Florida is concerned, the E.J. Steptoe story does have something of a coda. By the fall of 1849, a little more than two years after he was brevetted to lieutenant colonel at the Battle of Chapultepec (the commission is dated

Three. In Florida: The Second Seminole War

September 13, 1847, and the document is signed by President Polk on July 5, 1848), Steptoe returned to Florida, by then the nation's 27th state, during what historian Joe Knetsch calls an "interlude" between the Second and the Third Seminole War, which erupted in 1855. Steptoe stayed for only a year before returning to garrison duty at Fort Adams in Rhode Island. In November of that year General David E. Twiggs sent Steptoe with two artillery companies as red-leg infantry to newly erected Fort Chokonikla on the Peace River, about 45 miles southeast of Fort Brooke.[84]

The single document that most accurately reflects Steptoe's final deployment to the Sunshine State describes what could be called a study in frustrated reconnaissance. It traces his march with four officers and 48 men commencing on November 16, 1849, and ending on the 21st back at Fort Chokonikla, now marked by Paynes Creek Historic State Park about twenty miles south of Bartow. After two days getting lost and retracing their steps along the Pea (later Peace) River, Steptoe reached Fort Frazer (near present day Lakeland) about 32 miles north of Chokonikla. He found bridges and causeways across the river to be in poor repair, and on the 19th he dismounted half of his men and started on foot toward Fort Gardner, located on the Kissimmee River, which then meandered some forty miles to the east. After a ten-mile march, he found himself "unable to proceed farther from sickness & painful feet," at which point he put the command under Captain George W. Getty, who reported "all trace of the road ceased at once," although he did make it to the Kissimmee River.[85] Then, running low on provisions, the chagrined colonel headed back to Fort Chokonikla, reaching it on the evening of the 21st. He reported, a "good wagon road of twenty miles length" could be built from Chokonikla to Fort Frazer requiring only slight repairs to some bridges.

This rather anticlimactic conclusion to Steptoe's adventures in Florida indicates something of the tedium that awaited career soldiers and officers between wars. Fort Chokonikla had been established in July 1849 following an attack by a small band of Seminoles in which a trader named Dempsey Whidden and Captain George S. Payne were killed and others wounded. After they burned the trading post, the Indians were captured by fellow Seminoles under Billy Bowlegs (Holata Micco) and the aged chief Sam Jones (Arpeika), who wished to avoid confrontation. Billy Bowlegs, who was not bowlegged, became the main adversary after this and would remain hostile throughout the Third Seminole War (1855–1858).[86] He finally surrendered with John Jumper in March 1858, by which time Steptoe was a continent away commanding at Fort Walla Walla in the Washington Territory.

Chapter Four

In Mexico

By the time Congress declared war on Mexico, May 13, 1846, Edward J. Steptoe had been on active duty in the army for nine years, not counting his four years as a cadet at West Point, which with some justification he did. Commissioned a second lieutenant in July 1837, he had been promoted to first lieutenant a year later, and so he had remained despite his diligent service in Florida for nearly four years (1838–1841) during the Second Seminole War, for which he had been nominated for promotion by brevet to the rank of captain. The brevet rank was awarded in recognition of meritorious service but did not carry the pay accorded to full promotion in rank; nonetheless, brevetted officers were generally addressed by the honorific title. That he felt keenly about the rejection of the brevet is attested by a note he sent from Fort McHenry, Maryland, to the Adjutant General's office dated February 12(?), 1844.[1] Garrison duty at posts like Fort McHenry or Old Point Comfort (Fort Monroe, Virginia) could be pleasant, but uneventful and unlikely to lead to promotion. More than once the thirty year-old lieutenant must have second-guessed his choice of careers, and if he knew the Academy song "Benny Havens, Oh!" as written down in 1838, just a year after his graduation, he must surely have agreed with the third line of the opening stanza of what are said now to number in excess of a hundred: "In the army there's sobriety, promotion's very slow."[2] Actually, at least among the enlisted men there wasn't all that much "sobriety" in the army, but promotion in all ranks was notoriously slow.[3] The plea of a later stanza, however, was about to be answered: "May the Army be augmented, promotion be less slow; / May our country in the hour of need be ready for the foe."

Under the circumstances the United States was not particularly "ready for the foe," for it remained President James K. Polk's avowed intention to acquire the recently annexed Republic of Texas, Alta California, and all of the land in between mostly through feints and negotiations. As his last important presidential act John Tyler signed the joint resolution of Congress to that effect on March 1, 1845. Northern abolitionists rigorously opposed the annexation because Texas would enter the union as a slave state, and if war should break out over the acquisition, many feared that additional territories in the West would be open to slaveholders. In June of that year the Republic of Texas agreed to the annexation, and as David A. Clary succinctly observes, "Mexico was mad as hell."[4] K. Jack Bauer asserts, "It was in their inability to recognize that Mexican public opinion considered acceptance of the loss of Texas a shattering of national honor and dignity that the American leaders made their greatest mistake."[5]

That the nation of Mexico, which had separated from Spain little more than twenty years earlier, was bankrupt and wrapped in the throes of political chaos was well known north of the Río Bravo (Rio Grande to North Americans), but these conditions led to greater complexity than the newly elected President Polk appears to have anticipated. How was one to negotiate with a government in chaos? Between 1833 and 1855 "the presidency changed hands thirty-six times," 11 of those presidencies being served by Antonio López de Santa Anna, the hero (or villain from a Texan's perspective) of The Alamo and Goliad and the dominant force in Mexico throughout the war years.[6] Santa Anna retained the title "Savior of His Nation" despite his disastrous defeat at the Battle of San Jacinto on April 21, 1836. One historian has called him "the greatest scalawag in the history of the Western Hemisphere."[7]

The population of the United States numbered more than seventeen million in 1840, reaching nearly three times that of Mexico by the middle of the decade. Mexico's predicament was complicated by the fact that Mexico City, the administrative center of what had been New Spain, is located more than 2,500 miles from San Francisco in Alta California, though at the time San Francisco was a village of scarcely more than two hundred residents. In the coming conflict Mexico's central government could not have defended its broad territory even if its armed forces, supposedly numbering some thirty thousand had been well-armed, highly trained, expertly led, and several times as large. Moreover, the U.S. was a considerably more industrialized nation. Joseph Wheelan reflects on the three "enduring icons" of the age, "the steamship, the railroad, and the telegraph, all of which quickened America's pulse."[8] By 1845 the U.S. could boast more than 1,600 miles of railways; Mexico would not acquire railways at all for another twenty years.

Many in the United States opposed the war, notably the Whigs, even though both General Taylor and General Scott were of that party. Poet Henry Wadsworth Longfellow railed against this "shabby and to us disgraceful war with Mexico" in a journal entry dated May 27, 1846, two weeks after Congress officially declared war.[9] Writer and sage Henry David Thoreau would spend a night in jail and write one of his most admired essays, "Civil Disobedience," using the Mexican War as a point of departure, although the war was over by the time the essay was published in May 1849. Writing in his diary before Matamoros on March 26, 1846, Colonel Ethan Allen Hitchcock asserted, "We have not one particle of right to be here." "My heart is not in this business," he elaborated. "I am against it from the bottom of my soul as a mostly unholy and unrighteous proceeding; but, as a military man, I am bound to execute orders."[10]

The massacres of 180 Texans at the Alamo (including former Tennessee congressman Davy Crockett) and of about twice that number at Goliad in 1836, however, did not allow much sympathy for the outnumbered, poorly armed, and poverty-stricken enemy south of the Rio Grande. By August 1845, just six months after Polk's inauguration, Major General Zachary Taylor, age sixty and putative hero of the Battle of Okeechobee, fought on Christmas day 1837 during the Second Seminole War, was set up on the Nueces River at Corpus Christi, then known as Kinney's Post, and was prepared to move south to the Rio Grande when ordered. Popular with the troops as "Old Zach," and later to be renowned in the press as "Old Rough and Ready," Taylor accumulated an "Army of Observation" of between three and four thousand troops, which amounted to about half of the manpower authorized for the regular army at that moment.

Polk's minister John Slidell attempted to arrange for the purchase of the desired property, including Alta California and what was then known as "New Mexico," the intervening land between western Texas and California, from the Mexican government under President José Joaquín de Herrera. But by the first of January 1846 Herrera's government had been overthrown, and Major General Mariano Paredes y Arrillaga had named himself acting president. Taylor was promptly ordered to the Rio Grande, setting up near present-day Brownsville, across the river from a Mexican garrison at Matamoros.

At issue immediately was the question as to the southern boundary of the recently annexed state of Texas, whether it should be the Nueces River at Corpus Christi, or the Rio Grande about 165 miles to the south. After initial skirmishes, Taylor built up his defenses at the earthworks, dubbed Fort Texas, in front of Matamoros and moved about 2,500 of his troops toward Port Isabel, his source of supply on the coast, 23 miles to the northeast. As the small garrison at Fort Texas withstood a Mexican siege, Taylor began moving back toward them, but superior Mexican forces under Major General Mariano Arista at Palo Alto confronted him about five miles from Matamoros. Regarded as the first significant engagement of the Mexican War, the Battle of Palo Alto took place on May 8, 1846, and might be regarded as prophetic of things to come. Although outnumbered by at least a thousand troops, Taylor won the day convincingly due in large part to his deployment of mobile "flying artillery," Major Samuel Ringgold's light 6-pounders mounted on horse-drawn carriages (usually six-horse limbers drew both cannon and caisson, which carried ammunition). Ringgold, with whom Steptoe had served briefly when he was at Fort McHenry in 1843, was killed in that action.[11] In the resulting artillery duel the American forces lost just five dead and 45 wounded to Mexican casualties of 102 killed and 129 wounded.[12] In the subsequent Battle of Resaca de la Palma the next day, just a mile or so distant, the outcome proved even more disastrous for Arista's forces, which outnumbered Taylor's by about 4,000 to 1,700. While Taylor lost 33 killed and 89 wounded, the Mexican Army of the North lost at least 154 killed, 205 wounded, and 156 captured or missing.[13] The Mexican War offered excellent conditions for demonstrating the worth of the recently modernized and expanded artillery regiments.[14]

Lieutenant Steptoe's attitude toward his imminent involvement in the Mexican War is implicit in a letter he wrote to Ellen Wilkins Tompkins, the anxious wife of his former West Point classmate, Captain Charles Quarles Tompkins, who graduated the year before Steptoe. Dated September 14, 1846, and sent from Fort Moultrie, South Carolina, Edward's sensitive and thoughtful letter begins with his observation that he understands her distress; he then informs her that her husband's mission is not "fraught with toil & peril," but offers evidence of "the Government's confidence in his superior judgment & decision of character."[15] He suggests her husband will return soon, as the war with Mexico will be quickly resolved, and he reminds her that "an increase of reputation is inevitable to him, already one of the bravest & most estimable members of our body."

The latter observation doubtless refers to Tompkins' deployment to Florida during the Second Seminole War, where he was engaged in the Battle of Lockahatchee (Loxahatchee) in January 1838. Like Steptoe, Tompkins served with the Third Artillery; their paths may have crossed in Florida. The two young officers were promoted to first lieutenant within just two days of each other. Steptoe goes on to say he envies Tompkins "the visit to strange lands, the view of strange scenes & intercourse with strange peoples." As it happened, Captain Tompkins spent the war in garrison at Monterey, California, and he resigned his commission before the war ended, perhaps in "frustration" over the inactivity.[16] Mexico beckoned with the lure of the strange, the "exotic," and although Captain Tompkins did not experience the "increase of reputation" Steptoe thought would be "inevitable," it did provide exactly that for the ambitious lieutenant.

The first extant letter concerning the Mexican War that Edward sent home to his father in New London, Virginia, is dated October 10, 1846, and opens, "We have preparatory orders for the field at last."[17] His immediate destination was Point Isabel, a few miles northeast of Matamoros. He anticipates Tampico falling soon to the navy, "but Vera Cruz will probably be regularly besieged by land, and cannonaded into submission." For an artillery officer this consummation was devoutly to be wished. As to the capital of Mexico, Steptoe confidently affirms it will be "captured," but "not without some hard blows," and he mentions his concern that if the small farmers, "the Rancheros," get stirred up against them, "it will be a very different affair from the present warfare" being waged solely against the Mexican army. Steptoe dates the second page of his letter "Oct. 9" and indicates several days have elapsed since he began writing. In the interim he has chartered "a splendid ship" to take his troops to Point Isabel. He comments on Zachary Taylor and William Worth's costly victory at Monterrey (September 21–24), then a city of about ten thousand, maintaining it was "absurd" to "assault a Spanish town, to attempt to carry it by storm, when each house is a perfect fortification in itself." Taylor's victory over General Pedro de Ampudia's troops resulted in a nearly equal number of casualties on both sides, a rare experience for Americans during the Mexican War. True to his artillerist's nature E.J. writes, "A few pieces of heavy artillery would probably have battered the town from a distance & *forced* it to capitulate with very slight loss on our part."[18]

Toward the end of his letter, Steptoe writes a passage that many soldiers about to be exposed to enemy fire allow themselves in one form or another. His phrasing shows him to be devoutly religious and serious-minded: "Hope always for the best on my account—if it should be the will of heaven to number me amongst the slain, who shall say it is not right?" None of the extant letters from his deployment to Florida during the Second Seminole War reflect any such presentiment of death in battle, and as in most such cases, his sense of impending doom did not come to pass. "I hope always to do my duty," he adds in a sentence that echoes through the annals of military correspondence, although not always with the religious inflections, "& God grant that my efforts to serve my country may be worthy in his sight." That Steptoe had some misgivings about what lay ahead of him is also implicit in the next paragraph, where he reflects on his younger half-brothers John (Jack) and William, urging his father to "incite them to *strain* their energies and make for themselves a name," and on his half-sisters, to whom he sends his "ardent aspirations that they may be patterns of virtue & modest excellence." This expression of conventional sentiments of the age should also remind us that the thirty-year-old lieutenant's thoughts and feelings conformed to those of other young men of his moment. Steptoe was no wild Lord Byron straining at the leash of propriety.

The United States blockaded the important Gulf coast port of Tampico in mid–May 1846, and Santa Anna evacuated the garrison there at the end of October. U.S. forces began occupation at the end of November. E.J.'s first letter from Tampico is dated November 27, 1846. He informs his father that motivated by curiosity, an "immense concourse of people assembled" to watch their disembarkation, and he suggests, "A few cannon well planted & manned might have destroyed the whole of us," but "the supineness of this people has greatly benefited us."[19] He adds, "The common people are ignorant in the extreme & have no graver care than to provide themselves a little tinsel to deck themselves withal." After commenting on the violence of a "Norther," he writes of reconnoitering a position a few "extremely warm" days before, returning "by the moonlight": "How bright the moon and starlight is down here," he exclaims. On their return he found orders to "mount my company as Flying Artillery," as a mobile unit in effect: "A beautiful battery we have & I shall try to make it tell if we have another fight."

Although two of the six extant letters Steptoe was to send to his father from Mexico are dated in January 1846, the year indicated is obviously one of those errors many make around the first of the New Year. In his January 13 (not 1846, but 1847) letter Steptoe informs his father, "We have been so busily occupied throwing up lines of defense and drilling our command into efficiency that little leisure time has remained to us."[20] He adds, "We are something like a bird just fledged and anxious to spread its wings."

By the time Steptoe arrived in Mexico the war had been partially won; he was to participate in what amounted to the critical second phase: the seizure of Vera Cruz and the subsequent overthrow of Mexico City. To the far west, Brigadier General Stephen Kearny was consolidating federal control over California. A major portion of Zachary Taylor's command had just been ordered to join the forces of "Old Fuss and Feathers," Major General Winfield Scott, renowned for his resplendent uniforms, for the assault on Vera Cruz. But first, with Brigadier General John Wool's division and a company of Texas Rangers under Captain Ben McCulloch, Taylor would defeat a vastly superior force under Santa Anna and General Ampudia at the icy Battle of Buena Vista on February 23, 1847, the last major engagement in the north and Taylor's most important victory. He left Mexico shortly thereafter to pursue a political career that would take him to the White House in 1848.

Cullum's Register indicates after serving a year at West Point as an assistant instructor in infantry tactics (September 20, 1842–July 5, 1843) Steptoe spent three years in garrison duty at Fort McHenry, Maryland (1843–1844), Savannah, Georgia (1844–1845), and Fort Marion, Florida (1845–1846), leaving for Mexico from Fort Moultrie, South Carolina, traveling by sea.[21] Stuck at the rank of first lieutenant since his promotion on July 9, 1838, Steptoe may well have shared some of the enthusiasm young George B. McClellan, about to graduate second in his class at West Point and destined to serve as an engineer, expressed in a letter to his sister dated May 13, 1846: "Hip! Hip! Haarrah! War sure enough! Ain't it glorious!"[22] McClellan's boyish exuberance may be explained in part by the fact that he was still seven months shy of his twentieth birthday. A little more than 16 years later, commanding the Army of the Potomac, Major General McClellan would prevail at the Battle of Antietam on September 17, 1862, in what is regarded as the bloodiest single day of battle in American history. Young Lieutenant McClellan arrived at Tampico with General Twiggs' division on January 24, 1847, so he might well have encountered Lieutenant Steptoe there.

Perhaps, though, Steptoe might have agreed with the attitude toward war of another fellow officer, Second Lieutenant George Gordon Meade (West Point Class of 1835, two years before Steptoe), who had served a year in Florida during the Second Seminole War with the Third Artillery Regiment, but left before Steptoe arrived, resigning his commission to pursue a career in civil engineering. Destined for greatness at Gettysburg in July 1863 as commander of the Army of the Potomac, Meade reentered the army in 1842 serving on the staffs of generals Taylor, Worth, and Patterson during the Mexican War. He would be brevetted to first lieutenant for heroism at the Battle of Monterrey. In a letter to his wife dated May 28, 1846, Meade, like Steptoe, thirty years old and a good ten years older than McClellan, refers to the "terrible consequences" of combat and frankly states,

> For my part I have no hesitation in saying I have no stomach for it. I trust I shall always do my duty, from a stern sense of the propriety of assisting in the defense of my country, and giving my services to the Government by which I have been supported when there were no risks to run. But I candidly acknowledge I have no penchant for it; nothing but a sense of duty would keep me in it.[23]

The Mexican War served as the proving ground for the regular army, providing what could be described as qualifying exams for the war to come, even though the bulk of the troops were volunteers, as were most of the general officers, for Polk shared Andrew Jackson's distrust of any professional military establishment and also his faith in the militia. Polk's wariness applied both to the existence of a sizable standing army and to West Point and the cadre of officers he perceived to be elitist. Nevertheless, the regular army during this period grew by about 600 percent, from just under 6,000 enlisted men to more than 42,500; volunteer militia units numbered in excess of 73,500 men.[24] Historians agree almost unanimously that tension between officers and soldiers from the regular army and those from the volunteers severely complicated every phase of military operations. Disciplining the independent-minded citizen soldier proved impossible at times, and West Point educated junior officers with combat experience often found themselves outranked by officers from volunteer units whose only qualification for command was popularity with the troops who elected them. In his letter of November 27 Steptoe observes "the best people" left Tampico thinking the American troops were volunteers, but "Finding that we are regulars they are coming back." He adds, "The excesses of the volunteers are exceedingly injurious to our cause. Murder, rapine & _____ (?) atrocity follow in their path."

Informing his sister of General Taylor's "dangerous situation" following the Battle of Palo Alto, McClellan wrote, "may the Lord deliver him, for it is pretty certain that the Volunteers won't."[25] Meade's attitude toward the volunteers, as expressed in a letter to his wife from camp near Matamoros on May 27, 1846, reflects that of regular army officers in general and of West Point graduates in particular:

> The volunteers continue to pour in, and I regret to say I do not see it with much satisfaction. They are perfectly ignorant of discipline, and most restive under restraint. They are in consequence a most disorderly mass, who will give us, I fear, more trouble than the enemy.[26]

Fellow West Point graduate (Class of 1842) and future Confederate Lieutenant General D[aniel] H[arvey] Hill, then a lieutenant with the Fourth Artillery, served with Meade at Monterrey. Hill describes the Louisiana volunteers as "a lawless drunken rabble," adding that in Matamoros the volunteers "have murdered about twenty persons [...] have committed rape, robbery, etc., etc."[27] Hill was brevetted to captain and then to major after the Battle of Chapultepec a year later, in September 1847, where Steptoe earned his brevet rank of lieutenant colonel.

The extent to which such West Point alumni connected with one another throughout the Mexican War varied considerably. By January 1847 Meade had been detached from Taylor's staff and was in Tampico anticipating the action against Vera Cruz. Steptoe's extant letters do not mention Meade, who graduated just two years ahead of him, nor do Meade's mention him, but the total student body at the Academy in the mid–1830s numbered only around 250 cadets, so it is likely they would have been acquainted. In his letter of January 24 Meade, who had reported to General Robert Patterson, one of President Polk's many political appointees, claims Taylor "has been most outrageously treated by the Administration, which hopes to play off General Scott against him, and by depriving him of all his command."[28] His analysis, historians have confirmed, proved accurate. Elsewhere in his letters Meade notes "Colonel Polk" is "known to be prejudiced against West Point."[29] Perhaps Meade and Steptoe exchanged views on such matters before Meade, encamped at Vera Cruz, on March 13, 1847, came to the conclusion he had become "a perfect cipher" and shipped out to the United States, where he would work as an engineer on lighthouse construction for the next ten years.[30] Steptoe's battery also served under Patterson's command.

Meade's letters offer a valuable picture of Tampico as Steptoe would have seen it in January 1847:

> I find the place much larger than I expected and really quite delightful. There is a large foreign population of merchants, and in consequence the town has all such comforts as good restaurants, excellent shops, where everything can be purchased, and is in fact quite as much of a place as New Orleans. [...] Tampico is a delightful place, having fine cafes, and all the luxuries of a somewhat civilized town.[31]

Meade also mentions an elegant party at which "many beautiful Mexican girls" were numbered among the guests, and he reflects his wish that "when we take Vera Cruz the foolish Mexicans will come to terms."[32] But neither the early victories in the north, culminating in the Battle of Monterrey, nor the coming success at Vera Cruz would prove sufficient, as Meade—and increasingly the administration in Washington—realized: "I do not believe they will make peace till we have given them one or two terrible thrashings, and follow up our success by marching directly on their capital."[33]

Four of Edward's six extant personal letters were sent from Tampico, a city some military visitors described as Eden-like. But Justin H. Smith in *The War with Mexico* (1919) notes that the town posed a "hard problem" for the army because of the wide availability of liquor and gambling. He writes, however, of myriad "sights and amusements":

> The many strange and beautiful trees; the mullard [mullet] and sea-trout, schools of yellow jackfish, huge, pearly tarpon, and many other denizens of the rivers and lagoons; the buzzards coasting on air, the grunting ravens, and forty other kinds of birds; the long, slender pirogues of red cedar constantly bringing luscious fruits to the market; the many vessels coming and going.[34]

Surrounded by rivers and lagoons, Tampico can be very hot and humid in the summer, but from January into March, as Steptoe and the other forces now under the command of General Scott prepared for the amphibious assault on Vera Cruz about 240 miles to the south, temperatures usually held to the 60s. Although he focuses on other matters in his January 13/15 letter from Tampico, Steptoe observes "a more splendid country never was seen," and he draws particular notice (although in general terms) to the "varied & uncommon" resources: "These are tracts of land rich as land can be, of immense size, in market but no one willing to purchase on any terms—so unsettled are affairs here. Under our rule, I should like to see our young friends in Virginia seeking their fortunes here, for they could not fail of success."[35]

Like many officers, Lieutenant Steptoe was somewhat entrepreneurial. His letter of October 1846, cited above, concludes with a paragraph opening,

"My turpentine speculations [in Florida] advance very well." All that would be required, he informed his father from Tampico, was "a little capital."

Also posted to Tampico in January 1847, Captain Robert Anderson who, like Steptoe, served in the Third Artillery, breakfasted at a café in town on "fried fish, venison, steak, eggs, buckwheat cakes, fried bananas, and coffee, enjoying his meal so much," historian Richard Winders writes, "that he returned to the same establishment for a dinner of soup, baked fish, broiled and roasted duck, lettuce salad, and potatoes (Irish and sweet)—all washed down with champagne."[36] Officers did not dine on government rations, as did enlisted men, but drew on a daily stipend for that purpose. They ate apart from the troops, "and when possible, attempted to maintain an air of gentility, setting their tables with crystal, china, and silver."[37] On January 25, newly commissioned Second Lieutenant McClellan wrote in his diary, "Tampico is a delightful place—we passed a very pleasant time there and left it with regret. [...] Champagne suppers were the order of the day (night I should say) for a long time."[38] George Wilkins Kendall, reporter for the New Orleans *Daily Picayune*, summed it up in a dispatch dated March 14, 1847: "Everything in and about this place would go to prove the go-aheadity of the Anglo-Saxon race, and that everything is fast Americanizing. Here we have an American newspaper, the American theatre, the United States Hotel, the Union Restaurant, and an American court of justice."[39]

A few days before writing, Edward tells his father in his January 13/15 letter, some seven hundred regulars and volunteers "started out to assault Tuspan [Tuxpan], a Mexican town something over a hundred miles from this [closer to ninety miles]. We had not a single cannon but were destined to attack works defended by about two to three thousand men & I know not how many guns." Fortunately, he relates, an "express came through our camp on the second day" directing them to "remain quiet until further orders." The officers "were not reluctant to return for the project appeared to the whole of us quite Quixotic, tending toward madness." The "crude conception," as Steptoe describes it, was thought to be the scheme of "one of the 12 months (or as we term them, *Mustang*) Generals—a man of decision, energy & courage, but not apt to reason very closely or correctly." The identity of this political general in charge of mostly volunteers is uncertain, but at Vera Cruz a couple of months later Steptoe's battery was serving under General Robert Patterson, an Irish-born Pennsylvania politician who has been described as "affable" but "a poor commander" in the field.[40]

While Lieutenant Steptoe's attitude toward Polk's political generals appears to have been very much in line with that of the majority of regular army officers, he was impressed with the efforts of the "Expressman alluded to," a Texas Ranger who "rode day & night for 48 hours, breaking down three horses, the Mexicans on every side & their picket Guards frequently obstructing the way." Steptoe refers specifically to "the famous Col. Kinney, of whom you have seen accounts in the papers, a Texan ranger & spy, bold as an Arab & as wily. The cool desperation of these Texan adventurers is wonderful, & they will relate to you the most hardy exploits, & their 'hair-breadth 'scapes,' with all the indifference possible." Describing a dinner with Kinney and other officers while at Tampico, Captain Anderson refers to him parenthetically as a "Texan Danl. Boone" and calls him "an extraordinary man" who "probably knows more of the Mexican character than any one with the Army."[41] The ranger mentioned here is Colonel Henry Kinney (1814–1862), who settled in Texas from Pennsylvania in 1838 and by 1840 was ranching, trading, and possibly smuggling out of the village of twenty or so buildings known as Kinney's Post, later Corpus Christi, of which Kinney is considered the founder.[42]

In his mid-January letter E.J. mentions somewhat casually, "I am ordered to embark my company tomorrow morning with two of its cannon on board a steamer for secret service. What we are to do, or where going I have not the remotest idea." Nor, unfortunately, do we, except that in his third extant letter from Tampico, dated 12 days later and still bearing the erroneous year (his fourth letter, dated February 25, 1847, aligns him with the correct year), Steptoe writes, "My whole company and myself were ship wrecked the other day, but all escaped except two of my poor fellows who were lost." In a letter to his wife dated January 25, Captain Anderson, newly arrived from Fort Brooke, Florida, writes, "Lts. Steptoe and Judd have returned to this place from an expedition about fifty miles to the north a few days since,"[43] but he mentions nothing about a shipwreck. He does, however, note "two severe storms, one very severe," he felt fortunate to survive. In his recently reprinted journal Private Jacob Oswandel of the First Pennsylvania Volunteers, aboard ship headed for the Island of Lobos about sixty miles south of Tampico, describes an "awful storm" that occurred on the 10th and 11th of February, very likely the one Steptoe mentions to his father.[44] E.J. professes in his letter of January 27 to be "exceedingly busy" preparing his flying artillery company for the amphibious assault on Vera Cruz in hopes he will "put it in the way of distinction ere long."[45]

He also awaits General Scott's arrival to take command of his "gallant little army," a phrase Oswandel employs a dozen times in his journal and that historian Timothy D. Johnson appropriated for the title of his 2007 study of Scott's six-month campaign to take Mexico City.[46] Scott's assumption of command occurred the evening of February 19, when he arrived aboard the steamer *Massachusetts* to a "thunderous reception," one reporter noted, from the nine thousand troops waiting to embark.[47] In his January 27 letter Steptoe indicates "7 or 8000 men are assembled here now, regulars & volunteers. It is the largest body of soldiers I ever saw convened." In his letter of February 25 Edward informs his father without elaboration that he is "attached to Genl. Pillow's Brigade of Tennesseans," a volunteer militia unit.[48]

Historians are virtually unanimous in concluding that Gideon J. Pillow was the worst of Polk's political appointments to the rank of general. Known to be the president's personal friend and a political crony, Pillow had "no previous military background."[49] Justin Smith wrote, "Naturally Pillow felt inclined to look upon the soldiers as merely coal for his furnace, and they in turn generally detested him."[50] Writing from Mexico City on October 29, 1847, for the *Daily Picayune*, Kendall slammed Pillow as "the laughing-stock of the army."[51] Whether Steptoe harbored such doubts about his commanding officer we will probably never know. It may be he refused to indulge potentially insubordinate comments concerning a superior officer, even of volunteers, or it may be he was simply discreet. Scott's disputes with the ambitious and obstreperous Pillow eventually led to a court of inquiry, but President Polk came to his rescue.

The bottom line intention of Steptoe's January 27 letter home is a little self-promotion: "We hear that some new Regiments of the line are to be raised—please use your influence to get me a majority or the *first captaincy*, in one of them if several are raised. [...] It is said that 9 or 10 Regiments are spoken of—would that I could get the majority of one of them. They will be permanently in service tis thought. Please write to your representative on the subject." The next month Congress did create ten new regiments of regulars to serve for the duration of the war, but if Dr. Steptoe attempted to use his influence on his son's behalf, he apparently failed. Such efforts to influence promotion may appear unusual today, but in the army of the mid-nineteenth century an aspiring young officer would avail himself of any possible leverage. In a letter written from Tampico on January 27, 1847, McClellan, who had been commissioned a second lieutenant for scarcely six months, pleads with his father, like Steptoe's a physician, "I write particularly to beg you to try and get me an appointment in one of the new Regiments of Infantry—a Captaincy I want. I would not like to accept anything less."[52] For both Steptoe and McClellan brevet promotions would come soon enough.

In his February 25 letter E.J. writes, "The troops here have been embarking for several days for Lobos Island, the point of rendezvous preparatory for the attack on Vera Cruz."[53] The successful siege would open the door to Mexico City and possibly force the shaky government of President Valentín Gómez Farías to negotiate. His presidency would last a little under three months, to be followed by those of Antonio López de Santa Anna for the ninth but not the last time (about ten days), Pedro María de Anaya (one month), Santa Anna again (about four months), Manuel de la Peña y Peña (a month and a half), and Anaya again (about two months). Those six presidential sojourns account for the year 1847 in Mexico's chaotic history, and their brief visits to the office may also account as much as anything for the failure of peace negotiations short of the overthrow of the capital city itself.

Lobos Island (named for "sea wolves," or seals), located about sixty miles south of Tampico and ten miles offshore of Vera Cruz, measures about five hundred yards across. A correspondent for a Philadelphia newspaper wrote in February of 1847,

> The Island of Lobos is a lovely little spot, formed entirely of coral, about two miles in circumference [...]. It is covered (or was before we landed) with a variety of trees and shrubs, the highest of the former perhaps twenty-five feet high, and these are so thickly covered with vines that one can hardly get through them. There is hardly a tree or shrub, or plant growing here I have ever before seen. [...] Lemon, lime, fig, palm, cane, and a hundred other species of wood are growing with all the freshness and beauty of the Indies.[54]

Observing the temperature that day had risen to 92°, the Philadelphia reporter concluded, "The universal remark among the volunteers is, 'If this is winter, what will summer be?'" Within just a few days the area would be hit with a powerful "Blue Norther," the weather phenomenon that can bring howling winds and drop temperatures twenty to thirty degrees in minutes. "Another Norther," Captain Anderson wrote his wife, "is now *screaming* its approach."[55]

Although embarkation had to be put off for a couple of days, E.J. expresses considerable confidence in his "splendid Battery": "I have six fine Guns & more than a hundred horses to carry. Perhaps you may hear of 'Steptoe's Battery' yet—I hope in terms of commendation. Certainly a prettier command no officer ever had." In a letter to his parents dated February 4/5, 1847, Lieutenant McClellan expresses boredom with his life in Tampico, "for I like to be in motion. You have no idea of the charm and excitement of a march. I could live such a life for years without becoming tired of it. [...] You never saw such a merry set as we are. No care, no trouble, we criticize the Generals, laugh and swear at the mustangs and volunteers, smoke our cigars and drink our brandy—when we have any—go without when we have none. [...] We are living off the fat of the land—game, oysters, vegetables of all kinds, champagne, &c., &c., warm baths when we want them."[56] But ten days later he complains to his father that it is "certainly too late to attack Vera Cruz" because of the approach of the "vomito" (yellow fever) season.[57] A week after that, however, the antsy McClellan was "hourly expecting to embark for Vera Cruz" by way of Lobos Island.[58]

Joseph Wheelan opens his history of the Mexican War with a dramatic prologue recounting the amphibious landing at Collado Beach about two miles south of the fortified city of Vera Cruz, out of range of the 113 cannons on the outer walls and of the 136 cannon at the major defensive works of the fortress known as San Juan de Ulúa some thousand yards offshore.[59] The "first major American amphibious assault" in the nation's history would open up "a second front in the ten-month-old Mexican War" and it would come off without a single casualty among the 8,600 troops to be landed.[60] Captain Anderson tells his wife in a letter dated March 13, "the landing was a most thrilling and exciting affair."[61] The fleet of about eighty ships anchored off the tiny island of Sacrificios, where Spanish conquistadors nearly 330 years earlier had encountered the remains of recent human sacrifice. From that distance all could see the snow-covered peak of Mount Orizaba (nearly 18,500 feet elevation) some 75 miles inland. Cold, blustery northers would plague the siege and cause greater discomfort than Mexican shot and shell, but the day of the landing, March 9, featured cloudless blue skies and a "gentle, soothing breeze from the southeast, rippling but not breaking the surface of the sea, yet sufficient to permit the beaching craft to retract with ease."[62]

Private Oswandel, who mentions Steptoe several times in his journal, reports the "great enthusiasm" aboard ship as the landing commenced with "bustle and excitement" and bands played "Yankee Doodle" and "Hail Columbia." The lyrics suggest the spirit of exceptionalism and naïve jingoism that accompanied the vision of Manifest Destiny:

> Hail Columbia, happy land!
> Hail, ye heroes, heav'n-born band,
> Who fought and bled in freedom's cause ...

Longfellow and Thoreau may not have been caught up in that fervor, but ordinary soldiers like Jake Oswandel were, and so were their officers, from General Scott down to Lieutenant McClellan, and very likely including Steptoe.

Lieutenant D.H. Hill landed the next day "in great confusion." He notes the enemy "made a fatal mistake in not opposing us on the beach with desperate determination."[63] Serving with the Fourth Artillery under General Worth and the regulars, Hill complains of "dreadfully hot" days and of nights that are "damp and cold." The siege would last about twenty days, ending with capitulation of the Mexican garrison on March 28, but Hill's diary indicates the troops suffered from violent storms and "very cold" nights at least nine of those days. On the 27th, he writes, "an unusually fierce Norther was throwing sand by the hogshead upon the cannoneers."[64] Vicious fleas, prickly chaparral surrounding the city of between ten and fifteen thousand beleaguered inhabitants, and the challenge of wrestling artillery over huge sand dunes added to the discomfort. Hill estimates one of the dunes to have been "at least seventy-five feet in perpendicular height without the smallest bush or shrub on it."[65] Field artillery batteries usually featured the 12-pounder gun, weighing 1,800 pounds and with a range of something over 1,600 yards, and the 24-pounder howitzer, which allowed for higher trajectory.[66]

Hill notes on March 10 and March 11 that Lieutenant Steptoe had not yet shown up, but on the 11th he indicates half of his six-piece battery arrived.[67] Sounding perhaps more like an enlisted man than an Academy-educated officer, D.H. Hill complains more than once of "the deplorable imbecility of our chiefs," General David E. Twiggs being the most frequent recipient of his annoyance.[68] On March 15, the same day he reports having seen "an enormous green lizard almost as large as a young alligator" (surely an iguana), Hill records "the great victory, the greatest ever won by Americans" of General Taylor at "frigid Buena Vista."[69] Although outnumbered about three to one, Taylor suffered 272 dead and 387 wounded to Santa Anna's 591 dead and 1,048 wounded along with an additional 1,894 missing, most of whom may have deserted.[70] The batteries of both Lieutenant Braxton Bragg, who graduated in Steptoe's class at the Academy, and Captain Thomas W. Sherman, who graduated the year before, distinguished themselves as Buena Vista, some seven hundred miles to the north. On March 18 Hill notes, "Lt. Steptoe has arrived and landed. He is with Genl. Patterson."[71] But he adds that he thinks field batteries will be of little use during the siege, and in all likelihood only Steptoe's pair of 24-pounder howitzers would have been employed.

Of greater importance to the siege was the Navy's landing of four heavy Paixhan guns (32- and 68-pounders); the company of engineers under Captain Robert E. Lee and Lieutenants McClellan and Pierre Gustave Toutant Beauregard constructed the revetments "At the bombardment's height," Wheelan writes, "American batteries poured 180 rounds of shot and shell into Vera Cruz every hour."[72] Bauer reports during the four-day bombardment, "American artillery fired 6,700 shot and shell, weighing about 463,000 pounds, into the city."[73] While the U.S. lost only 13 killed and 55 wounded, "at least 350 Mexican soldiers and 400 civilians lay dead, the total wounded uncounted."[74]

General Scott orchestrated this victory by investing the city of Vera Cruz on the western side, stringing out his troops a mile or so from the city walls and moving his artillery batteries to within just a few hundred yards. From that distance American troops could hear the screams of the citizens, including women and children, as the Mexican soldiers shouted "to show their bravery, and indifference," Hill writes, "whilst our men, really feeling a total disregard of the havoc going on, were singing and playing flutes."[75]

Outnumbered three-to-one by Scott's troops, the garrison under General Juan Morales dared not risk much in the way of sorties. As to the anticipated attacks from their rear, these appear to have been rare. Lieutenant Hill writes on March 26 of having learned that "Col. Harney with some of his Dragoons and Lt. Steptoe with his Battery had had a skirmish with a large body of the enemy and had driven them back destroying a strong barricade on the road."[76] In his letter dated March 27, 1847, his last extant personal correspondence from Mexico, Steptoe writes rather dismissively: "I have not been brought into action yet but yesterday two of my Guns were required to break through a barricade the Enemy had reared on a bridge some miles out. I sent them & then followed on. The Enemy fired fast & close but seven or eight shots of canister dispersed them. I lost one of my men only which was a very small loss considering the Mexicans were only about 30 yards from our Guns."[77]

E.J. candidly informs his father, "the Town & castle [Ulúa] capitulated today after a short but fierce fight. It was a fight solely between the *heavy* artillery of the two armies & as my Guns were Field Pieces I took no other part than to guard an avenue to the city & prevent ingress & egress to the Enemy. But I was stationed on a height & saw the whole. For three days the air was literally filled with flaming, hissing Balls. You could hear our shells crushing through roofs of houses & bursting with a noise like distant thunder & a flash of lightning. The Enemy shot splendidly, but thanks to a watchful Providence harmlessly, considering their rapidity of fire." The Third Artillery Regiment, including Steptoe, was briefly garrisoned at Ulúa, but even if he saw it only from a distance, it must have reminded him of Fort Marion (Castillo de San Marcos) in St. Augustine, Florida, a "castle" he knew very well. Captain Anderson sardonically reports being "delighted to receive orders to leave the pleasant quarters of the Fortaleza de Ulua" where he had "the honor of being bitten by day and night by fleas which might have legitimately descended from the Conquerors of this Country. Defend me from a summer residence in the justly celebrated Ulua!"[78] Lieutenant Steptoe, D.H. Hill notes, "fired the national salute on the plain where the ceremony of surrender took place."[79] "Whither we go hence," Steptoe wrote his father, "I cannot tell—probably to Jalapa with the chance of a combat en route. The Enemy may possibly come to terms if any Government can be found bold enough to compound with us."

As it happened, no such bold government came to Mexico's rescue. General Scott did indeed head toward a respite in the comfortable mountain city of Jalapa (elevation 4,680 feet; population around 5,000), about 68 miles by line of march to the northwest in the Sierra Madres, leaving the threat of yellow fever and the vomito season behind him in Vera Cruz. Lieutenant Steptoe was also correct in his anticipation of "a combat en route." This would occur at a village called Cerro Gordo ("fat hill"), located about 16 miles east of Jalapa (Xalapa), in the middle of April. Actually, by this date it was "Captain

"The Battle of Cerro Gordo" (April 18, 1847), presumably featuring General Winfield Scott, "Old Fuss and Feathers," in full dress uniform on horseback waving his troops forward. Captain Steptoe was brevetted to major for his action on Atalaya Hill. Courtesy Library of Congress.

Edward J. Steptoe," for his promotion, after nearly nine years as a first lieutenant, is officially dated March 3, 1847, although he would not likely have been informed of it while in the midst of combat at Vera Cruz. Perhaps his father had put in a good word on his behalf with the congressional delegation from Virginia, but more likely his time had come at last.

Steptoe and his battery accompanied Colonel William S. Harney's command as part of Brigadier General Twiggs' division as it advanced from Vera Cruz moving along the National Highway northwestward toward Jalapa on April 2. In a diary entry McClellan notes in passing "Steptoe was with Twiggs," and he had been assigned to Harney before.[80] Harney, whose path Steptoe probably crossed in Florida, served as Scott's cavalry commander and would be brevetted to brigadier general following the battle at Cerro Gordo. The bull-necked Twiggs has been described as "recklessly aggressive" and overly inclined to frontal assaults, but at Cerro Gordo General Patterson countermanded his orders for a "potentially suicidal attack."[81] April 9 was "extremely hot," Private Oswandel wrote, "dusty and hot."[82] Although winter uniforms were authorized from the first of October through the end of April, troops had probably shed their traditional sky-blue wool shell jackets (offers wore dark blue) for white cotton ones.

Nearly halfway from Vera Cruz to Jalapa, Steptoe and his dusty column crossed the Antigua River over a deep gorge at the National Bridge (Puente Nacional) on the National or "Royal" Highway (Camino Real). "The road—all the way very hot and dusty," wrote Lieutenant Colonel Ethan Allen Hitchcock in his diary for April 15.[83] In his April 11 journal entry Private Oswandel describes the bridge as "fine, substantial" and "well constructed," and he draws attention to "a beautiful stream of water, called Rio Antiqua, or Old River," noting that several of the men bathed in the stream that evening.[84] The troops endured sporadic firing from guerrillas, and attacks from the chaparral-covered hills (mostly gnarly dwarf oak, long-spine cholla, and prickly pear) remained frequent even after the Battle of Cerro Gordo and the occupation of Jalapa. Passing through the small town of Puente Nacional three months later, Richard McSherry, a Navy physician serving with the Marines accompanying General Franklin Pierce on their way to join Mississippi politician and political General John A. Quitman's division for the attack on Mexico City, found the scenery "majestic—reminding me forcibly of Harper's Ferry—though more primitive." McSherry found the stream reminiscent of "our own Shenandoah."[85]

Historians have assigned much of the credit for the victory at Cerro Gordo to the reconnaissance work of Lieutenant Beauregard and Captain Robert E. Lee, who discovered that seizing the hill of Atalaya would allow U.S. troops to flank the Mexican left, essentially attacking from the rear, while General Pillow's division launched a diversionary attack. Scott specifically cited Lee for his role in setting up Steptoe's battery, which "served with effect."[86] Fortunately for the Yankees, Santa Anna deployed only about 3,000 of the 12,000 troops at his disposal, holding the remainder in reserve. Three of Steptoe's heavy 24-pounders were manhandled up Atalaya, where they outdueled Mexican artillery on the higher hill (between five hundred and six hundred feet) known as El Telégrafo.[87] Assaulted from front and rear and bombarded by Steptoe's battery, the Mexican forces on El Telégrafo retreated, and the three-hour Battle of Cerro Gordo ended in the headlong flight of Santa Anna's troops, leaving Jalapa, the "city of flowers," to General Scott. Jalapa welcomed Scott's troops, even though Santa Anna was a native son whose hacienda, Encero, was located about seven miles away.

Of the 8,500 or so U.S. troops engaged at Cerro Gordo, casualties amounted to 63 killed and 368 wounded. Mexican forces suffered the usual disproportionate casualties, about 200 killed, nearly a thousand wounded, and as many as 3,000 captured, most of whom had to be paroled, as Scott had no way to provide for them. American dragoons and troops of the Fourth Illinois in the ensuing pursuit seized Santa Anna's personal carriage along with $20,000 in coin and one of Santa Anna's wooden legs, "which for years afterward was kept on display in the Illinois state capitol."[88]

Private Oswandel was attracted to verse, and although his taste was not particularly admirable, his inclusion of a ditty known as "The Leg I Left Behind Me," to be sung to the popular Irish tune "The Girl I Left Behind Me," merits quotation of the opening lines:

> I am stumpless quite since from the shot
> Of Cerro Gordo peggin',
> I left behind, to pay Gen. Scott,
> *My grub, and gave my leg in.*
> I dare not turn to view the place
> Lest Yankee foes should find me,
> And mocking shake before my face
> *The Leg I Left Behind Me.*[89]

The meter succeeds in the third line if "Gen." is pronounced as a monosyllable ("jen"). British versions of the lyrics date back to the 1790s and of the music to the first decade of the 19th century.[90] The original song remained popular with American soldiers on the frontier, through the Civil War, and for decades thereafter.

Scott ordered his quartermasters not simply to commandeer supplies at Jalapa, but to pay for them, although a certain amount of foraging and pillaging did occur, most of it to be blamed on the volunteers. Ironically, Scott's policy of attempting to curry favor with local residents meant purchasing rather than requisitioning cattle owned by Santa Anna himself. Jalapa served for upwards of three months as a sort of R-and-R station while Scott awaited the arrival of reinforcements for his assault on Mexico City, commencing with battles at Contreras and Churubusco in August. For his role at the Battle of Cerro Gordo Captain Steptoe was brevetted to the rank of major dating from April 18.

No other extant personal letters from E.J. Steptoe tell of his experiences during the Mexican War, but fellow officers mention him in several accounts, and he would be brevetted to lieutenant colonel on September 13, 1847, for "gallant and meritorious conduct" (the standard phrasing of the day) at the Battle of Chapultepec before Mexico City. During his sojourn in the resort city of Jalapa, E.J., like others on the expedition, may have been stricken with the beauty of the local señoritas. Sergeant Thomas Barclay of the Second Pennsylvania Infantry notes, "While tramping around we saw several beautiful women, who will compare favorably with the lasses in the States, although as a matter of course they are not so handsome as the girls we've left behind us."[91] A correspondent for the *Boston Advertiser* writing from Jalapa on May 3, was more "discriminating": "Many [ladies of Jalapa] are of unmixed Castilian descent, and quite beautiful."[92] Captain Steptoe was single, good looking, with fine dark features, and just 31 years old. Thanks to his West Point education, he knew some French; perhaps, like Dr. McSherry, he also learned some Spanish. Several of his letters indicate he had an eye for attractive women.

Private Oswandel reports in his journal for May 23, 1847, that General Worth's division had been engaged in "a little fight" with some two thousand of Santa Anna's cavalry about ten miles from Puebla, and Steptoe's battery, with those of Duncan and Bonneville, "got into position" and "commenced to fire, and the way our fellows poured the grape, canister and shell in and among them was a caution. [...] The victory was complete, and the enemy fled in all directions." After that, Worth proceeded into Puebla "without the firing of a gun."[93] E.J.'s battery would assemble with Quitman's division at Puebla, about 75 miles east of the capital and the second largest city in Mexico. "One of the most beautiful cities I have ever seen," Colonel Hitchcock recorded in his diary.[94] Scott's troops began their triumphal entry on May 14.[95] "Friends, think of it," Oswandel exulted, "a little over four thousand, marching into a city with a population of seventy-five or eighty thousand, without firing a gun!"[96]

Steptoe and others in Mexico at the time probably paid little heed to news that the Latter Day Saints, or Mormons as they were commonly called, had arrived in the Utah Territory and on July 24, 1847, their leader, Brigham Young, looked out on the valley of the Great Salt Lake and famously declared, "This is the place." A little over seven years later Steptoe would be offered the governorship of that territory by Franklin Pierce, a brigadier general commanding volunteers in 1847. The future fourteenth president, Pierce suffered a severe knee injury when his horse was shot from under him at the Battle of Contreras on August 19.

The troops, including what journalist George Wilkins Kendall described as "Steptoe's admirable battery,"[97] left Puebla on August 8 hoping, in Dr. McSherry's words, "to enter the famed capital of Mexico" on the thirteenth of August, "the anniversary of the triumph of the great Spanish conqueror," Hernando Cortez, over the last Aztec emperor, Cuauhtémoc, in 1521.[98] In letters and diaries from soldiers and officers referring to the storming of the "Halls of Montezuma," one rarely encounters anything like a 20th- or 21st-century uneasiness over assuming the mantle of new conquistador. Mexico's generally recognized socio-economic and political chaos was among several factors, which included animosity toward Roman Catholicism and at least some degree of racism or ethnocentrism.

An entry from the journal of Sergeant Barclay, whose infantry regiment of Pennsylvania volunteers served with Steptoe's battery in Quitman's division, puts it well enough:

> But Mexico torn by civil internal convulsions, pressed by a foreign war, the center of her territory invaded and in possession of the foe can only preserve her nationality by sacrificing territory to her affectionate sister of the north. [...] [T]he young of the present generation may see the day when the "Stars and Stripes" which now float in triumph over the City will be the banner under whose folds the inhabitants of all Mexico will find shelter and protection. The Anglo-Saxon race, that land loving people are on the move. [...] However great a calamity war may be and however much we may regret the sad consequences which follow in its train mankind will have no cause to mourn a change of things in this Country.[99]

Sergeant Barclay goes on to celebrate the "spirit of the age" and to lament the influence of "the holy fathers who like locusts of Egypt darken the land."

How much of that ethos Captain Steptoe might have shared is uncertain, but Barclay's straightforwardly asserted views appear to represent the prevailing sentiment in the United States at the time. "Every man is a creature of the age in which he lives," wrote Voltaire in the middle of the 18th century, "and few are able to raise themselves above the ideas of the time." It seems unlikely that Steptoe would have been numbered among those few.

Although portions of Quitman's division were engaged, Steptoe's battery was apparently not involved in the important action known as the Battle of Contreras on August 19–20, 1847, where Captain Lee again distinguished himself. Left with most of Quitman's division to defend the supply depot and hospital at San Agustín. Steptoe's battery did not participate in the Battle of Churubusco, at a Franciscan convent located three or four miles northeast of Contreras, also on August 20. This may have been fortunate for Steptoe, as the action at the head of the bridge over the Churubusco River proved costly for Captain Francis Taylor's battery, which lost more than two dozen men before being forced to withdraw. The day would be carried by the infantry, sometimes in hand-to-hand fighting, and Scott's forces triumphed, but at the loss of more than 130 killed. An armistice followed during which Polk's appointed commissioner, Nicholas Trist, attempted to negotiate a peace treaty, but to no avail, as Santa Anna used the time to strengthen his defenses. Historians regard the Battle of Churubusco as "the bloodiest day of the whole war," accounting for more American casualties than any other battle, the dead and wounded numbering more than a thousand.[100] Mexican casualties, including more than twelve hundred captured, numbered nearly two thousand.

Hostilities against the capital recommenced on September 8 with General William Worth's assault on the heavily defended Molino del Rey ("King's Mill"), located about a thousand yards from the Castle of Chapultepec, where the Mexican military academy was located. The Battle of Molino del Rey has been described as a "pyrrhic victory," the dead and wounded by some accounts being about equal at nearly eight hundred per side.[101] Among the severely wounded was Assistant Surgeon James Simons, who along with Steptoe had greeted Lieutenant William T. Sherman on the dock at Fort Pierce in the fall of 1840. Captain Anderson, who was also wounded in the battle, refers to it in a letter to his wife as a "murderous affair."[102] At this point, as the crucial assault on what McSherry calls "the dread castle of Chapultepec," located about seven miles from the center of Mexico City, was about to get underway, Captain Steptoe's company was brought into action.[103]

"On the evening of the 11th," lieutenant of engineers P.G.T. Beauregard reports in his brief reminiscences of the war, "I put Steptoe's battery of two 12-pound and two 24-pound howitzers in position to fire in the morning against the works at San Antonio."[104] Although he was brevetted to both captain and major for his action at Contreras and Churubusco and at Chapultepec, Beauregard, who graduated second in his class at West Point a year after Steptoe, would leave Mexico "an embittered and unhappy man," feeling he had been neglected in official reports.[105] He would be serving as the Confederacy's first brigadier general on April 12, 1861, when he ordered the attack on Fort Sumter against Major Robert Anderson. "As soon as the batteries were completed," the exhausted Beauregard reports, "I turned them over to my friend Captain Steptoe of the artillery, who was to command them."[106] (Steptoe would be known by his brevet rank of major several months later.) At daylight on September 12 in "an ostentatious display" both Francis Taylor's and Steptoe's batteries "boldly fired against the southern edge of the city" in a diversionary action that was to last the better part of two days.[107]

In his reports of September 18, 1847, General Scott indicates on the 11th "Twiggs, with Riley's brigade and Captains Taylor's and Steptoe's field batteries—the latter of 12-pounders—was left in front of those [southern] gates to manouevre, to threaten, or to make false attacks, in order to occupy and deceive the enemy."[108] This "stratagem," he notes, was "admirably executed," thus "holding a great part of the Mexican army on the defensive."[109] The diversionary fire against the Garita de Niño Perdido (Gate of the Wild or "Lost" Boy) did much to ensure the success of the assault on Chapultepec (the word translates as "grasshopper hill"). New Orleans *Daily Picayune* correspondent Kendall wrote on October 14, "The important part taken by the batteries of Steptoe and Taylor, in diverting the enemy in the direction of La Piedad and Niño Perdido I am fearful were not even alluded to [in the official reports]. If I live to get home, full and most complete justice shall be done to all who took part in the glorious achievements."[110] Lester R. Dillon considers Chapultepec to have "furnished the war's best example of integrated fires and a coordinated artillery-infantry."[111]

In the assault on the castle, D.H. Hill volunteered to lead a detachment from the Fourth Artillery, what he called a "forlorn hope" of a "storming party."[112] Elsewhere on the field of battle Lieutenant James Longstreet, who graduated near the bottom of the West Point Class of 1842 and served as a Lieutenant General for the Confederacy, was badly wounded while carrying the regimental colors. His friend Lieutenant George Pickett retrieved them and reached the top of the hill. The officers joined again famously, and tragically, at the Battle of Gettysburg in July 1863. Army Lieutenant Ulysses S. Grant and Navy Lieutenant Raphael Semmes, who would command the Confederate raider, the CSS *Alabama*, during the Civil War, fought side-by-side on the causeway leading to the Garita de San Cosme, Semmes serving with a company of Marines. Also figuring importantly in the assault were 23-year-old Lieutenant Thomas J. Jackson (West Point Class of 1846) of the First Artillery, later to be renowned as Confederate General "Stonewall" Jackson, and Lieutenant Colonel Joseph E. Johnston, leading four companies of light infantry, who would rise to the rank of brigadier general in the U.S. Army before resigning his commission to serve eventually as full (four-star) general for the Confederacy.

American losses in the Battle of Chapultepec amounted to 130 killed and 703 wounded; Mexican losses are approximated at about three thousand, including 823 taken prisoner.[113] Such raw statistics do not address the carnage. Included among the Mexican dead, for example, are the *Niños Héroes*, six young cadets between the ages of 13 and 19, who were killed in the assault and who are still venerated as martyrs. The last one surviving is said to have wrapped himself in the national flag and thrown himself from the parapet in order to keep it from falling into enemy hands. Dr. McSherry's account is quite graphic:

> Their dead bodies lay in masses of tens, twenties, or more, wherever there had been concentration; some there were gasping in the last agonies, with their dark faces upturned to the sun, like fish thrown on shore by the angler, writhing and struggling in death; others lay motionless, but an occasional gasp, an upheaving of the chest, alone gave evidence that the vital spark had not entirely fled.[114]

McSherry continued his way "among the fearful mutilations of the human body lying around. [...] I was soon earnestly engaged in my occupations, lopping off crushed limbs, and dressing wounds." He notes the "remarkable stoicism" of the wounded: "In one instance, while taking off the forearm of a rifleman, a sturdy son of the Emerald Isle, with a shattered wrist, he conversed calmly during the operation, uttering not a groan; and the arteries were scarcely tied, before he was smoking a pipe borrowed from a comrade."[115] It is unlikely McSherry had any anesthetics at his disposal.

Essentially the war with Mexico was over, but the aftermath would carry into the next year. Because he was the only staff officer available who could speak Spanish, Lieutenant Beauregard was sent to consult with the Mexicans after they showed a white flag the morning of September 14. By two o'clock that morning Santa Anna and his army had already left the capital on the road to Guadalupe Hidalgo. "After leaving a garrison at the *garita* and at the citadel [Chapultepec]," Beauregard exclaims, "we marched toward the main plaza of the city with only about three or four regiments and Steptoe's battery!"[116]

"Strange and almost incredible seems our victory," wrote D.H. Hill on September 18. Hostilities in the capital continued, however, as mobs alternated with rooftop snipers to make life on the streets of Mexico City perilous for Scott's troops for several days, and guerrilla warfare raged throughout the country, particularly at Puebla, where Brevet Colonel Thomas Childs was forced to withstand a 28-day siege by some four thousand troops under Brigadier General Joaquín Rea (rains had made roads from Mexico City impassable). Troops under Brigadier General Joseph Lane, who had led Indiana volunteers at Buena Vista, lifted the siege on October 12, but only after he permitted his troops to ransack the village of Huamantla in "a drunken spree of pillage, murder, rape, and wanton destruction."[117]

By September 20 Lieutenant Hill was sightseeing in Mexico City, visiting the great cathedral, built between 1573 and 1813, and a museum connected with the University of Mexico. On the 22nd he notes, "I called to see Capt. Steptoe this evening. He is occupying Genl. Spinosa's house, by far the most magnificent I have ever seen. Whilst there the General came in and showed his resignation and asked if he would be permitted to occupy his house. 'Twas a strange sight that of a Mexican General asking an American Captain permission to occupy his own house."[118] Steptoe may have accompanied his fellow officer on sightseeing ventures. This not-so-welcome tourism would be about Mexico's only gain from the war.

On November 29, 1847, far to the north in what would become the Washington Territory, a tragedy was played out that might be regarded as prologue to the climactic event of Steptoe's military career. In 1836, under the auspices of the American Board of Commissioners for Foreign Missions (largely Presbyterian), Dr. Marcus Whitman, a physician, and his wife Narcissa established a mission among the Cayuse Indians about six miles west of present day Walla Walla. After Marcus Whitman led a group of wagon trains in 1843 along what became the Oregon Trail, relations with the local tribes grew strained, and following a measles epidemic in 1847, which the Cayuse blamed on the Whitmans (notably on Dr. Whitman as a false shaman), the tribe attacked the mission killing the Whitmans and a dozen others in what has been called the Whitman Massacre. The Cayuse War that followed would continue sporadically into 1855. In the summer of 1856 Steptoe would begin building Fort Walla Walla near the site of the Whitman mission.

Hill next refers to Steptoe in a diary entry dated December 15, 1847, in which he describes General Scott's arrest of the politically ambitious Generals Worth and Pillow on various charges including bribery. Details of the inquiry, in which Worth and Pillow were exonerated, are not especially pertinent here. President Polk had long wanted to rid himself of Scott, whom he regarded as a political adversary, and he used the fracas to remove him from command and replace him with Major General William Butler, the transfer occurring on February 19, 1848. Scott left Mexico City on April 23 and embarked from Vera Cruz on May 2 with slight fanfare. "Genl. Butler is a creature of Mr. Polk's appointment," Hill wrote in his diary, "and of course a fool."[119]

In a mid-December entry Hill notes in passing that "Steptoe's battery of two twelve-pounders and two twenty-four pound Howitzers is assigned to the Division of Volunteers under Genl. Patterson."[120] Patterson had returned to Mexico in the fall, following General Lane's troops into Puebla in October, and resumed his former command, which devolved on General Quitman, then serving as Military Governor of Mexico City. Private Oswandel writes in his journal of visiting Mexico City on Christmas day 1847 "for the purpose of eating our Christmas dinner" and to visit the "curiosities" of the capital, including "the great Cathedral, which stands on the very spot where the old halls of Montezuma once stood."[121] He observes the building was "illuminated with five thousand wax lights," he saw "an image of our Saviour in a [rocking] cradle," and the organ was "playing to its utmost extent." He and his comrades enjoyed dinner at the Laqunda or Lake Hotel. Perhaps Steptoe and his fellow officers celebrated in similar fashion.

On February 2, 1848, the long awaited and carefully negotiated Treaty of Guadalupe-Hidalgo was signed, officially ending the war with the United States being granted virtually everything it wanted. The official ratification and conclusion to the war came on May 30, 1848; General Butler's Orders #122 to the army ("the homeward march will be at once commenced") is dated May 29.[122] By that date "Old Rough and Ready," General Zachary Taylor, famous for rarely wearing any matching parts to a regulation uniform, had taken office as the nation's twelfth president. The Whig hero of Monterrey and Buena Vista, and Polk's longtime adversary, would die after just 16 months in office, his place to be taken by his unheralded vice president, Millard Fillmore, the last Whig to serve as president. If Steptoe stayed with Patterson's division, which seems likely, he may have been on the steamer *Massachusetts*, which landed Patterson and his staff at New Orleans on July 12, 1848, although his name is not mentioned in the *Niles Register* for that date.[123] By mid-August of that year Steptoe was back in garrison at Fort McHenry.

Writing just a couple of years after the war ended, Brevet Major Isaac Ingalls Stevens, who served as adjutant with the Corps of Engineers from Vera Cruz through the capture of Mexico City, summed up his sentiments, grandly analogizing the American victory to that of Philip of Macedonia and Alexander the Great over the Persians:

> We prevailed over the Mexicans for the same reasons that the Greeks conquered Persia. [...] The people of Asia were living in their past renown, and were in the full fruition of the accumulations of past generations. They succumbed to a people having a future which they were resolved to achieve. [...] So of the people of Mexico. Their future is their past. They have neither the spirit of enterprise, nor the individuality of the people of the United States. They have not had our two hundred years of discipline and of culture, in the full enjoyment of regulated liberty.[124]

These sentiments, ringing with the pomp of Yankee exceptionalism, echoed those of most Americans, at that time, probably including Captain Steptoe. Stevens was a third classman the year Steptoe graduated from the Academy. Whether they were acquainted at West Point or in Mexico, their paths would cross importantly about eight years later in Washington, where Stevens served as the first territorial governor.

* * *

We know very little for certain about Steptoe's personal experiences in Mexico after the siege of Vera Cruz. Like Captain Anderson he must have choked on the dust during the advance to Jalapa. He may have been attracted to the Castilian ladies as were Sergeant Barclay and news correspondent George Kendall. Surely he stood in awe of mounts Orizaba and Popocatepetl. As in Florida, he was under fire, but although he was in harm's way, we have no evidence he was ever placed in desperate circumstances as was Captain Anderson at El Molino del Rey. We can only conjecture as to how he spent such holidays as July 4, of which Anderson writes, "The anniversary of our glorious independence. Many, very many years must pass before the common people, the public of this miscalled Republic, will be sufficiently enlightened to enjoy the blessings of independence."[125] Private Oswandel writes of being roused out of bed at 4:00 a.m., and although he mentions the appeal of pulque, his comments on the Fourth of July 1847 focus mostly on a dusty march rounded off with a driving downpour. Steptoe's experiences on that day would have mirrored those of the bedraggled private.

On November 11 that year Steptoe turned 32, recently promoted to the rank of captain and twice brevetted, largely unscathed by combat, and confident he had made the right choice of profession, although his promotion to major (and to that pay grade) lay almost seven years ahead. Most likely he celebrated the New Year, 1848, in Mexico City looking forward to his return home, but that lay more than six months ahead. In his official correspondence through the summer of 1848 Steptoe signed himself "Capt. 3rd Arty" but by August of 1850 he had added "Bt. Lt. Col."

Although no personal letters are extant from Steptoe's last months in Mexico, a few letters he sent from Jalapa to the Adjutant General's office in June 1848 indicate the nature of his activities. His letter dated June 22 pertains to pay for troops who had served under his command. He concludes tersely: "You can perceive from the Muster Rolls, that not many of my original Company remain to get this benefit—death has carried them off mostly."[126] Entering the city in April 1847, Oswandel likened the place to the Garden of Eden, the air being scented with the aroma of orange blossoms: "I was astonished to see how neat and clean everything looked, in and around the city, not only the streets and houses, but the citizens, themselves."[127] Steptoe's last posting in Mexico would be comfortable. He devoted his attention mostly to his men, as indicated by a pair of letters sent on June 23, 1848. The first, to the Adjutant General, requests the pay of light artillery for the "officers & men of my Battery" who have "suffered much by losses during this campaign."[128] Steptoe's letter outlines his unit's activities from the siege of Vera Cruz in March 1847 through the occupation of Toluca in May 1848, and it mentions the men's losses in the shipwreck off Tampico on January 19, 1847, along with additional losses from a ship that went down off Charleston in December 1846. The second letter commends to General Jones' attention a Lieutenant H. Brown for his "gallantry, zeal, energy, & intelligence." Throughout his career Steptoe often demonstrated his concern for his men and for their welfare.

In a note to the Adjutant General dated August 16, 1848, from Fort Monroe, Virginia (Old Point Comfort), Steptoe requests a four-month leave of absence starting the first of September to visit his family, "from whom I have been separated now just six years."[129] He explains his health has been "considerably impaired" and adds "some matters of private business" require his attention "urgently." It may well be his father's financial problems were involved, as a Deed of Trust dating December 7 offers four slaves as "collateral on a debt of $1000 owed to Edward J. Steptoe."[130] Other letters sent to the Adjutant General's office in August 1848 pertain to his inquiry about troops under his command receiving "certificates of merit" that would entitle them to pay increases, for which he considers them "eminently deserving" and, on August 30, his acknowledgement of receipt of his commission as brevet major.[131] Most likely Brevet Major (soon to be Brevet Lieutenant Colonel) Steptoe spent some time with his family in the Lynchburg, Virginia, area, perhaps visiting nearby Red Sweet Springs or White Sulphur Springs for his health, as he had done before.

The gold rush was underway in California, but for the next few years it appeared Steptoe's destiny would keep him in the East and out of the action, for his next posting would be to garrison duty at Fort Adams in Newport, Rhode Island, in 1849. Steptoe left Fort Adams for service in Florida between 1849 and 1850, returning to garrison duty at Fort Adams from December 1850 through June of 1853. Subsequently, he was garrisoned at Fort Wood, New York, destined to be the location for the Statue of Liberty.[132]

Chapter Five

The Gunnison Affair

Brevet Lieutenant Colonel Edward J. Steptoe, age 38 and a veteran of the Second Seminole War and the Mexican War, served at Fort Wood, New York, between July1853 and July 1854 as a member of a commission "to examine into the relative advantages of civil and military supervision of National Armories."[1] It was not the kind of duty that would likely enhance his career. His attention might have been drawn to an item published in the *New York Times* on December 1, 1853: "Late and Important from the Plains—Massacre of Captain Gunnison and Eight of his Party by Indians." The brief report from St. Louis concerned an officer he would have known well, as Captain John W. Gunnison graduated second in the same 1837 class at West Point as Edward:

> Captain Gunnison and twelve of his party had departed from the rest, and while at breakfast a band of Indians, intending to destroy a Mormon Village near at hand, came upon them and fired with rifles, and then used bows and arrows. Shots were returned by the Gunnison party, but they were overpowered, and only four escaped. Gunnison had 26 arrows shot in his body, and when found, one of his arms was off.[2]

In some respects the newspaper overestimated the tragedy (Gunnison and seven were killed, not eight, and his body was penetrated by 15 arrows, not 26), but the facts may have been even more gruesome. H.H. Bancroft in his *History of Utah* (1889) indicates several men's arms were cut off, "their entrails cut open and torn by wolves," and "it is related that Gunnison's heart was cut out while he was yet alive, and that it was so full of blood that it bounded on the ground."[3]

Captain Gunnison, of the topographical engineers, was surveying potential routes for what would become the Transcontinental Railroad, which would not be completed until after the Civil War, in 1869. By mid–October 1853 Gunnison's survey party, which included thirty mounted rifles under Captain Robert M. Morris, were in the vicinity of the town of Fillmore, located about 140 miles south and a little west of Salt Lake City. Hard weather was closing in. At sunrise on October 23 Lieutenant Edward G. Beckwith's journal indicates a low of 15 degrees, and two days later dark clouds threatened an early snow.[4]

At about this point in the historical narrative the issue becomes increasingly intricate and somewhat murky. On October 22, with some wagons in need of repair, Gunnison visited the hamlet of Fillmore, fortified by Governor Brigham Young's orders against possible Indian attacks, as were most towns in the territory. "What the Captain learned while in Fillmore," historian Robert Kent Fielding notes, is "a matter of conjecture,"[5] but Bishop Anson Call apparently did inform Gunnison of recent hostilities. Call had been leading the construction at Fillmore for two years. Located at the geographic center of the territory, it served as the capital for about a year (1855–56); the three-story single wing of the elaborate building as designed by Truman O. Angell and fashioned out of rose-colored sandstone, has been turned into the Territorial Statehouse State Park Museum. Construction was in progress during Gunnison's visit and all but complete when Steptoe arrived in the fall of 1854. Gunnison and Steptoe would have seen a couple dozen houses built mostly out of cottonwood logs, facing Chalk Creek and connected with walls of large stones, mortar, and mud-and-straw, eight to ten feet high, so they became part of the outer fortification.

Gunnison also met with Young's Indian agent, Dimick Huntington, who reported an incident in which a party of emigrants headed for California "inflamed an otherwise friendly band of local Pahvants" by killing one of their number and wounding others. Yet Huntington apparently advised the captain, whom he had met four years earlier when Gunnison was engaged in a survey of Utah Lake in 1849, that he had "appeased" the angry Pahvant Utes.[6]

Gunnison proceeded west and north of Fillmore, crossing what is called the Sevier Desert on present-day maps and then following the narrow, serpentine Sevier River. Operating on limited intelligence and concerned about the weather, Gunnison split his force in order to hasten the completion of his survey. Fielding observes, "The fact of their mid-point location between the two remaining survey objectives in this area may have led the Captain to propose that the expedition be divided into two parties."[7] This decision, opposed by Captain Morris, the junior officer, had fatal consequences.

Recently named territorial governor, Brigham Young's policy was to convince the tribes that Mormons differed from "Americans" in their attitudes toward Indians, who are described in the *Book of Mormon* as descendants of Laman who left Israel around 600 BC. The Mormons had begun settling in the territory only in the summer of 1847, so they had been in place just half a dozen years at the time of the massacre. Despite the theological basis for their Indian policy, Brigham Young and the Saints, as they often called themselves, were not naïve about their relationships with the tribes, individual bands of which might be friendly while others might prove hostile. Moreover, individual warriors, most often the younger, within any given band sometimes operated on their own, stealing horses or cattle, demanding food or munitions from the settlers, or avenging wrongs, generally along lines of justice that required blood for blood. Nevertheless, as Bancroft and others have noted, "the Mormon maxim with regard to the Indians was that it was cheaper to feed them than to fight them."[8] Secretary of War Charles M. Conrad expressed similar sentiments in 1851.[9]

Wagon trains headed through the territory on the way to the California goldfields after 1849 brought gentiles who had little or no understanding of either the Mormons or the various tribes, but irrespective of their influence, relations between Mormons and Utes were strained to the breaking point. The title of Howard Christy's essay published in the *Utah Historical Quarterly* in 1973 is suggestive: "Open Hand and Mailed Fist: Mormon-Indian Relations in Utah, 1847–52." In a battle near Fort Utah, present-day Provo, in the winter of 1849 a force of a hundred militia killed as many as forty Utes, including their leader Big Elk, "with orders to take no prisoners except women and children," to be employed as servants in Mormon households.[10] Utah historians provide numerous additional accounts of misunderstanding and bloodshed prior to establishment of the Territory of Utah in 1850.[11] The territorial population according to the 1850 census was only 11,354, and although that number had at least doubled by 1852, settlements other than Salt Lake City remained vulnerable.

In September 1853 a band of Utes killed and mutilated four Mormons. The Mormons retaliated by shooting down nine Indians who had come into Nephi looking for food.[12] These events may be related to the so-called "Walker War" that erupted in July of that year and came to a negotiated end in July 1854.[13] A noted horseman and raider whose band included Utes, Shoshones, and Paiutes, Chief Walker (Wa-kara, sometimes translated "Hawk of the Mountains") initially established friendly relations with the Mormons and was baptized in that faith. Given those recent events, historians have alternately accused Brigham Young and Mormon leaders like Anson Call of intentionally misleading Captain Gunnison, or accused Gunnison of being foolhardy for splitting his command in the face of a potential enemy.

Meanwhile, Colonel Steptoe was enduring the tedium of garrison duty at Fort Wood, the eleven-pointed star-shaped fortress in New York harbor that today serves as the base for the Statue of Liberty. The nature of that tedium may be gleaned from his communications with the Adjutant General

Five. The Gunnison Affair

in the early months of 1854: a request for an updated copy of military regulations (February 4); request for information on how to process copies of clothing receipts for men from his company who were deceased or had been discharged from service (March 2); notes on the post's muster roll that a Lieutenant Symonds took with him when he left (April 2); requests for advanced pay to officers attached to his command and "now under orders for California" (April 12).

The request of March 2, 1854, regarding clothing receipts requires additional details. On Christmas Eve 1853 the newly launched steamship *San Francisco* sank in a heavy gale off Cape Hatteras with the loss of more than two hundred lives, including about 160 men from the Third Artillery Regiment.[14] Crews from three ships in the vicinity were able to save some five hundred lives, but Steptoe's men lost much of their belongings, as did Steptoe himself. The equipment and personal items, including some of Steptoe's uniforms, had been sent by steamer in anticipation of his command's arrival that summer at Benicia, California. In a letter dated April 4 Steptoe advises the Adjutant General, "Nearly all my personal effects were embarked (& lost) on the 'San Francisco'" and requests reimbursement. His earlier letter of March 2 pertains to the needs of "several destitute women—widows of men lost on the San Francisco, and importunate for the settlement of their husbands' accounts."

Surprisingly, although Governor Young investigated immediately, the federal government left the Gunnison Massacre unresolved for more than a year. On May 10 Adjutant General Samuel Cooper supplemented Colonel Steptoe's original orders of April 1, 1854, to proceed from Fort Leavenworth and to deliver about 800 horses and 448 mules to Benicia, with an order to bring the perpetrators of the massacre to justice. Colonel Cooper's tone may be unintentionally casual:

> As your command will pass through the country of these Indians on the route to California, it is the wish of the Department that you should visit their towns, if not lying too much out of the line of march and time will permit, for the purpose of holding them to a strict account for their conduct in respect to this atrocious massacre. They must be made to comprehend that such outrages are not to be perpetrated upon our citizens or soldiers with impunity, and that the Government, in every instance of the kind, will visit upon them the severest penalty.[15]

Steptoe and his train left Fort Leavenworth in the Kansas Territory on May 29, 1854, and arrived in the vicinity of Salt Lake City at the end of August. The trial of the alleged perpetrators of the "atrocious massacre" did not get underway until March 1855.

Although plagued by heavy rains for two weeks, Steptoe wrote the Adjutant General that his "march to the Pacific" was "very well organized &

appointed" and that the "whole detachment" was setting out "with buoyant spirits."[16] He informs Cooper he has organized the detachment of dragoon recruits into a "mounted force of 50 men" under Lieutenant Benjamin Allston (West Point Class of 1853) and the remaining 34 into a company under Lieutenant Sylvester Mowry (West Point Class of 1852). Captain Rufus Ingalls, also a West Point graduate (Class of 1843), served as assistant quartermaster on the Steptoe Expedition, as it has been called. Ingalls had served with distinction during the Mexican War under Colonel Kearny in what would become New Mexico Territory.[17] In his letter, Steptoe tells the Adjutant General that Ingalls has "shown much management & good judgment in all his arrangements, and I doubt not that he will accomplish satisfactorily the difficult tasks assigned to him."

Ingalls left a detailed account of the expedition tracing events from the departure at Fort Leavenworth via the Big and Little Blue Rivers, the Platte (stopping at Fort Kearny, Nebraska Territory), the Sweetwater, Sandy, and Green rivers in present-day Wyoming, and the Bear River into the Salt Lake valley.[18] The force consisted of nine officers and 150 soldiers; in addition, "the Quartermaster's department employed 130 citizens as teamsters, ostlers, herders, and laborers."[19] The seventy heavy baggage wagons, each drawn by six mules, and seven light wagons to which were attached strings of thirty to forty horses would be under Ingalls' authority. Ingalls notes the recruits were at first "imprudent in food and drink," but reports he received Colonel Steptoe's full cooperation.[20]

Shortly after leaving Fort Leavenworth, cholera struck the command, killing as many as ten soldiers. In a letter to the Adjutant General concerning muster rolls dated June 30, 1854, Steptoe draws attention to "the number of desertions recorded on the Rolls. This was, I believe, mainly due to absolute panic amongst the men when the cholera made its appearance."[21] Although penalties for deserters could be harsh, the rate of desertion for troops on the frontier, particularly new recruits, could become elevated for various reasons, including the lure of California gold. Robert M. Utley cites figures to the effect that "in an army of 10,000 nearly 1,300 would receive their discharge each year, while nearly 1,500 would desert. In 1856, with the Army expanded to more than 15,000, 3,223 men deserted.[22]

Ingalls describes the weather as "very changeable," the roads "quite muddy," and the rivers high. The command arrived at Fort Kearny, a journey of around 250 miles, on June 21 and stayed there two days before moving up the South Fork of the Platte, which they forded on July 6. In his letter of June 30 written from "Camp Cooper, S. Fork of the Platte, 116 miles from Fort Kearny," Steptoe assures Colonel Cooper "the health of the troops" is "entirely restored and their efficiency greatly improved." The "horses & train," he adds, are in "admirable condition": "Since leaving Fort Leavenworth to the present moment not an animal has died or become unserviceable."

No trees were available for building rafts, Ingalls wrote, and the crossing of the muddy, swollen Platte spanned between eight hundred and nine hundred yards. Edward Steptoe was getting his first taste of the American West, and Ingalls observes they began to sight Indians, mostly Pawnee, between Fort Kearny and Fort Laramie, which they reached on July 16, but they kept their distance. Steptoe had seen Seminoles in Florida, but neither the Plains Indians nor their environs were familiar. The Indians he would encounter over the next four years of his life, the climactic years of his military service, would rank among history's finest light cavalry, and the setting would not be the humid swamps and flat, palmetto-strewn hammocks of Florida, but the arid, grassy hills and buttes of the inland Northwest. "Altogether," Steptoe's letter of June 30 informs the Adjutant General, "my expedition has thus far been perfectly successful." In a note sent on the 27th, however, Steptoe requests additional muster rolls and advises he will likely be detained by winter in Salt Lake City.

Early in his account of the expedition, new dragoon recruit William Antes, born in Germany, described seeing numerous Indian warriors head to or from battle with other tribes. "They are dirty, lazy beggars," he wrote, echoing typical American attitudes of the day, and as "expert a lot of thieves as one could hope to meet with,"[23] At Fort Laramie he mentions "some five hundred Indians paid their respects" led by a chief wearing "an orderly Sergeant's jacket, with Captain's epaulettes, a stovepipe Hat, and a Dragoon's Sabre."[24] They encountered thousands of buffalo, Antes wrote. While encamped several weeks later at Salt Lake City in Union Square (later Tabernacle Square), Antes watched tribal war dances performed for their benefit, and noted that Steptoe said "we enjoyed it greatly," which "brought a roar of delight" from the Indians.[25]

At Fort Laramie in the dry heat of mid–July Ingalls mentions having conversed with some Sioux warriors. A month later Second Lieutenant John Lawrence Grattan and his command would be massacred, a total of thirty soldiers and civilians killed in an attack triggered by a soldier who shot down a Brulé Lakota chief named Conquering Bear. By that date (August 19, 1854) Steptoe's command was nearing the valley of the Great Salt Lake. Ingalls observes the expedition forded the North Fork of the Platte on July 31 and proceeded northwest to the Sweetwater: "The whole distance is over a miserably poor, sterile, arid country. There is no timber—no trees—very little grass and *good* water; but an abundance of poisonous alkali springs."[26] Perhaps to keep their spirits up along the trail or beside the campfires the troopers and the civilian herdsmen sang songs written by the most admired songwriter of that moment, Stephen Collins Foster, whose "Oh! Susanna" had become the anthem of the 1849 California Gold Rush. Minstrel shows and parlor singing around the piano were common pastimes for the American middle class, and by 1854 Foster's popular tunes included "Camptown Races," "Old Folks at Home," and "My Old Kentucky Home."

Ingalls writes of encountering scarce grass as they marched through South Pass, "very nearly on the summit of the 'back-bone' of the continent" on August 11, heading toward the Green River. From there they traversed mountainous terrain across the Wasatch Range before descending some three thousand feet into the Salt Lake valley, reaching what was then known as Great Salt Lake City at the end of August, a journey of 1,216 miles conducted over 64 marching days at an average of 19 miles per day by Ingalls' reckoning.[27] Figuring in "layover days for leisure or cholera," historian David A. White makes it to be more like 15 miles per day.[28] After reaching California the next spring, Ingalls would report negligible losses in livestock. The animals were delivered in better condition than would have been predicted because they were kept corralled for protection against the Indians and provided with ample forage. Because Steptoe's supplemental orders necessitated wintering over, he sent the horses and civilian herdsmen into Rush Valley south of the city.

Colonel Steptoe's letter to Cooper from "Great Salt Lake City, Utah," dated August 30, 1854, begins, "I have the honor to report that my command will reach this place tomorrow. I left it on 27th encamped on Weber river, 50 miles distant—all in fine health & condition."[29] He explains it was his hope to "*hut* the command some 40 or 50 miles from this city where timber, water, & grain would be abundant & convenient," but not having found such a place, he was "compelled to winter the officers & soldiers here, and most of the animals in the valleys south & north." Because no such economical "hutting" proved feasible, Steptoe was also compelled to quarter his officers and men among the Mormons under less than ideal circumstances.

It would be informative to know whether Steptoe had encountered his old classmate John Gunnison's book, *The Mormons or Latter Day Saints*, published in Philadelphia in 1852, or Major Howard Stansbury's reconnaissance report of his expedition to the Great Salt Lake, which appeared the same year. Although he reported favorably on the would-be State of Deseret, Stansbury cautioned his readers the "intimate connection of church and state seems to pervade every thing that is done."[30] The long-title form of Gunnison's book is instructive: "The Mormons, or Latter-Day Saints, in the valley of the Great Salt Lake: a history of their rise and progress, peculiar doctrines, present condition, and prospects, derived from personal observations, during a residence among them." Apparently intended to be a moderate and objective

Panoramic view of Salt Lake City in 1853. Brevet Lieutenant Colonel Steptoe spent a challenging eight months in the valley of the Great Salt Lake from the first of September 1854 through April 1855 on his way to Benicia, California, with livestock. His efforts to bring to justice the Pahvant Utes responsible for the massacre of Captain John Gunnison and his command in October 1853 were largely thwarted. Steptoe felt obliged to decline President Franklin Pierce's offer of the territorial governorship of Utah. Used by permission, Utah State Historical Society.

commentary on the controversial and persecuted religion about which relatively little was known except that they accepted polygamy, Gunnison's volume "was not perceived as objective or friendly by the Mormons."[31]

In addition to tracing the history of the Mormons, Gunnison commented on their social life and institutions, commending them as "the most enterprising people of the age" and describing their parties and "lively meetings" in which he observed "the most sprightly dancing" and "hearty goodwill, from the highest dignitary to the humblest individual."[32] He also touched admiringly on the Mormons' support of education, including their liberal appropriations for a university which, like West Point, would be "eminently practical in its character."[33] As to their loyalty to the nation, Gunnison cited their participation in the Mexican War and claimed "they embraced the earliest opportunity of declaring their adherence to the great charter of liberty and national glory" (the Constitution).[34] "The dignity of labor is held sacred by the Mormons," Gunnison wrote, and "usefulness is their motto."[35]

As to that *other* "peculiar institution" of the age, along with slavery, polygamy, Gunnison could not restrain his own views: "they pretend to see a more rational application of a generous soul in loving more than one wife."[36] The verb "pretend" speaks loudly here, as does his phrasing when it comes to describing the lot of the plural wives:

> That the wives find the relation often a lonesome and burdensome one, is certain; though usually the surface of society wears a smiling countenance, and to all who consent from a sense of duty or enthusiasm the yoke is easy.[37]

In this sentence the noun "yoke" speaks loudly. But overall Gunnison's book comes across as sensible and judicious. His attitude toward the Mormons closely resembles that of Captain Howard Stansbury, also of the topographical engineers, who led the 1849–1850 expedition into the Salt Lake valley and whose account, also published in 1852 and widely read, describes them as an "energetic and far-seeing people."[38]

It must have been a curious meeting, that first handshake between Brigham Young, President of the Church of Jesus Christ of Latter Day Saints, Governor of the Utah Territory, and Prophet, the "American Moses," and Brevet Lieutenant Colonel Edward J. Steptoe, West Point graduate, veteran of the Second Seminole War and the Mexican War, and career army officer. Born in Vermont in 1801, the son of a Revolutionary War veteran, Brigham Young was 54 years old and stood a barrel-chested five-feet-ten. He was a gifted orator, a charismatic leader, and probably the most notorious American living at that moment. By the time he met Steptoe, Young had accumulated 48 of his eventual 55 wives, his first wife having died and at least half a dozen of those marriages having ended in divorce, and he had sired more than fifty children.

How much the two men knew of each other must remain as conjectural as the nature of their first conversation, although the latter almost certainly concerned practical matters: where to place the livestock for adequate forage, how to quarter the officers and troops in Salt Lake City, what to do about arresting the Indians responsible for the Gunnison Massacre. They likely met in Governor Young's recently built home, now known as the Beehive House, located in the center of downtown Salt Lake City just off Temple Square. The simple two-story structure was expanded considerably in later years. Even when it became obvious Steptoe was being groomed for the governorship, Young and other Mormon leaders regarded him, in the words of Orson Hyde, a member of the original Quorum of the Twelve Apostles, as "a noble-minded and honorable man."[39]

In an article titled "Biography of Col. Steptoe" appearing in the *New York Evening Post*, dated December 20, 1854, a journalist celebrating his forthcoming nomination as territorial governor may or may not have been guilty of hyperbole in noting that "on account of his strict observance of the rules of the Episcopal Church, to which he belongs, and his general uprightness, he received the title of 'the immaculate Steptoe.'"[40] Colonel Steptoe, "as his friends say," continued the reporter, is "of remarkably handsome and commanding appearance, courteous and dignified manners, irreproachable private life, and his qualifications as a scholar and a civilian would secure him eminence should he turn his attention to legislative and political life." The colonel "wields a ready pen," the writer adds, that proved to be "of great service in promoting the election of General Pierce to the presidency."

Initial relations between Steptoe's men and the Mormons appear to have been amicable, most likely because of the rent the U.S. government paid for housing the troops and because of the boost to the local economy. But relations deteriorated soon enough and perhaps predictably. In addition to his primary orders, to move the large herd of livestock to Benicia from Fort Leavenworth, and to his secondary orders, to bring to justice the perpetrators of the Gunnison Massacre, Steptoe was operating under tertiary orders, to investigate a proposed road between Salt Lake City and the eastern border of California. As David Henry Miller puts it in his unpublished thesis, Secretary of War Jefferson Davis "decided to cut administrative costs to a minimum by assigning Colonel E.J. Steptoe, who was already on his way to Utah, the task of letting contracts and supervising the actual construction of improvements."[41] The war department's inclination to pursue a southern route starting at Cedar City, some 250 miles south of Salt Lake City, eventually proved unfeasible, but Steptoe signed contracts for road widening and for bridging the Provo River forty-odd miles south of Salt Lake City.

If economic factors sweetened what many saw as an incursion of military forces inimical to their culture and institutions, other factors proved threatening. Fielding suggests, "It is probable that Brigham Young welcomed the presence of the troops in his vicinity at this time, both for revenue and for protection."[42] One church leader estimated the troops would expend as much as $400,000 during their stay in the territory.[43] Chief among the perceived threats to the theocracy, however, was speculation President Pierce intended to replace their governor and religious leader (and prophet), Brigham Young, with Colonel Steptoe. Various historians have suggested the Mormon leadership was well aware of that prospect before Steptoe himself was informed of Pierce's decision, which the Senate approved on December 13, 1854, but of which the colonel was apparently not officially advised until the first week in February. In a letter dated February 7, 1855, 3:00 a.m., to his friend Edward Bicknall in Providence, Rhode Island, Lieutenant Mowry writes he was playing cards when "the District Attorney walked in with the news of the mail—and Col. Steptoe's appointment to the Governorship," to which "we all gave about four thousand cheers" and "took large drinks of whiskey and water."[44]

Presumably, most Mormons did not share Mowry's enthusiasm. In his journal, attorney Seth Millington Blair declared in December 1854 that his feelings ignited "like a Lucifer match" at the prospect of gentile troops in the city and at the "very idea of a damned Gentile Governor & him a Military Character" at that.[45] But Albert Carrington, editor of the weekly *Deseret News*, commended President Pierce in the March 8, 1855, edition for resisting "the howlings, and the scratching, and whining at the door of the 'white house,' of the hungry hunters of office who wish to fatten upon the spoils."[46] When "compelled to give way," Carrington observes, Pierce "acted with all magnanimity by appointing the gallant Lt.-Col. Steptoe to be our Governor, an appointment that could not have been more acceptably made, outside the ranks of our own population."

Had Blair somehow acquired access to a letter from Lieutenant Mowry to his friend Edward Bicknall, dated September 19, 1854, he would have found his suspicions confirmed. After hearing Church President Heber C. Kimball speak before some three thousand at the tabernacle, advising the Mormons to treat the soldiers well but warning the soldiers to keep "'hands off' the women," Mowry writes, "The whole looked very much as if he and Brigham were afraid we were going to f___k our way through the town. Perhaps we shall. Brigham's daughter in law is the prettiest woman I have ever seen yet. Her husband is on a mission and she is as hot—a thing as you could wish." Mowry goes on to describe his plans to use "tact and shrewdness" in order to "conduct an intrigue successfully."

Miller asserts, "Steptoe represented the first tangible threat to Mormon political sovereignty within the territory."[47] But he also describes Steptoe as a man without political ambitions and as "one of the most open-minded, capable, and honest federal representatives to set foot inside the Mormon empire during the eighteen-fifties."[48] Editor Carrington went even further in his praise: "We have the honor of a personal acquaintance with the Colonel, and so far as our observation and judgment extend we have found him to be in every particular an intelligent, honorable, and upright officer, citizen, and gentleman."[49] This item appeared more than two weeks *before* the controversial Gunnison trial got underway on March 21, 1855; moreover, Carrington confidently declares Steptoe has already refused to accept the appointment as territorial governor, and for reasons the colonel was in fact to give Secretary of State Marcy and President Pierce some seven weeks later.

In September 1854, however, the urgent matter of bringing to justice the perpetrators of the Gunnison Massacre absorbed Steptoe's attention, and he informs the Adjutant General he has hastened back to Salt Lake City from

Rush Valley, where he left the livestock and their civilian herders for the winter, in order to witness the public execution of "two Indian criminals on the 15th instant."[50] Historians have concluded Governor Young wished to impress upon Steptoe the likelihood that the Indians responsible for the massacre would be brought to a strict accounting. Moreover, as Miller observes, Young emphasized the two murderers had been arrested "through negotiations with friendly Indians."[51] Miller stresses Mormon relations with the Pahvants had remained amicable during the Walker War; moreover, their attack on Gunnison had been carried out during that war and was therefore an act of war rather than murder.[52]

In a letter to Colonel Cooper dated October 4, Steptoe explains why he has not seized "a proper number of their chief men as hostages," namely because the "Pah=Utahs [...] have taken the alarm & gone some 150 miles south."[53] This letter is particularly significant because it provides the first evidence of Steptoe's creation of a military strategy. Prior to this, throughout his deployments to Florida and Mexico, he had followed orders handed down by superior officers. That he had done so effectively is proven by his promotions and brevets in rank, but in the Utah Territory he was for the first time left to his own devices. "Under the circumstances," he writes, he was "confident" his orders to hand over the accused murders "would not be obeyed" and "would probably cause their [the Indians'] immediate dispersion."

> The best policy, in my judgment, is to lull their suspicions, if possible, and use the first opportunity to capture them. Accordingly, I shall leave here on the 12th instant, with the mounted men of my command, ostensibly as an escort to the U.S. judges who then set out on their southern judicial tour. This will enable me to see the country and, if a favorable opportunity offers, to seize those criminals—about 30 in number. It is not likely, however, that their tribe—supposed to be, generally, more or less implicated—will suffer them to be taken without resistance.

"If this plan shall fail," Steptoe continues, "I propose to make a rapid night march upon them when the weather has become a little colder & they are obliged to quit the mountains." Had he pursued this strategy, a major confrontation might have occurred, or, perhaps more likely, the Indians would have dispersed. Clearly, though, Colonel Steptoe was willing to undertake aggressive offensive action in the field.

Between the date of this dispatch and his next, sent to Cooper on November 10, Steptoe met with Governor Young and Chief Justice John F. Kinney[54] at Nephi, about 85 miles south of Salt Lake City and agreed to appeal to Chief Kanosh of the Pahvants, who was then living at Fillmore, "assuring him of personal safety & requesting to see him" to arrange a negotiated surrender of the perpetrators. He sent a similar dispatch to Walker, "Chief of the Utahs, generally."[55] When he reached Fillmore, the colonel found Kanosh awaiting him with a few warriors, but not Chief Walker, who "declined to come." Steptoe notified Cooper "it seems that about 25 Pavants & some Pi=utes, or 'White Knives,' were directly concerned in the massacre; most of whom came to see us, but warily—only a few at a time. It is probable that all would have presented themselves together upon my assurance of safety, but that could only have been given in sincerity & good faith." Miller takes Steptoe's refusal to deceive the Indians as evidence of the "extreme personal honesty that accompanied all his transactions."[56] Steptoe does not indicate in his correspondence that he suspects Mormons were complicit in the Gunnison incident despite rumors to that effect circulating in the East.

In his letter of November 10 Steptoe explains that under the circumstances during his six days at Fillmore he would never have been able to capture more than "a half dozen of the criminals, leaving the rest to avenge the seizure upon the residents & travelers." He informs Adjutant General Cooper, "After a very careful consideration of the matter, I concluded not to seize any of these men at present, but to see what could be accomplished through the Chiefs"; in short, he decided to follow the advice of Governor Young, deferring to his greater experience, more thorough knowledge of the circumstances, and diplomacy. Steptoe was brought to this decision also by his awareness that the "people of Fillmore" were "almost without defences, and with their stacks of grain so near to their houses that a few Indians might in as many minutes, do them great injury." "I felt reluctant," Steptoe continues, "to create for them an enemy whom they would be left to combat alone." He reports having offered the

Chief Kanosh (1821–1884) of the Pahvant Utes in 1870 at about age fifty; he was in his mid-thirties when Steptoe attempted with slight success to deal with him in order to bring the killers of Captain Gunnison and his command to justice. A long-time friend of the Mormons, Kanosh signed the treaty that ended the Walker War in 1854 and was baptized into the Church of Jesus Christ of Latter-Day Saints in 1858. Used by permission, Utah State Historical Society.

Five. The Gunnison Affair

chiefs two horses apiece and "some small presents," but they "declined to give an answer to the proposition before seeing Walker." He relates having advised Kanosh to expect his return in the spring, and he asks to be informed whether the Department of War should consider it best "to capture as many of these Indians as possible, at every hazard."

The meeting at Fillmore confirmed Colonel Steptoe's recognition he would be obliged to winter his command in the Salt Lake valley; moreover, he must have realized he would not be able to bring to justice anything like the thirty or so Indians involved in the action on the Sevier River. Subsequent events, including the breakdown in relations between his troops and the Mormon citizenry, were predictable if not inevitable. When he composed a pair of letters to the Adjutant General's office ten days later, Steptoe sent copies via California due to "the irregularity of the mails at this season." He hoped to receive a response from Washington before April.[57] He describes himself as "a good deal embarrassed to determine upon the best course towards those Indians—personal & professional feeling urging me in one direction and considerations of expediency in another."

One of the most peculiar events with respect to Brigham Young's continuing control of the territory was the willingness of Colonel Steptoe and Justice Kinney to sign a petition by the territorial legislature drafted in December supporting Governor Young's incumbency. The opening sentence indicates the signers believe Young to possess "the entire confidence of the people of this Territory, without distinction of party or sect" and they find him to be "a firm supporter of the constitution and laws of the United States."[58] Miller suggests while Steptoe believed it would be best to remove the governor and prophet from office, he knew Young would nevertheless continue to exercise "absolute authority in Utah" and "would remain *de facto* governor even if he were not reappointed."[59] Steptoe deferred to Kinney, a year his junior but the senior federal official in the territory at the time. A traveler who met Kinney in September of 1855, six months after Steptoe's departure, described him as, "A short, fat man, decently attired and of respectable appearance, [...] smoking a long porcelain pipe."[60] The entrepreneurial and rather controversial judge would play a vital role in the court proceedings in March 1855.

Of perhaps equal concern to the Mormons and of greater concern to Steptoe were the strained relations between his troops and the citizenry, particularly the young women, attracted, as Fielding observes, by "The Gallantry of Epaulettes." Inebriation and gambling, two mainstays of soldiers and officers in billets or on post throughout the period, drew the censure of Mormon authorities, and on December 23 a brawl broke out after a performance at the Social Hall Theater in Salt Lake City followed by a more serious incident on Christmas day. "Fists, sticks, clubs and stones were freely used on both sides," according to one Mormon account of the melee. Although Lieutenant Mowry estimated as many as three hundred were involved, shots were fired, and about twenty soldiers were arrested, no one was seriously injured. In his letter to Bicknall, Mowry insists the "affair" was "commenced by the citizens." Yet, despite the ruckus, the following evening Governor Young and other leading members of the church hierarchy attended a military ball in honor of Colonel Steptoe. Moreover, the audacious Lieutenant Mowry acquired the governor's approval to ask his daughter-in-law for a dance, and Hosea Stout, the territory's first attorney general, wrote in his diary, "About midnight we took supper an excellent one too & returned to the dance continuing the fantastics till about three in the morning when all returned well satisfied."[61]

Relations with the military in Utah had deteriorated considerably by the first couple of months of the New Year (1855); nevertheless, Brigham Young publicly praised "the gallant gentleman who is now in our midst," if he should be appointed governor, adding "there is not a man, out of the Kingdom of God, that I would listen to sooner, and feel more confidence and cordiality towards, than him." From these remarks, however, Miller deduces Young "was fairly certain by this time that Steptoe had either not received his commission, or would probably refuse it once it arrived."[62]

The spirit of cordiality was not universally shared in the Mormon community. Andrew Love, alderman and school trustee in Nephi, who served in the territorial legislature in 1852, wrote in his journal, following the trial in March: "Our streets are once more clear of the gentiles & Thank the Lord, be ware of the leven of the gentiles, Their atmosphere is poisonous to Mormonism."[63] Love questioned the motives of "those who are so active in bringing them to justice": "Are they men of pure hearts & clean hands or is it not probable There is some stain of innocent blood on *Their* skirts, be ye carefull that the judgement ye meet out to others don't fall timely upon your own heads."[64] Love served as a juror in the trial.

As to the Gunnison affair, by the first of February Colonel Steptoe was aware that capturing all those implicated would prove impossible: "It is probable that he [Kanosh] *cannot* surrender them, as I have recently heard that not only he, but his whole Tribe, were directly, or *indirectly*, concerned in the affair."[65] He informed the Adjutant General he was awaiting Kinney's decision as to whether he must take the field against the Indians. On February 24 he apprised Colonel Cooper he had sent Major John F. Reynolds, Lieutenant Allston and 23 men to Fillmore to receive the surrender of seven Pahvants: "The number *seven* was specified because Captain Gunnison & party numbered *eight*, and the Chief [Kanosh] claims one life for a Pah=vant killed by an Emigrant in the spring of last year."[66] He advises Cooper he thinks it "decidedly best to accept this proposition as it will be in accordance with the Indian policy pursued by Gov. Young, and will probably obviate all trouble with the Utahs for which the southern settlement, especially, are but ill prepared." Judge Kinney set the hearing for March 19.

Fielding asserts an assemblage of fifty or more painted warriors resisted even the arrest of those seven, two "old and blind" and one "a squaw."[67] His observations are drawn from reports of interpreter, George Washington Bean, who wrote some years later that Kanosh "knew the real killers would never be revealed."[68] Accounts of the indictment and subsequent trial of what by then had dwindled to just six of the twenty-odd perpetrators of the massacre read like a comedy of the absurd. Fielding describes the apprehension of only six alleged murderers as "a singular defeat for Colonel Steptoe's Indian diplomacy" and "a victory for Brigham Young."[69] Moreover, he concludes Young was motivated in his decision not to assist Steptoe by his awareness of President Pierce's intent to offer him the governorship. Significantly, no official transcript of the proceedings was kept, so all accounts of the grand jury hearing and the trial were made by participants therein, all of whom must be seen as having had vested interests in the outcome.

Presiding over the affair held in Nephi, Chief Justice Kinney had arrived in the territory on January 1854 and would stay through 1857. Miller describes him as "a long time quasi-friend of the Mormons, whose political ambitions far exceeded his abilities."[70] J[ohn] H[anson] Beadle, quondam editor of the *Salt Lake Reporter*, described Kinney as a "Jack" Mormon, which at the time indicated a Gentile sympathetic to that religion.[71] In his 1870 "exposé" entitled *Life in Utah; or, the Mysteries and Crimes of Mormonism*, Beadle cites Catherine Waite's rather improbable account of how Steptoe was "ingeniously trapped by two of Brigham's 'decoy women,'" that is, blackmailed, into signing the petition in December to retain Young as territorial governor. He insists the judge "spared no pains to keep on good terms with his Mormon customers."[72] By all accounts the prosecuting attorney, Joseph Hollman, turned up inebriated on the day of the grand jury hearing and was compelled to apologize for his comportment when court reconvened the next day. Lieutenant Mowry, familiar to the jury for his "amatory intrigues with Brigham Young's daughter-in-law," assisted Hollman. Miller notes Mowry was "only recently admitted to the bar" and although "a man of considerable intellectual ability," was regarded as being "of questionable moral character."[73]

In a journal entry dated March 15, 1855, Andrew Love reports the weather was "snowing & blowing" and observes, "Well to some [sic] up the whole we have a real gentile crowd in our Midst & the Spirit appears to be spreading, Ah Israel be carful."[74] The "upcoming trial," according to Miller, "generated a holiday atmosphere in the small central Utah town."[75] When the grand jury met on March 19, Love, who served as a juror during the trial but did not sit on the grand jury, wrote, "Steptoe & Holeman both drunk in afternoon on Monday & continue well heated."[76] While Miller recounts the inebriated condition of prosecuting attorney Hollman, he says nothing of Steptoe's conduct, although he did have access to Love's journal.[77] One might suspect Love confused Lieutenant Mowry, who assisted Hollman in the prosecution, for Colonel Steptoe, but in his journal he adds, "Col. Steptoe drunk & acting very foolish."[78] In a private meeting with Brigham Young recorded months later, on July 10, 1855, Judge Kinney admitted to drinking "more liquor last winter than I have done in all my life," adding that "Col. Steptoe did drink a good deal in my house and was often high."[79]

No other evidence regarding Steptoe's drinking habits before or after this event has surfaced, but if in fact he had a drinking problem, his liver ailments would surely have been exacerbated by any alcohol abuse. In her exposé of Brigham Young published just after the Civil War, Mrs. Waite asserts "the uniform course of Judge Kinney has been to aid and abet Brigham Young in his ambitious schemes."[80] She later describes Kinney as "pompous and conceited," "never declining to drink when invited," and "an open apologist and advocate of polygamy."[81] Perhaps, then, one should not regard Kinney's testimony as unimpeachable, and one might go so far as to question his conduct of the trial, despite his later expressions of outrage over the jury's lenient verdict. Historian Norman F. Furniss, however, argues Kinney's "duplicity" and hypocrisy were aimed at the Mormons and consigns such obviously anti-Mormon treatises as those of Waite and Beadle to the vast emptiness of "interstellar space."[82] The most peculiar result of Judge Kinney's "secret antagonism to the Church" was that he would be elected territorial delegate from Utah to the 38th Congress (1863–1865).

Defense attorney for the Indians was Almon Babbitt, who had practiced law for twenty years and had served in the Illinois legislature. He built the case for the defense "entirely on his presumption that the Indians could not be charged with the crime of murder because, at the time, their tribes were at war with the United States and with the people of the Territory of Utah."[83]

Details of the trial held over three days in the crowded courtroom are available in both Miller's thesis and Fielding's book-length study of the Gunnison Massacre. Only three of the accused Indians handed over by Chief Kanosh were indicted. Hollman and Mowry called three Mormon witnesses for the prosecution, two of whom had helped bury the remains and testified they had overheard two of the defendants talking of their participation in the attack. Miller and Fielding agree "the most important testimony" was presented by "an attractive young Indian" woman who could implicate all three of the accused and others who had not been charged.[84] Predictably, the all-Mormon jury proved not amenable to the case presented by the federal government. Although Judge Kinney ordered them either to find the accused guilty of murder in the first degree, for which hanging would be the sentence, or to exonerate them entirely, the jury handed in a verdict of manslaughter, for which the sentence would be three years in the territorial penitentiary.

The rationale for the lenient verdict after only four hours of deliberation remains a mystery, although both Miller and Fielding have registered some suppositions. Given that the jury had disobeyed his instructions, why didn't Judge Kinney declare a mistrial? Miller submits the "testimony of the witnesses appears to have proved very conclusively that the murder had been premeditated and that the three defendants, if not the main perpetrators, had been unquestionably involved."[85] Fielding concludes Judge Kinney might have ignored the verdict and pronounced the death sentence in spite of the jury's decision, but he asserts such a move would certainly "alienate the Mormons, prejudicing attitudes toward the Judge and affecting future jury trials."[86] Miller and Fielding concur that trying the case before a different jury would have been costly and time consuming and would not likely have led to a different verdict. Moreover, Fielding notes, Steptoe "must soon be on his way to the west coast." Within a week of their incarceration at the territorial penitentiary, all three of the Indians escaped, "and no great effort, to my knowledge, has been made to arrest them again," Steptoe informed the Adjutant General in a letter dated April 15, 1855.[87] Two weeks later Steptoe's expedition departed the territory, heading for California.

The response to the verdict at the national level was doubtless driven by Lieutenant Mowry's communication to the *New York Daily Times*, dated March 28, 1855, three days before news of the Pahvants' escape was received. Accompanied with a reporter's account of the proceedings and including Joseph Hollman's observations, the item filled nearly four full columns of the front page under this heading: "'Interesting from Utah'—Trial of the Indian Murders of Captain Gunnison—Verdict of Manslaughter Only—Mormon Interference with the Cause of Justice—INFAMOUS DICTATION OF BRIGHAM YOUNG—Full and Interesting Report of the Trial of the Murderers."[88] Mowry portrayed the verdict of manslaughter as "an infamous outrage upon justice," "contrary to the letter and spirit of the law," and a "wanton" insult "to the friends of the lamented dead, and to the good sense of every well judging man." He declared the American people should "reflect upon this monster of Mormonism," and concluded, "Let the separate organization of Utah be abolished, and her broad and beautiful valleys be portioned out between Nebraska, New Mexico, and California. Then, and only then, with the aid of strong military force, can the law have its legitimate supremacy among this God-forsaken community."

In response to Mowry's assault on the "monster of Mormonism" Governor Young wrote a 22-page, handwritten letter (with appendices) addressed to Secretary of War Jefferson Davis and dated September 8, 1855, but not published until 1995.[89] In his vindication, Young maintains Steptoe "very properly pursued the peaceable course" of attempting to negotiate with Kanosh, as he advised.[90] While he does not mention Judge Kinney or Colonel Steptoe by name, Young asserts at Nephi "there was more drunkenness than sobriety" and "Bacchus, much to our surprise, found among his worshippers, and devotees, the highest, as well as the lowest; the civilian clothed with Judicial ermine, as well as *Gallant Militaire*," all paying "humble adoration to the God of inebriation."[91] As indicated above, Young based his argument for leniency toward the Pahvants on grounds that the Gunnison Massacre had been committed in time of war. Significantly, Young indicates he saw to the recapture of the three escaped Indians, a matter not generally reported in eastern newspapers and unknown to Steptoe.

In Steptoe's letter of April 15, not written in his own hand possibly because he may have suffered a minor stroke (perhaps mild cerebral ischemia) that left him temporarily partially paralyzed,[92] he advises the Adjutant General there was "a suspicion in my mind from the first that these prisoners would not be permitted to suffer death nor any other severe punishment." He informs Colonel Cooper he suggested Judge Kinney allow him to take the prisoners to California to stand trial:

> The fact probably is, that the Governor saw a collusion between The Government and Indians inevitable, and sympathizing mostly with the latter caused them to be informed that whatever number should be surrendered for trial would escape any serious penalty.

The result, Steptoe notes disgustedly, was that "the few persons tried for participating in the murder of Capt. Gunnison have received no punishment whatsoever." Moreover, he writes that should Cooper advise the Secretary of War in this matter and "if he should hold the Pahvants to a further accountability the troops will receive but scant aid or countenance from the Mormons." Steptoe's concluding statements are particularly revelatory of his state of mind during the weeks before leading his command out of Utah:

> It is a real pleasure to me to get this matter off my hands however much as I may regret the result. To square my duty and inclination with a proper respect for the legal authority of the Governor and the condition of the people has been no easy task, but all my annoyance is lost in sincere regret that any citizens of our country should be found so disregardful of this high obligation to the laws as many connected with this affair have shown themselves to be.

Ten days later, in a short communiqué again dictated, Steptoe notified Colonel Cooper that although his command had "pushed out some fifty miles on the route to California," it would not be "prudent" to advance any farther until more grass became available around the first of May. He also reports the "growing ill feeling of the Inhabitants towards the Troops—very fully reciprocated by the latter." This, he indicates, has given him "constant uneasiness."[93] Steptoe informed the Adjutant General of his intention to take the two artillery companies along the northern route, following the Humboldt River through what is now northern Nevada, then proceeding along the San Joaquin River in northern California toward Benicia, while Lieutenant Mowry would take the horses needed at Fort Tejon, located about seventy miles north of Los Angeles, by the southern route.

The slow progress of his march out of the Valley of the Great Salt Lake may be attested to by the fact that Steptoe's next letter to the Adjutant General is dated May 15, in camp just 120 miles from the city. Written in his own hand, this letter is not signed in his usual manner as brevet lieutenant colonel of the Third Artillery Regiment, but as Major of the Ninth Infantry, his promotion having been accorded on March 3, 1855, perhaps amounting to tacit approval of his efforts in Utah to that date. His promotion was confirmed, however, prior to the Gunnison Massacre trial.

On April 25, the day he sent word to the Adjutant General that he and his command had "pushed out" from Salt Lake City, Steptoe wrote a short letter to William L. Marcy, Secretary of State, and a lengthy letter to President Pierce, both in his own hand. In his letter to Marcy, Steptoe indicates he received official confirmation of his appointment as Governor of Utah on the 23rd and it came as no surprise "as the newspapers had prepared me for it."[94] In short, he surely knew the Mormons had suspected and feared such a move from the moment of his arrival. After all, as previously mentioned, both Steptoe and Kinney had signed a petition drafted by the Utah Territorial Legislature on December 21, 1854, indicating their awareness that "the incumbent Governor [Brigham Young] was the unanimous choice of the people."[95] Steptoe assures Marcy "the appointment was never sought by me, directly nor indirectly."

Additional details in his letter to Marcy are worth noting, as the appointment placed Steptoe in an awkward position, realizing as he did that his tenure as governor would have been quite untenable. "Be pleased to say to the President," he writes, "that having never in my life avoided any just responsibility, the imputation of doing so now could not fail to distress me." Choosing his words carefully, Steptoe concedes "it is fair to apprehend that my refusal of the proffered honor would be regarded by the Nation generally as a timid shrinking from responsibility which I have not sought, but do not fear." He then agrees to accept the office for one year, "long enough to solve the problems of this people's loyalty & to establish to some extent at least their political character," but only "provided, that the President will then place me in some situation corresponding to that I might have accomplished in the Army." He conceives no chance of making a "political reputation" in the territory, but predicts the likelihood of "privation & annoyance" awaiting "any Governor, not a Mormon, who may be sent here." He indicates he would accept "a mission abroad, or position at home either *military* or civil"; that is, he suggests his willingness, under certain circumstances, to abandon his career in the army.

Steptoe's six-page letter to President Pierce accompanied his note to Secretary of State Marcy.[96] He writes the appointment "has embarrassed me much," and he is uncertain what to do, particularly as the position of governor has been offered with no apparent "promise of unusual support." In his opening paragraph Steptoe bluntly states his sense of conditions in Utah:

> Remember that there is such a state of things here as perhaps never existed before in any land—fanaticism in the mass of the people and a religious oligarchy, or rather *Monocrasy*, while corruption is every where in every branch of the public service.

Steptoe admits he "wrote differently once & recommended the reappointment of Gov. Young," probably alluding to his signature on the petition mentioned above, "but I was not so well informed then as now." Brigham Young "certainly did then appear to me to be a rational man—either from principle or from policy," but he now thinks otherwise. Steptoe's tone here resembles that of Mrs. Waite's writing 11 years later. He makes clear his concern is by no means limited to Young's character:

> [H]ere has been planted in the very heart of the confederacy & almost unheeded, the germ of a mighty State; here are 40 or 50,000 white citizens of the Republic with scarcely a trace of nationality amongst them, who have never experienced the fostering watchful care of the Government or one paternal effort to guide them aright; and they have gone on cultivating follies & vices which possibly the whole influence of the Nation may not be able now to check without a civil war.

That these alarming observations did not lead sooner to the ill-advised Utah War or Mormon War, sometimes known as "Buchanan's Blunder," which occurred two years later in May 1857, may owe to the fact that President Pierce was in the spring of 1855 more deeply involved with events known as "Bleeding Kansas." Following the Kansas-Nebraska Act of 1854, pro-slavery settlers had begun to enter the Kansas Territory, and the Border War that would bring abolitionist John Brown to the forefront of national attention was underway.

In his letter to Pierce, Colonel Steptoe attempts to educate and warn the president about the dangers of Mormonism. Polygamy, he advises, "is but one of its features;—put them all together and you will form as much a *political* as a social monster." From Steptoe's perspective, "these people, persevering, industrious & brave, are working under the spur of fanaticism for a *political* end which it is the policy of their leaders at present to obscure by religious cant." Lashing out at the Mormon leadership, he appeals to President Pierce: "Permit me to say that in your whole range of duties not one, in my opinion, merits your deep concern more than this," and he again raises the specter of "civil war" if Mormonism is left unchecked. But Steptoe also warns against "persecution," as "Persecution has made Mormonism what it is and its followers would rejoice to encounter it again." In this he comes close to one of Gunnison's observations in the last chapter of his book on the Mormons, where he argues that "to enforce rulers over them from abroad, by the power of the bayonet, will entail perpetual war," and asks rhetorically "what would be gained," answering,

> Nothing but the same as persecution has heretofore given, increase of Mormon power. Indeed we are not sure but the leaders would like a display of force, in order to raise the cry of persecution, and turn the attention of the people upon foreign objects.[97]

Gunnison's conclusions are more temperate than Steptoe's. Reflecting on the principle of "the right of sovereignty," Gunnison describes the Mormons as "a mighty moral force among the threatening cloud of savages on our frontiers," and he counsels "generosity on the side of power, towards those who achieved so much in fertilizing a barren region."[98] He concludes while the "system" was once "aggressive," it is now "on the defensive—then it was violent, now it is politic." The thousand-mile distance from the rest of the nation "hems it in and renders it harmless"; moreover, "the industry of its supporters makes it useful to the country."[99] In short, Gunnison advises, let them alone and pray they will eventually conform "into the one Catholic [that is, universal Christian] Church."

Steptoe informs Pierce that as he has ascertained the "feelings of the people," at least half "would prefer to see me in the office" of governor, but he adds he has advised those with whom he has conferred that should he decline the appointment, "no Mormon, in my opinion, could ever be appointed and that none ought to be." Moreover, "I do beg you by every consideration of this people's interest to remove Gov. Young." In this context, Steptoe reminds Pierce of Young's manipulation of the jury during the Gunnison trial: "the Governor's mandate to a sworn jury was superior to right. I give you this as a single evidence of his want of sympathy with the Nation."

At this point, however, Steptoe turns to a sympathetic reading of the Latter Day Saints that echoes Gunnison's sentiments: "These people have merits—excellent merits; they are the most industrious I ever saw—they are temperate, frugal, polite, unostentatious, docile." He admits his soldiers and officers "have quarreled with them and harsh words & blows have been exchanged," but he claims to have kept himself "entirely aloof from them & treated them without injustice"; moreover, "they have ever been kind & courteous to me." He commends Judge Kinney as a "keen observer" and "an able, upright, fearless officer" who "can give you a true relation of events here." Steptoe clearly attempts to distinguish between the Mormon people and their leaders, particularly Brigham Young, and he even suggests his "conviction [...] that the wintering of my command here has given a shock to Mormonism from which, if judiciously followed up, it may never entirely recover."

In conclusion, Steptoe writes, to accept the appointment as offered "would be an utter waste of life to me." But he tactfully adds, "Then pray decide for me & rest assured, my dear Genl., that whichever way you decide will be entirely satisfactory to me." If he should return to the territory, he continues, "I will work for it with all my might and do my utmost to make the people obey & execute the laws *themselves*; soldiers will be needed to control the Indians not the Mormons." Nevertheless, "if I continue with my Regt., not one regretful look shall I ever turn towards Utah." He signs the letter "Ever faithfully yr. friend."

While *The Deseret News* reported on the arrival of Steptoe and his command in its September 7 edition, dating that event to August 31, listing the officers by name, and indicating approvingly that Steptoe would settle his civilians and livestock in the Rush Valley, the paper made no mention of his departure. The editions of May and June were filled with grasshoppers; that is, with anxiety about their predation on the crops. Throughout the months of Steptoe's sojourn in Utah *The Deseret News* focused on events of the Crimean War that pitted the crumbling Ottoman Empire with its allies Britain and France against Russia even more than on local issues. The front page was normally taken up with "The History of Joseph Smith," including his correspondence, and with "Discourses," sermons, or "Teachings" by such Mormon luminaries as Heber C. Kimball or Brigham Young. "Fine and pleasant weather," the paper said in its April 25th edition, "rather dry for the young and tender plants." But nothing was said about the departure of Steptoe and his sometimes troublesome troops.

Steptoe sent the irksome Lieutenant Mowry, who had attempted a liaison with Governor Young's daughter-in-law and had apparently succeeded with a Miss Tanner, "who does me the honor to sleep in my bed for the present and for so long as I will keep her,"[100] to Benicia on the southern route, leaving Rush Valley on April 30. What became of Miss Tanner, not quite 15 but "well developed for her age," is uncertain, but according to Mowry, "More than half the women want to leave with us, or with somebody. Everybody had got one except the Colonel and Major."[101] The almost equally difficult Captain Ingalls had also transgressed, having been involved in some way with the abduction of a "minor child, aged twelve years," the upshot of which was a trial and the payment of a hundred dollar fine.[102] The details remain unclear, but Fielding suggests something of a Mormon "underground railroad" was involved and cites one account to the effect that more than a hundred Mormon women "begged of the soldiers to take them to California."[103] Ingalls accompanied Steptoe, taking the northern route. Fielding observes the arrival at Benicia of Steptoe and his troops with an undisclosed number of Mormon women "caused a titillation which bemused the nation."[104] Governor Young, Fielding adds, "was more angry with the women than the soldiers."[105]

Lieutenant Mowry's report to the Adjutant General from Benicia is dated July 23, 1855. In it he offers details regarding the southern route to California, and he takes the opportunity to excoriate the Mormons for "exorbitant" overpricing of grain. He advises Colonel Cooper of the Mormons' "disposition to annoy and embarrass in every possible way, and to extort the greatest sum of money for the least possible services."[106] He attached a separate report on the Indians, mostly various bands of Utes, noting Steptoe's observation that they "had been taught that the Mormons were superior people to the Americans, and that the Americans were the natural enemies of the Indians, while the Mormons were their friends and allies."[107] Mowry clearly concurred, claiming he found two Mormon missionaries with every band, "whose sole object was to impress upon the Indians the belief in the inferiority and hostility of the Americans, and the superiority and friendship of the Mormons." Moreover, he reports having found them well armed "with good rifles," whereas just two years previous "they were armed with nothing but bows and arrows of the poorest description." Mowry's suspicions of Mormon dealings with the tribes combined with his personal animosity would contribute to the evolution of the nation's policy toward the Mormons during President Buchanan's administration.

On May 16, 1855, Edward wrote to his father from camp 150 miles northwest of Salt Lake City in response to a letter posted on the fifth of February but received only the night before. He complains of irregular correspondence, but finds himself at fault as much as members of his family and refers to himself as "a nomadic, wild, military Arab."[108] He indicates he has "neither accepted nor declined the appointment, but stated it could *not* be accepted in the shape offered." If he were to accept, his "army position would be sacrificed & the time passed here—alone, isolated as I should be—would be very unhappy," even though his relations with the Mormons have been as "pleasant as they possibly could be under the circumstances." He insists it is his "conviction" that "the Mormons & I would have no trouble whatever," and he adds, "No Mormon, I *know*, can be the successor of Gov. Young, and I also know that he *will* have a successor." As the army prepared for the Utah War in April 1857, President Buchanan appointed as governor Alfred Cumming, former superintendent of Indian Affairs in Missouri, but for the two-year interim Young continued as territorial governor by default.

Captain Ingalls' observations on the journey from Salt Lake City north and west to Benicia indicate the march was mostly uneventful. He admires such rivers as the Weber and Ogden, and he notes of the Bear, "the valley of this river is quite picturesque."[109] The soil was good, Ingalls reported, and the grass abundant for forage, and they followed good roads as far as the Humboldt River in northern Nevada. This region through to California, however, he found to be "infested by nomadic tribes of Indians, generally of the lower order of beings," who were especially to be "dreaded" because "their native propensity to rob and murder is sharpened, excited, and refined by contact with white men of notoriously bad characters."[110] He reports while the troops were never molested, the Indians frequently pestered the drovers, so Steptoe had to provide military escort for the livestock.

At Lassen Meadows in northern California, Colonel Steptoe sent Ingalls with fifty dragoons and some horses north to Fort Lane near the Rogue River in southern Oregon Territory. Kurt R. Nelson notes that miners and settlers in the Rogue River valley "were waging a private vendetta against the Indians, who responded in kind," with some two dozen Indians killed by gunshot or hanging by the end of September.[111] Steptoe arrived at Benicia by July 10 via the old Carson Valley route, sending a brief note to President Pierce on that date. Four days later he wrote to the Adjutant General regarding figures for the military road to be built from Salt Lake City. Benicia Barracks had been established in April 1849, and it served as western headquarters of the Third Artillery Regiment, Steptoe's old unit, and the Second Infantry Regiment. Since 1852 it had been designated Benicia Arsenal, the first ordinance supply depot in the West. During the few months of Steptoe's sojourn he might have witnessed the construction of the camel barns intended to stable the nation's short-lived Camel Corps, although no camels were housed there until sometime in 1857 (the corps was deactivated during the Civil War).

We have no record of Steptoe's first impressions of the Pacific Ocean or of his first visit to the brash gold-rush city of San Francisco that had soared from a town of about a thousand in 1848 to more than 25,000 by the end of 1849. In 1855 San Francisco was probably as well known for vigilante justice as it was for anything else, but Levi Strauss had been turning out his denims for a couple of years by then, and Edward might have availed himself of some of Ghirardelli's chocolate, which had opened up there in 1852, the same year Wells Fargo set up in business. In a brief letter dated August 15, 1855, from

Five. The Gunnison Affair

San Francisco, Colonel Steptoe expresses his gratitude for the services of Mormon adventurer Porter Rockwell, who guided his troops in their trek from Salt Lake City, commending him as "an honest, indefatigable, fearless man," whose "practical, good sense, and bold, hearty, honest conduct saved it [the command] from repeated disaster."[112] The colonel does not elaborate on the nature of the disasters.

Steptoe's commendation of Orrin Porter Rockwell makes an odd postscript for this chapter of his life. Known as "the Destroying Angel of Mormondom," Rockwell served as bodyguard to both Joseph Smith and Brigham Young, and is said to have been a leader of the Mormon vigilante or guerrilla group known as the Danites. The exploits, genuine or imagined, of "Old Port" have been chronicled in biographies and featured in film as well.[113] As biographer Harold Schindler notes, on Rockwell's death the anti–Mormon *Salt Lake Tribune* hyperbolically claimed he had committed "at least a hundred murders for the Church."[114]

* * *

So far as Steptoe is directly concerned, the rest is epilogue, or perhaps aftermath. The national attitude toward Mormonism was much affected by the outcome of the Gunnison trial and the interpretations of Mormon views via such officers as Lieutenant Mowry and Captain Ingalls. Captain Ingalls' comments on Mormonism in his report on the Steptoe Expedition are of particular interest here, as they both parallel and to some extent elaborate those of Mowry cited above. He indicates his awareness of Gunnison's "praise of them" in *The Mormons, or Latter-Day Saints*, but writes,

> If these "saints" had not sometimes raised the veil and disclosed to us their real intentions, feelings, and character, we too should eulogize them. We possessed opportunities for observing the *shady* side of this people, while the officers referred to [Stansbury and Gunnison] always saw them in sunshine.[115]

As with Steptoe's observations to President Pierce, Ingalls commends the "great mass of the people" as "quiet, good men," but he adds they are "chiefly foreigners of the lower orders who do *in all things* exactly as they are told to do by their Prophet Brigham Young."[116] Although he takes note of their "remarkable industry," as did both Gunnison and Steptoe, Ingalls warns it is "far from voluntary," and he explains their apparent independence is actually "an abject submission to the will of the iron-handed priesthood." He insists they strive to "seem virtuous," but once the curtain is drawn "one sees what is generally regarded in other communities as sensuality and corruption." As to the Gunnison case and Mormon Indian policy, Ingalls echoes Mowry: "It is generally believed that the Indians there are taught to consider Mormons and Americans as different people. It is *certain* the Indians make a distinction." He concludes by lashing out against the miscarriage of justice that resulted from the trial, appealing for a change in the territorial government that would assure separation of Church and State, and commending the appointment of "any upright and pure man—for instance Colonel Steptoe" as governor.[117]

But Colonel Steptoe was directing the construction of Fort Walla Walla in the Washington Territory when the Utah or Mormon War got underway a few months after the inauguration of Democratic President James Buchanan on March 4, 1857. The specific rationale for sending the 2,500-man expedition to Utah, ostensibly to quell a Mormon "uprising," has never been firmly established. One historian concludes, "In assessing the factors that led to the ordering of armed forces to Utah, one is well advised to observe the part played by ignorance and misinformation."[118] According to Will Bagley, "None of the grandiose conspiracy theories devised to explain the Utah War provide a credible explanation of the president's actions, but politics inevitably played a part."[119] In the event, the federal government misjudged everything from the Mormons' temperament to the weather and terrain. Some Mormons may have had disputes with Brigham Young and the priesthood, but they were not about to rebel, nor were they about to receive the army with open arms and offer to provide forage and provisions.

The military force under Colonel Edmund Alexander, and ultimately under the command of Colonel Albert Sidney Johnston, who would distinguish himself as a Confederate general before being killed at Shiloh in 1862, left Fort Leavenworth on July 18, 1857, and would not come into contact with elements of the Mormon militia known as the Nauvoo Legion until early October. Blizzards closed down any significant military activities that winter. Young was compelled to accept the appointment of Alfred Cumming as governor in mid–April 1858, but allowing the unopposed entry of federal troops, in the process of being augmented by some three thousand reinforcements, was another matter. Scorched earth and structures as a tactic began with the torching of Fort Bridger on October 7, 1857.

On April 6, 1858, President Buchanan issued a pardon to the inhabitants of Utah, including Brigham Young, for their "seditions and treasons." Had it not been for the infamous Mountain Meadows massacre in September 1857, the casualties of the Utah War would have been negligible.[120] That atrocity involved an emigrant wagon train of Arkansans headed for California that was attacked by Mormon militia disguised as Paiute Indians and some number of Paiutes themselves in the southwestern corner of Utah. Between 100 and 140 men and women were killed, most of them taken under a white flag of truce: only 17 children under age eight were spared. Young's declaration of martial law in mid–September, as federal troops approached Salt Lake

City, along with what might be described as an atmosphere of nearly apocalyptic paranoia and hysteria likely contributed to the motives for the massacre.[121] Although it may plausibly be argued that the Utah Expedition initiated by President Buchanan did bring the Mormons out of their isolation and compelled them into eventual conformity with the Union, the costs were high. The Church of Jesus Christ of Latter Day Saints would not officially outlaw polygamy until 1890, and Utah would not acquire statehood until 1896.

No direct line of cause-and-effect can be drawn between Colonel Steptoe's experiences in Utah and that dark episode in Mormon history, but some speculation may be unavoidable. In an essay entitled "Sex, Subalterns, and Steptoe: Army Behavior, Mormon Rage, and Utah War Anxieties," William P. MacKinnon proposes that although the Steptoe Expedition "did not cause the Utah War," it "created a civil affairs atmosphere so poisonous that it aggravated deteriorating Mormon-federal relations while stiffening Brigham Young's resolve to bar the U.S. Army from Utah."[122] Perhaps a more severe verdict at the Gunnison trial, leading to the execution of three or even seven perpetrators of the massacre, would have obviated the perceived necessity of Buchanan's Utah Expedition along with the so-called Utah War and the massacre at Mountain Meadows. And if such a verdict had been attained, perhaps the anxiety in the East over the perceived threat of Mormonism and polygamy would have been quelled; moreover, Steptoe might have accepted the appointment to serve as territorial governor for at least one year.

But what then, one wonders. Miller speculates, as did Steptoe, that he "would be relegated to a mere figurehead"[123] while Young reigned as prophet and president of the church. On the other hand, given his initial welcome by Governor Young and other church leaders, perhaps Steptoe would have found himself accepted. Unlikely as it may seem, given some of his written comments on the Mormons after the trial, he might have acquired a Mormon wife and family, and history might have turned out quite differently. In a letter to his son William Junior, dated February 22, 1850, Dr. Steptoe reflects on Edward's desire to serve in the West and speculates, "His pay will pay his debts & support him genteelly if he never marries—but he had better marry if he ever intends doing so." In later correspondence from Fort Walla Walla with his half-sister Nannie, the subject of matrimony would come up more than once. In his 1850 letter to William, Edward's father adds, "I know he can get as much future as he wants."[124]

Chapter Six

In the Washington Territory: Building Forts at Walla Walla

By the end of November 1855 Major (Brevet Lieutenant Colonel) Edward J. Steptoe was in garrison at "Old Point Comfort," Fort Monroe, Virginia, at the mouth of Hampton Roads, regarded upon its completion in 1834 as "The Gibraltar of Chesapeake Bay." The impressive fortress, which Robert E. Lee helped construct between 1831 and 1834, boasted 32-pounder cannons and would play an important part in the Civil War, where it was commanded by General Benjamin Butler in support of the federal naval blockade.[1]

In a note sent from Washington, D.C., to his father, dated October 9, 1855, Edward refers to his letter dispatched while en route from Salt Lake City to Benicia, California, and indicates he expects to be sent back West via St. Louis in the spring. He mentions being "not well—not quite recovered from Panama fever or something of the kind which assailed me on the Isthmus."[2] Coincidentally, on that same day a young second lieutenant named Philip Sheridan arrived at Portland in the Oregon Territory; within six months he and Steptoe would meet under fire at the Cascades settlements in the Washington Territory.[3] While staying in Washington, D.C., that fall Steptoe may have visited the recently completed red sandstone Smithsonian Castle, construction on which had begun in 1847 while he was serving in Mexico.

Part of the October 9 letter is missing, but significantly, Edward says he is writing "from my old room in the President's house." This refers to his former comrade-in-arms during the Mexican War, Franklin Pierce, whose appointment as governor of the Utah Territory Steptoe had recently declined. In September 1852, during his presidential campaign, Pierce had been accused of cowardice for backing down during a confrontation in Mexico City at the Aztec Club, a society of officers who participated in the Mexican War. An intoxicated Captain J. Bankhead Magruder, an artillery officer serving under Pierce, supposedly slapped the general, but that report had been challenged as a false rumor. Pierce turned to Steptoe to clear his name, and Edward responded with a letter in support of Pierce's account of the event.[4]

In early autumn of 1855 Franklin Pierce remained sanguine about the likelihood the Democratic Party would support his reelection. A so-called "Doughface," a Northerner who was sympathetic to the South, Pierce had championed the Kansas-Nebraska Act of 1854 and with it, the concept of "popular sovereignty," the cornerstone of states-rights and, ipso facto, slavery ideology. The act nullified the Missouri Compromise of 1820 and would potentially open the new territories to slavery. During the summer of 1855 Free-soilers (or Free-staters) and pro-slavery advocates held separate territorial conventions in what would soon be known as "Bleeding Kansas." In October, as Steptoe was settling in at the White House for a few days, abolitionist John Brown was entering Kansas. The newly-created Republican Party, which attracted anti-slavery Northerners from the Democratic Party, Whigs, and Free-soilers, was beginning to flex its muscle. His party would soon abandon Pierce in favor of yet another "Doughface," the bachelor James Buchanan of Pennsylvania, who took office on March 4, 1857.

In a letter to the Adjutant General, Colonel Samuel Cooper, dated October 11, 1855, Steptoe offers advice as to the quartering of troops in Utah, indicating "at no time after the first of the year would a force of 2 or 300 men be distressed for subsistence" and "in years ordinarily productive, a Regiment [about 600 men] would find there ample supplies."[5] He adds "prompt payments" would likely "attract whatever supplies could be furnished, especially in the southern settlements which have no market whatsoever for their produce." He also advises that inhabitants of the territory should be informed "as early as possible" if troops are to be sent so they can plant crops accordingly, as "the church would no doubt make exorbitant demands."

Steptoe's most important observations, however, are of a more sweeping nature and may well have had some influence on the next administration's decision (Buchanan's) in the summer of 1857 to send a force of some 2,500 troops to put down what was described as an "uprising" among the Mormons: "As to the moral influences which troops established in the Territory would probably exercise, I scarcely think it can be over estimated. At present there are no national influences in the country—not a conspicuous emblem, civil or military, of the Federal Government, and I am satisfied there are many persons in the Mormon community who only require something positive & permanent near which they may take their stand as good, reliable American Citizens." Moreover, Steptoe adds, the Indian tribes in the Utah Territory need to be "assured that the Government has power to control them."

In subsequent letters sent to the Adjutant General from Washington, D.C., dated October 13 and November 7 of 1855, Steptoe acknowledges receipt of his commission as major with the Ninth Infantry Regiment, and he appeals for compensation for Lieutenants Mowry and Allston, who commanded detachments of recruits during his expedition from Fort Leavenworth into the Utah Territory the previous summer. Steptoe apparently did not re-cross the Plains, but accompanied Colonel George Wright and other officers of the Ninth Infantry to the Pacific Coast via Panama, arriving on January 21 or 22, 1856, at Fort Vancouver on the Washington Territory side of the Columbia River. There he would see the imposing Hudson's Bay fort established in 1824 about five miles from the mouth of the Willamette River. The army had set up its Vancouver Barracks on a twenty-foot rise overlooking the fort in 1849, but the fur trading post was still in operation in 1856, although it was becoming dilapidated (it burned down in 1866).

Numerous businesses set up operations just outside the walls: shipyard, tannery, hospital, distillery, sawmill. Fruit orchards and a dairy were also established so that by the time the U.S. military arrived in the spring of 1849, a thriving community existed. The fort has been reconstructed. On the bluff a few officers' residences, still standing, would have been new buildings when Steptoe arrived. One of those is known today as "Grant's House," though Captain Ulysses S. Grant was stationed at Vancouver Barracks for only a couple of years (1852–1853). The primary resident in 1856 was Grant's former West Point roommate and Steptoe's quartermaster during the expedition to Utah, Captain Rufus Ingalls.

Lieutenant Lawrence Kip, whose journal was first published in 1859 as *Army Life on the Pacific*, describes Fort Vancouver as "probably the most pleasant of our posts on the Pacific coast. The place is healthy and the scenery around beautiful."[6] The population of the newly settled town of Portland, across the Columbia, numbered only 821 according to the 1850 census, but it had increased to 2,874 by 1860, and historian Jewel Lansing observes at its chartering in January 1851 it was the largest city in the Oregon Territory, and there was then "no Seattle, no Tacoma, no Boise, no Spokane."[7] Kip notes the nearness of Fort Vancouver to Portland and Oregon City, about twenty miles south on the Willamette River, "prevents the young officers from being, as at many other western posts, deprived of the refining influence of female society. Many are the occasions on which they find it necessary to drop down to these places." Steptoe's marching orders, however, would take him not southward, but eastward along the Columbia toward the newly established Fort Dalles, nearly ninety miles away.

"It is a river of imagination," writes William Dietrich in *Northwest Passage: The Great Columbia River*. "It is the most beautiful big American river in the grandeur and variety of the landscape."[8] Like Lewis and Clark when they descended the river, Colonel Wright and Colonel Steptoe's officers and men were probably more concerned with the rapids than they were with scenic beauty. But Steptoe may well have been impressed, if not awed, by the sublime beauty of the Gorge. The middle of the 19th century, after all, remained as Wordsworth and other Romantic poets defined it, an age of the sublime, the proper response to which was awe. It would be a stretch of the imagination, however, to suppose the two colonels were steeped in poetry.

As he made his way upriver toward Fort Dalles a couple of months after his arrival, Steptoe would see on his starboard side, about 15 miles east of Fort Vancouver, a feature known today as Crown Point rising some 733 feet above the river. Another ten or 12 miles would bring him opposite the spectacular Bridal Veil Falls, which drops through the basalt at sixty to a hundred feet at the upper falls and another forty to sixty feet at the lower. Another seven or eight miles would place him opposite 848-feet-high Beacon Rock, as Lewis and Clark named it, an imposing andesite monolith on the port or Washington side.

In *Fighting for Paradise* Kurt R. Nelson writes the territories of Oregon and Washington "experienced total war in the 1850s, with nearly thirty percent of the white and American Indian populations directly engaged in periodic combat."[9] Steptoe was serving in Mexico City when Marcus and Narcissa Whitman along with ten others were massacred on November 29, 1847, by Cayuse Indians at their mission, known as Waiilatpu, near a former fur trading post that was known variously as Fort Nez Perce or Fort Walla Walla ("many rivers"). That event gave rise to the Cayuse War, which extended through May of 1850 and involved members of the Palouse and Umatilla tribes as well as the Cayuse. Although five Cayuses were tried and hanged on June 3, 1850, hostilities lasted into 1855. Moreover, as Robert Ignatius Burns observes in *The Jesuits and the Indian Wars of the Northwest*, tribes to the west of the Cascades, including the Klamaths, Tilamooks, Klickitats, and Snoqualmies, also took up arms.[10] Even before the Whitman Massacre, white incursions on Indian lands in the Oregon Territory had ballooned from about two hundred families in 1842 to a population of more than five thousand by 1845. The discovery of gold in California in 1848 triggered even greater numbers, some 53,000 immigrants in the decades between 1840 and 1860.[11] At mid-century the Indian population in the Oregon Territory (comprising the present states of Oregon, Washington, and Idaho) has been estimated at something under 25,000.[12]

Burns indicates before 1855 the American army was "an absurdly small affair, seldom reaching a total of 11,000 men."[13] Congressional legislation in 1855 allowed for perhaps another 2,700 men. Terms like "perhaps" are well chosen, as units were rarely maintained at full strength. A frontier company of any designation (dragoon or cavalry, infantry, artillery) might boast the allotted number of 74 privates, but Robert Utley indicates the "set maximum" was "rarely reached." He explains some three-fourths of the total was "stationed on the frontier," but of those, "only about one-third could be counted on as effective for any but a passive mission of guard and escort."[14]

The thousand or so regular army troops available in the Oregon and Washington Territories by that year were frequently supplemented with militia. Nelson posits "nearly 6,000 troops—over 850 regular U.S. Army troops and over 5,100 militia troops" took the field between 1855 and 1858.[15] Citizens in the territories were inclined to trust in their own Indian fighting capabilities based on past successes in the Rogue River Wars and in the Cayuse War. Friction increased when Brevet Major General John E. Wool took command early in 1854. Utley observes the army "steered a torturous course," alternating "between protecting innocent Indians from slaughter by angry settlers and joining with improvised volunteer units to run down Indians accused of robbery or murder."[16]

General Wool would exacerbate the situation. Utley describes him as a "stiff-necked professional of forty-two years' service" who was "possessed of a contemptuous temperament" and "tended to regard anyone who differed with him as a scoundrel."[17] In particular, given the federal commitment to treaties and reservations, Wool opposed settlers who would appropriate Indian lands, and this opposition led to conflict with the governor of the recently established Washington Territory which, in early 1853, was split off from the Oregon Territory. Isaac Ingalls Stevens, who graduated at the head of his 1839 class at West Point and had served with distinction in the Mexican War, was named Washington's territorial governor. He would also act as the territory's Superintendent of Indian Affairs. Burns describes Stevens as a man of "keen and cultivated" intellect and "flamboyant" manners, possessed of "an iron will impatient of opposition."[18] Steptoe would likely have been acquainted with him, as Stevens had graduated from the Academy just two years before he did. Both officers had been brevetted for gallantry at the Battle of Chapultepec and were great supporters of President Franklin Pierce.

The span of time between 1853 and 1858 is known as "The Great Outbreak," a period that saw hostilities between Indians and white settlers raging from the Puget Sound to the Rogue River in southern Oregon. The most powerful leader to emerge among the tribes from the inland Northwest or Northern Plateau region was Yakama war chief, Kamiakin, whom Nelson describes as "a voice of Indian unity in a manner not heard since the days of Pontiac or Tecumseh."[19] Kamiakin's father was Palouse, his mother Yakama, so he was not full-blooded Yakama and would not likely have claimed to speak for them, although Governor Stevens and various Indian agents, like most officials who dealt with the tribes from the earliest days, preferred to believe they were dealing with the "head chief" who spoke for his entire people.[20] It was a matter of convenience and efficiency—values not necessarily shared by Native Americans.

Governor Stevens' description of the chief as he saw him at the Walla Walla Council in late May 1855 is worth noting because Kamiakin, directly or indirectly, would become Steptoe's major adversary:

> He is a peculiar man, reminding me of the panther and the grizzly bear. His countenance has an extraordinary play, one moment in frowns, the next in smiles, flashing with light and black as Erebus the same instant. [...] He talks mostly in his face, and with his hands and arms.[21]

In his biography of Isaac Ingalls Stevens, his son Hazard Stevens describes Kamiakin as "a man of fine presence and bearing, over six feet in height, well built and athletic." According to his recent biographers, Kamiakin at first "cautiously welcomed White newcomers in the region," and in the late 1840s and early 1850s he cooperated with two Oblate missionaries in establishing St. Joseph's Mission on Simcoe Creek, later relocated to Ahtanum Creek near present-day Yakima, Washington.[22] He raised various crops, which he irrigated from a canal. By fall of 1853, however, surveying parties, one of which was led by Captain George McClellan, caused Kamiakin to grow "increasingly disturbed."[23]

The treaty signed by the various tribes at Walla Walla (the Yakama-Palouse-Klickitat, the Walla Walla-Cayuse-Umatilla, and the Nez Perce) in mid–June 1855 did not accomplish the easy settlement of some 17,000 square miles of Indian lands that Governor Stevens intended.[24] Students of Native American history and culture would argue the governor's assertion that the combined tribes "are to be considered as one nation, under the name of 'Yakima,' with Kamiakun as its head chief" amounted to wishful thinking, as did the premise that Kamiakin was "duly authorized" to speak on their behalf.[25] With the discovery of gold north of the Spokane River near Fort Colville a few weeks later, Kamiakin found it easier to convince other chiefs to join his tribal confederacy.[26] In southern Oregon the Rogue River Indians reignited a war with miners and settlers that had ended in 1853, and Qualchan, son of Kittitas or Upper Yakama Chief Owhi and close friend to Kamiakin, killed six white gold seekers (the number varies) in early September 1855.

Several Yakama chiefs opposed Kamiakin's efforts to unite the Northern Plateau tribes, and Owhi initially refused to join, but as Utley phrases it, Kamiakin "adroitly maneuvered by enticing Owhi's son Qualchin into murdering two gold-hunters," and Owhi then "resignedly" joined the "formless alliance."[27] When Indian agent Andrew Jackson Bolon set out from Fort Dalles to investigate the killings, four Yakama warriors seized him on September 23, 1855, and cut his throat. Brevet Major Granville Haller was dispatched from Fort Dalles with two companies of the Fourth U.S. Infantry (86 men) to seize the perpetrators, but a force of at least five hundred Yakama and Klickitat warriors (perhaps Cayuse and Walla Walla as well) attacked on October 5 at Toppenish Creek and compelled him to retreat with a loss of five men killed and 17 wounded.[28] Thus began the Yakama War of 1855 in which Steptoe would find himself engaged in March 1856.

Reprisals for the murder of Agent Bolon and for the defeat of Major Haller followed in November 1855 with a force composed of about 350 regulars under Major Gabriel Rains, who would serve the Confederacy as a brigadier general at Shiloh and elsewhere, and a similar number of Oregon volunteers under militia Colonel (and quondam general) James W. Nesmith, who would go on to become Superintendent of Indian Affairs for the territories and later U.S. Senator for Oregon. They struck Father Pandosy's mission on Ahtanum Creek, and burned down Kamiakin's home, but because the Indians did not engage with the troops, the expedition was regarded as a failure.

Saved from the plundering and conflagration was a remarkable letter Kamiakin dictated to Father Pandosy on October 6, presumably while the battle with Haller's troops was underway on Toppenish Creek. "Write to the soldiers and tell them we are quiet, friends to the Americans, that we are not thinking of war at all," the letter begins.[29] Kamiakin expresses his irritation at Governor Stevens' conflation (or confusion) of the Yakama with the Cayuse and his anger at the reservation system that took them out of their native lands and "into a strange land among a people who is our enemy." The Yakama language is Sahaptin while the quite different Cayuse language has never been reliably classified. Kamiakin chastises the Americans (whites) for executing Indians, but not hanging whites, "though there is no place where Americans have not killed Indians." He also refutes the notion that Indians had no knowledge of livestock or agriculture before the whites arrived: "They tell us that our ancestors had no horses or cattle, nor corn nor seeds nor instruments to garden, that we have received all of these riches from the Americans." The Indians, he declares, have been treated "as dogs."

"You have fired the first shot," Kamiakin tells Governor Stevens. "Our heart is broken." He explains that miners fired on them because they would not give up their women, so they were compelled to defend themselves. As to Agent Bolon, "he strongly insulted us" and "threatened us with death," so they felt obliged to defend themselves in this matter as well. If the whites (Kamiakin uses only the word "Americans") will "retire and treat us in a friendly way, we will consent to put down our arms and to grant them a parcel of land from each different tribe, as long as they do not force us to be exiled from our native country." He was well aware of the odds against his people:

"We are resolved to be cut down and if we lose the men who keep the camp in which are the wives and our children we will kill them rather than see them fall into the hands of the Americans to make them their playthings. We have hearts and self-respect."

Major Rains, commanding at Fort Dalles and serving in the field as a brigadier general of Washington territorial volunteers, wrote a substantial response to Kamiakin dated November 13, 1855, accusing him of lying about his desire for peace: "You came in peace—we come in war. And why? Because your land has drunk the blood of the white man. [...] You know that you murdered white men going to the mines who had done you no injury, and you murder all persons [he mentions Agent Bolon], though no white man had trespassed on your lands."[30] Rains probably spoke for most of the settlers in the territory when he dismissed the notion of trespass and wrote, "We will not be quiet, but war forever, until not a Yakima breathes in the land he calls his own. The river only we let retain this name to show all people that here the Yakimas once lived. [...] The country is ours already, as you must see from our assembled army; for we intend to occupy it, and make it too hot to hold you."

After reminding Kamiakin of the treaty he signed with Governor Stevens (not ratified by Congress for another four years), Rains concludes: "Our warriors in the field are many, as you must see; but if not enough, a thousand for every one more will be sent to hunt you, and to kill you; and my kind advice to you, as you will see, is to scatter yourselves among the Indian tribes more peaceable, and there to forget you ever were Yakimas." In the event, the chief accepted part of Rains' "kind advice" by scattering among other tribes, but there is no evidence he ever forgot he was Yakama.

On December 4, 1855, Oregon volunteers under Lieutenant Colonel James K. Kelly, attempting to exact vengeance for Major Haller's defeat, seized the Walla Walla Chief Peopeo Moxmox (Yellow Bird) under a flag of truce, and when angry Indians closed in on his troops near the old Whitman mission, the guards murdered the aging chief (probably in his late fifties) and his companions. The "stately old Wallawalla chief," who had signed the May 1855 treaty along with Kamiakin and others, was killed, Alvin Josephy writes, because "his intelligence and pride had made him too dangerous to the Americans." The volunteers "had a ghoulish time, mutilating his corpse and cutting off his fingers, ears, and bits of his scalp as souvenirs."[31] Kamiakin was among numerous chiefs who regarded Peopeo Moxmox as a friend or at least as a respected adversary; his mistreatment would not be forgotten. The atrocity called into question both the integrity of Governor Stevens and the reliability of his treaty.

Complicating matters for General Wool, the Rogue River Indians' renewal of hostilities to the south presented him with a war on two fronts by fall of 1855. Members of the Nisqually, Green River, and Klickitat tribes attacked small settlements in the Puget Sound area in December 1855, and in January 1856 a group of Yakamas joined in, so that in effect a third front opened up briefly, effectually tying down additional forces through the month of June. Wool would focus, however, on the eastern front (employing the term "front" loosely), where forces under Colonel Wright built fortifications and confronted the Yakamas, who allied themselves with elements of the Walla Walla, Cayuse, Umatilla, and Palouse, to list only the most prominent tribes engaged.

In his memoirs, then Second Lieutenant Philip Sheridan, a 25-year-old dragoon officer and 1853 West Point graduate, writes of heading up the Columbia from Fort Vancouver by boat in late March 1856 in order to confront the tribes as "represented in the person of old Cammiackan, chief of the Spokanes."[32] Here Sheridan provides an unusual phonetic spelling of Kamiakin along with evidence of typical confusion among the whites, mistaking Kamiakin's tribe, the Yakama (a Sahaptin-speaking people) for the Spokane (a Salish-speaking people). Sheridan would emerge as the Union army's most effective cavalry leader during the Civil War and command troops in the Plains Indian wars, where he would (perhaps erroneously) be credited with declaring "the only good Indian is a dead Indian."

Sheridan's destination, with his troop of forty dragoons, was a pair of settlements on the Cascades of the Columbia, forty-odd miles to the east of Fort Vancouver. The rapids there had become a prime salmon fishing site for the Cascade tribes. Lewis and Clark endured a rainy and foggy day when they encountered the rapids on October 30, 1805. Clark notes they "landed on an Island close under the Stard. Side at the head of the great Shute." Steep mountains on both sides of the river were "thickly Covered with timber, Such as Spruc, Pine, Cedar, Oake, Cotton[wood], &c., &c."[33] About 150 yards wide at that point, the Columbia drops forty feet in two miles and presented a challenge to navigation even by steamships. "A number of the Savages came to our Camp and Signed to us that they were Surprized to See us," Sergeant John Ordway reported, "they thought we had rained down out of the clouds."

Frances Fuller Victor in *The Early Indian Wars of Oregon* indicates the "great importance" of the Cascades settlements and the five-mile portage, which were defended by a blockhouse built between them. Early in March, as Colonel Wright, with Steptoe second in command, began moving his 250 troops the ninety or so miles from Fort Vancouver to Fort Dalles, "a large amount of army stores and baggage was temporarily detained at the Cascades, offering a great temptation to the Yakimas and Klickitats."[34] Moreover, two of the three companies left at Fort Vancouver had been sent north to Fort

Steilacoom, and the single company at the blockhouse between the upper and lower Cascades, known as Fort Rains, had been drawn down to just ten men under Sergeant Matthew Kelly. In what Nelson describes as "an unusual display of discipline and coordination," Indians on the morning of March 26 simultaneously attacked the blockhouse and both the upper and lower Cascades communities, separated by six or seven miles of unnavigable rapids.[35] At the sawmill on the upper rapids, Victor writes, "B.W. Brown, his eighteen-year-old wife, and her young brother were slain, scalped, and thrown into the river."[36] As forty men, women, and children barricaded themselves in the Bradford Storehouse in the upper Cascades settlement, a small steamboat got underway and headed east to alert Colonel Wright at Fort Dalles.

Meanwhile, Lieutenant Sheridan and his dragoons boarded another steamboat and proceeded upriver, followed by a contingent of Oregon Territorial Volunteers raised in Portland. The settlement at the lower Cascades having been overrun, Sheridan's orders were to relieve the blockhouse in the middle Cascades. For that purpose he left Fort Vancouver at 2:00 a.m., March 27, landing in the lower Cascades, where he confronted "hostiles" who dared him to fight with "loud shouting, and much blustering" and "by the most exasperating yells and indecent exhibitions."[37] As he led his men through some underbrush on a narrow neck of land, "the enemy opened fire and killed a soldier near my side by a shot which, just grazing the bridge of my nose, struck him in the neck, opening an artery and breaking the spinal cord. He died instantly." Taking a few men from his command, Sheridan towed a boat along the south side of the island and moved into position the next morning (the 28th) opposite the besieged blockhouse.

By this time, Sheridan notes, the advance of Wright's command had arrived "under Lieutenant Colonel Edward J. Steptoe," who agreed with Sheridan's opinion that when they attacked, the Yakamas "would take to the mountains" and the Cascade Indians would cross over the island they had just left. In his account of the combat at the upper Cascades, L.W. Coe, one of the beleaguered citizens at the Bradford Storehouse, indicates Steptoe's dragoons reached them at 6:00 a.m. on the March 28. As they were about to swoop down on the Indians, however, someone sounded a bugle, and most of them escaped.[38] Victor lists the names of 17 who died in the two days and nights of siege and the day of combat that followed in what has been called the Battle of the Cascades or the Cascades Massacre. Lieutenant Sheridan captured several Cascade Indians and had nine of them, including Chief Chenowith, "sentenced to death and duly hanged" after a hasty military trial. Steptoe saw to it the lieutenant received a commendation for his part in the battle.

Steptoe's next assignment would be to join Colonel Wright in the field in pursuit of Kamiakin and the Yakamas. On May 11 their troops confronted some fifteen hundred warriors from the Yakama and other tribes under Kamiakin at the Naches River, but the exchange of fire was brief and the Indians scattered. Wright then ordered Steptoe to establish Fort Na-Chess located nine miles north of the mouth of the Naches River, where it joins the Yakima. That confluence is today located in the city of Yakima. The fort, essentially a supply depot, was a gabion structure composed of woven willow basket-like containers filled with dirt, stone, and other rubble. Settlers in the vicinity called it "Fort Basket." Nearby, Fort Simcoe, established at about the same time by Major Robert S. Garnett lasted somewhat longer, as the federal government used it as headquarters of the Yakima Indian Agency after 1859.[39]

Father Burns suggests Colonel Wright "walked his men fatuously over empty, endless landscapes."[40] Frances Fuller Victor wrote: "The history of Wright's operations [...] shows a summer spent in trailing Indians from place to place, from fishery to fishery, and over mountains before thought impassable for troops, dragging after them their season's supplies, and accomplishing nothing but to collect the non-combatants of the disaffected tribes upon a reservation in Oregon, where they were secure from the turmoil of war, and at liberty to spy on each other."[41] Ethnologist and geologist George Gibbs (1815–1873) pronounced the pursuit "a perfect farce."[42] Colonel Wright informed Major W[illiam] W[hann] Mackall, a West Point classmate then serving in San Francisco as Assistant Adjutant General of the United States, to the effect that "the whole country should be given to the Indians; they require it; they cannot live at any one point for the whole year."[43] Significantly *not* among those Indians were Kamiakin and his followers, who moved east into the Palouse country, the land of his father's people, rather than accept the peace terms mediated between Colonel Wright and Chief Owhi of the upper Yakamas and the war chief Burns calls "Kamiakin's disreputable brother Skloom."[44]

Steptoe subsequently joined Colonel Wright at Fort Dalles prior to moving east to build a fort at Walla Walla. Fort Dalles was in the process of evolving from a "dreary" and "isolated" spot on the Columbia into "an equal, even overshadowing rival to Fort Vancouver."[45] Writing of his visit in late June 1858, Lieutenant Kip noted many changes since his visit three years earlier, when the post seemed to him "the most unattractive on the Pacific."[46] Immigrants passing through Fort Dalles or its predecessor Camp Drum in the early 1850s would have seen little in the way of civilization, nor would they have found much in the way of a break from the bleak landscape they had traversed since leaving the old Hudson's Bay post known as Fort Walla Walla (a.k.a., "Old Fort Walla Walla"), located where the Walla Walla River joins the Columbia. "A most desolate place," lamented Sylvester Mowry in September 1853, about a year before he would perform at Salt Lake City in his role as Steptoe's most troublesome lieutenant, "with nothing to recommend it except wolves, coyotes, rattlesnakes and skunks."[47]

The building of Fort Dalles fell to assistant quartermaster Captain Thomas Jordan, who entrusted the architectural plans to a German immigrant named Louis Scholl, who coincidentally had met Colonel Steptoe when he was in the Utah Territory.[48] Scholl embraced the costly "Picturesque" mode of New York architect Andrew Jackson Downing, who modeled his rural residences after the English cottage style, favoring verandas, entrance porches, bay windows, and pointed gables. What Steptoe and Wright would have found in March 1856, however, was a motley assemblage of overcrowded barracks constructed haphazardly and insufficient for the "sudden and great vicissitudes," as Captain Jordan phrased it, of the climate. The dozen officers, including Jordan, were cooped up in "a shabby log hovel divided into six rooms."[49]

In his six-page report to U.S. Quartermaster General Thomas S. Jesup on the construction dated August 29, 1857, Captain Jordan takes pride in detailing the features of the new officers' quarters. "The officers' quarters are in the cottage form," Lieutenant Kip wrote near the end of June 1858, "and for taste are superior to those we have seen at any other post."[50] Priscilla Knuth observes the town of The Dalles grew quickly around the expanded military post, as civilian employee rolls grew from just five in March to "a peak of 290 in November 1856."[51] Captain Jordan came under sharp criticism for his extravagance, but Steptoe must have been impressed by what he saw just one year after his initial visit.

In August 1856 Colonel Wright ordered Steptoe to establish a fort in the Walla Walla River valley, about thirty miles east of the old Hudson's Bay fort on the Columbia. Edward's letter to his father dated August 22, 1856, and sent from Fort Dalles informs him he will march in the morning "to establish a Post some 150 miles east of this place, on the Walla=Walla."[52] How many letters Steptoe wrote home between his previous extant communication, dated October 9, 1855, and this, one can only surmise, but he opens by thanking his father for acknowledging his previous letter "so promptly," by noting that he is "much pressed for time," and by apologizing for having "procrastinated" to the point that he is writing at 9:00 p.m. and has four or five letters yet to compose.

Since he last wrote, Steptoe says, "I have encountered no stirring life: The Indians in the South all wanted peace & it was granted to them." "You would be amused," he continues, "if you could see my household & general arrangements—very much like those of an emigrant (except that there are no Females)." In addition to three horses and a wagon, his entourage consisted of "one black boy, one little Indian boy (whom I bought out of slavery & who is a most promising servant by the way)," a cow and a dozen chickens.

Whether the "black boy" was a slave is unknown, but although others in his family in Virginia were slave-holders, we have indications elsewhere that both Edward and his father were opposed to slavery in principle.

Indeed, his next observation speaks directly to the coming maelstrom: "If you in the East separate politically, I think my best course will be to occupy some choice spot in this country: a vast Empire is to be formed in the Pacific some day, undisturbed by the questions which seem to trouble the Atlantic States so much." He regrets "for many reasons" the failure of the Democratic Party to re-nominate Franklin Pierce and predicts "the election of Buchanan will be no relief to the South—that is no *permanent* good. I *was* in hope that the great battle for the Union & the rights of the South would be fought under Pierce, Douglas, or some other man equally prominent in defending the principles which they proclaimed so bravely." Edward, while declaring his concern for the "rights of the South," appears content to separate himself from the approaching hostilities. He expresses concern over the region of his birth and heritage, but he significantly refers to "you in the East," effectively distancing himself. Moreover, he shows some personal interest in the "vast Empire" of the Pacific Northwest, and one reason for that may have to do with his chronic illness, as he implies indirectly in another passage: "My health remains very good: this climate is considered remarkably fine—very dry & very genial."

Steptoe's troops proceeded about 132 miles east along the Columbia to the site of the old Hudson's Bay Fort Walla Walla. At that point, having ridden in a somewhat northerly direction for the previous twenty or so miles, the troops headed due east for thirty miles, following the winding Walla Walla River before passing the site of the 1847 Whitman Massacre seven miles west of today's city of Walla Walla. They halted somewhere along what is now Five Mile Road, a little over five miles east of the present downtown business district, and there Colonel Steptoe set up camp in preparation for the arrival of Governor Stevens and his escort.

In a proclamation dated August 21, the day before his letter to his father, Colonel Steptoe tersely asserts the U.S. military's policy in the western territories: "No emigrant or other white person, except the Hudson's Bay Company, or persons having ceded rights from the Indians, will be permitted to settle or remain in the Indian country or on land not settled or not confirmed by the Senate and approved by the President of the United States." In this document Steptoe was expressly carrying out the orders of General Wool, commanding the Department of the Pacific and nemesis of Governor Stevens. Added to the proclamation was a paragraph that might at least somewhat have appeased the pro-development governor: "These orders are not, however, to apply to miners engaged in collecting gold at the Colville mines."[53]

Six. In the Washington Territory

The tenor of the relationship between the military commander and the territorial governor is implicit in a passage from Hazard Stevens' biography with respect to the first Walla Walla treaty council held in late May of 1855, nearly a year before Steptoe arrived in the territory. The governor urged Wool to occupy the Walla Walla valley "with a strong military force [...]. This, like other sound and indeed necessary measures recommended by the governor, was ignored by the self-sufficient Wool and his officers, until they were obliged to adopt them from necessity."[54]

In a letter addressed to Stevens dated February 12, 1856, General Wool indicates he intends to prosecute the war against the Indians "with all vigor, promptness and efficiency" with his additional forces, "provided the extermination of the Indians, which I do not approve of, is not determined on, and private war prevented, and volunteers withdrawn from the Walla Walla country."[55] Wool's provisions, particularly the one regarding withdrawal of the volunteers, did not sit well with Stevens. The general informs the governor at the end of the letter that he has directed Colonel Wright to "take the Walla Walla country at the earliest moment practicable" and that he has ordered him "to give protection to the Cayuses from the depredations of the volunteers." He explains if such behavior continues, the Nez Perce might enter the war and thereby require "a much larger force than we now have."

Governor Stevens' "caustic reply," as his son described it, ran more than 2,300 words and is dated March 20, not quite a week before the attack on the Cascades settlements. While he acknowledges that atrocities committed by "some turbulent men of the Oregon volunteers" did cause injury to some friendly Cayuses, Stevens insists the affair was "grossly exaggerated," and he proceeds to point out the general himself had found it necessary to call on volunteers, "and thus I have your testimony as against yourself in vindication of the necessity of calling out volunteers." The governor loads much of his venom into a single brief paragraph:

> I have a right to hold you to a full knowledge of our condition here. If you say you were misinformed, then you are not fit for your position, and should give place to a better man. If you were informed, then your measures as a military man manifest an incapacity beyond example.[56]

Hazard Stevens asserts Wool was unable to answer his father's letter "which so clearly exposed and justly rebuked his reprehensible course and conduct," except with a note from his aide.[57]

The tone of this exchange may be as relevant as the particulars or even the concepts involved (civilian versus military control, popular sovereignty versus federal authority, volunteer militia versus professional military) to the next significant episode in Steptoe's deployment to the Washington Territory. After the Battle of the Cascades and fruitless pursuit of the Yakamas over the next two or three months, Governor Stevens sent territorial volunteers under Colonel Benjamin F. Shaw into the Walla Walla valley. Shaw then proceeded into northeastern Oregon along the Grande Ronde River at the site of present-day La Grande, Oregon, where, in mid–July 1856, he encountered a gathering mostly of people from the Walla Walla, Cayuse, and Umatilla tribes. The volunteers swept into the village and, according to Stevens' biographer, Kent D. Richards, killed "at least sixty, many of whom were women and children"; Shaw's troops also seized their supplies and killed two hundred horses.[58] In a furious letter dated August 19 to Colonel Thomas, Assistant Adjutant General at Army headquarters in New York City, General Wool asserted the "whole object" of the volunteers sent by Governor Stevens was "to plunder the Indians and prolong the war."[59] After that, a significant military presence in the Walla Walla valley was deemed essential, particularly if Governor Stevens were to proceed with his plans for a second council in that area in the middle of September.

The Battle of Grande Ronde constitutes something of the backstory for Steptoe's urgent need to establish a fort near the treaty site. Given recent events, one might question the governor's insistence upon this second council, the first one having produced no clear evidence of success. Hazard Stevens deals with the effort in a chapter entitled "The Fruitless Peace Council"; Burns describes it as a "dismal failure" and as "eventuating in another fiasco."[60] Governor Stevens opened proceedings on September 11. By the fifth of that month Colonel Steptoe and his four or five companies (about 350 soldiers in all) were hastily assembling winter quarters on Mill Creek, a few miles from present-day downtown Walla Walla. Steptoe's troops constructed a blockhouse by September 20, with stockade to follow.[61] Initially named "Fort Steptoe," construction was completed in just two days. Steptoe would later supervise the building of two, more elaborate, forts at Walla Walla, the first of them within the present downtown business district (October-November 1856) and the second on higher ground about one mile out of town (occupied beginning February 1858).

Given his orders from General Wool, Steptoe's relationship with Governor Stevens was destined to be prickly. Hazard Stevens writes indignantly, "It is impossible [...] to acquit Wright and Steptoe of a lack of candor in concealing from the governor the real character of Wool's instructions, and in leading him to expect their faithful cooperation and support."[62] Richards, however, indicates the governor had known the colonel in Mexico and "admired his coolness and efficiency as an artillery officer. Steptoe had a reputation as a conscientious, dedicated officer destined for increased responsibilities."[63] Moreover, as Waldo E. Rosebush has observed, Stevens knew Colonel Wright "was under the strictest orders from Wool not to recognize

Six. In the Washington Territory 135

the volunteers in any way."[64] In his biography of Kamiakin, A.J. Splawn suggests the Indians also knew of this rift between regular army and the volunteers. According to Splawn, Kamiakin said "the regular army had no respect for Governor Stevens and he thought that Colonel Steptoe's command would not help Governor Stevens if the Indians should attack him; wherefore he thought it a good time to kill Governor Stevens and all his escort."[65]

With Colonel Wright remaining at Fort Vancouver, Colonel Steptoe commanded as the senior officer during the entire period of the ill-fated council near the site of what would become the first Fort Walla Walla (the blockhouse). Because the period of enlistment for the volunteers who had accompanied him was to elapse on September 8, Stevens released all but a single company of those troops, even as the tribes, some of them in a less than cordial mood, were gathering at the council site near Steptoe's hastily assembled fort six miles away. Utley notes, "An angry four thousand Indians representing nearly all the tribes between the Columbia and the Rockies" arrived for the parley, and Governor Stevens' talk of "unconditional surrender and compliance with the yet unratified 1855 treaties" would not prove conducive to a new treaty.[66]

When Stevens requested two of Steptoe's companies for protection on the morning of the 10th, the colonel refused, "incredible as it may seem," Hazard Stevens writes, "giving several lame excuses" and informing the governor that his instructions from General Wool did not authorize "any arrangements whatever of the kind you wish."[67] He urged the governor to move nearer his own encampment on Mill Creek. The council convened on the 11th in spite of the governor's and Colonel Steptoe's concerns. The largest tribe in attendance was the mostly friendly Nez Perce, whose amicable relations with the whites dated to their fateful meeting in 1805 on the Weippe Prairie in what is today the Idaho panhandle when they came to the rescue of Lewis and Clark, whose men were near starvation. The Yakama, Cayuse, Walla Walla, and Umatilla, among other tribes represented, were generally much less well disposed.

Governor Stevens' attitude toward the regular army is made explicit in his son's biography (Hazard, then fourteen, accompanied his father during the conference): "The fact was that these regular officers had idealized the Indians, accepting as true the falsehood of Kam-i-ah-kan, sympathized with the savages, and were 'down' on the settlers and volunteers."[68] Predictably, given the obvious bias of his biography, Hazard Stevens cites his father's expressions of regret over recent hostilities and presents his claim that he had "labored only for their good as their friend." He mentions no reference on the governor's part to the massacre on the Grande Ronde perpetrated by his own volunteers, yet fewer than two months had passed since that event. "Most of the Indians," Josephy suggests, "listened in hostile silence."[69]

By the end of the second day of the council, September 12, Hazard Stevens reports, "So hostile were the Cuyuses, Umatillas, Walla Wallas, and others, and so much did more than half of the Nez Perces sympathize with them, that the friendly Nez Perces danced the war-dance during the whole night."[70] The more belligerent among them threatened the friendly chiefs, and all seemed to be awaiting the arrival of Kamiakin, who was in the vicinity but did not attend the council. In a confidential letter addressed to Steptoe on the morning of the 13th, Governor Stevens claimed to be "seriously embarrassed" at the lack of a military presence on the council grounds and requested a company of troops be sent. Steptoe responded that he, too, was embarrassed—by the governor's request.[71] On the 14th Stevens moved the council to within a few yards of Steptoe's encampment, as the colonel had advised.

After a two-day hiatus, the council reconvened on the 16th but achieved nothing of consequence, and on the morning of the 19th Governor Stevens began his march back toward Fort Dalles. Richards observes that on the 17th the governor met with Quiltenenock, of the Ile des Pierres (the Sinkiuse, a Salish-speaking tribe along with the Yakama), not realizing he had supported Qualchan's attack on the Colville miners the previous fall, and it was he and not Kamiakin who had been involved in hostilities during the weeks before Agent Bolon's murder: "The governor dismissed Quil-ten-e-nock by firmly repeating that Kamiakin was the head chief."[72] Historians Robert H. Ruby and John A. Brown, writing on the Cayuse tribe, posit Quiltenenock's intent was to impress upon the governor that his tribe had not been signatory via Kamiakin to the 1855 treaty ceding their lands, but Stevens "brushed off the chief" and abruptly ended the talks.[73] Steptoe's reading of the council is made explicit in his letter to Colonel Wright describing the governor's insistence on holding the conference before his establishment of the post as "unfortunate." Describing a meeting at his tent with Nez Perce and Cayuse chiefs on the 17th Steptoe writes: "I told them plainly that my object in coming here was to establish a military post, and thereby to preserve the peace; that I would protect the good and punish the bad; that I would defend their rights against all aggression whatever [...]. I told them, moreover, that they must cease fighting *instantly*, and forget their animosities toward the whites."[74]

Nevertheless, at one o'clock on the afternoon of the 19th, hostiles from the Nez Perce, Yakama, Palouse, Walla Walla, and Umatilla tribes under the leadership of Qualchan, Lokout, and Quiltenenock attacked the governor's column, which consisted of 69 volunteers under Colonel Shaw and about fifty packers and fifty Nez Perce under the always reliable Lawyer.[75] Splawn asserts they all acted under Kamiakin's general orders.[76] At the same time Indians set fire to the grass near Steptoe's bivouac, so he ordered Stevens to move his column back toward him, but the governor and his volunteers had already circled their wagons and were engaged against as many as 450 warriors. Colonel Shaw and 24 volunteers were nearly annihilated in a trap which they narrowly escaped.[77]

The Indians kept up fire throughout the night, as the governor sent a warrior named Nez Perce Dick to Steptoe's encampment. He arrived around 11:00 p.m. and just before midnight Steptoe dispatched his company of dragoons along with a mountain howitzer to the governor's rescue. The Indians withdrew, and at daybreak Steptoe deployed his main body of troops to accompany Governor Stevens' column back to Fort Dalles, leaving a company to continue building the blockhouse at the site on Mill Creek. Kamiakin meanwhile headed eastward toward the Palouse country, land of his father's people. Steptoe had informed the Indians he had peaceful intentions, but the attack on Governor Stevens' wagon train apparently changed his mind. Historians have tended to cite two of Steptoe's declarations: First, "My mission is pacific. I have not come to fight you but to live among you. [...] I trust we shall live together as friends."[78] Second, in a letter to Colonel Wright dated September 26, "In general terms, I may say that in my judgment we are reduced to the necessity of waging a vigorous war, striking the Cayuses at the Grande Ronde, and Kam-i-ah-kan wherever he may be found."[79] Wright wrote he was "gratified" the Walla Walla treaty had not been ratified, as most of the Nez Perce would have resisted any attempt to enforce it, and that would have attracted the "combined resistance" of the other tribes.[80]

When Wright and Steptoe returned from Fort Dalles to the blockhouse at Walla Walla, arriving on October 17, they decided to move the site about six miles from the junction of Mill Creek with the Walla Walla River. This "cantonment" was located near what is today the corner of First Avenue and Main Street. Thanks to a drawing probably rendered in 1857 by Eugène de Girardin, a friend of an officer in Steptoe's command, we have a good indication of the appearance of the second Fort Walla Walla, timber for which was taken from the Blue Mountains about ten miles distant.[81] Enlisted men's barracks were completed by Christmas of 1856. In the first of his Returns from U.S. Military Posts, dated November 1, 1856, covering events of August through October, Steptoe informed the Adjutant General that his command consisted of ten sergeants, six corporals, four buglers, one musician, one farrier, and 124 privates serving under nine commissioned officers distributed over one company each of dragoons and artillery and two companies of infantry. Another 40 officers and enlisted men were listed on Detached Service that took them off the post for various reasons. The officer cadre consisted of his Assistant Surgeon, John F. Randolph, three captains, two first lieutenants, and three second lieutenants. Steptoe also employed 21 "citizens," mostly as wagon-masters, teamsters, and herders.[82] By January 1857 Steptoe's command at Fort Walla Walla numbered 259 enlisted personnel (224 privates), including 14 sergeants, 12 corporals, 8 musicians, and 1 farrier. The number of commissioned officers on the post rarely numbered more than ten. By the summer of 1857 Colonel Steptoe and his commissioned officers commanded more than 320 enlisted men.

During his stay in October 1856, as Governor Stevens became involved with Indian unrest west of the Cascades, Colonel Wright tried his own hand at Indian diplomacy, meeting with between forty and fifty chiefs to produce what has been described as "a new quasi-treaty of promises."[83] Historians indicate no major chiefs attended and no Yakamas, Walla Wallas, or Spokanes participated. Essentially, Wright repudiated the treaty Governor Stevens had created in the first Walla Walla council of 1855, which had won few adherents among prominent tribal leaders. With the establishment of Fort Walla Walla, Wright declared, the Indians would be protected and peace would prevail. He did not believe the U.S. Senate would ratify Stevens' treaty, which it did not accomplish until the spring of 1859, and he supported General Wool's decision to close Indian lands in the interior to white immigration.

Governor Stevens was righteously indignant. In his report to the Secretary of War, he declared Wright had "made a concession to the Indians which he had no authority to make," and in doing so he had accomplished only "the semblance of a peace."[84] Splawn, in his biography of Kamiakin, argues "a cooler-headed, less domineering and more fair-minded man than Governor Stevens" might have averted the expanding war, but he also observes, "The policy of General Wool played into the hands of Ka-mi-akin without doubt."[85] The immediate consequence of the building of Fort Walla Walla, with its strong garrison, and of Colonel Wright's "quasi-peace," to use Stevens' term for it, was to bring about a year or so of relative calm in the region.[86]

Colonel Steptoe's first extant personal letter from Fort Walla Walla, addressed to his half-sister Nannie, is dated October 27, 1856.[87] He briefly refers to the building of the second Fort Walla Walla; he claims to be "not much given to writing" and to having been "lately much taken up by professional duties." This letter reveals Steptoe's sense of place: "Look up the Columbia River on the map till you see its tributary, the Walla Walla, and on this latter 'The Mission'—about 5 miles above the last place I am erecting a post." This refers to the "cantonment." "The Walla Walla River flows through a valley surrounded by hills & mountains," Edward continues: "this valley being so shut in has a very fine climate, is very fertile and is intersected by streams every where. I find much to interest & amuse me—what with supervising the work, shooting grouse, & catching trout, the time moves not unpleasantly along."

On the other hand, the amusements of fort-building, bird-hunting, and fishing, while pleasant enough pastimes, did not necessarily equate to a pleasant life. "In the Army," the colonel laments, "we are not our own masters, and the character of our duties exacts most of our time;—we have little leisure until age or sickness overtakes us." This letter records the first clear evidence of Steptoe's dissatisfaction with the direction of his life: "It is a source of regret to me always that inexorable Fate has so long separated me from you all— and that we must probably continue to be separated for I know not how long." The poignant nostalgia amounts to a sort of confession that all is not well. Born around 1834, Nannie would have been in her early twenties at this time. She later married a cousin and physician from Memphis, Tennessee, John Wesley Eldridge, who served as a major of artillery for the Confederacy. Whatever he does, Steptoe writes, "or however long absent," his affection will continue: "And sometimes I dream that in the Providence of God the time will yet come when we all will be again assembled & happy." He tells Nannie he would especially like to be home in the fall, as it is his "favorite season."

This correspondence is among the most intimate of E.J. Steptoe's extant personal letters. He would turn 41 within two weeks, and when he tells Nannie about his command, he reflects the single "want" they feel most is "female society." In that context he addresses her objection to his not having married: "Alas! dear Nannie, who can suffer more than I from that fact:—it is a sad, sad reflection for me, nor is it any relief to remember that one [presumably a woman mentioned in Nannie's letter] & often I might have been married." He adds she "may be sure that with a heart so warm in its feelings memory is often busy and then it is that I experience probably the keenest sorrow of my life." For his sister's "consolation," he explains he is "by no means averse [...] to marriage, and if an opportunity presents itself I will not hesitate to seize it:—what I regret is simply that such things *might have been* long years ago—*such* opportunities lost never to be met again!" Edward then waxes philosophical: "age & death must overtake us all sometime, and if we have striven diligently to perform our duty in the sphere allotted to us, perhaps the retrospect of *this* will obscure the other." These views might be written off as conventional expressions of sentiment for a man of that era, but a deeply melancholy mood shadows this letter in its most personal moments.

At the end of his letter, Edward offers to write "an earnest request" to President Pierce on behalf of their brother William, Jr., "to give him the Superintendence of one of the armories if possible," but such a letter would not likely have availed, given that Pierce was in his final months in office.[88] More significant is his brief summary of the "brush" he experienced a few weeks earlier "with some Indians;—not much damage done however,—none to my people." This refers to the strike against Governor Stevens, whose "130 men" were attacked and surrounded by "4 or 500 Indians." "No time was to be lost," he writes, "and although it was 12 o'clock at night I sent out Troops who attacked them briskly & rescued the Governor." He does not elaborate, no more than he did in a letter he wrote to his father nearly twenty years earlier, when he mentioned being wounded in an engagement against the Seminoles. The next day, he reports, there was some "skirmishing around my camp," but they are "now all quiet & begging for peace."

In a letter to the Adjutant General, Colonel Samuel Cooper, dated November 1, 1856, Steptoe begins, "This Post is now, no doubt, permanently established, for there is probably not one other in all this Department which will in the future exercise a stronger, or more extended influence upon the Indian Tribes."[89] He requests the fort be named a "*double Ration* Post." The day after Christmas Steptoe sent a considerably more significant communiqué to Jefferson Davis, Secretary of War, as it addresses the issue of settlement in the territory. In response to the governor's letter declaring General Wool's policy of prohibiting settlers from returning to the Walla Walla valley was "clearly an illegal order" that the settlers were "under no obligation to obey," Colonel Steptoe quotes from the "notice thrown out by me in August last" (dated August 21—see above) and explains his understanding of the phrase, "Persons having ceded rights from the Indians."[90] Such settlers would include, according to Steptoe, "all those white persons who had lived in this valley previous to the late disturbances, either with the consent, or by invitation of the Indians." He indicates about half a dozen such persons were residing near Fort Walla Walla and are "preparing to resume the cultivation of their fields"; others would arrive soon. He adds, in his opinion, "the old, or former, settlers, at least, ought to be encouraged to return at once as they seem to have always lived in harmony with the Indians and the latter could not fail to gather from them some knowledge of agriculture and of the customs of civilized domestic life." (In a note dated December 13, 1856, Steptoe directed that a Umatilla Indian named Mis-ta-kai-ya-wa was under his "protection" and "must not be molested" as he is "at present employed by me to give useful information respecting the cantonment."[91])

Steptoe's next, and concluding, paragraph, however, begins with the word "but": "But there is a class of land claimants here—no doubt had in mind by Gov. Stevens when writing to me—respecting whom I am constrained to request some definite instructions; I refer to those who assert 'claims' under the late 'Donation Act' of Congress." A forerunner of the Homestead Act of 1862, the Donation Land Claim Act of 1850 opened up the Oregon Territory for white settlement by granting 320 acres for any white male 18 or older, or 640 per married couple, provided it was lived on and cultivated or "proved up" for four years. Needless to say, Native American inhabitants were not consulted, although "American half-breed Indians" were included among acceptable land owners.

Governor Stevens' 1855 treaty, still not ratified and a bone of contention among the tribes, would eventually provide some fiscal compensation in the form of annuities and reservations that would include schools and medical facilities and provide assistance in setting up farms: "Mills, schools, mechanic arts, and all the usual aids to civilization were assured."[92] Steptoe explains General Wool's order "clearly forbids me to recognize" claims presented under that act "without the consent of the Indians." His dilemma, and that of the army, at least as long as Wool was commanding the Department of the Pacific, is implicit in the following sentence: "It would be idle for me to give an opinion for, or against, their recognition, as I do not know where the claims lie, what Indian rights (if any) would be interfered with in locating them, nor can foresee whether our relations with the surrounding Tribes during the coming year will, or will not, be peaceful."

In the event General Newman S. Clarke replaced the uncooperative Wool in March 1857, making his first visit to the Columbia district in June, amid what Burns describes as "revelry and merry gunfire."[93] "I know that Gov. Stevens contends for the validity of these claims," Steptoe wrote just months before Wool's ouster, "*irrespective* of the wishes or interests of the Indians, and I have therefore to ask that instructions may be given me how to act in the matter." He concludes, "[I]n the present state of things collision between the judicial & military authorities is by no means unlikely." The year 1857 would pass "largely without incident," at least in the vicinity of Fort Walla Walla.[94] Burns asserts, however, "Numbers of Indian leaders were righteously hanged by the authorities as opportunity offered, or betrayed and assassinated by individuals," even though the army "opposed this policy of petty retribution."[95] Nevertheless, Kamiakin's recent biographers write, "From the start of 1857, a nearly eighteen-month interregnum of relative calm prevailed in the Inland Pacific Northwest."[96]

Isaac Ingalls Stevens spent the year in Washington, D.C., as territorial delegate to Congress blaming General Wool for Indian problems and advancing his proposals for a railroad to be built through the Cascades (the eventual Northern Pacific). He also devoted his efforts in support of the reservation system and ratification of the Indian treaties. Kamiakin bided his time, "nursing grudges against his white adversaries and those Yakima chiefs who had sought peace."[97] William Compton Brown places him at the Palouse River about 15 miles northwest of present-day Colfax, Washington, building fences, corrals, and cabins.[98] Increasingly, his name was linked with that of Chief Tilcoax of the Palouse. The Swiss Jesuit Father Joseph Joset, who had worked among the Coeur d'Alenes since the mid–1840s, reported both chiefs attempted to draw that tribe into the coming fray during the winter of 1857–58.[99]

Meanwhile, General Clarke set about reinforcing troops in the region, dispatching companies from the First Dragoons, the Third Artillery, and the Fourth and Ninth Infantry to Fort Walla Walla early in 1857. By that spring Colonel Steptoe was in the process of building the third Fort Walla Walla, about a mile west of the cantonment. Covering some 613 acres, this fort would be constructed of adobe block, later boarded over and painted white, and boasting two-story officers' duplexes (four of which are still standing), barracks, and parade grounds as well as stables, a blacksmith shop, granary, storehouses, and a sawmill.[100] Typically, a military post of this size required similar acreage nearby to provide forage for the livestock (640 acres or about one square mile).

Brevet Captain Oliver Hazard Perry Taylor (West Point Class of 1846), the son of a commodore, arrived in June to command the First Dragoons. A Mexican War veteran, he had tangled with the Apache in New Mexico. His wife of five years and their two children joined him in September. Serving in Taylor's company was 23-year-old North Carolinian William Gaston, an 1856 graduate of West Point, who had yet to experience battle. The officer cadre at Fort Walla Walla in 1857 also included Captain Charles S. Winder, a Marylander and 1850 West Point graduate then on sick leave. He had been promoted to captain for his courageous action when on board the *San Francisco* when it sank in 1854. Four years later, in 1862, serving as a brigadier general under Stonewall Jackson, he was killed at the Battle of Cedar Mountain. The 25-year-old Pennsylvanian, David McMurtrie Gregg (West Point, 1855) would, like Lieutenant Gaston, see his first combat under Steptoe's command. He went on to serve with distinction as brigadier general and cavalry commander in the Army of the Potomac throughout the Civil War. These officers would play important roles in the battle at Tohotsnimme in May 1858.

Left in command at Fort Walla Walla at the time of that engagement was Brevet Major William N. Grier, an 1835 graduate of West Point who had been posted to the First Dragoons, where he served in the Indian Territory and elsewhere on the frontier, being brevetted to major after the Battle of Santa de Rosales near Taos, New Mexico. Like Captain Winder, he had seen combat with the Apache. During the Civil War he was brevetted to colonel after the Battle of Williamsburg in 1862 and to brigadier general near the end of the conflict. The senior captain serving at Fort Walla Walla, the Missourian Frederick T. Dent, graduated from West Point in 1843 and participated in the siege of Vera Cruz and in the battles at Churubusco and Chapultepec. In 1864 he was named aide-de-camp to his brother-in-law, Lieutenant General Ulysses S. Grant.

On June 1, 1857, Edward wrote to Nannie reflecting on a "severe" winter. His opening sentences are reserved for another sister nicknamed "Queen," who had apparently been ill: "I remember her only as a merry, active little sprite and so I'm resolved she shall remain—no young lady indispositions will be put up with. And that sweet voice of hers, it has rung in my ear many a day. She would never let me hear it if she could prevent—would never sing when asked, but I did occasionally listen to her little songs, unobserved by her."[101] Most likely he is referring to Lucy Steptoe Rose (1845–1924), who was about 11 years old at the time. Edward's memories of her reveal a sentimental dimension to his personality we do not see elsewhere: "Tell her there is a little portrait in my trunk of a saucy untamed little creature at which her old soldier brother frequently looks, and he will come back to her one of these days expecting to find her just as merry & capricious as before."

Her letter also informed him of William Junior's plans to come out West, about which he declares himself "truly right glad," as "his energy & talents would no doubt be quite lost in old Va." But in something of an about-face, he advises William not to try the Pacific: "It is too late to make a fortune here unless one has a fortune to start with, and this whole region has become the refuge of bad unscrupulous men with whose way of doing business a high toned man like William could have no sympathy." William, who was about 28 at this writing, remained in Virginia, serving the Confederacy along with at least one other of Edward's half-brothers (Patrick) and a dozen or more cousins and in-laws.

In response to an obituary notice of his maternal uncle, Edward writes, "Alas—I am now the oldest male member of my mother's family;—how long shall I continue to be? Ah, Nannie if it be one year or ten years, at longest it will be like the fleeting of a shadow. Thank God the answer to the question gives me not much concern. May we all my dear Sister meet once again in the happier land is my constant prayer." This sentiment might be described as typical of the age. The colonel is not revealing a death-wish or anxiety over the prospect of imminent demise, but what might be regarded as conventional sensibility and piety. He adds "professional duties" absorb his time and his health is "quite good." In a letter to Dr. William Steptoe dated April 8, 1861, however, Surgeon John Randolph indicates Steptoe may have suffered a mild stroke that caused temporary paralysis of the right side sufficient to require him to dismount his horse and ride in a carriage on his return to Fort Walla Walla from Fort Vancouver five months later, in October 1857.[102] In effect, Edward's frequent reassurances of his good health suggest reluctance to cause his distant family concern as to his wellbeing.

Something of the nature of his professional duties, aside from the ongoing construction of the third Fort Walla Walla, to be occupied by mid-February 1858, is implicit in a letter Steptoe sent to the Adjutant General requesting his pay be adjusted to reflect his brevet rank of lieutenant colonel, commensurate with the nature of his command of "at least four companies of Troops of different Corps" (infantry, dragoons, and artillery) from the first of January.[103] "When it is considered how harassed I have been," he continues, "by the restless crowd of Indians arriving at this Post, that there is no Indian Agency here, & that much of the brevet pay I would receive has been already expended in small presents to the Indians as evidence of kind feelings towards them, the application now made can scarcely seem unreasonable." Some were calling the small settlement growing up around the fort, "Steptoeville."[104]

In mid–July 1857 troops sent into Utah by President Buchanan were about to ignite the Utah or Mormon War and gold miners were increasing their incursions up the Columbia into the Colville region some seventy miles north of present-day Spokane: a "rabble of miners," Father Burns calls them.[105] Burns describes the Utah War as "a clumsy maneuver intended to upset Mormon control in Utah"; the invasion is sometimes called "Buchanan's Blunder."[106] Suspicions ran high that Mormons were arming the Indians and inciting them to violence throughout the Washington Territory. Those suspicions would soar with the Mountain Meadows Massacre on September 11 when Mormon militia and Paiute Indians killed upwards of 120 men, women, and children from a wagon train of Arkansans on their way to California.

On October 19, 1857, Steptoe wrote to Major Mackall, in San Francisco, complaining that Indian agent J. Ross Brown had informed Chief Lawyer of the Nez Perce the 1855 treaty would "*certainly* be ratified and enforced," a statement made "in very bad taste, to say the least" and "in direct opposition" to what the army had been telling the Indians.[107] He concludes, "in my opinion any attempt to enforce that treaty will be followed by immediate hostilities with most of the tribes in this part of the country; for which reason it does appear to me greatly desirable that a new commission be appointed, and a new treaty made, thoroughly digested and accepted by both sides."[108] In forwarding Steptoe's letter to Army headquarters in New York, General Clarke chastised Brown for suggesting Governor Stevens' controversial treaty had been ratified, and he recommended a new commission be formed to concoct a treaty less objectionable to the tribes.

No such new treaty would be forthcoming, and ratification of the 1855 treaty still lay two years into the future. In the meantime Superintendent of Indian Affairs Nesmith wrote to Mackall on November 18 indicating he had ordered his agents to inform the Indians the treaty was "void" until ratified, but he also enclosed a copy of his September 1 annual report recommending (contra General Wool) that "steps be taken to throw open the Walla Walla valley to settlement" and arguing that "as the treaties have never been ratified, the country is open to settlement."[109] His report indicates his awareness that the interior tribes have been "great sufferers by reason of the occupation of their country by the whites" for which they "have never received compensation," but at the same time he stresses the Indians have been informed "until these treaties were ratified they could expect nothing from the government in the shape of annuities or subsistence." During the severe winter of 1857–1858 Colonel Steptoe sent Captain Taylor and his dragoons back to Fort Dalles, where more adequate forage was available.

One of the first communications Steptoe received in the new year was Major Mackall's letter of January 12, 1858, on behalf of General Clarke "to say that he desires you to recall your dragoons and horses as early as the state of the roads and the grass, or your supply of forage will permit."[110] Clarke also directed Steptoe, via Mackall, to acquire intelligence on tribes "south and east towards Fort Hall and the Salmon river" (the vicinity of present-day Pocatello, Idaho), and observed "through the Mormons the Indians are being inclined to hostility," adding "a conflict in Utah may be the signal for trouble on the frontier, and it is not improbable that the Mormons may move north." Reports, "unofficial but reliable," that Mormons were arming Indians in the vicinity had been circulating since the fall of 1857, and Steptoe had seen evidence of that in his expedition to Benicia in the spring of 1855. General Clarke "wishes you to be prepared in advance for either contingency," Mackall wrote to Colonel Steptoe. "Full and prompt report of all information, and your opinion founded theron, is desired."[111] The relative calm of 1857 was about to be disrupted.

Chapter Seven

"Chapter of Accidents"

THE YEAR 1858 WOULD PROVE something of an *annus horribilis* for Brevet Lieutenant Colonel Edward J. Steptoe, the high-water mark of his military career and its climax, leading to a painful although not genuinely tragic or catastrophic end. "Steptoe's Disaster," some labeled it, but it really did not come to that, nor was it "Steptoe's Last Stand," the defeat of his 150-odd men at a site near the present-day town of Rosalia in eastern Washington about 35 miles south of Spokane. The action is known as the Battle of Tohotsnimme (Tohotonimme) or Pine Creek, but if the victors get to name the event, historians should probably stay with the former and reserve the English term for the subsequent Battle of Four Lakes fought by a large and well-armed punitive expedition under the command of Colonel George Wright on September 1. Contemporary maps refer to "Ingossomen Creek," from the Coeur d'Alene word "Hngwsumn," or "rope-making place." Beset by hundreds of Indians and outnumbered at least four to one (estimates vary, but most accounts indicate a thousand Indians, a ratio of something like seven to one),[1] Steptoe and his troops managed to escape late at night on May 17 with the loss of seven killed, six severely wounded, and seven slightly wounded, according to his report filed from Fort Walla Walla on May 23; a single solder listed as missing made it back to safety. This episode in Steptoe's life has been so thoroughly documented and interpreted that the commentators' perspectives could amount to a subject of inquiry in their own right.

The standard texts are B.F. Manring's *The Conquest of the Coeur d'Alenes, Spokanes and Palouses* (1912), supplemented by Mahlon E. Kriebel's *Battle of To-hots-nim-me* (2nd edition revised, 2012).[2] Manring's book was the product of "long research," he writes in a prefatory note dated August 1, 1911, from Garfield, Washington, where he served as mayor in 1910. He communicated directly with Steptoe's half-sister, Nannie Steptoe Eldridge, with Brigadier General David M. Gregg, who had served as a lieutenant on that expedition, with pack-master Thomas B. Beall, and with other survivors and relatives of officers and men involved in the battle. He reprints in full most of the relevant documents written prior to the battle and thereafter, including Steptoe's official report and that of Father Joseph Joset, S.J., of the Coeur d'Alene mission, to Father Nicholas Congiato at Fort Vancouver. Manring extends his account, about half of the text, through Colonel Wright's expedition, which culminated in the Battle of Four Lakes on September 1 and the Battle of Spokane Plains five days later.

Among other treatments of the battle to be found in books, the most important, or in various ways engaging (listed chronologically—*not* in order of importance or degree of reliability) are Frances Fuller Victor's *The Early Indian Wars of Oregon* (1894), R. Ross Arnold's *Indian Wars of Idaho* (1932), A.J. Splawn's *Ka-mi-akin: Last Hero of the Yakimas* (2d ed., 1944), Waldo E. Rosebush's *Frontier Steel* (1958), William Compton Brown's *The Indian Side of the Story* (1961), Robert Ignatius Burns' *The Jesuits and the Indian Wars of the Northwest* (1966), Robert M. Utley's *Frontiersmen in Blue* (1967), Robert H. Ruby and John A. Brown's *The Spokane Indians: Children of the Sun* (1970), Jerome Peltier's *Warbonnets and Epaulets* (1971), Clifford E. Trafzer and Richard D. Scheuerman's *Renegade Tribe: The Palouse Indians and the Invasion of the Inland Pacific Northwest* (1986), Carl P. Schlicke's *General George Wright: Guardian of the Pacific Coast* (1988), Edward J. Kowrach and Charles E. Connolly's *Saga of the Coeur d'Alene Indians* (1990), Richard D. Scheuerman and Michael O. Finley's *Finding Chief Kamiakin* (2008), and Kurt R. Nelson's *Fighting for Paradise* (2007) and *Treaties and Treachery* (2011). Burns describes both Splawn's and W.C. Brown's accounts as "untrustworthy," and the same may be said for many of the accounts at one point or another, those of Manring, Burns, Scheuerman and Finley, and Kriebel being the most reliable and useful. Several substantial essays on the engagement have also appeared in periodical form, dating back to T.C. Elliott's "Steptoe Butte and Steptoe Battle-Field" in the *Washington Historical Quarterly* (1927) and including Jack Dozier's "The Coeur d'Alene Indians in the War of 1858" in *Idaho Yesterdays* (1961), Helen Addison Howard's "The Steptoe Affair" in *Montana: The Magazine of Western History* (1969), and Randall A. Johnson's "The Ordeal of the Steptoe Command" in *The Pacific Northwesterner* (1973). In effect, someone has spoken out on the battle in nearly every decade since the 1890s, and voices from both sides have spoken, sometimes in the process either perpetuating or creating errors.

More than 150 years after the event frequently addressed questions remain not fully resolved: Why didn't Colonel Steptoe take more men with him? Why did they take an indirect route toward Colville? Why didn't they take more ammunition? Why didn't they carry sabers? And from the Indian perspective: Why or perhaps how did they fail to annihilate Steptoe's command? What role did the Nez Perce play? Did Chief Timothy (Tammutsa) act as the army's guide in addition to helping them cross the Snake River? Did the Coeur d'Alene make some sort of deal to allow Steptoe and his command to escape? And where was Chief Kamiakin?

All of these questions and others were proposed months and years later. Colonel Steptoe's first important communiqué of 1858 is dated January 29 in response to Major W.W. Mackall's urgent letter of January 12 sent from Benicia, California, where he served as Assistant Adjutant General: "Measures were taken at once to insure the full efficiency of this command, whenever it may be required for active service."[3] Steptoe proclaims himself "quite sure" the Indians have "discussed" the "expediency of availing themselves of this Mormon revolt [the Utah War that commenced in May 1857 and lasted until July 1858] to recover some real or imagined rights." In particular he draws attention to the Snake Indians (Northern Paiute and Bannock) between Fort Walla Walla and Fort Hall (near present-day Pocatello, Idaho) who are "represented to be great friends of the Mormons" and are "well armed and provided with ammunition." Of the Indians in his immediate area, Walla Walla and Cayuse, Steptoe evinces little concern, but of the Palouse, Yakama, and Spokane, "there never has been a doubt on my mind that very slight encouragement would at any time suffice to revive their late hostile feelings." He indicates his intention of sending three companies of dragoons toward Fort Boise (about two hundred miles to the southeast) once travel conditions permit, and he concludes that although he doubts the Mormons will emigrate north from the Utah Territory, he thinks it "more than probable" they will arm "all the Indians living on the principle routes to Utah."

As it happened, however, Steptoe's letter to Mackall, dated April 17, proposed an "expedition to the north" once Captain Taylor returned from Fort Dalles with the horses he had been wintering there. His concern derived from reports Palouse Indians had killed two miners at the Palouse River, near present-day Colfax, on their way to the Colville gold fields; moreover, "some forty persons living at Colville [about seventy miles north of present-day Spokane] recently petitioned for the presence of troops at that place."[4] Steptoe also informed Mackall, "a few nights ago" several Palouse Indians made off with livestock belonging to settlers in the area, "both whites and Indians," including 13 head of cattle owned by the army's commissary department. Curiously, he adds his "impression" the Palouse "did not suppose these animals to be in our charge or they would not probably have taken them." In his account of the theft, Splawn asserts Tilcoax of the Palouse intentionally stole the livestock at Kamiakin's request and Kamiakin notified the tribes of Colonel Steptoe's planned expedition to Colville.[5] The interior tribes were also agitated over plans to build a military road between Fort Benton, on the upper Missouri River, to Fort Walla Walla, what would be known as the Mullan Road.[6]

About two weeks earlier, on April 5, Steptoe wrote two personal letters, one to his father and one to his sister Nannie, that reveal his state of mind at this point. Edward's tone is somber: "As the years roll on I feel more & more the isolation of my lot and a keener regret that the time past was not improved so as to make this separation from those so dear to me unnecessary."[7] The sentiments appear those of a much older man stricken with what the German Romantics would refer to as *Weltschmerz*: "It is a sad thing when one no longer finds excitement a pleasure nor feels a desire for new friendships." He complains specifically about his chosen profession as perhaps "the greatest misfortune" of his life, feeling he has "few real qualifications" for a military career and regretting that it has cost him "so much domestic enjoyment."

He turns philosophical, to employ the term loosely. When he becomes expansive in his observations, Steptoe reaches after some conceptual depth, usually with melancholy results: "Alas!, my Father, it is only when the substance has escaped our grasp forever that we discover how perseveringly we have been chasing a shadow." This expression of sentiment approaches sheer pessimism. The excitements of military life on the frontier have not sustained him—excitement itself is no longer "a pleasure." Even though he finds the Walla Walla valley "pretty compared with others west of the Rocky mountains," they are "not like the valleys in the East." Unlike the hardwood covered hills of his boyhood, the Blue Ridge Mountains and the readily accessible Shenandoah Valley, the trees that "skirt the streams" and deck the mountains "are rarely seen elsewhere." And the native bunchgrass, while "long, nutritious" and "excellent for animals" makes "nothing of a sward." He concedes the climate may be better than Virginia's, but writes, "I have suffered unusually this winter from colds—catarrh—indeed can scarcely say I have been well one day since Xmas." He laments "the keenness of regret has left me old in every thing except true affection for my relatives & friends."

The letter Edward wrote to his half-sister dated the same day was not quite so dark. He tells her he intends to visit his family and friends in Virginia in the fall or winter if possible. Yet even that anticipated pleasure he describes oxymoronically as "a *sad* delight," as he anticipates so many changes and "every one looking so much older—especially myself," his uncle dead and his family gone.[8] "Ah—my dear little sister," he continues, "I cannot tell you what a sharp sorrow will be mingled with my joy when we all meet again." Edward's next statement seems rather startling, however, given his apparent nostalgia for the familiar Virginia countryside expressed in his letter to his father bearing the same date: "If it were not for my relatives, believe me nothing should ever tempt to revisit Virginia—nothing whatever." He may have been thinking of the precarious political state of affairs, the nation's "house" that was so clearly "divided against itself." (Lincoln would deliver that famous speech based on Mark 3:25 in his debate with Stephen A. Douglas on June 16, 1858, almost exactly one month after Steptoe's defeat.) Edward does not elaborate, but moves to marriage, a familiar topic in letters to his sister, and his doleful tone continues: "Alas—who in the world today regrets half so much as I do my lonely state. No one seems to have trifled away life as I have and perhaps no one living was ever more punished in mind & feeling for opportunities neglected."

Again, he complains of his illness: "This past winter has been especially grievous to me—sick, isolated—brooding painfully over the past & almost hopelessly on the future, I have grown ten years older in one, apparently." Steptoe may have suffered a minor stroke while in Utah in 1855, and he surely experienced another in October 1857 that left him temporarily paralyzed on his right side and unable to ride a horse (see above). Surgeon John Randolph, however, considered him fit in the spring of 1858.[9] In the same paragraph he advises Nannie to tell her brother William "to take our brave brother Jack's example rather than mine as he values happiness," and he informs her that Jack (John) "has exhibited what I never had, true moral courage & *self reliance*." Although Edward does not elaborate, he may be referring here to his half-brother's pursuit of a career in medicine. John Reed Steptoe is described briefly in *Colonial Families of the Southern States of America* as "a much beloved physician, and a zealous Episcopal Churchman."[10] Edward sends his regards to his other half-brothers, William and Patrick. Like John, Patrick also became a physician. From his letters concerning turpentine investments in Florida during the Seminole War and comments on business opportunities in Mexico during the Mexican War, one can deduce the colonel was entrepreneurial. Near the end of this letter, he writes of his purchase of "some property this side—in Cal. & shall do so in Oregon likewise, which will no doubt be valuable in a few years." Apparently he was considering the reinvention of himself as a Westerner.

Within a month, Colonel Steptoe was preparing to embark on what proved the last military expedition of his 25-year career. On May 2, 1858, he informed Mackall of his intention to set out within four or five days "with about 130 dragoons and a detachment of infantry for service with the howitzers, and to move directly where it is understood the hostile party is at present."[11] That location would take him not on the direct route north from Fort Walla Walla to Colville, but northeast some seventy miles and then northnorthwest about sixty miles, moving through what is today the town of Colfax, on the Palouse River, where the two miners headed for Colville had been

Seven. "Chapter of Accidents"

killed by Palouse Indians, and then on to Tohotsnimme Creek about 25 miles north of Colfax. On the way they would see what was then known as Pyramid Peak, a 3,612-foot high quartzite "island" that juts more than a thousand feet above the loess that provides the fertile farmland surrounding it. Now known as Steptoe Butte, it is the site of a 150-acre state park. Travelers sometimes mistake this geological feature for the Steptoe battle site, some 14 miles to the northwest.

On Thursday morning May 6, Colonel Steptoe moved out with three companies (C, E, and H) of the First Dragoons and 25 men from Company E of the Ninth Infantry, all mounted, along with two mountain howitzers (twelve-pounders), several friendly Nez Perce Indians, and a pack train of thirty or so drovers under the supervision of Thomas Beall. This would total 158 "effectives" under six officers, counting Steptoe himself. Some historians assume Steptoe must not have expected a major confrontation, given the size of his detachment: "A typical combat force would have fielded two of the remaining three companies."[12] At this point, though, one might consider Utley's calculations concerning military strength at the company level during the 1850s. He begins his chapter, "The Frontier Army, 1848–61," with observations on Company E of the Fourth Infantry stationed at Fort Jones, "a strategic post in northern California" in August of 1853, pointing out while the company "was authorized 3 officers, 8 noncommissioned officers, and 74 privates," the muster rolls listed only 34 names.[13] When it came to the matter of "effectives," men fit for duty, the numbers were often much lower.

According to the Returns from U.S. Military Posts for Fort Walla Walla submitted for the month of April 1858, Steptoe had at his disposal just 270 enlisted men described as "for duty." Another 103 enlisted men were listed for "extra duty," generally a designation that signifies some form of punishment; 18 were listed as "sick" and 14 under arrest or confinement. The post at Walla Walla numbered a dozen commissioned officers, 24 sergeants, 24 corporals, and 11 musicians.[14] He left at Fort Walla Walla only B Company and the remainder of E Company of the Ninth Infantry, and I Company of the First Dragoons. He would be leaving the important post manned by about half of its full complement. Given the number of settlers and Indians in the vicinity and taking into account the cattle thefts mentioned above, the colonel could hardly have drawn down his resident force any further. About two-thirds of the troops in his command appear to have been new recruits.

As to the Indians, there has also been considerable conjecture. Ought Steptoe to have calculated upwards of a thousand might assemble against him? Lieutenant Lawrence Kip, who wrote soon after accompanying Colonel Wright on his punitive expedition, describes the Palouse as "a feeble tribe"

Fort Walla Walla in 1857 (known as "The Cantonment") sketched by Eugène de Girardin, said to be a friend of one of Steptoe's officers. Located in what is today downtown Walla Walla, the drawing shows Mill Creek along the tree-line to the viewer's right; the seven or eight buildings to the right are officers' housing; buildings to the left of the gap at the top are commissary stores and the long low buildings below the stores are stables; to the right of the stables are barracks; outside the rough oval (the parade ground) are the corral and additional stables, perhaps for mules; buildings and tents in the foreground are thought to be residences for soldiers' families. Information is from Robert A. Bennett's *Walla Walla: Portrait of a Western Town, 1804–1899* (Walla Walla: Pioneer Press, 1980): 41.

and suggests Steptoe thought "his force was considered quite sufficient to overawe them."[15] While no accurate census exists, the total number of the Palouse people in the mid–1850s has been estimated at about five hundred, including men and women of all ages. But if the Palouse were slight numerically, they were by no means "feeble." Other tribes were thought non-hostile, including the Coeur d'Alene and the Kettles, or were presumed to be peaceful, and no doubt many of the people were. But all of the tribes, even the friendly Nez Perce, included warlike factions.

Burns describes the difficulty of calculating the number of warriors available from any given tribe, suggesting that no more than 150 Coeur d'Alenes (his particular focus) "could have been mustered."[16] Most of the northern tribes, like the Kettles and Spokane, apparently numbered no more than five hundred persons each, considerably fewer than half of them warriors. Any Cayuse, Yakama, and Walla Walla who joined in were expatriates, expeditionary forces from outside their tribal bounds, perhaps mercenaries, and the same could be said of any Nez Perce involved on the side of what has been called the "confederation" or "alliance," although such terms might imply more organization than appears to have been the case. It was something of an ad hoc affair. In his letter of May 29, 1858, filed with Major Mackall a week after his return from the engagement and four days after his initial postcombat communications, Steptoe reckons he faced "about half of the Spokanes, Coeur d'Alenes, and probably the Flatheads [Kutenai], nearly all of the Pelouses, a portion of the Yakimas, and I think a small number of Nez Perces, with scattered families of various petty tribes."[17]

The tribes were aroused over the increasing encroachment of miners on their way to the gold fields near Colville and over Lieutenant Mullan's preliminary work on the military road from Fort Benton to Fort Walla Walla. Mullan would serve under Colonel Wright in the coming Battle of Four Lakes. Indians in the region were also aware of former governor Stevens' plans for the Northern Pacific Railroad. The tenor of Steptoe's May 2 letter to Mackall suggests he did indeed underestimate the "probability of considerable disturbance among the neighboring tribes."[18] They were more than disturbed—they were alarmed and angry. In fact, Steptoe adds, all too casually as it would happen, "I hope to check it." The pronoun "it" refers here to the "considerable disturbance."

One of the commentators more sympathetic to Steptoe, Randall A. Johnson, observes "trouble was coming to a fast boil and Steptoe erred in not recognizing its extent," and he conjectures the colonel might have thought advice he received about the "growing unrest" was "deliberately meant to deceive."[19] Considerably less sympathetic is Jerome Peltier, who surmises, "Steptoe was so naïve that he thought that words alone would calm the upset northern tribes."[20] Although Steptoe intended to "investigate the temper of the Palouse and awe them with a show of force," Robert Utley writes, "no one expected any trouble."[21] "Nobody really expected a fight," Carl P. Schlicke suggests in his biography of George Wright, "a few arrests and perhaps a light skirmish or two—but mainly, they believed, this was to be a training exercise for Steptoe's new recruits, a fact-finding expedition, and a pleasant spring excursion to impress the Indians and allay the fears of the whites."[22]

Writing of the Palouse, Trafzer and Scheuerman phrase it this way: "The colonel anticipated little resistance, although he hoped to engage a few Palouse warriors."[23] He expected to defeat any hostile Palouse easily, and he anticipated "no trouble from the Spokanes, Coeur d'Alenes, or their neighbors." Writing of the Spokanes, Ruby and Brown propose that Steptoe planned "to paw, but not maul, troublesome Indians there and along the way, particularly the Palouses."[24] Father Burns, noting Steptoe was prepared for a skirmish rather than a battle, offers an apt enough metaphor: "He was prepared, so to speak, for a light rain but not for a flood."[25]

Burns states bluntly "Steptoe's men were badly armed," and some version of that view has been ratified by nearly every commentator on the battle.[26] On the one hand, former artillery officer that he was, Steptoe trailed a pair of mountain howitzers, sufficient to intimate his aims might not be as peaceable as he would later claim (on the battlefield, that is, in a parley with Father Joset and Coeur d'Alene Chief Vincent); on the other hand, his men carried only forty rounds of ammunition apiece, a "light supply," Manring and others have noted, that would prove to be "a thing of grievous consideration."[27] At least two additional matters pertaining to armament have received ample attention over the years: the decision not to equip the dragoons with the customary sabers and their use of what might well be described as "the infamous musketoon." In his after action report, Steptoe pointed out that two of the companies were armed with "musketoons, which were utterly worthless in our present condition."[28]

The much abused Model 1847 Springfield Musketoon, however, "incapable of speeding a ball accurately beyond the average throwing distance of a man," was the standard firearm for dragoons at that time.[29] Waldo E. Rosebush is content to let Steptoe's chief packer Beall, age 84 and commenting contemptuously on the action nearly sixty years afterward, describe the frequently maligned weapon: "muzzle loaders, short twenty-two inch barrels with swivel ramrods; and big mouthed like a garrison soldier and not much better. They load them with what they call 'buck and ball.' Cartridge case of paper contains one large ball and three buckshot. Couldn't kill a rooster across the barnyard."[30] One company of dragoons was equipped with new Sharps breech-loading .52 caliber carbines, but these were not generally available, at least in the inland Northwest, at that date. The mounted infantry contingent from Company E was armed with the Mississippi or Yager rifles popularized by Colonel Jefferson Davis's troops during the Mexican War. This Model 1841 .54 caliber percussion lock muzzle-loader, although admired for its range and accuracy, was considered difficult to load and not suitable for use on horseback; nevertheless, it remained in service into the Civil War, especially by Confederate troops..

Some commentators blame Steptoe for arming his troops with the standard musketoon, but they carried what they had available. No evidence suggests Steptoe possessed confidence in that weapon or that he preferred the musketoon to firearms left at Fort Walla Walla. Some dragoons carried the Colt cap-and-ball, six-shot revolver that had become widely used by the early

Seven. "Chapter of Accidents" 155

1850s, but others apparently still used the Model 1842 .54 caliber Aston, a handsome muzzle-loader reminiscent of dueling pistols. Rosebush provides photographs of two of the three Colt revolvers discovered on the battleground.[31] When Colonel Wright rode out from Fort Walla Walla in August, his seven hundred troops would be armed with freshly issued Springfield Model 1855 caliber rifle-muskets and Model 1853 breech-loading Sharps carbines capable of firing eight to ten rounds per minute.

But why only forty rounds of ammunition per man? As several historians have noted, the army's commander-in-chief, General Winfield Scott, found the "small supply of ammunition" to be "surprising and unaccounted for."[32] Forty rounds per man, however, was the standard field issue for that time and remained the capacity of the cartridge box used during the Civil War.[33] Additional rounds would normally be carried in the pack train. Manring asserts that Beall, "who had charge of the packing," found the baggage "exceeded the carrying capacity" and speculates "in cutting down the amount a part of the ammunition probably inadvertently was eliminated."[34] Rosebush, limiting his conjecture to an endnote, supposes the fault might have been Beall's, but because Steptoe was "a high-minded Virginian," he refused to make Beall "the goat."[35] In comments made sixty years after the battle, Beall stated he did not think any more ammunition was set out of the magazine for the expedition by the quartermaster in charge, and he sent four pack mules to the magazine at Fort Walla Walla, but only three loaded mules returned.[36]

As to the sabers, commentators have been fond of quoting Private Victor C. DeMoy of Company C, a former officer in the French army, swinging his rifle by the barrel and crying, "My God, for a saber!"[37] Or, as Rosebush rather fancifully phrases it, "Mon Dieu, wat would ay geef for mon sabreur!"[38] (Those with a smattering French would know the word for saber is "sabre." Those with access to a French dictionary will discover a "sabreur" is a cavalryman.) DeMoy was mortally wounded in the battle, but his supposed plea notwithstanding, the cavalrymen of that period did not universally admire the flashy saber. According to Utley, Captain William Hardee, a cavalry officer of some distinction who would rise to the rank of lieutenant general in the service of the Confederacy, found the weapon a noisy encumbrance. Utley suggests the saber was rarely used, "but it figured importantly in too many engagements of the 1850s to be discounted altogether."[39] In his *Survey of U.S. Army Uniforms, Weapons and Accoutrements*, David Cole writes, "Despite images of the dramatic cavalry charge with lifted sabers gleaming in the sun, less than one per cent of all the casualties in the Civil War were inflicted by an edged weapon of any type, saber or bayonet."[40] In any event, Steptoe's expertise was in artillery; one might speculate, however, that he had more confidence than was warranted in his pair of 12-pounder howitzers. In his combat report he laments having to bury them: "What distresses me is that no *attempt* was made to bring them off."[41]

Departing Fort Walla Walla on May 6, Colonel Steptoe and his troops proceeded north and east, crossing the swollen Touchet River (pronounced "*too*-shee"), the largest tributary of the Walla Walla, after about a twenty-mile march. Another 15 to 20 miles brought them to the Tucannon River. "The early rising sun this May morning of 1858 cast its bright beam across the vast green stretches of the Spokane and Palouse prairies, shining out from the horizon edge of a clear blue sky," or so R. Ross Arnold expresses it in the opening sentence of *Indian Wars of Idaho*.[42] Most writers of detailed treatments of the expedition and battle do indulge their penchant for lyricism. Burns describes the wind-molded hills ahead as follows: "Rolling Palouse lands swelled and dipped around them, for all the world like an ocean frozen in action."[43]

After crossing the Tucannon they followed Pataha Creek over what is now called Alpowa Summit. Later, they crossed the Snake River and moved onto the plateau where, Mahlon Kriebel suggests, "The basalt bluffs were ablaze with yellow balsamroot interspersed with spikes of lavender lupine and clumps of pink phlox" as they moved away from the sagebrush in the lower canyon into the bunchgrass above.[44] They encountered fields of camas in the meadows, a member of the lily family blooming in deep blue swaths and much valued by all of the tribes in the region. Women digging with digging sticks ceremonially harvested the "sweet and nutritious" roots or bulbs, and then steamed or baked them, or they "could be eaten raw or cooked as a mush." Trafzer and Scheuerman, writing of the Palouse, indicate "a woman could gather enough camas in three or four days to feed a large family for an entire year."[45]

Within a week of his return to Fort Walla Walla, Colonel Steptoe sent three letters bearing the date May 23, 1858, each directed to Major Mackall, the Assistant Adjutant General serving near San Francisco. In the lengthiest of these, the primary battle report, he writes that having heard of "hostile Pelouses" on Nez Perce land "near Al-pon-on-we" (Alpowa Creek), he moved his forces to that point "and was ferried across the Snake by Timothy, a Nez Perce chief."[46] A band of thirty or so Palouse had been reported crossing the Snake, and they likely spread news of the army's approach. In a subsequent note Steptoe informs Mackall he had "vast difficulty in getting the dragoon horses over the Snake river, which is everywhere wide, deep, and strong, and without the assistance of Timothy's Nez Perces it would have been utterly impossible for us to cross, either going or returning."[47] The site, known as Red Wolf's Crossing, where Timothy and Red Wolf had established a permanent camp, is located about six miles west of present-day Clarkston, Washington. When he passed through in the summer of 1855, Governor Stevens found "a village of about thirteen lodges of Nez Perces" and "a fenced field of thirty acres, well watered by irrigation from the Al-pa-wha, and containing a fine crop of corn and a promising orchard." He described the Snake River there as "swift and dangerous."[48]

When Steptoe and his party of nearly two hundred, counting civilian packers and some Nez Perce who joined him from Timothy's band, arrived at the Snake in May, they found high water from the spring runoff. Nez Perce canoes ferried the troops across the swollen river, as they had done for Governor Stevens' party, and guided the horses as they swam against the swift, muddy current.

After splashing ashore on the north side of the Snake, Steptoe and his troops and pack train, accompanied by several Nez Perce warriors and perhaps with Chief Timothy as their guide, left the steep basalt canyon behind and made their way up the four-and-a-half mile draw along what Indians would have called Sklassams, now known as Steptoe Creek, just a trickle most of the year, but offering ample water for horses in May. "An easy grade up a lateral creek," as Governor Stevens remembered it.[49] The ravine is accessible off Wawawai Road, Washington Route 193, and is labeled "Steptoe Canyon." At the top, Steptoe encountered Smokle Creek, today known as Union Flat Creek. "The Pelouse tribe ought to be the first one struck at," Steptoe wrote in one of his May 23rd post-combat communiqués to Mackall, "as it is the most hostile, and was guilty, a few weeks since, of murdering two white men on the Colville road."[50]

In the early portion of that account, describing his journey northward toward his moment of destiny, Steptoe employed an adverb he might later have wished he could retract: "leisurely." The Palouse Indians, Steptoe wrote, "fled towards the north, and I followed leisurely on the road to Colville."[51] Nearly everyone who has written about the battle has picked up on that ironically freighted word, often by way of substantiating the view that Steptoe was perilously if not negligently unaware of what lay ahead. Commentators have divided over whether Timothy accompanied the expedition. Those who argue that he did not act as Steptoe's guide have based their view primarily on what one might call negative evidence—the fact that Steptoe does not so indicate in his account of the battle. Manring, while he professes his desire to "ascribe to Chief Timothy the full meed of praise thus accorded him," notes also that then Lieutenant Gregg had "no recollection of his presence on the expedition."[52] He therefore reluctantly concludes that Timothy "did not accompany the command in any recognized capacity."[53]

The main source for those who believe Timothy did accompany the column, as the majority of commentators do, from Frances Fuller Victor to Robert Ignatius Burns, is a writer named George F. Canis, whose account appeared in *The Washington Historian* of July 1900, reprinted in the Ye Galleon edition of Manring's book with the caveat that "certain points in the Canis account are very questionable historically."[54] The editor of Ye Galleon Press supports Manring's contention that Timothy did not participate in the expedition after his people helped the troops cross the Snake, and Kriebel apparently agrees with Manring.[55] Canis relied on chief packer Beall's say-so, but William Compton Brown insists a study of Beall's "narrations" will prove him an "unreliable source of information."[56] Tradition, as attested by the monument at the battle site in Rosalia, sides with Timothy's presence, as his name appears chiseled in the stone. Baptized by the Reverend Henry H. Spalding in 1838, Timothy (Tammutsa) was regarded as one of the most important Nez Perce chiefs who could be relied on as an ally to the whites. Most historians confidently state he acted as Steptoe's guide and played an important role in the battle, but that role may have been double-faceted.

In what one might regard as a conspiracy theory, some maintain Timothy's intention from the outset was to lead Steptoe into a confrontation with his tribal enemies to the north, certainly including the Palouse and the Coeur d'Alene. Scheuerman and Finley state the case most forcefully in their biography of Kamiakin: "The actions of Steptoe's ally, Chief Timothy of the Nez Perces, helped inflame tribes to the north. He sent envoys to tell opposing bands to fear for their horses and lives. Timothy had feuded with Tilcoax and spoiled for a fight with the abrasive Palouse leader. But Timothy most likely also directed the Nez Perce guides to remain silent about this dispute when around soldiers."[57] These historians suggest it was Timothy who led the expedition well to the east of the more direct trail to Colville. But if it was indeed his intent to confront members of the Palouse tribe implicated in the murders near Colfax, then Steptoe would have swerved intentionally. That Timothy might well have desired a confrontation of the sort indicated may be likely enough, but this does *not* necessarily prove he plotted to lead the command into a trap. The second facet of Timothy's role, and the one traditionally accepted, maintains he managed to extricate the troops from their perilous dilemma on the night of May 17 by leading them along an unguarded trail between the Coeur d'Alene and Spokane camps.

In an essay published in the *Pacific Northwest Quarterly* in 1947, Father Burns notes "the frank admission of guilt by Chief Timothy" when Father Joseph Joset charged him with having "instigated the war."[58] Burns' essay is comprised primarily of commentary on the battle written by Father Joset in 1874, in which he offers a more thorough version of events than is available in the statements he wrote during the months immediately following the battle (quoted in full in Manring's book). Father Joset played a major role in the coming engagement as the "outstanding peacemaker," albeit an unsuccessful one.[59] A Swiss Jesuit born in 1810, the diminutive (5'3") Joset had established the tribal mission on the Coeur d'Alene River. Known then as Sacred Heart it is now called Cataldo and is located 24 miles east of the city of Coeur d'Alene. Burns indicates about forty Coeur d'Alene lived around the mission at the time, with other bands, none numbering more than a hundred or so, scattered around Lake Coeur d'Alene and along the St. Joe River.[60]

In April Coeur d'Alene Chief Vincent told Father Joset "the Paluses are trying every means to excite our yong [sic] people against the Whites."[61] He informed Father Joset, "if the troops are coming to pass the river [the Spokane, that is] I'm sure the Nez Perces are going to direct them upon us"—a "significant statement," Burns maintains, "deserving to be remembered in view of subsequent ambiguous events."[62] A few weeks later Vincent informed Father Joset that Steptoe's soldiers were approaching an area where Tilcoax and a party of Palouse were digging camas.[63] There, Steptoe's Nez Perce scouts taunted Tilcoax claiming, "soon your wives, your horses, and your goods shall be ours."[64] Tilcoax is then said to have encountered a band of Coeur d'Alenes camped with Chief Vincent near present-day Oakesdale, Washington, about ten miles southeast of Rosalia. To the Coeur d'Alenes, whose Salish language differs from that of the Palouse (like the Nez Perce, theirs is Sahaptin), "the canny Palouse translated Timothy's remarks in altered terms": "Coeur d'Alenes, your wives, your horses, your goods shall very soon be ours."[65] Presumably, Tilcoax was seeking to build an impromptu alliance based upon mutual distrust of the Nez Perce, whose decades-long friendship with the whites was well known.

Father Burns carefully delineates the baffling complexity of the tribal world: more than two dozen tribes, many of them speaking distinct dialects representing two quite different language groups, and many of those tribes divided in their hostility to the American interlopers. The Nez Perce, for example, were split between the "conservative [...], more traditional, rather sedentary party" that welcomed the Presbyterian missionaries as they had Lewis and Clark, and the "more numerous and wilder buffalo hunters," who annually moved into the plains of Montana in pursuit of buffalo.[66] The latter engaged in frequent combat with the Blackfeet and tended to be "anti-Whites" and "adamant trouble-makers."[67] Timothy appears *not* to have been among the latter. His incitement of the Palouse, and perhaps of the Coeur d'Alene, could be regarded as a display of personal bravado rather than betrayal of Steptoe's command.

Burns portrays the Spokane chief known as Spokane Garry as an opportunist who "helped form a pro–American, pro–Protestant [as opposed to

French and Catholic] faction among his portion of Eastern Spokanes," but Robert H. Ruby and John A. Brown, in *The Spokane Indians: Children of the Sun*, describe the "restless" Spokanes as "epicentral to the disgruntled tribes."[68] Garry struggled to control the war faction of his tribe, as did Chief Sgalgalt, who would join Chief Vincent of the Coeur d'Alene in a battlefield parley with Steptoe, but the angry young men among the tribes followed a chief named Polatkin into battle. Ruby and Brown contend he was won over by Owhi's son Qualchan, a Yakama chief who was married to one of Polatkin's daughters and was a nephew of Kamiakin.[69] The web of interrelationships among the Indians of the Northern Plateau tribes was more complex than settlers and soldiers might have suspected. In the month following Steptoe's defeat, Kamiakin and Qualchan were named the most dangerous of the Indian leaders. Yet most historians believe Kamiakin was a reluctant participant, agreeing only after yielding to the "fiery rhetoric" of Tilcoax.[70]

The nature of Kamiakin's role has long divided those who have written about the battle. A.J. Splawn, Kamiakin's early biographer, ostensibly quotes the chief: "We now have the opportunity to kill this whole command, thereby making the white man afraid forever to attempt to pass through our country."[71] R. Ross Arnold has Kamiakin joining in on Sunday night (the battle raged all day Monday) and immediately assuming leadership. As night fell, according to Arnold, "Kamiakin begged his warriors to continue the fight, declaring, 'We can finish them in a short time then lie down and sleep.'"[72] After Steptoe's parley with Vincent, Indians swarmed in from every direction "urged on by the aggressive Kamiakin."[73] Randall A. Johnson goes so far as to declare "Kamiaken himself, recognizing [Lieutenant] Gaston's courage and effectiveness, marked him for death and detailed his best marksmen to do the job."

At the other end of the speculative spectrum, William Compton Brown flatly asserts, "there has never been a scrap of proof that Kamiahkin was there at all."[74] Burns poses the question, "Did Kamiakin direct the Steptoe encounter?" And he answers, somewhat equivocally, "Kamiakin does not seem to have been on the scene, or to have arrived rather late in the battle, or even to have influenced its course."[75] But Burns then suggests Kamiakin was only "unavailable at first," or "perhaps he may even have held aloof from Tilcoax's unplanned, harebrained scheme until overwhelming success chanced to crown it," and then, taunted by the Palouse chief before the others, "he, too, joined in."[76] Kamiakin's most recent biographers, Scheuerman and Finley, maintain he was caught completely off-guard and in the spring of 1858 hoped "a new era of peace had emerged." When he "eventually" appeared on the scene, he united with Vincent in advising "constraint," but when "upbraided" by Tilcoax, he acquiesced.[77] Rosebush and Helen Addison

Seven. "Chapter of Accidents"

Drawing of Chief Kamiakin (1800–1877), whose father was Palouse and mother Yakama, by Gustav Sohon (1855). Kamiakin was Colonel Steptoe's most significant adversary during his two years' service in the Washington Territory (1856–1858), climaxing with his defeat in the Battle of Tohotsnimme near present-day Rosalia, Washington, in May 1858. Kamiakin led an array of tribal allies in the Yakima War that started in the fall of 1855 and ended in defeat at the hands of Colonel Wright in September 1858. Used by permission of the Washington State Historical Society.

Howard have it that Kamiakin not only acquiesced, but urged the Indians to attack on the night Steptoe's command escaped and argued they should "make a grand concerted charge" on the position before midnight. "If he had succeeded," Rosebush concludes, "the end of Steptoe and all with him" would have been assured.[78] Coeur d'Alene Chief Vincent features centrally in Mahlon Kriebel's account, which does not mention Kamiakin at all.

One striking feature of the battle as it unfolded is the relatively personal nature of the comments available from both sides, and another peculiar feature concerns various quirky or bizarre episodes like the ones just recounted concerning Timothy's Nez Perce taunts and Kamiakin's uncertain role. After all, as Lieutenant Kip so memorably wrote, "An Indian war is a chapter of accidents."[79] By the time Steptoe's column neared present-day Rosalia, they had been on the march for ten days and had covered something over 120 miles since leaving Fort Walla Walla. Perhaps the soldiers' minds were on girls back home, or what to do after their enlistment was up (maybe head for the gold fields of Colville), or how they would respond if attacked.

Many of the men were raw recruits, half excited and half frightened of what might lie ahead. Some of the officers and the Nez Perce guides knew they had jumped a party of thirty or so Palouse warriors at the Snake River, and some were aware they had startled several Coeur d'Alene camas diggers as well. But Captain Charles Sydney Winder, who commanded the detachment of the Ninth Infantry, wrote on June 2, 1858, safely returned to Fort Walla Walla, that after marching "about 150 miles" over ten days, "scarce an Indian had been seen, except a few friendly ones."[80] Most commentators agree both the Palouse and the Coeur d'Alene were encroaching on Nez Perce territory, so that may account for Timothy's challenges, or to those sent out by his scouts, but Steptoe's men probably knew nothing of this, not that the Nez Perce taunting would necessarily have enflamed the gathering hostiles more than they already were.

By May 13 the column had reached the Palouse River, where they encamped and where Colonel Steptoe scribbled a note to Major Grier, whom he had left in command of Fort Walla Walla. In his note, dated May 14, Steptoe expressed confidence his command would give the Indians "a good drubbing," even though he understood "quite a number of the Spokanes" had joined them.[81] What the colonel may originally have planned as a reconnaissance-in-force, primarily intended to acquire intelligence while avoiding direct confrontation, was about to become open battle. As a matter of what Burns calls "routine prudence," Steptoe ordered Grier to send troops to the Snake with additional provisions (perhaps more ammunition). Grier sent 66 men, nearly half of the remaining garrison available for duty, under command of Captain Dent.

Although Indians had been seen from a distance ever since his column

Seven. "Chapter of Accidents" 163

had crossed the Snake, no direct contact was made before Steptoe's command reached Tohotsnimme Creek and set up camp the evening of Saturday, May 15, with what Manring calls "the usual quietude."[82] "The night passed serenely," Rosebush writes.[83] Lieutenant Mullan's careful topographical map, drawn soon after the battles at Four Lakes and the Spokane Plains, is conveniently displayed in Rosebush's *Frontier Steel*, complete with two U.S.G.S. maps, an overlay, and a handy one-page commentary on the physical details of the area.[84] The creek is identified as "Ingossomen," as mentioned above, which Scheuerman and Finley connect with the Coeur d'Alene name.[85] Their line of march would take them along the stream through the heart of what is today downtown Rosalia. Along both sides are gently sloping hills, most of which rise a few hundred feet above the creek bed and are today part of the residential area or cultivated fields, mostly planted to wheat. The highest elevation in the vicinity, where Steptoe would pull his forces together for what might well have been a truly disastrous "last stand" rises 721 feet above the stream.[86]

At reveille on Sunday the 16th, Manring writes, "the soldiers assembled in high spirits" and the dragoons' mounts "having fed to their satisfaction on the nutritious bunch grass, displayed good fettle."[87] The troops "assembled in a holiday mood," Rosebush assures us, and the sky "was bright and clear, the sun warm."[88] Although they were told hostile Spokane Indians had assembled ahead of them, nothing happened until around 11:00 that morning when, as Captain Winder wrote to a friend a couple of weeks later, "we found ourselves opposed by a body of Indians, painted and dressed for war, bows strung, and guns loaded. At first sight with my glass I could count but 70, in a few seconds as if by magic, the moment one or two rode up to talk they appeared all around us, some 800, and in half an hour from 1000 to 1200."[89] In a brief parley with some of the chiefs, Colonel Steptoe declared his intentions to be peaceful, hardly consistent with the note he dispatched to Fort Walla Walla the day before. He requested help crossing the Spokane River to the north, but the Spokanes refused and increased their threats.

Steptoe warned his men to be ready for action, but not to fire unless fired upon. His troops were about to enter a ravine, but seeing "it was their purpose to attack us in this dangerous place," Steptoe turned his column to the northwest and set up a defensive encampment near a pond or small lake that has been variously identified, but which Rosebush believes to have been Squaw Creek, perhaps over its banks.[90] Kriebel identifies it as Sanders Creek, located about six miles from where they stayed the previous night. "We formed for defense," Winder writes, "and marched two miles or more to water, they charging around us, yelling, whooping, shaking scalps and such things over their heads, looking like so many fiends." He informs his friend the troops "behaved nobly, and kept cool."

Some Indians later said Steptoe "should have turned due south immediately, to demonstrate his good intentions," and then the battle could have been avoided.[91] But such optimistic 20–20 hindsight seems rather unlikely under the circumstances. Kriebel emphasizes Chief Vincent's role in this matter. Nearly all of the commentators, including Burns and Rosebush, agree the Indians decided not to attack because it was Sunday, but given their provocative demonstration, perhaps that, too, is unlikely.[92] Somewhat more likely might be a premise that the chiefs had not yet had an opportunity to coordinate their plans for an attack, although Burns emphasizes the individualistic nature of such combat, involving single engagements.[93] There does appear to have been an "Indian strategy" though, and that was "to keep the soldiers on the run" all the way back to the Snake River. Burns also surmises Chief Vincent of the Coeur d'Alenes and Chief Sgalgalt of the Spokanes argued and pleaded vigorously, hoping to "restrain [their warriors] from violence until Father Joset could arrive," which he managed after traveling by canoe and horseback at full speed to the Indian camp, about six miles northeast of Steptoe's encampment. Vincent explained that Tilcoax and the Palouse had taunted the Coeur d'Alene, said they were "like cowards and women," and although Joset exhorted to the best of his ability, he realized he "had no or very little effect" on the young, who spent the night drumming, singing of war, and performing war dances, much to the misery of the soldiers in the distance.[94]

Head packer Thomas Beall relates a tale of how 24-year-old Second Lieutenant William Gaston of North Carolina requested that he sing a lugubrious song called "Arkansas Bay," but Beall didn't feel up to it. The lieutenant was suffering from a cancer in his neck that he believed terminal. Kurt R. Nelson observes, Gaston "expressed to his fellow officers a desire to die a warrior's death rather than be slowly consumed by the agonizing cancer."[95] His wish would be fulfilled the next day leading Company E of the First Dragoons guarding the exposed flank of the column as it turned back toward the Snake River.

The scene the next morning, Monday May 17, "beggars description," Captain Winder wrote to his friend. Lieutenant Gregg provided a vivid account that has served as a source for most of those who have commented on the battle.[96] He indicates the order of march as the command headed back toward the Palouse River: "H company [dragoons, under Gregg] in advance, C [dragoons under Captain Taylor] in the centre, with the packs, and E [dragoons under Gaston] in rear."[97] Captain Winder commanded the 25 men of Company E, Ninth Infantry, mounted along with the two howitzers, following Company C. Rosebush notes the column, including 85 pack animals and beef cattle, stretched out over a mile and a quarter.[98] Burns describes it as a "long

Seven. "Chapter of Accidents"

serpent of blue [...] winding and bobbing in the dim daylight along a little valley." Father Joset rode up to Colonel Steptoe, who knew his name, and apprised him of the "disposition of the Indians."[99]

The troops broke camp by 6:00 a.m. (Captain Winder claims they were up by two), and by eight o'clock they were under attack, so Father Joset's parley, which Steptoe mentions in the third of his May 23rd communiqués, must have taken place early in the morning. As he had explained to the chiefs the afternoon before, the colonel indicated he was "much surprised" at their "hostile demonstration," as "they had always talked peaceably to him."[100] He added if he had known "the Spokans and Coeur d'Alenes dreaded the presence of the armed force, he would not have come without having notified them" and "he was happy to return without spilling blood." Steptoe's observations might be described as disingenuous, with respect to the former observation and unaccountably optimistic with respect to the latter. But the priest arranged what amounted to a sort of horseback diplomacy, as Steptoe had no intention of holding up the column as it doubled back toward Fort Walla Walla. First, Father Joset assured the colonel any rumors he might have heard that he had provided ammunition to the Coeur d'Alene were utterly false ones circulated by the Palouse. Then Joset attempted to renew the parley of the previous evening, but he was able to bring only Chief Vincent.

At this point a bizarre episode occurred, as a Nez Perce scout named Levi struck Vincent with his whip and taunted him: "Proud man, why do you not fire?"[101] Burns interprets this exchange as evidence the Nez Perce were "angry and frustrated": "They could see their once-in-a-lifetime chance for spectacular revenge upon Tilcoax go a-glimmering."[102] Kriebel writes, "Steptoe immediately reprimanded the scout."[103] Chief Vincent "bore the brunt stoically," Father Joset indicates in his 1874 narration, and "every thing being explained to mutual satisfaction they shook hands and we were returning when we met the people coming on."[104]

At this point another strange episode occurred. "The crisis was past," Burns writes, or at least it seemed so, when "an influential tribesman named Melkapsi" struck a sub-chief named Jean Pierre Kumpaskat, and when another Coeur d'Alene sub-chief named Victor, who would be mortally wounded in the combat that followed, rebuked him, Melkapsi lashed out at him as well. It was all Father Joset could do to part them.[105] Then the exhausted Joset, apparently believing he had defused the situation, returned to the camp at Silé (Sila or "Seelah"), a popular camas gathering site for all the tribes in the area about 15 miles distant from Steptoe's column as it moved to the south. About an hour later, Indians aroused Father Joset from his tent and informed him the attack had started.

"At 8 o'clock," Gregg reports, "the Indians appeared in great numbers about the rear of the column, and just as the advance was crossing a small stream they began firing. In twenty minutes the firing became continuous."[106] "The initial attack was sporadic," historian Jack Dozier writes, "consisting of individual attacks by honor-seeking braves."[107] According to Joset, it was not the Palouse, but a Coeur d'Alene chief named Paschal Stellam who led the first charge, "shooting in blind anger," and soon accompanied by about a dozen young Coeur d'Alenes.[108] Predictably, traditional tribal accounts vary. One Coeur d'Alene version has it that Qualchan of the Yakamas, accompanied by five Palouse warriors, fired the first shots.[109]

Topographical engineer that he was, Lieutenant Mullan, writing about four months after the battle, carefully describes the area, for which he also composed a map:

> At this point the pine timber had become more sparse and much scattered, save a few detached clumps where it was more dense. At eight and a half miles from the Lahtoo [Latah, now called Hangman Creek, flows into the Spokane River], this prairie bottom, which runs north and south, is intersected by a cañon running at right angles to it and fifty yards wide. It was at the southwest corner of this intersection that the rear guard of Colonel Steptoe's command, under Lieutenant Gaston, was fired upon in the retreat of May 17, 1858. The trail that Steptoe followed, which, at the intersection spoken of, was to the west of a small willow creek, in a mile to the south crosses it to the east and ascended a hill some 250 feet high where a first position of the howitzers was taken.[110]

With Lieutenant Gregg leading the advance company, Lieutenant Gaston "on the hills to the left," Captain Taylor on the right, and, according to Mullan, Sergeant William C. Williams of Company E, First Dragoons, commanding the rear, the southeasterly retreat "entered the valley of the Ingossomen [Tohotsnimme or Pine] creek." When Mullan wrote his account in late September the stream was just two feet deep and 15 yards across, the water "lying in long canal shaped basaltic basins," but in May, with the spring runoff, it would have been much deeper and faster. To the south Mullan saw "a few clumps of scattered cotton-wood."[111]

When the troops finally were compelled to return fire, they "unfortunately," Burns asserts, "brought down three of the most popular Coeur d'Alenes," including Victor.[112] "We labored under the great disadvantage of having to defend the pack-train while in motion and in rolling country peculiarly favorable to the Indian mode of warfare," Steptoe writes in his combat report.[113] Lieutenant Gregg, in the vanguard with Company H, reports he "was ordered to move forward and occupy a hill that the Indians were making for, and upon which they would have a close fire upon the head of the column." Around 11 o'clock he and Lieutenant Gaston, leading Company E of dragoons, charged against "a large body of Indians," leaving 12 dead.[114] Subsequently, Captain Taylor and Lieutenant Gaston, holding the flanks, made repeated short charges as the Indians struck at the pack train. "The Indians rode off the Palouse Hills at breakneck speed, firing guns and shooting arrows. In small lightning waves, they raced forward, retreated, regrouped, and dashed out again in a most unorganized and haphazard manner," write Trafzer and Scheuerman of the Palouse. The same appears to have applied to all of the tribes involved.[115] "In their first excitement," Rosebush writes, echoing Steptoe's report, "some soldiers fired in the wildest manner."[116]

The killing of the three Coeur d'Alene warriors spurred the Indians to even greater fury. The day was very hot, and with water supplies running low, Colonel Steptoe angled his withdrawal toward Tohotsnimme Creek to the southwest. With Taylor and Gaston holding the flanks, Gregg and Winder covered the rear, including the jittery pack animals, as the long column moved against "the frenzied, yelling horde of savages."[117] A little before noon "pandemonium broke loose anew among the Indians" and enemy fire "raked the whole command constantly."[118] It was about then that Lieutenant Gaston, the recent West Point graduate who was suffering from cancer, fell, to be followed within half an hour by the dashing Captain Taylor.

Assistant Surgeon John F. Randolph did what he could for Captain Taylor, but he was beyond help. In his report Steptoe commended Randolph, a fellow Virginian, for his "skill and promptness."[119] According to Lieutenant Gregg, after enduring "a constant and raking fire," the three companies under the heaviest attack managed to reach a hill near water, where they were quickly surrounded and where Colonel Steptoe prepared to make a stand.[120] Manring describes the hill as "the point of a long ridge whose terminus dropped off to the creek in a steep incline."[121] The exhausted and thirsty soldiers began digging shallow rifle pits while the wounded along with the picketed horses and mules were placed "close together on the centre of the flat inclined summit."[122] The Indians were close, Lieutenant Gregg wrote, "and so daring as to attempt to charge the hill."

Towards dusk, with thirst and fear running high and ammunition running low, the officers were reduced to crawling on their hands and knees to encourage their troops "amid the howling of the Indians, the groans of the dying, and the whistling of balls and arrows."[123] "It was manifest," Steptoe wrote in his report, "that the loss of their officers and comrades began to tell upon the spirit of the soldiers; that they were becoming discouraged, and not to be relied upon with confidence," partly because some were "recruits but recently joined."[124] Realizing some of the men were down to their last two or three rounds of ammunition and that without rest during what promised to be a long night "they would be still further disqualified for stout resistance on the morrow, while the number of enemies would certainly be increased," the colonel and his officers resolved, as Gregg put it, "to run the gauntlet."[125] Father Joset reported the Coeur d'Alenes told him of Nez Perce scouts shouting encouragement to the attackers: "'Courage! you have already killed two chiefs'" (presumably Gaston and Taylor).[126] Manring speculates this may have been connected with some "treacherous design" on the part of the Nez Perce, who may have intended to foment strife with their old enemies from the outset, or "very probably" it was "an effort at diplomacy on the part of the Nez Perces, at this critical period when it seemed that certain doom awaited all."[127]

Did Steptoe argue, as some commentators have written, "there remained no other course for them but to stay and die like brave men"?[128] He mentioned no such bravado in his battle reports of May 23, nor is the die-with-your-boots-on mentality to be found in the reports of Captain Winder or Lieutenant Gregg. It seems likely he thought of other massacres: of Major Dade in 1837, of Captain Gunnison in 1853, of Lieutenant Grattan in 1854, at the Cascades in 1856. In a letter to Manring dated February 3, 1909, Gregg wrote: "The Colonel a most gallant officer, at first did not see that it would be possible to escape, and expressed the opinion that it only remained for us to meet our fate like brave men. In a second interview, I expressed my opinion that if we remained until the morrow not a soldier would survive to tell the story of the fight, that if we attempted an escape probably one half of the command would be saved at the loss of the other half. Col Steptoe agreed that the movement should be undertaken."[129] Writing some fifty years after the event, Gregg might, or might not, have claimed more credit than he deserved for the crucial decision to withdraw.

Steptoe reported he "determined" to "make a forced march to Snake river" and "After consulting with the officers, all of whom urged me to the step as the only means in their opinion of securing the safety of the command, I concluded to abandon every thing that might impede our march."[130] Being an artillery officer, he confessed "deep pain" over the necessity of burying the howitzers. Also left behind were many of the supplies and "disabled animals." Sergeant Michael Kenny describes them as "leaving all our Provision all our Blankets and 100 Pack mules 20 wounded Horses two howitzers and every thing we had onley the Animals we wrode."[131] They set off at about 10:00 p.m. "in perfectly good order" on their desperate 85-mile trek.

How the command managed to accomplish this feat, heavily outnumbered and surrounded as they were, has received considerable speculation ranging from sheer luck in finding an unwatched space between the Coeur d'Alene to the southeast and the Palouse to the west, to the good offices of Chief Timothy, to the collusion of the Coeur d'Alene. Manring has Steptoe send "a small party" down the hill to "reconnoiter." After meeting no opposition, they report back and the troops silently slip away.[132] Rosebush, among others, credits Timothy with finding a "gap" in the "Indian cordon." Burns suggests another Nez Perce scout might have served rather than Timothy and the Spokanes may have been responsible for the break in the Indian lines.[133] Kriebel, Brown, and others credit (or blame) the Coeur d'Alene for arranging a "deal" that would permit the troops to ford Tohotsnimme Creek, leaving the provisions to them as the first tribe to sweep into the deserted camp around midnight.[134]

Joseph Seltice's rather fanciful version proceeds from the premise that the ford across the creek and the strategic Coeur d'Alene position were "placed there by the Savior at the creation of the earth for Steptoe's fight" and the tribe "shared a feeling of humanity for the remaining troops," so they sent two Indians, Andrew Seltice and Sebastian, under a white flag with an offer to help the soldiers get away, after which hands were shaken all around and Chief Vincent ordered the Coeur d'Alenes to beat their drums and sing war songs to cover the sound of the retreat.[135] He does not mention their rushing the hill to seize the provisions. In his 2001 book on the Coeur d'Alene, anthropologist Rodney Frey credits Vincent with allowing the troops "passage through their lines that night, provided they leave their weapons behind," but there is no evidence the soldiers abandoned their firearms other than the howitzers.[136] "By Indian laws of war," Brown asserts, "the Coeur d'Alenes were entitled to keep all that pelf."[137] Father Joset, who met with the colonel at Fort Walla Walla within a month of the attack, credited Steptoe with "throwing them his provisions" as "an inducement to delay" and thus saving his command owing to his "sagacity."[138] Father Joset also lamented the "bad success" of the colonel, who he regarded as "the zealous protector of Indians," maintaining that his retreat "will do him infinite honor."[139]

Regardless of the explanation one accepts, it does seem "strange indeed" that "not one of those Indians heard the soldiers" and none of them, equipped as they were with "fresh mounts," chose to pursue the bedraggled column the next day.[140] Trafzer and Scheuerman, in their study of the Palouse Indians, propose it was neither Steptoe's "capable handling" of the withdrawal nor the "lure of booty," but an aspect of the Plateau Indians' view of warfare that saved their lives. The Palouse "never intended to annihilate Steptoe's troops," they maintain, although some individual warriors may have wished to do so: "they *allowed* Steptoe to escape" (italics mine).[141]

Six days after the battle, aided by Chief Timothy's Nez Perce, Sergeant Edward Ball arrived at Fort Walla Walla somewhat the worse for wear, but able to recount one of the happier stories to arise out of the debacle. He had been among a small contingent left to keep the fires burning to convince the Indians that troops were still present, but after overindulging in the remaining liquor supply, he passed out and spent the night in some bushes. A couple of

Drawing of Chief Timothy (1808–1891) of the Nez Perce by Gustav Sohon (1855), drawn at the treaty council in May of that year at Walla Walla. Timothy (Tasmmutsa, Tamootsin) was in his mid-forties when he helped Colonel Steptoe's troops move toward the battle at Tohotsnimme or Pine Creek, near present-day Rosalia, Washington. His role in the battle has remained a subject of controversy to this day. Used by permission of the Washington State Historical Society.

months later he would appear among the soldiers and officers especially commended by Colonel Wright after the Battle of Four Lakes on the first of September, where it was reported he charged some Indians and unhorsed and killed one of them. Ball's good luck would hold through the Civil War, during which he served as an officer, and through the Battle of the Little Bighorn in 1876, by which time he was serving as a captain commanding Company H in the Second Cavalry.[142]

Had the consequences of the Steptoe battle—which in just three more years would be regarded as little more than a skirmish—been no greater than those following Major Haller's equally disastrous engagement with the Yakamas in early October 1855, it might amount to no more than an historical footnote. After all, Haller's casualties were nearly identical to Steptoe's: five killed and 17 wounded, a significantly higher percentage of the troops involved, as Haller's force numbered just 86 men.[143] But the consequences of Steptoe's engagement proved momentous. Steptoe may have "managed," as Father Burns claims, "one of the cleverest retreats in Indian-fighting history," but that was not the prevailing view at the time, nor has it been since.[144] His lot was not that of Major Dade, or Lieutenant Grattan, or Captain Gunnison, after all, hard as it was, and it would not be his fate to lead an ignominious "last stand" á la Custer.

At the end of his third letter to Major Mackall dated May 23, Steptoe cites Father Joset to the effect that the combined tribes "had bound themselves to massacre any party that should attempt to make a survey," and adds he makes "no question that Lieutenant Mullan's party has been saved from destruction by late occurrences."[145] In his biography of Captain Mullan, Keith Petersen suggests Steptoe was reaching for "silver linings" in an effort "to salvage what remained of his reputation," but he also cites his letter to Steptoe of June 1, in which Mullan writes, "Your encounter with the Indians has saved my party from disaster ... probably from a complete massacre."[146] In a letter sent to Major Mackall on May 26, 1858, from Fort Dalles, Colonel Wright concurred with Steptoe's observation, proposing that "had Lieutenant Mullan preceded Colonel Steptoe his whole party would have been sacrificed."[147] Petersen concludes, as many have, that Steptoe was "a disgraced and ruined man," but contrary evidence exists, as will be shown hereafter.[148]

Certainly, in his letter to the Secretary of War dated July 15, 1858, General Winfield Scott summed up Steptoe's defeat as a "disastrous affair."[149] On the other hand, as renowned military historian John Keegan observed in *The Face of Battle*, "All battles are, in some degree, and to a greater or lesser number of the combatants, disasters."[150]

California newspapers received and published unconfirmed reports from the *Oregonian* by the first of June: three officers and fifty men supposedly killed. That dire overestimate would be picked up and published elsewhere, for instance on page one of the *New York Herald* for June 28.[151] By the ninth the estimate in the California papers was down to nine killed and 19 wounded.[152] But the ten who did lose their lives, including three Nez Perce scouts, and the 13 wounded would surely weigh heavily on the mind and heart of an officer who was by all accounts, but especially as evidenced in his personal correspondence, a sensitive man and a career soldier who had in recent months begun to question his own fitness for duty. His most painful task would be to inform the widow of Captain Taylor, married a little less than five years and the father of a young son and daughter. Taylor's family had joined him at Fort Walla Walla only a couple of weeks before the expedition. Burns describes Taylor as "an uncomplicated man" and an "exacting and hot-tempered" young officer (he was 32) "loved by his men."[153]

The account that filtered into the world via the *Oregonian* and such California papers as the *Sacramento Daily Union* and the *Daily Alta California* was that of 25-year-old Lieutenant Gregg, the Pennsylvanian in command of Company H, First Dragoons. Predictably, he comes off rather well, although his rendition is not egregiously self-promoting: "Leaving the men to defend the first hill, and deploying my men, I charged the second [group of Indians] and drove them off."[154] Gregg points out "three friendly Indians" were killed in the battle, a statistic that tends to be overlooked even in some recent accounts. Ten of Steptoe's men, not seven, lost their lives in the Palouse hills that day, including "one half-breed B[o]y," who served as Steptoe's interpreter. Quite possibly this refers to the "little Indian boy" Steptoe mentioned in his letter of October 9, 1855, the "promising servant" he had "bought out of slavery."[155]

News writers did not hesitate to editorialize, and they were none too concerned about the facts. The writers for the *Daily Alta California* and the *Sacramento Daily Union* echoed the journalist for the *Oregonian* to the effect that Steptoe's command was "decoyed into a position by the cunning treachery of Kamiakin, and the duplicity of friendly Indians, in whom the officers of the regular army place entirely too much confidence." The writer for the Sacramento paper added the "most formidable were the Flat Heads." Quite aside from the uncertainty as to Kamiakin's involvement in the battle, the role of the Flatheads (Kutenai or Kalispel tribes) was apparently much exaggerated in this account. The June 13 issue of the *Daily Alta California* places the fight in "the Pallome country," and its June 9 issue features the column crossing "the Pioneer river." The word "disastrous" echoes throughout early news accounts, probably providing General Scott with his choice of adjective in describing the battle. *Harper's New Monthly Magazine* reported inflated figures and erroneous information in its August 1858 issue, proclaiming Step-

Seven. "Chapter of Accidents"

toe's command numbered four hundred and they were attacked by fifteen hundred Indians on the Snake River. The September issue corrected those figures and quoted Steptoe to the effect that "the war had been maturing for some time; but if I could have beaten the enemy at the start, all future difficulty might have been prevented."[156]

*   *   *

As it happened, there was to be little in the way of "future difficulty": The alacrity with which a reprisal was arranged seems remarkable. Lieutenant Lawrence Kip, who attended the Walla Walla Council in 1855 and was stationed at Fort Dalles, at the time of the battle was in San Francisco, but he rejoined his company at Fort Vancouver by June 18 and by the 24th they had reached Fort Dalles. His journal account of the two battles with the Plateau Indians in September 1858 was published just a year after the action.

Kip briefly describes the "routine" for the garrison at Fort Dalles, including dress parade at nine and an hour's drill starting at 9:30, rifle practice at noon, another drill at five, and guard duty at six. These drills, Kip observes, were not the usual *"pro forma* business," but were "invested with a reality, since all are conscious that our success in the field depends perhaps upon the state of our discipline."[157] He also found "time for sociability," a "delightful reunion" with brother officers from different regiments, and an "exceedingly fine" regimental band. On the 28th he mentions Colonel Steptoe's arrival from Fort Walla Walla en route to Fort Vancouver to meet with Major Mackall. Steptoe overtook Kip's entourage a few days later on his return to Fort Walla Walla.

Lieutenant Kip's column headed for Fort Walla Walla at three in the afternoon of July 7, marching just six miles before camping for the night. He describes the area as "barren and desolate, unfit for culture, except a few spots on the river."[158] It would take the column 12 and a half days to reach its destination, varying in progress from five to thirty miles a day (an average of a little more than 14 miles a day). Kip complains of "stifling dust" and "exceedingly hot" weather, the sun "hot as the tropics" and producing "an intolerable glare." The 21-year-old lieutenant describes the landscape as a "sun-burnt plain, perfectly lifeless" except for "a miserable crop of salt week [saltweed] and wormwood."

Arriving at Fort Walla Walla on July 19, Lieutenant Kip's column encamped between the "dragoon cantonment and the infantry post," which were located about a mile apart. Colonel Wright's forces took shape quickly, with two companies of the Fourth Infantry sent toward Fort Simcoe, from which they would proceed on August 15, augmented by troops already there to total about three hundred men. On the first of August Kip notes the arrival of Wright and his staff, who reviewed the troops. The expedition, numbering "about seven hundred men," left around a hundred in garrison under Colonel Steptoe.[159]

In his comments quoted in the September issue of *Harper's*, Steptoe mentions his "fear that many lives will be lost before a satisfactory adjustment can be made."[160] The writer for *Harper's* observes the Superintendent of Indian Affairs in Oregon recommended "the troops be withdrawn at once" because the Indians "promise to create no further difficulty if the troops are withdrawn and their rights respected." The writer does not editorialize, but concludes the piece with the superintendent's statement that "our true policy [...] is to send a peacemaker to them." Colonel Wright was no peacemaker. As it turned out the many lives lost would not be those of his fellow soldiers, but of the combined Indian tribes under the leadership of Kamiakin and Tilcoax. Perhaps a hundred Indians would lose their lives in the Battle of Four Lakes and the Battle of Spokane Plains, with the cost of "but one man slightly wounded" for the army, according to Colonel Wright's report.[161]

Lieutenant Kip notes in his journal that by August 8 they had reached the Touchet River under Captain Erasmus D. Keyes of the Third Artillery, an 1832 graduate of West Point who had missed out on the Mexican War and the promotions thereunto appertaining.[162] In August 1858 Keyes' command consisted of a company of dragoons and six companies of artillery with two 12-pounders and two six-pounders.

At the Tucannon River on August 11 the troops began to erect the works to be known as Fort Taylor, named after Captain O.H.P. Taylor, who had been killed in the Steptoe battle. Kip narrates Lieutenant John Mullan's risky hand-to-hand combat in the Tucannon with an "exceedingly athletic savage." The officer who would build the Mullan Road was getting the worst of it when the Indian stepped into a deep hole and lost his grip, after which he managed to escape.[163] On the 18th Wright arrived with additional troops and a supply train. Meanwhile, Major Robert S. Garnett, moving northward out of Fort Simcoe, defeated a force of Palouse and Yakama warriors on the 15th and executed five for murder.[164] A week later a force under Lieutenant George Crook, then Garnett's second in command, summarily executed five more suspected murderers.[165]

On August 20, as the 680 troops of Colonel Wright's command made its way north from Fort Walla Walla, Colonel Steptoe wrote to his sister Nannie *not* about his battle three months earlier or about the punitive force on its way to exact revenge, but about religion. He begins by commending her for having "fairly surrendered" herself to "One [God] who will never forsake you—who will guard & guide you through this troubled life into the eternal calm above."[166] As for his own religion, Steptoe writes, it "has always been too much of a *spasm*—for which a wayward, faulty youth is probably much responsible." Just what sort of waywardness Colonel Steptoe has in mind is impossible to say, unless he is once again reflecting on his ill choice of a military career. He explains he hasn't the time to "discuss business matters," but "if I live [...] I shall then [in the winter] consult with all of you upon what is best to be done." The scant information available in the few other extant family letters suggests their father had not prospered. Edward thanks his sister for her interest "in getting me married," commenting, "never in my life has the need of a companion been so strongly felt by me as during the last 2 or 3 years. [...] You rightly conjecture that the roving life of deprivation & annoyance becomes more & more irksome, but the difficulty is to get rid of it."

Details of the retaliatory battles and of what Colonel Wright would describe as "retributive justice" concern Colonel Steptoe only indirectly. On August 25, marching in intense heat after a storm had torn down their tents a few days earlier, Wright's command crossed the Snake on flatboats with the assistance of the Nez Perce. In addition to the troops, the column included some two hundred packers and teamsters and thirty Nez Perce scouts, in army uniforms, under command of Lieutenant Mullan. By the 31st, in the area known as Four Lakes, about ten miles southwest of what is today downtown Spokane, Colonel Wright was prepared to confront the Indians that had assembled on the hills about three miles ahead. His letter to the Adjutant General bearing that date carries the following "return address": "Headquarters Expedition Against Northern Indians, Camp at the 'Four Lakes,' W.T., 121 miles North of Fort Walla-Walla." He concludes his letter, composed at seven p.m., with what would prove to be justifiable confidence: "I shall look after them tomorrow, after my men have had a night's rest."[167]

Colonel Wright, Captain Keyes, and Lieutenants Kip and Mullan have provided detailed accounts of the Battle of Four Lakes. Four days later, in what might be described as a separate battle, or as an extension of the former, or perhaps even as a mopping-up operation, Wright's forces defeated the Indians once again at what he called in his report the Battle of Spokane Plains. Armed with the new, long-range Springfield Model 1855 rifle-muskets and supported by experienced artillerymen manning the mountain howitzers, Wright's command overwhelmed the outnumbered tribes (Spokane, Palouse, Yakama, Coeur d'Alene and others) under Chief Kamiakin: "The loose Indian confederation that Kamiakin and Tilcoax sought to sustain over the objections of the Jesuits and peace chiefs included an impressive number of experienced fighters, although virtually every tribe other than the Palouses remained split into hostile and neutral factions."[168] While some accounts claim upwards of five thousand Indians were involved, both Colonel Wright's and Lieutenant Kip's reports suggest an extra zero somehow got inserted.[169]

Kip's vivid commentary merits quotation of at least a few passages. From the top of a hill "the whole scene lay before us like a splendid panorama," Kip writes, and on the plain below, "Every spot seemed alive with the wild warriors we had come so far to meet. [...] Mounted on their fleet, hardy horses, the crowd swayed back and forth, brandishing their weapons, shouting their war cries, and keeping up a song of defiance." With boyish enthusiasm Kip describes "the bravery of their war array, gaudily painted and decorated with their wild trappings. Their plumes fluttered above them, while below skins and trinkets and all kinds of fantastic embellishments flaunted in the sunshine."[170]

Colonel Wright waxed dramatic in his after battle report to the Adjutant General as he described Major Grier's squadron of the First Dragoons in action: "At a signal, they mount, they rush with lightning speed through the intervals of skirmishes, and charge the Indians on the plains, overwhelm them entirely, kill many, defeat and disperse them all."[171] The colonel's account omits Kip's portrayal of Major Grier's voice "ringing over the plain" and shouting "'Charge the rascals!'" Kip also offers a memorable image of Lieutenant Gregg as he "clove the skull" of an Indian warrior with his saber.[172] A couple of rounds from a howitzer sent the remaining scattered Indians into retreat, and at two in the afternoon, after something under four hours of combat, Wright reports, "The battle was won."

Four days later, on September 5, the scene pretty much repeated itself when Colonel Wright's command encountered "from five to seven hundred warriors" (he identifies them as Spokanes, Coeur d'Alenes, Palouses, and Pend'Oreilles or Kalispels) about five miles to the north. The Indians set fire to the grass and attacked the pack train, but Wright acted promptly and Major Grier "dashed gallantly through the roaring flames." The howitzers then opened up and the Indians were "routed."[173] "The battle was won," Wright echoes himself. Two brothers of Spokane Chief Garry were killed; Kamiakin was wounded but managed to escape. How many other Indians died is unknown,[174] but the aftermath of the two battles has proven controversial.

Finding himself "embarrassed" with hundreds of Indian horses seized by his troops, mostly the property of Palouse Chief Tilcoax, many of those horses "very wild," Colonel Wright "determined to kill them all," with the exception of a few found serviceable by the quartermaster. "I deeply regretted killing these poor creatures," he writes, "but a dire necessity drove me to it."[175] The slaughter of the horses, variously reported to number from as low as six hundred to as high as a thousand, has been explained as analogous to the destruction of a modern enemy's trucks and tanks, or as an example of harsh but effective psychological warfare. Whatever the explanation, the killings had a huge impact on all of the Indians of the Northern Plateau: "What nature of mankind, they asked, could kill horses—stallions, geldings, mares, and colts—in such a cold-blooded manner?"[176] Captain Keyes, writing 25 years after the event, claimed the "actual tally was 690" and declared it "a cruel sight to see so many noble beasts shot down." They were all "sleek, glossy, and fat," Keyes wrote around 1883, and "I fancied I saw in their beautiful faces an appeal for mercy." Noting that toward the end of it "the soldiers seemed to exult in their bloody task," he concludes, "such is the ferocious character of men."[177]

Wright's forces proceeded to destroy Indian lodges and food caches up the Spokane valley as they moved toward the mission on Lake Coeur d'Alene. Kamiakin and Tilcoax retreated into the Bitterroots, but the aging Yakama Chief Owhi, a brother of Kamiakan's father-in-law, who had achieved some degree of notoriety for leading an attack on the village of Seattle in early 1856, was captured and killed when he tried to escape at the Tucannon River. Wright seized Owhi's son Qualchan, who rode into camp for a parley assuming he would be immune from capture. The colonel's brief account in his September 24 letter to the Adjutant General speaks volumes: "I seized Ow-hi and put him in irons. I then sent a messenger for Qual-chew [Qualchan] desiring his presence forthwith, with notice that if he did not come I would hang Ow-hi. Qual-chew came to me at 9 o'clock this morning, and at 9 ¼ a.m. he was hung."[178] Qualchan is said to have struggled desperately with the soldiers, as did his young wife Colestah, daughter of Chief Polatkin of the Spokane, who had also been taken hostage. Six other Palouse warriors were hanged that day.[179]

After a couple of years spent living among the Flathead in Montana, Kamiakin returned to his home in the Palouse around 1860, settling on Rock Lake, about ten miles from the Steptoe battlefield, where he died in 1877, in his late seventies. Tilcoax joined friendly tribes in Montana and did not return to the Palouse region; the date of his death is uncertain. Remnants of the Palouse tribe eventually were settled as a distinct band among the Colville, whose sizable reservation begins about fifty miles west and slightly north of Spokane. The gold had mostly played out by the 1880s.

The next day, September 25, Colonel Wright sent Major Grier with three troops of dragoons to the Steptoe battlefield under orders to retrieve the remains of Captain Taylor, Lieutenant Gaston, and other soldiers buried there. In his letter to the Adjutant General dated September 30, 1858, Colonel Wright wrote he informed the Palouse if he "ever had to come into this country again on a hostile expedition no man should be spared"; he would "annihilate the whole nation."[180] In his appended list of nine "Results" Wright touched upon a broad range of achievements, from "The Spokanes, Coeur d'Alenes and Pelouses entirely subdued" to the "recovery of two mounted howitzers abandoned by the troops under Lieutenant Colonel Steptoe."[181] On October 7 at Fort Walla Walla the remains of Taylor and Gaston and of the other men were "buried with military honors, the ceremony being invested with all the pageantry which was possible, to show respect to the memory of our gallant comrades."[182] The feelings of Colonel Steptoe during these services can only be imagined.

On October 10, just three days after volleys were fired over the graves, Colonel Steptoe left Fort Walla Walla and the West, never to return.

Chapter Eight

Last Years

Colonel Steptoe's long sea voyage back to his home in Virginia would have been a dolorous occasion under the best of circumstances, but the trip was doubtless rendered even more melancholy by his traveling companion, Major Robert Garnett, who had constructed Fort Simcoe and led an expedition that moved northward as part of Colonel Wright's strategy to trap the Northern Plateau tribes in a pincers maneuver. This punitive action followed Steptoe's defeat by just three months. The major's "subsidiary campaign," as Father Robert Ignatius Burns describes it, involved about three hundred troops, but proved "brief and ineffectual." When he returned, the major discovered his "pretty bride of twenty months" had died of a fever. His nine-month-old son died a week later.[1] Whether the two officers, both Virginians and West Point graduates, both veterans of the Mexican War, bonded in some special ways during the months-long sailing from San Francisco to the Isthmus of Panama and then on to New York remains conjectural. Commanding the department of what was then known as Northwestern Virginia, Garnett would become the first Confederate general to be killed in action during the Civil War, falling at the Battle of Corrick's Ford, near Parsons (now West Virginia) on July 13, 1861.

An item from an unidentified New York newspaper cites the *San Francisco Herald* on the subject of Steptoe's departure from the West:

> Col. Steptoe, one of the most gallant and meritorious officers in the army of the United States, leaves California by steamer today.
> In the military history of our country the name of Col. Steptoe stands prominent for gallant and oft-repeated services and the country owes him a debt of gratitude which every generous-hearted American citizen will find a pleasure in acknowledgeing.
> Had Col Steptoe's command in Oregon been armed with Sharpe's carbines instead of worthless and condemned old musquetoons, the result would have been a signal and immediate chastisement of Indian insolence.

The journalist proceeds to credit Steptoe for his well-executed retreat and to comment on the subsequent defeat of the Northern Plateau tribes, but his focus remains on Steptoe, and he concludes "wherever that gallant officer is known on the Pacific coast, his name is coupled with eulogy for his capacity as a soldier, and praise for his conduct as a true gentleman."[2]

The trip from San Francisco via the Isthmus of Panama to New York would last two to three months, so presumably Steptoe had hardly arrived at Washington, D.C., before writing to the Adjutant General on December 4 to request a Court of Inquiry. Since his arrival he had heard of "some misrepresentations" with respect to "the number of Savages engaged" and "the necessity for the forced march of the troops in retreat."[3] He informs Colonel Cooper that Lieutenant Gregg, who had commanded a company of the First Dragoons during the battle, is now in Pennsylvania "and can give the fullest information upon all the points of inquiry." Significantly, given that much has been made of his ill health in the aftermath of the battle, Steptoe insists it will "give me the highest satisfaction to return at once to the Dept. Oregon" to obtain additional witnesses should the court be convened there. Apparently no such inquiry or further investigation was undertaken.

In a note to the Adjutant General dated February 23, 1859, Steptoe indicates he has been "testing relative merits of small arms nearly six weeks from Dec. 3rd to Jan. 15," but he hopes "the time thus taken from my leave of absence will not be considered a part of it."[4] The letter was sent from Forest Depot, Virginia, in Bedford County about seven miles southwest of Lynchburg. He most likely spent the last evening of the hard old year 1858 with his family, perhaps with his sister Nannie, then 25 years old and (again "perhaps") ready to introduce him to one Mary Rosanna Claytor, about ten years younger than her bachelor brother, whom she had been urging toward marriage for several years. Mary Rosanna Claytor, then 32, was a member of a prominent family engaged in the tobacco industry, Lynchburg's economic focus.[5]

Whether their courtship began on the eve of 1859 remains conjectural, for Edward may have been too ill by then. The colonel had in his possession a diagnosis of his illness penned by his Assistant Surgeon at Fort Walla Walla, John F. Randolph, dated October 9, 1858: "I do hereby certify that I have carefully examined this officer and find that he has great derangement of the liver, attended with dyspepsia and general nervous debility—and that in consequence thereof he is in my opinion unfit for duty." Randolph adds he cannot say when Steptoe will be capable of resuming his duties, "probably not for months or years."[6] Significantly, Steptoe did not present that letter to the Adjutant General for several months after his return to the East. In a brief note dated March 17, 1859, he acknowledges receipt of orders to report to Fort Moultrie, on Sullivan's Island outside Charleston, South Carolina. Had

Eight. Last Years

he gone, he might well have been stationed there in December 1860, when Major Robert Anderson moved that garrison to Fort Sumter in the face of South Carolina's secession. Apparently Steptoe intended to comply with the orders in hopes of deriving some benefit from the change and travel, but he reported his health had "not been at all good for some weeks."[7]

The orders were presumably countermanded, as Steptoe sent a subsequent letter dated April 19, also from Forest Depot. It begins, "In the belief that no military operations in the Dept. of Oregon are contemplated at present," suggesting he anticipated being sent back West.[8] He then forwards Assistant Surgeon Randolph's note, cited above, and requests an official leave of absence "for the benefit of my health." Until quite recently, he writes, "I supposed my general health to be improved by this trip to the East, but I find myself at times very weak—prostrated in fact, & unfitted for any duty." He then proposes the "exercise of travel" as "probably most beneficial" and in that context requests permission "to go beyond the limits of the U. States." This rather peculiar request, given the apparent severity of his illness, may have been connected with events unfolding in northern Italy.

French forces in northern Italy under Napoleon III, combined with Sardinian or Piedmontese troops, began maneuvering in opposition to Austrian influence in the region, intending to unite the various Italian states. Outright combat began April 29 and the so called Austro-Sardinian War or the Second Italian War of Independence would last only months, ending by mid–July with defeat of the Austrian forces. In an item appearing in newspapers dated May 25, 1859, Steptoe is listed among ten officers, including Colonel William W. Loring, with whom he served in Mexico, as taking ship "to go beyond the United States, with the understanding that they are to put themselves in communication with the antagonizing armies in Italy so as to note military operations."[9] Transatlantic crossing from New York to London could be accomplished by side-paddled steamer in about ten days, so the group of officers would most likely have reached the front in time to witness the decisive Battle of Solferino on June 24. Manring indicates Steptoe postponed his plans, but in a letter to former President Franklin Pierce dated June 18, 1860, Steptoe writes, "I never once heard of you in Europe without feeling the desire to write you." Presumably, that statement refers to his visit the previous year.[10] Steptoe's visit to Europe is also mentioned in an item from the *Richmond Daily Dispatch*.

In a letter to his sister Nannie dated August 3, 1859, however, Edward mentions nothing of a visit to Italy. He wrote from Alleghany Springs, presumably the thermal waters located about twenty miles southwest of Roanoke. In this letter, apparently the last extant personal letter he wrote, Edward proposes conveying her and "Pa" to "the Falls of Niagara, stopping a day in Washington & two in N. York," noting the trip "can be made from Lynchburg in 10 days easily without fatigue."[11] His handwriting appears shaky, but in a letter mailed from Havana, Cuba, several months later, his hand seems quite firm. Once at Niagara Falls, Edward indicates he would not return to Virginia, and his father would accompany Nannie back home. He tells her he cannot say who is at the springs, and his head aches "so much from the hot dusty travel today that I have small inclination to write more than necessary." He then reflects on other visits to springs in the region: "The W[hite]. Sulphur benefitted me but the Sweet Springs not at all—I caught cold there & did not get over it the whole stay."

Whether the family made the trip to Niagara Falls is uncertain, but if so, they may have been in New York when news came of abolitionist John Brown's raid on the federal armory at Harpers Ferry, then still within the State of Virginia, on October 16, 1859. Harpers Ferry was located nearly two hundred miles northeast of Lynchburg, but the world was shrinking with the spread of railroads and the telegraph. By 1860 the Orange & Alexandria Railroad would extend its lines to Lynchburg, effectively establishing direct rail service to the nation's capital. By the end of the 1850s Lynchburg could boast 45 tobacco factories, most of which employed leased slaves.[12] One noted "tobacconist," Samuel Leftwich Claytor, had been in business with Steptoe's maternal grandfather, Captain Henry Brown, and married Brown's daughter Mary in 1817.[13] Their daughter, Mary Rosanna Claytor (1826–1887), would become Edward's wife in January of 1860. Nothing concerning their courtship is presently known.

The year 1860, would doubtless bring some happiness to Colonel Steptoe in his marriage and some last months of calm before the storm of secession and civil war gripped the nation. The descent into the maelstrom must have been obvious to any thoughtful person, but the year began auspiciously enough for the new couple with a "complimentary supper" held in their honor at the Norvell House the evening of January 30.[14] Presumably, this dinner was intended as a celebration of their recent marriage. Among the 25 "managers" listed on the announcement for the fete are at least five physicians, a Colonel J.M. Langhorne, and Professor Lycurgus G. Matthews, who taught Latin and literature at Lynchburg College, a Methodist school that had moved from Uniontown, Pennsylvania, when racial integration threatened Madison College there in 1855. Edward would turn 45 that fall.

That spring Colonel and Mrs. Steptoe traveled to Havana for his health, and also to enjoy a honeymoon. In March he wrote to Adjutant General Cooper, requesting extension of his leave of absence for medical reasons. "I have delayed doing this to the last moment," he writes, "in hope of being able to avoid it, but am finally satisfied that a farther relief from active duty, or retirement from the public service altogether, are my only alternatives."[15] Steptoe asked for "6 months additional leave" and appended a statement beginning, "I certify on my honor that my health, although better than it has been, is such as to make my return to duty at present both imprudent & improper." He then spells out his ailments as he understands them: "deranged liver & stomach producing general, and at times very great nervous derangement & debility—and especially when some exposure often trifling in degree, causes me to take cold." He adds it is impossible for him "to foresee how long this may continue." In addition to the strokes previously noted, the "deranged liver" may have resulted from a variety of causes, including hepatitis, or malaria or yellow fever possibly contracted while deployed to Florida or to Mexico. He appears never to have possessed a very robust constitution.

Colonel Steptoe would have been at home when Abraham Lincoln won the Republican nomination for president on May 18, but it is unlikely he or his family anticipated Lincoln's election in November. Only the four-way division of the popular vote would bring that to pass. Lynchburg favored John Bell of Tennessee, who represented the new Constitutional Union party composed largely of former Whigs who opposed secession. Lincoln's name did not appear on the ballot. Had the northern Democrats under Stephen A. Douglas and the Southern Democrats under John C. Breckenridge united, they might well have won the election with a compromise platform.

On May 3, 1860, Steptoe wrote to Colonel Cooper from New Orleans in response to having read in the newspaper of "a recent order requiring all officers absent on account of their health to return to their departments without delay—even if unable to resume the discharge of their duties."[16] This left him with no alternative, as he saw it, but to resign his commission, which he would regret, but would accept "without hesitation as without a murmur." If the Secretary of War agreed, however, Steptoe hoped for an extension of his leave of absence for another six months, after which he would feel compelled to resign if unable to perform his duties.[17] He informs Cooper that a return letter would reach him at Forest Depot, which suggests he and his wife might have taken up residence at his parents' home, Cedar Grove, located a couple of miles north of the New London Academy. His father was then in his seventies and his stepmother, Mary Dillon Steptoe, the only mother he had known since the age of seven ("Ma" in his letters) would have been about 63

Mary Claytor Steptoe was nearing the end of her first trimester of pregnancy when news came of Lincoln's election on the third of November. Five days before Christmas, South Carolina, became the first state to secede. A brief news item printed in the *Sacramento Daily Union* on October 11, 1860, reports a "gallant officer of the army, Colonel Steptoe, of the artillery, is lying ill somewhere in the East, of sickness so severe that it is thought he cannot recover."[18] The item is of interest not only because it informed readers of Steptoe's ongoing health problems, but also because it attests to his high reputation in the West, despite his defeat in the Washington Territory in 1858.

New Year's Eve of 1860 involved celebrations fraught with anxiety. South Carolina announced it was raising regiments; President Buchanan, still in office until the inauguration of Lincoln in March, refused to extract federal troops from that rebellious state. Newspapers were full of the talk of war and of "compromise before war." An item datelined Richmond, December 28, declared "The seizure of the forts at Charleston by South Carolina gives great joy here. The secession feeling here has attained an intensity which no one could have predicted a week ago. I observe many ladies on the streets wearing secession rosettes."[19] On December 31, the *New York Times* praised Buchanan's decision not to remove Major Anderson's troops from Fort Sumter as "A Gleam of Hope."[20]

But hope's gleam went dim over the next few months as one by one, starting with Mississippi on January 9, 1861, the other ten states seceded to form the Confederacy. General P.G.T. Beauregard commenced the bombardment of Fort Sumter on April 12, and Virginia seceded on the 17th. On June 10, 18 Union soldiers under command of General Benjamin Butler were killed at the Battle of Bethel Church on the Virginia Peninsula near Hampton. Confederate forces under Colonel John Magruder and Colonel D.H. Hill, outnumbered more than two to one, suffered only eight casualties (one killed) to more than seventy for the Union. Magruder and Hill, like Beauregard, were West Point graduates who had served with Steptoe in Mexico. Hill mentioned Steptoe in his diary (see Chapter Four), and he commented on Steptoe's service as an artillery officer during the Mexican War in his "eloquent" essay on "the military spirit and genius of the Southern people" delivered at Wilmington, North Carolina.[21] A brief news item in the *New York Times* dated June 11, 1861, just a day after the Battle of Bethel Church, indicates Colonel Steptoe and his family had arrived at the Donegana Hotel in Montreal. Their daughter Rosanna Eliza had been born on April 20.

The *Richmond Daily Dispatch* for September 11 published a list of 28 Virginia officers listed for assignment "in Lincoln's Army," beginning with Brevet Lieutenant General Winfield Scott and including, fourth on the list, Lieutenant Colonel Edward J. Steptoe, who was offered command of the Tenth U.S. Infantry Regiment.[22] A note appended to the list singled out Steptoe: "The friends of Col. Steptoe have asserted with confidence that he, too, would be true to his State and to his name, and we are unwilling to place his name on the list of Scott traitors. Before the commencement of our present troubles, in consequence of ill health, he obtained furlough with a view to a somewhat protracted absence from the country. He returned from Europe, however, some weeks since, and was in Montreal the last we heard of him." In an item in the *Dispatch* dated March 7, Edward's half-brother William, about three years his junior, is listed as second lieutenant in a company of volunteers organized at Liberty. The *Dispatch* kept fairly close tabs on Colonel Steptoe, reporting on August 19 that he was still in Montreal as of the 15th. The paper also noted his resignation from the U.S. army dating from the first of November 1861.

On October 10, 1861, Steptoe wrote to the Adjutant General's office from Philadelphia, where his father had sent him for treatment. According to Manring, he would remain there "for some months."[23] Significantly, the letter is not written in his own hand, and the signature, which is in his own handwriting, is scarcely legible, probably indicating the effects of another stroke:

> My prospect of recovery is so uncertain—never having recovered my powers of speech and having only partial use of my right side—I feel assured I can never again render military service. Under these circumstances I feel it best to resign my commission in the Army which I hope there will be no difficulty in accepting.[24]

This letter is addressed to Colonel Lorenzo Thomas, an 1823 West Point graduate and like Steptoe a veteran of the Seminole and Mexican Wars. Colonel Cooper had resigned and was serving the Confederacy as full general. Attached to the letter are affidavits of two Philadelphia physicians to the effect that Steptoe's "health is such as to render it quite infeasible for him to visit Washington or to perform any military duties for the present."

B.F. Manring, probably taking his cue from correspondence with Nannie Steptoe Eldridge, whose physician husband served as an artillery officer for the Confederacy in Tennessee, writes, "The war between the states was a matter which distressed Colonel Steptoe sorely. He was loth to break his fealty to his native state, which cast its fortunes decidedly with the South, yet he regretted profoundly the imminent prospect of the dismemberment of the Union."[25] In addition to his younger half-brothers William and Patrick, Edward could count several cousins who served in the Confederate forces, one of whom, Second Lieutenant Charles Yancey Steptoe of the 44th Virginia Infantry, was twice wounded in action, at Gaines Mill and at Fredericksburg. All three of his Uncle Thomas's daughters married Confederate soldiers, his daughter Frances (Fanny) Steptoe being wed to Colonel Richard Carlton Radford of the 30th Virginia Volunteers, Second Virginia Cavalry, known as "Radford's Rangers." Edward's brother, William, Jr., later served as a captain in that unit, which served under the overall command of General Jubal Early, fellow West Point graduate of the Class of 1837 with Edward, and a family friend. Several of his wife's Claytor relatives also served with the Confederacy.

Promoted in September to permanent (as opposed to brevet) lieutenant colonel of the Tenth U.S. Infantry, Steptoe's official resignation was recorded on November 1. He may never have regained his power of speech or full mobility. As the war swirled around Lynchburg, he presumably returned to a town that became an important hospital center for the Confederacy. His old comrade-in-arms, Jubal Early, was like Edward and his father a Whig who opposed secession. Like Edward, Early experienced his first combat against the Seminoles near Fort Pierce. Stationed in Monterrey during the Mexican War, Early contracted chronic rheumatism and saw no action. When the Civil War broke out, General Early organized three regiments.[26]

Known by his men as "Old Jube" or "Old Jubilee," Early was a self-acknowledged disciplinarian. His most notable moment in the war occurred during the Shenandoah Valley Campaign of 1864, when he brought his troops to the outskirts of Washington, D.C., leading skirmishers against outlying fortifications on July 11 and 12. Lincoln himself stood under fire observing the artillery duel from Fort Stevens, and the raid caused some panic in the capital. In his memoirs Early explains the broad and navigable Potomac, which could have exposed his troops to naval action from Washington, should "cause the intelligent reader to wonder, not why I failed to take Washington, but why I had the audacity to approach as I did, with the small force under my command."[27]

So far as the ailing Steptoe is concerned, the most momentous event of Early's career occurred a month earlier, in mid–June of 1864, as federal troops under Major General David A. Hunter led a force of some 18,000 toward Lynchburg. Because of the city's remoteness from Richmond, the primary target of the Union command during most of the war, Lynchburg had been unscathed. The Hill City by that time was home to four iron foundries; moreover, it had become "one of the largest military medical centers west of Richmond and one of only two locales for the treatment of diseased and crippled horses."[28] In addition to the James River and the Kanawha Canal, the city was connected by half a dozen roads and three railroads. Voters in the city had approved of secession unanimously in May of 1861, and by the end of the war "approximately 80 percent of the white male population" would serve in the Confederate army.[29]

Hunter's troops razed the campus of the Virginia Military Institute at Lexington, about fifty miles east of Lynchburg, plundering private homes and the library at Washington College, which dated back to the mid-18th century and which would be renamed Washington and Lee in 1870, after the death of its post-war president, Robert E. Lee. General Lee sent the sometimes obstreperous Early and his weary and numerically diminished corps of some 8,000 by quick march and then by rail toward Lynchburg. Counting some

250 cadets from VMI and 1,800 walking wounded and local militia, Early could muster up to 11,000 troops to face Hunter on June 17. Among Hunter's leading officers, commanding an infantry division, were the later renowned Indian fighter George Crook, who had served under Colonel Wright in his campaign against the Northern Plateau Indians after Steptoe's defeat six years earlier. Hunter's troops attacked from the west, sweeping through Liberty (present day Bedford). Also in Lynchburg at the time was General D.H. Hill, another of Steptoe's former comrades-in-arms from the Mexican War. Hill or Early may or may not have stopped by Colonel Steptoe's home to pay their respects.

Through the hot, muggy evening of June 17 reinforcements arrived by rail for General Early, although perhaps not as many as Hunter supposed. On the afternoon of the 18th attacks and counterattacks combined with artillery barrages, which resulted in Hunter's forces failing to make any significant gains. His troops retreated toward Liberty that evening. Early would return to Lynchburg after the war to practice law and to champion the so-called Lost Cause movement that promoted the Old South as the demesne of chivalry and genteel agrarian values.

Details of Steptoe's last days remain conjectural. Assuming he had returned from Philadelphia, he no doubt heard the not-so-distant shelling during the hot days of mid–June 1864, a familiar sound to the ailing artillery officer. His father had preceded him in death on December 31, 1862, at age 77; his stepmother Mary Dillon Steptoe outlived her husband by thirty years, dying at age 94. She likely helped Edward's wife take care of him in his last days. Dr. Steptoe was buried at the Callaway-Steptoe Cemetery in New London. The typescript of a newspaper clipping from the *Lynchburg Daily Virginian* refers to his work as "the family physician of Jefferson" when he was in residence at his western Virginia retreat at Poplar Forest and indicates Jefferson was "an intimate friend & companion."[30] Noting that Dr. Steptoe was nearly eighty, the writer asserts for more than fifty of those years "he had been actively engaged in the laborious duties of his calling" and adds "He was truly a good and honest man, a friend and benefactor to the poor." About two and a half months after the battle, on September 1, 1864, Edward and Mary Steptoe's two-and-a-half year-old daughter Rosanna died. The cumulative effect must have been devastating on the already suffering colonel who died on April 1, 1865, as Richmond was being evacuated and Lee's forces were moving toward Appomattox Courthouse, a little over twenty miles east of Lynchburg.

Although Manring notes that Colonel Steptoe "joined the Episcopal church in 1851 and continued thereafter a consistent member," he was buried in Lynchburg's Presbyterian Cemetery.[31] He was more than seven months removed from his fiftieth birthday. Manring observes Steptoe's widow, whose grave is located alongside his, outlived him by "about ten years," but in fact she lived another 22 years, passing away in 1887.[32] Oddly, no obituary for Colonel Steptoe appears to be extant, probably due to the chaotic events of that period,[33] but the eulogy inscribed on his monument, hyperbolic in the mode of the era and distinguished by stilted diction and syntax, makes a fitting enough end for this last chapter of his life:

> A soldier by avocation and profession, he was *sans peur et sans reproche*.[34] A grateful Government testified to its sense of the value of his services by advancing him through various gradations to the elevated rank he held in its military service, ere he had reached the high noon of existence; crowning all with the graceful tender, through an Executive [Franklin Pierce] who had been his companion in arms, in a foreign land, of exalted civil position [governor of Utah Territory], which he declined.
>
> Religion and Patriotism were beautifully blended in the character of him who sleeps beneath, for he was not less a soldier of Christ than of his country. Like the Captain of his salvation, he was "made perfect through suffering" and hath now entered into the joy of his Lord.[35]

Epilogue: Legacy

SOME MIGHT SAY THE WORST THING that happens to a person is to be consigned to oblivion; others maintain better oblivion than infamy. Some historians have come down hard on Colonel Steptoe. Elwood Evans (1828–1898), mayor of Olympia (1859–1861) and territorial legislator in the 1870s, made extensive contributions to *The History of the Pacific Northwest: Oregon and Washington* (1889), and in Volume One he berates the military for its role during the mid-nineteenth century: "Glorious duty for American troops to protect the blood-stained murderers of our people, to stand guard that the spirit of treaties shall be violated, that Americans may not occupy America and every part of its domain!"[1] His acerbic tone rings with the self-righteous confidence of Manifest Destiny.

"It was Kamiakin's real aim," Evans continues, "to draw Colonel Steptoe and his little command from the post and serve them as he had Haller's detachment in 1855, in the Yakima country." He portrays Kamiakin as a subtle plotter, "wily chieftain and conspirator, the ablest savage general west of the Rocky Mountains."[2] Evans proceeds to denounce Steptoe in terms that would have eradicated any trace of a legacy, had his view prevailed: "All agree, 1st That the command of Lieutenant-Colonel Steptoe was very badly worsted by the hostiles, and that they made a very miraculous escape from the trap set by Kamiakin; and that it would have been much more magnanimous and creditable in the commander to have admitted how greatly he was indebted to the friendly Indian, Timothy, for that escape. 2d. That he was criminally negligent in starting upon such an expedition without ammunition. 3d. That he largely magnified the number of the hostiles by whom he was attacked; that Lieutenant Gregg's estimate is about correct as to the number in the hostile party; that the war party consisted of Spokanes, who furnished the largest number, Palouses, Coeur d'Alenes, Yakimas, Walla Wallas and Lower Pen d'Oreilles [Kalispel]."[3] The next year (1890), however, noted historian Hubert Howe Bancroft's considerably more temperate and objective account was published as Volume 31 in the *History of Washington, Idaho, and Montana, 1845-1889*.[4] And as the foregoing chapters have demonstrated, historians have not quite closed their books on Colonel Steptoe.

At the end of his essay on Steptoe, Ernest J. Whitaker poses the question, "Should Edward Steptoe be remembered by historians only for his 'defeat,' and the derogatory connotation that entails?"[5] Colonel Whitaker (West Point Class of 1941) goes so far as to ask, "was Steptoe's engagement with the Indians in May 1858, truly a 'military defeat' in the first place?" He cites Father Joset to the effect that "in the eyes of reflecting men, who know his situation, his retreat will do him infinite honor."[6] Historians have disputed this matter over the years. Steptoe surely underestimated the strength and animosity of the Palouse tribe and overestimated the peaceful temperament and neutrality of the Coeur d'Alene and the Spokane. Had he suspected the presence of Kamiakin in the area, he might not have proceeded along the fateful route he selected and which Chief Timothy and the Nez Perce apparently recommended. From a somewhat Machiavellian perspective, though, one might argue his "blunder" forced the hand of the federal government and brought about a swift end to the troublesome threat posed by the Northern Plateau tribes. By the end of September, in little more than four months' time, Colonel George Wright put a decisive end to all present or potential hostilities. The antithesis of that result was the prolonged conflict with the Seminoles in Florida, in which Steptoe had been engaged as a young lieutenant.

From another perspective, Edward Jenner Steptoe's legacy might be said to have consisted of the handful of items listed in his widow Mary Rosanna Claytor Steptoe's will and codicils, dated in December 1883, four years before her death on April 7, 1887. To his brother William she left her husband's portrait, uniform sword, and epaulettes.

To her "true friend," Catherine T. Eccles Mary Steptoe left her pew in St. Paul's Episcopal Church in Lynchburg. From 1856, the women of the church had provided education for "underprivileged children," and its "tradition of fine music began in 1826, when a new organ, the first west of the Tidewater, was installed."[7] Her obituary in the *Lynchburg News* describes Mary Steptoe as a woman "possessed of an ample fortune" who "from her plenty dispensed sweet charity among many of the unfortunate poor of the city."[8]

For residents of the inland Northwest, the obvious legacy of Colonel Steptoe is the imposing geological formation known as Steptoe Butte, elevation 3,612 feet, a pink quartzite island known in earlier times as Pyramid Peak and towering some thousand feet above the rolling dry cropland around it. Manring recalls being told as a 12-year-old boy in 1878 it was already being called "Steptoe Butte," as early maps of Washington Territory attest.[9] Today the butte comprises a state park of about 150 acres. According to the Washington State Parks website, it is "famous for its stark, dramatic beauty and the panoramic view it provides of surrounding farmlands, the Blue Mountains, and other neighboring ranges and peaks. From the top of the butte, the eye can see 200 miles."[10] Manring waxes more poetic: "From the top of Steptoe butte one beholds a panorama that can hardly be excelled in grandeur from the summits of noted mountains of far greater proportions. The hills stretch away from its base in every direction like the billows of a stormy sea; here and there a long depression indicates the course of a hollow leading down to its confluence with a spring branch and that to its distant connection with a creek away in the distance."[11]

Entrepreneur James H. "Cashup" Davis built a hotel on the butte in 1888, and it experienced brief popularity, but supplying the would-be resort proved too costly, and by 1908 the hotel with its "spacious auditorium" and gallery, roof deck and observatory equipped with telescope was abandoned.[12] Pharmacist, farmer, and conservationist Virgil T. McCroskey (1876–1970) donated the land to the state of Washington between 1945 and 1946. A plaque on the summit describes the geologic "steptoe," used as a technical term for many years, to designate "an isolated hill, or mountain, of older rock that is surrounded by younger lava flows."[13] Basaltic rock covered with a varying layer of volcanic soil encompasses the pink quartz of Steptoe Butte, the rolling hills largely resulting from wind erosion. Cashup Davis's hotel burned down in 1911, the year Manring was writing his account of the Steptoe battle and its aftermath. As a geologic term, "steptoe" is in the process of being replaced by the Hawaiian word "kipuka."

Curiously, the etymology of the surname "Steptoe" derives from the Anglo-Saxon (Old English) for a feature that connects with its current, or at least recent, geological definition: "dweller on a steep ridge of land."[14] The Surname Database website indicates the derivation involves the word for "steep" (AS "stēap") and "hoh," the word for "heel, ridge of land, cliff, or precipice" ("hoh" is Old High German for "high").

Other place names, like Steptoe Butte, are also directly connected with Colonel Steptoe. Walla Walla, where he erected three forts, was initially called "Steptoeville" but was changed to its current moniker in November 1859.[15] In eastern Nevada the long basin running about one hundred miles between the Shell Creek and Egan mountain ranges is known as Steptoe Valley, and between the early 1890s and 1926, when a fire destroyed much of it, thrived the Nevada mining town of Steptoe City (its post office closed in 1940).[16] The sites in Nevada are connected with Steptoe's march from Salt Lake City to Benicia, California, in the spring of 1855. Also connected would be the Steptoe Valley Mining and Smelter Company and Steptoe Lodge #24 in Cherry Creek, Nevada (population 72 according to the 2010 census).

In addition to Steptoe Butte in the inland Northwest, notably Washington and Idaho, Colonel Steptoe's name has been appropriated for various city street names and for the unincorporated town of Steptoe, Washington, population according to the 2010 census around 180, located 43 miles south of Spokane.[17] A post office was established there as early as 1876. Some of those who live in family housing at Washington State University in Pullman, about two dozen miles to the south of Steptoe, might reside at Steptoe Village, built in the 1970s, "the largest apartment complex in family housing."[18] In Colfax, Washington, the county seat of Whitman County and the site near which two miners were killed, prompting Steptoe's expedition in May 1858, not far from where Chief Kamiakin's family raised livestock, Henry Spalding, son of missionaries, established the Steptoe Grange in 1874.[19] The *Morning Oregonian* for January 30, 1890, reported a squabble in eastern Washington over the proposed creation of Steptoe County out of Spokane and Whitman counties. Rising up from the Snake River into the Palouse, one may take a dirt and gravel road following a feature known as Steptoe Creek along which the colonel and his troops marched toward their battle near present-day Rosalia, which has since 1970 celebrated the engagement with an annual event held the first weekend in June known as "Battle Days" (parade, rodeo, dance, and the Step-N-Toe fun-run, as it was labeled in 2010).

For tourists and some residents these place names may bear no resonance, despite the highway sign posted on U.S. 195 outside Rosalia and the battlefield site (the brown-and-white signage indicates "Steptoe Battlefield") with granite obelisk placed in the town by the Daughters of the American Revolution in 1914 "to great fanfare and the presence of several veterans of the battle."[20] Visitors to Rosalia (population around six hundred) can take an auto tour of the battle area guided by a brochure that lists seven interpretive sites. The Battle Days Museum, which has a small exhibit on Steptoe and the battle, is located in the Rosalia city hall on 5th Avenue.[21] Founded in 1872 by T.J. Favorite and named after his wife, the town was incorporated in 1894.

Probably Colonel Steptoe's most notable literary moment occurs in a story by renowned Spokane-Coeur d'Alene writer Sherman Alexie, who grew up in eastern Washington on the Spokane Indian Reservation and whose 1998 film, *Smoke Signals*, was filmed on the Coeur d'Alene Reservation in the Idaho panhandle. "The Trial of Thomas Builds-the-Fire," from *The Lone Ranger and Tonto Fistfight in Heaven* (1993), features one of his most important recurring characters, a young Indian who suffers from a dangerous "storytelling fetish accompanied by an extreme need to tell the truth."[22] In the "evidence" he presents on his own behalf during the supposed trial, Thomas variously assumes the character of a young pony slaughtered by Colonel Wright after the battles of Four Lakes and Spokane Plains; the persona of

Qualchan, hanged after those battles; and the identity of a 16-year-old warrior named Wild Coyote, who participated in the attack on Steptoe. Alexie's account of Thomas Builds-the-Fire's testimony regarding the battle amounts to yet another version of "the facts":

> They [Steptoe and his troops] tried to negotiate a peace, but our war chiefs would not settle for anything short of blood. You must understand these were days of violence and continual lies from the white man. Steptoe said he wanted peace between whites and Indians, but he had cannons and had lied before, so we refused to believe him this time. Instead, we attacked at dawn and killed many of their soldiers and lost only a few warriors. The soldiers made a stand on a hilltop and we surrounded them, amazed at their tears and cries. But you must understand they were also very brave. The soldiers fought well, but there were too many Indians for them on that day [800 by Wild Coyote's count]. Night fell and we retreated a little as we always do during dark. Somehow the surviving soldiers escaped during the night, and many of us were happy for them. They had fought so well that they deserved to live another day."[23]

Certain details of Thomas's testimony hew to the facts of the battle as we know them, while others (the killing of "many" soldiers, for example) do not. As to the mystery of the troops' escape, Thomas remains as uncertain as most historical commentators. He confesses to having killed a couple of the soldiers "with premeditation," but claims they were "good men" and that he "did it with sad heart and hand." Of course he loses his case and is sentenced to "two concurrent life terms in Walla Walla State Penitentiary."[24]

A popular literary and film legacy also exists thanks to western novelist Will Henry's *Pillars of the Sky*, originally published by Random House in 1953 under the title *To Follow a Flag*. The previous year the novel had appeared in condensed form in *Zane Grey's Western Magazine* under the title "Frontier Fury." Paperback Bantam editions followed in 1956, 1970, and 1991, attesting to Henry's evolving reputation as a writer of Westerns. Born Henry Wilson Allen in Kansas City, Missouri, in 1912, he worked as a screenwriter beginning in 1937, adopting the pen name Will Henry (among others) in 1952, when the first of his fifty-plus novels was published. The only writer to date to have won as many as three Spur Awards for Best Novel of the American West, Henry died in California in 1991.

In his fictional account of the Battle of Tohotsnimme, Henry renames Steptoe as Brevet Lieutenant Colonel Edson Stedloe. As the novel opens, Sergeant Emmett Bell, for the historical Edward Ball, is accompanied by Timothy and two other Nez Perce scouts. Ball was ordered to destroy the liquor supply as the column retreated; his nearly miraculous escape provided the most entertaining sidebar of the battle. Consequently, he is not altogether Henry's "invention," as Dale L. Walker asserts in his introduction.[25] Walker correctly identifies several historical models for Henry's characters, including Lieutenant William Gaston (Wilcey Gaxton) and Captain Oliver Hazard Perry Taylor (Captain Oliver Baylor), but he errs in identifying Stedloe with *William Jenner Steptoe*. In his study of Henry's fiction, Robert L. Gale describes Stedloe/Steptoe as "a flawed but honest officer," Bell/Ball as "a renegade soldier of unquestioned loyalty and great panache," and Timothy as "a pro-white Christian Indian scout of great dignity and honor."[26] Henry's one-page "Author's Note" dismisses Rosalia as "a busy place full of busier people," the monument as "ugly" and "forgotten," and Chief Timothy as "forgotten" as well.

Henry makes Sergeant Bell, his main character, stereotypically scornful of commissioned officers, including Stedloe, but he describes the colonel as "no martinet." Stedloe tolerates Bell's occasional bursts of insubordination, and actually enjoys the noncom's "refreshing lack of deference" toward the officers.[27] The six-two, sandy-haired, slovenly Sergeant Bell likes a good pull on his bourbon-filled canteen and is "the picture of the factual frontier cavalryman—drunk, dirty, and disrespectful."[28] Not Assistant Surgeon Randall/Randolph, but Sergeant Bell, blunt and straight-talking, informs young Lieutenant Gaxton/Gaston that he is suffering from "lung fever" and is clearly a doomed man. This frank conversation early in the novel sets up the invented romance of the lieutenant with Calla Lee Rainsford of Lynchburg, Virginia, who is supposedly awaiting the stricken officer in Colville. In that context the reader discovers Sergeant Bell graduated from West Point, third in the Class of 1854, known then as Emmett Devereaux Bellew and at one time in love with Miss Rainsford, daughter of the disapproving General Henry Clay Rainsford. Stedloe, according to Robert Gale, is "strange," Bell is "more than strange," and Calla "is most strange."[29]

Will Henry conducted fairly good research, noting such details as Steptoe's suspicion the Mormons might be supplying arms to the Indians and his concern over the failure of Congress to ratify Governor Stevens' 1855 treaty with the tribes.[30] He raises the ante when he has Timothy report that a small wagon train heading south from Colville has been attacked, all seven of the white drivers killed and scalped, and a young white woman and her black servant taken captive by Kamiakin and the Palouse.[31] Henry's colonel embraces the theory offered in some historical accounts that the Nez Perce plotted to get the army into a confrontation with Kamiakin's Palouse warriors. The kidnapped white woman is none other than General Rainsford's daughter, Calla, and Stedloe is an old family friend.[32]

Henry's Colonel Stedloe/Steptoe, seen largely through the eyes of the seasoned, cynical, and obstreperous Sergeant Bell, is "a reasonably good egg as far as Academy hatches went," but also a bit "crazy" and inclined to run a command "like no other officer in the lousy service."[33] In the battle, which surprisingly, given Henry's research on other details, takes place atop the "3,600 foot cone of Stedloe's butte," Bell and Timothy rescue the damsel-in-distress, and Timothy engineers the troops' escape.[34] Calla's black servant Maybelle prefers to stay behind as Kamiakin's "squaw." Several times in the novel we are reminded of Chief Timothy's allegiance to "following the flag."

Most details of the battle and of the officers and soldiers involved follow historical accounts rather accurately, although the mountain howitzers appear in the novel to have been far more effective than in history ("little short of salvational," as Bell sees it, to his surprise, as they cause "fear and confusion" among the Indians[35]). So far as the historical Steptoe's "legacy" in fiction is concerned, however, the most significant passage, given his "magnolia-fancy Virginia rhetoric" and "patrician nose," is this:

> Stedloe was actually one hell of a gentleman and a damn fine officer. One of those rare ones from the Point who understood and genuinely loved his men. He was the kind who had probably stood about forty-ninth in a class of fifty at the Academy, but who ranked Number One with the dogfaces of any command he had ever held.[36]

Henry places this judgment in the thoughts of Sergeant Bell, himself a West Point graduate, the lead character of the novel, and the narrator the reader is clearly intended to trust.

The final three pages of the novel are given over to Timothy, who thinks of Bell and Calla Rainsford heading back to Virginia and of the "patient-eyed" Colonel Stedloe's promise of a full military pardon for Bell. Although Timothy asserts it is "a fool's flag" marked with the red of Indian blood, he concedes he and his tribe must agree to follow it.

In 1956 George Marshall directed a film of the novel on location near Joseph, Oregon. In the Hollywood version (Universal International), Colonel Stedloe/Steptoe's role, played by Willis Bouchey, is diminished considerably in favor of Sergeant Bell's (Jeff Chandler). Other notable actors include Ward Bond as Dr. Joseph Holden, who runs a church and clinic on Indian lands (his part resembles that of the historical Father Joset), Lee Marvin as Sergeant Lloyd Carracart, and Dorothy Malone as Calla Gaxton (not the lieutenant's former fiancée, as in the novel, but his wife—and he is promoted to captain). Marvin's character acquires an Irish brogue drawn from a minor character in the novel. Among the numerous deviations from the novel and from its generally careful adherence to historical events are the shift in time to 1868, hence post–Civil War, and of place to the Oregon Territory. Sergeant Bell, a former captain in the Confederate army, is charged with maintaining the policing operations at the mission. Colonel Stedloe arrives with his troops to construct a road (reminiscent of the Mullan Road) through reservation lands to enable settlement to the north. The Christianized Indians, who are portrayed sympathetically, believe their treaty rights have been abrogated, so they take to the warpath.[37]

The film was shot over about six weeks in the summer of 1955 amid the spectacular scenery of eastern Oregon's Wallowa Mountains, as opposed to the more muted beauty of the actual setting among the rolling hills of the Palouse. The Wallowas were once part of the sprawling Nez Perce Reservation and are the site of the grave of Old Chief Joseph (1785–1871), an early Nez Perce convert to Christianity who resisted federal efforts to shrink the lands by about ninety percent following discovery of gold there in 1863. His son, Young Chief Joseph (1840–1904), led the tribe's famous exodus toward Canada in 1877, pursued by troops under General Oliver O. Howard. The flight ended with the Battle of Bear Paw in northern Montana Territory, where units of the Seventh Cavalry defeated the Indians whom they outnumbered more than two to one.

In what may be regarded as typical casting for Native American roles during the 1950s, Chief Timothy is portrayed by Charlie Chaplin's half-brother Sydney (an Englishman) and Kamiakin is played by the Syrian-born actor Michael Ansara, who portrayed Cochise in the television series *Broken Arrow*. Although several shots depict the dramatic Wallowa Mountains as the "pillars of the sky," some of the terrain resembles that found near Rosalia—low-lying bare hills marked with scattered stands of pine, except the hills are decked with sagebrush instead of bunchgrass, as in the Palouse region of eastern Washington.

As the film begins, Sergeant Bell arrives at the mission with the bodies of some prospectors, including that of a young boy. His first words, sarcastically aimed at Doctor Holden, are, "Looks like I'll be hanging some more of your flock, doctor." The colonel comes off as irascible and high-handed, a "nervous man" the Irish Sergeant Carracart declares, but Stedloe defers to the hard-drinking Bell, as does his counterpart in the novel. Unlike the novel, the movie adheres to Fifties moral values, the screenwriters seeing to it that Captain Gaxton is not killed in action, which would have allowed his beautiful widow to be married off to the nonconformist Sergeant Bell. The couple will instead be reunited in their properly conventional marriage. After the battle, the Indians besiege the mission and Doctor Holden confronts Kamiakin only to be shot and killed before he can offer words of peace. Bell and Timothy then arrive on the scene, and the sergeant delivers a stirring speech in which he denounces the Indians for having abandoned their Christian faith. Having missed his opportunity to shoot Bell, Kamiakin charges at him, but is shot and killed by the now repentant Indians, who promptly make peace. Bell then discovers his lost faith and takes over the doctor's mission.

So far as the movie pertains in any positive way to Steptoe's legacy, it involves the colonel's presumed wisdom in acquiescing to the stereotypical good sense of the NCO: The boozy noncom, representative of the common man with his practical knowledge based on real-life experience, always proves superior to the college-educated professional. It's a Hollywood axiom. The Hollywood colonel also has a moment when he helps finish off a warrior who is about to alert the others during the late-night escape. But movie-Stedloe's best moment occurs when the troops have moved to high ground in preparation for what they assume will be their last stand, and he asks *"was* it the best I could do"? Sergeant Bell says that considering their orders it was, and he is proud to be serving under him.

In 1976 KHQ television in Spokane produced a documentary film entitled "The Day of the Comet and the Retreat of Steptoe," a reenactment of the battle and the subsequent Battle of Four Lakes shot on site near Rosalia and Spokane. The thirty-minute film is archived at the Eastern Washington University library in Cheney, but is non-circulating. (I am indebted to KHQ for providing me with a DVD of that documentary.)

The Library of Congress holds a drawing made by Gustav Sohon (1825–1903) a few months after the defeat "on the battlefield," according to Robert Ignatius Burns, "with the help of Coeur d'Alene and soldier survivors."[38] At age 17 Sohon migrated to the U.S. from Prussia and joined the army in the early 1850s, completing his enlistment in 1857, after which he joined his friend Lieutenant John Mullan, where his knowledge of Indian languages proved invaluable, as it had earlier when he assisted Governor Stevens. He made portraits of numerous tribal leaders from the region and paintings and drawings of the landscape, of Indian life, and of such events as Colonel Wright's battles with the Northern Plateau tribes, including one of the slaughter of Palouse Chief Tilcoax's horses.

Eastern Washington artist Nona Hengen has painted several canvases depicting scenes from the battle, two of which are featured on the cover of Mahlon Kriebel's *Battle of To-hots-nim-me*. Her DVD, "Painting in the Details," combines her photographs and paintings to present a vivid account of the events. A recent watercolor by Walla Walla native and renowned illustrator Norman Adams features Colonel Steptoe implausibly in full dress uniform along with a color-bearing sergeant, apparently intended to represent Edward Ball. While the full-dress uniforms and parade-ground headgear seem out of place on the battlefield, Adams' illustration draws attention to the notorious musketoon dangling from the sergeant's belt and a .44 cal. Third Model Colt Dragoon revolver looking to weigh every bit of its four plus pounds in the colonel's hand.

Anthropologist Rodney Frey in his study of the Coeur d'Alene relates an account of the battle in which the tribe's drummers beat their drums to

Steptoe monument in Rosalia, Washington, placed by the Daughters of the American Revolution in 1914 on the site from which his troops escaped on May 17, 1858. Photograph courtesy Georgia Tiffany.

Epilogue

drown out the sound of Steptoe's troops retreating from Tohotsnimme (Hngwsmn) Creek. Noting that "many of the 'spoils of war'" went to the Coeur d'Alene, Frey refers to a Veterans Powwow he attended in 1993 and again in 1996 where he saw "a saber from the Steptoe Battle," and he offers a photo of the putative "Steptoe Saber" in his book.[39] "The lives lost at the Steptoe Battle, both Indian and soldier," Frey adds, "are commemorated during the annual Memorial Warriors Horse Ride, or also known as the *Hngwsmn* Ride," which moves from the tribal headquarters in Plummer, Idaho, to near the battle site.[40] When the sword is brought out at a family gathering or worn during a special dance, he was told, "'you are honoring the soldier who had given his life for it and the Indian men who took it from the soldiers.'" Shawn Lamebull, a registered Yakama and doctoral student in American Studies at Washington State University, reflects on a dance known as the "Duck and Dive" that may pertain to the battle with Steptoe's forces: One repeated movement in the dance imitates how Indians ducked to avoid the errant cannon-fire unleashed by Steptoe's mountain howitzers which were manned by inexperienced and panicky recruits.[41]

Steptoe Butte the 3,612-foot high quartzite formation formerly known as Pyramid Peak, located about fourteen miles away from the site of the battlefield. Used by permission of the Eastern Washington State Historical Society.

In an item written about Steptoe Butte for the *Moscow-Pullman Daily News* and published in the weekend edition for February 11–12, 2012, journalist Bill London revisited the battle that took place near there more than 150 years ago, concluding with the observation that "despite Steptoe's dismal performance, the nearby mountain was named for him."[42] In about two weeks Terence L. Day, local history enthusiast and information specialist at Washington State University, responded in a letter to the editor that Steptoe's performance was "far from dismal" and reflected on the irony of how Colonel Custer became a "national hero," while military historians have overlooked Colonel Steptoe's "brilliant performance."[43]

Legacies are measured in different ways: place names, items exhibited in regional museums, personal and official correspondence stowed away in archives available to all but rarely read, historical commentaries, fictional appropriations, even reenactments. Colonel Edward J. Steptoe left no immediate descendants, so those who can claim descent today are connected with the families of his aunts and uncles, his half-brothers and half-sisters. In writing this biography I have contacted Mrs. Anne Leyden, a great-great granddaughter of Edward's uncle, Dr. Thomas Eskridge Steptoe (1798–1880), like his brother a physician educated in Philadelphia. Also, I communicated with Robert M. Steptoe, Jr., a highly regarded attorney and chair of the firm of Steptoe & Johnson, a law firm with its home office in Phoenix and several offices abroad. He is a great-great grandson of Thomas Steptoe.

In fact, I imposed on Dr. Robert Stepto, Professor of English at Yale University, and his wife Michele, who also teaches in the English department there, in quest of the notable Steptoes of the nation who are African American and trace their origins to Edward's uncles and half-brothers, virtually all of whom kept slaves. Professor Stepto, whose family dropped the terminal e from the name, is the author of *From Behind the Veil: A Study of Afro-American Narrative* (1979, 2d edition in 1991), a memoir, *Blue as the Lake: A Personal Geography* (1998), and a collection of essays, *A Home Elsewhere: Reading African American Classics in the Age of Obama* (2010). Michele indicated they had visited the Steptoe-Calloway graves in the Lynchburg area while investigating their family history. And I also imposed on Javaka Steptoe, noted artist and illustrator, particularly of children's books, and the son of the renowned writer and illustrator John Steptoe (1950–1989), whose best known book is *Mufaro's Beautiful Daughters* (1988). His father was born in Brooklyn, but Javaka noted his family is from Virginia and his grandfather (John) and uncle (William) bear given names common among the white Steptoes. I think there's a fitting and distinctly American irony that the story might end here, with some reflection on the descendants of Steptoe slaves, the traffic in which Edward Steptoe's father believed was "demoralizing the country."

Chapter Notes

One. Privileged Boyhood

1. Joseph Martin, *A New and Comprehensive Gazetteer of Virginia and the District of Columbia* (Charlottesville: Moseley & Tompkins, 1835), 141.
2. In 1845 Henry Howe wrote, "it is now a broken down village, fast going to decay." *Historical Collections of Virginia* (Charleston, SC: Babcock, 1845), 213.
3. James A. Bear and Lucia C. Stanton, eds., *Jefferson Memorandum Books*, Vol. 1 (Princeton: Princeton University Press, 1997), 255.
4. Julian P. Boyd, ed., *The Papers of Thomas Jefferson*, Vol. 6 (Princeton: Princeton University Press, 1952), 204.
5. John L. Abbott, "Presentation of the Portrait of James Steptoe to the Circuit Court of Bedford County" (October 16, 1953): 13. Manuscript located in Jones Memorial Library, Lynchburg, Virginia.
6. Bear and Stanton, Vol. 2: 1314n. Indicates that "itemized accounts of his [Dr. William Steptoe's] treatment of the Poplar Forest slaves" are archived at the University of Virginia library in Charlottesville.
7. Ann Smart Martin, *Buying into the World of Goods: Early Consumers in Backcountry Virginia* (Baltimore: Johns Hopkins University Press, 2008), 101–102.
8. "Steptoe Portrait Returns to Courthouse." http://www.bedfordbulletin.com/content/steptoe-portrait-returns-courthouse
9. Martin 103.
10. Edna Jones Collier, "The Old Virginia Gentleman," *American Monthly Magazine* 38.1 (January 1911): 1. The essay pertains mostly to Edward's grandfather.
11. In the biographical note appended to his study of Steptoe's battles with Indians in the Washington Territory, B.F. Manring perpetuates a couple of errors that occasionally appear in historical or biographical accounts: that the "J" stood for "Jevnor" and that Edward was born in 1816. B.F. Manring, *The Conquest of the Coeur d'Alenes, Spokanes and Palouses* (Spokane: John W. Graham, 1912), 266. Although Manring was in contact with Steptoe's sister Nannie, she was elderly (born in 1834, she would have been in her midseventies at the time). Some misunderstandings appear to have occurred.
12. John Redman Coxe, ed., "Medical Commencement," *Philadelphia Medical Museum*, Vol. 4, Medical and Philosophical Register: lix. William Steptoe's younger brother, Thomas Eskridge Steptoe (1798–1880) also received his medical education in Philadelphia, according to his great-great grandson Robert Steptoe, an attorney and Chairman of the Steptoe & Johnson PLLC firm (email correspondence dated November 21, 2011).
13. An application for listing on the National Register of Historic Places filed in 1982 describes Federal Hill as "a three-part, woodframe, Palladian-type house built in 1782," the main block consisting of "a 2½-story pedimented gable roof flanked by one-story wings." http://www.dhr.virginia.gov/registers/Counties/Campbell/015-0003_Federal_Hill_1982_Final_Nomination.pdf.
14. Daisy Imogene Read, *New London Today and Yesterday* (Lynchburg, VA: J.P. Bell, 1950), 75; photograph 28. I am indebted to Melvin Lester, Co-Chair of the Friends of New London, Virginia, Inc., for providing me with this information.
15. Manring 267. I've drawn information on Captain Henry Brown and his family mostly

from Barbara Brown Eakley, *The Browns of Bedford County, Virginia, 1748–1840* (Bowie, MD: Heritage Books, 1998).
16. Dr. William Steptoe to William Steptoe, Jr., Special Collections, University of Washington Libraries, Accession #4908-0001, Box #1, Folder #41.
17. Abstracts of Steptoe Wills & Deeds recorded in Bedford County, 1848–1859 http://files.usgwarchives.net/va/bedford/slaveabs/ss100005.tx
18. See the visitor guide, *Thomas Jefferson's Poplar Forest*; also http://www.poplarforest.org/retreat/landrest; the brochure for the landscape walking tour lists sixteen species of trees on the site today.
19. Martin 137.
20. Howe 213.
21. An elaborate website provides some family history, several photographs, and an account of the restoration efforts now underway (http://www.historicivycliff.com/Home_Page.php). Ivy Cliff was sold in August 2013 but the YouTube video currently (July 2015) remains active.
22. William Clarke's *The Boy's Own Book of Games* was first published in Boston and New York in 1829 as "A popular encyclopedia of the Sports and Pastimes of Youth," not that Edward Steptoe or any other boy would have needed such a reference work. Nevertheless, reprinted in 1996, it provides a handy sampling of what boys were up to in the 1820s.
23. Manring 266–267.
24. Reprinted in S. Allen Chambers, Jr., *Poplar Forest and Thomas Jefferson* (Little Compton, RI: Fort Church Publishers, 1993), 93. Published for The Corporation for Jefferson's Poplar Forest.
25. Peaks of the Otter http://en.wikipedia.org/wiki/Peaks_of_Otter; Natural Bridge (Virginia) http://en.wikipedia.org/wiki/Natural_Bridge_%28Virginia%29
26. I've drawn most of the material on Lynchburg's history from Clifton and Dorothy Potter's *Lynchburg: A City Set on Seven Hills* (Charleston, SC: Arcadia, 2004). This text expands on their earlier title, which incorporates Jefferson's quotation: *Lynchburg: "The Most Interesting Spot"* (Lynchburg: Beric Press, 1985). See also Philip Lightfoot Scruggs, *The History of Lynchburg, Virginia (1786–1946)* (Lynchburg: J.P. Bell [1970?] and Richard B. Lloyd and Bernard K. Murdy, *Lynchburg: A Pictorial History* (Virginia Beach: Donning, 1975).
27. Howe 212 (facing).

28. Stella Pickett Hardy, *Colonial Families of the Southern States of America: A History and genealogy of Colonial Families Who Settled in the Colonies Prior to the Revolution*, 2d ed. (Baltimore: Genealogical Publishing, 1958), 487. Among other errors, Hardy lists E.J. Steptoe's year of death as 1861; it was April 1, 1865. The Steptoe family is listed among 66 in Hardy's book.
29. Potter and Potter, *Lynchburg: A City Set on Seven Hills*, 26; Howe 212.
30. Potter and Potter, *Lynchburg: "The Most Interesting Spot"* 30–31.
31. Potter and Potter, *Lynchburg: A City Set on Seven Hills* 39.
32. Ibid., 17.
33. Martin 141.
34. *The Virginian* (December 21, 1826); microfilm, Jones Memorial Library, Lynchburg, Virginia.
35. Scruggs 55–56. The list is excerpted from a much longer one which Scruggs draws from Anne Royall's *Southern Tour* (1830) or *Mrs. Royall's Southern Tour*, Vol. 1.
36. Martin 137.
37. Martin 138.
38. Lloyd and Mundy's *Lynchburg: A Pictorial History* offers an artist's conceptual map of the town as it might have appeared in the 1820s (pages 140–141).The Federal style mansion, completed the year Edward was born, has been restored and is maintained by the Lynchburg Museum System. Daily tours are available "Point of Honor" (http://www.pointofhonor.org/history/index.php).
39. *The Virginian* (Monday, November 5, 1827). This issue of *The Virginian* appeared on Edward Steptoe's twelfth birthday.
40. *The Virginian* (April 6, 1827), Microfilm, Jones Memorial Library, Lynchburg, Virginia.
41. *The Virginian* (December 21, 1826), Microfilm, Jones Memorial Library, Lynchburg, Virginia.
42. Joseph Martin indicates there were "15 practising [sic] physicians" in the town as of 1830.
43. Kenneth S. Greenberg, ed., *Nat Turner: A Slave Rebellion in History and Memory* New York: Oxford, 2003) xi. See also Herbert Aptheker, "The Event," 59; Thomas c. Parramore, "Covenant in Jerusalem," 70.
44. Manring 267.
45. William S. Powell, "Carolina—A Brief History," http://www.unc.edu/about/history.html. Additional information for this section has been drawn from William D. Snider's

Notes—Chapter Two

Light on the Hill: A History of the University of North Carolina at Chapel Hill (Chapel Hill: University of North Carolina, 1992) and *True and Candid Compositions: The Lives and Writings of Antebellum Students at the University of North Carolina* (http://docsouth.unc.edu/true/chapter/chp02-01/chp02-01.html).

46. "Catalog of the Philanthropic Society" http://docsouth.unc.edu/true/philanthropic/philanthropic.html

47. http://docsouth.unc.edu/true/chapter/chp03-01/chp03-01.html; information for this section has been drawn largely from Erika Lindermann's "Overview: 1830–1839" and "The School Day and the School Year" from *True and Candid Compositions: The Lives and Writings of Antebellum Students at the University of North Carolina.*

48. (http://docsouth.unc.edu/true/chapter/chp02-01/chp02-01.html).

49. Snider 52. Although an outspoken opponent of slavery, at the time of his death Gaston owned some 200 slaves. http://docsouth.unc.edu/browse/bios/pn0000574_bio.html

50. E.J. Steptoe to Nannie Steptoe, Special Collections, University of Washington Libraries, Accession #4908-1, Box #1, Folder #31.

Two. At West Point

1. Of his 32 extant letters to family members archived at the University of Washington, only this one is undated. A tentative date of 1837 has been attached to this letter, but internal evidence pertaining to the terms in office of congressmen and senators like George Poindexter of Mississippi (in office between October 15, 1830 and March 3, 1835) and George M. Bibb (Senator from Kentucky, 1829–1835) invalidates that assumption; moreover, Senator William Wilkins of Pennsylvania was to resign his seat on June 30, 1834 to serve as U.S. minister to Russia. Near the end of this letter Steptoe refers to his effort to gain information about "selections," and on that account I have made the assumption above.

2. In addition to internet sources for my commentary on Washington, DC, I have drawn on Constance McLaughlin Green's *Washington: Village and Capital, 1800–1878* (Princeton: Princeton University Press, 1962) and Joseph R. Passonneau's handsomely illustrated *Washington through Two Centuries* (New York: Monacelli Press, 2004).

3. Jon Meacham, *American Lion: Andrew Jackson in the White House* (New York: Random House, 2008), 245.

4. Charles M. Wiltse, *John C. Calhoun: Nullifier, 1829–1839* (Indianapolis: Bobbs-Merrill, 1949), 187.

5. Meacham 245.

6. Fleming 16. After graduating from Dartmouth, Thayer took just a year to complete his work at West Point, graduating in 1808, after which he spent two years in Paris studying military education at the engineering school, L'École Polytechnique.

7. For much of the information included in this chapter I have drawn on Stephen E. Ambrose's *Duty, Honor, Country: A History of West Point* (Baltimore: Johns Hopkins, 1966, 1999), Thomas J. Fleming's *West Point: The Men and Times of the United States Military Academy* (New York: William Morrow, 1969), and James L. Morrison, Jr.'s *"The Best School in the World": West Point, the Pre-Civil War Years, 1833–1866* (Kent, Ohio: Kent State University Press, 1986).

8. Matthew Arnold, "Literature and Science," *Norton Anthology of English Literature: The Victorian Age,* 8th ed. (New York: W.W. Norton, 2005), 1422.

9. Ambrose 73.

10. Ambrose 75.

11. Fleming 91.

12. E.J. Steptoe to Dr. William Steptoe, Special Collections, University of Washington Libraries, Accession #4908-0001, Box #1, Folder #3.

13. Morrison 49.

14. *Cadet Life Before the Mexican War,* Bulletin #1 (West Point: The Library, 1945): 6.

15. Theodore Crackel, *The Illustrated History of West Point* (New York: Harry N. Abrams, 1991), 102, 106, 129.

16. Morrison 70.

17. *Register of the Officers and Cadets of the U.S. Military Academy, 1834* and *1837.* http://digital-library.usma.edu/libmedia/archives/oroc/v1829.pdf

18. Morrison, Appendix One, 155–159.

19. Fleming 46; Morrison 71.

20. *Cadet Life* 12.

21. Fleming 92.

22. *Cadet Life Before the Mexican War,* 10.

23. Cullum initiated what is known as "Cullum's Register," which provides an index of USMA graduates dating from 1818, including class rank in "order of merit" and summaries of their military careers. Upwards of one thousand cadets graduate annually today, as compared to about fifty in Steptoe's day.

24. William Fraser, USMA Archives, Box #139.

25. John Pope, USMA Archives, Box #268.
26. Ibid.
27. E.J. Steptoe to Captain Henry Brown, Special Collections, University of Washington Libraries, Accession #4908-0001, Box #1, Folder #4.
28. Barbara Brown Eakley, *The Browns of Bedford County Virginia, 1748–1840*. Westminster, MD: Heritage Books, 1998. Brown mentions Edward in his will along with his other grandchildren.
29. Shelby Foote, *The Civil War, A Narrative: Red River to Appomattox* (New York: Random House, 1974), 203.
30. Jubal A. Early, "Autobiographical Sketch," *Memoirs* (New York: Konecky & Konecky, 1994), [viii].
31. *Cadet Life Before the Mexican War* 18, 19.
32. Jeremiah Mason Scarritt, USMA Archives, Box #286.
33. E.J. Steptoe to Dr. William Steptoe, Special Collections, University of Washington Libraries, Accession #4908-001, Box #1, Folder #5.
34. George Walton, *Fearless and Free: The Seminole Indian War, 1835–1842* (Indianapolis: Bobbs-Merrill, 1977), 37.
35. Eakley 56.
36. E.J. Steptoe to Dr. William Steptoe, Special Collections, University of Washington Libraries, Accession #4908-0001, Box #1, Folder #6.
37. Morrison 161–162; see also E.J. Steptoe to Dr. William Steptoe, Special Collections, University of Washington Libraries, Accession #4908-001, Box #1, Folder #6.
38. Morrison 98.
39. In a letter to his sister Nannie dated July 11, 1855, their cousin Tom refers to him as "Ned," but no evidence has surfaced to suggest he preferred that nickname.
40. Morrison 85.
41. E.J. Steptoe to Dr. William Steptoe, Special Collections, University of Washington Libraries, Accession #4908-001, Box #1, Folder #7.
42. "Chesterfield Railroad" http://en.wikipedia.org/wiki/Chesterfield_Railroad
43. James D. Dilts, *The Great Road: The Building of the Baltimore and Ohio, the Nation's First Railroad, 1828–1853* (Stanford: Stanford University Press, 1993), xvi–xvii.
44. Fleming 98.
45. Morrison 90.
46. Morrison 89.
47. Morrison 78.
48. Nearly forty years would pass between that renowned oration and Everett's speech at Gettysburg, then more generally acclaimed than President Lincoln's "address."
49. E.J. Steptoe to Dr. William Steptoe, Special Collections, University of Washington Libraries, Accession #4901-001, Box #1, Folder # 7a.
50. Ambrose 149.
51. E.J. Steptoe to William Steptoe, Jr., Special Collections, University of Washington Libraries, Accession #4908-001, Box #1, Folder #17.
52. *Cadet Life Before the Mexican War* 12. Steptoe's letter to William appears to be misdated January 10, 1842, and it was mailed from West Point, but other sources (including an item in the *Army and Navy Chronicle* for March 19, 1842) indicate he did not leave Florida until March of that year. Apparently the letter should be dated 1843.
53. E.J. Steptoe to Dr. William Steptoe, Special Collections, University of Washington Libraries, Accession #4908-001, Box #1, Folder #7a.
54. E.J. Steptoe to William Steptoe, Jr., Special Collections, University of Washington Libraries, Accession #4908-001, Box #1, Folder #9.
55. Among other places, the image appears in the front matter of B.F. Manring's *The Conquest of the Coeur d'Alenes, Spokanes and Palouses* (Spokane, WA: Inland Printing, 1912). Manring, was in contact with Steptoe's sister Nannie, who mentions in one letter her brother's disinclination to be photographed in uniform. The painting, on wood, is not dated and not attributed to any artist. It bears striking similarities to the photograph, which is in private hands. The name and address of a photographic studio in Philadelphia is inscribed on the back of the painting.

Three. In Florida: The Second Seminole War

1. John K. Mahon, *History of the Second Seminole War*, Revised Edition (Gainesville: University Press of Florida, 1992) 182. While I've relied on Mahon's account of the Seminole wars in this chapter, I have consulted several texts, including Joe Knetsch's *Florida's Seminole Wars: 1817–1858* and *Fear and Anxiety on the Florida Frontier*, Virginia Bergman Peters, *The Florida Wars* (1979), Edwin C. McReynolds' *The Seminoles* (1957), and James

Notes—Chapter Three

W. Covington's *The Seminoles of Florida* (1993). Army surgeon Jacob Rhett Motte's journal, written between 1836 and 1838 and published in 1953 as *Journey into the Wilderness* by the University Press of Florida provides often colorful observations presented with literary flair. John T. Sprague's *The Origin, Progress, and Conclusion of the Florida War* (1848; facsimile edition, Gainesville: University Press of Florida, 1964) is, as Mahon notes, "indispensable."

2. James Mason Scarritt, USMA Archives, Box #286.

3. Mahon 106, 104. See also Frank Laumer, *Dade's Last Command* (Gainesville: University Press of Florida, 1995), 241–243 and Mark F. Boyd's "Florida Aflame: The Background and Onset of the Seminole War, 1835," *Florida Historical Quarterly* 30.1 (July 1951), available in monograph form.

4. "Official Account of the Massacre of the United States Troops by the Indians." *New York Spectator.* January 27, 1836. http://www.fultonhistory.com/Fulton.html Newspaper journalism was a volatile business in the early nineteenth century, with gazettes often flourishing for just a few years before vanishing. David Shedden's chronology of Florida newspapers for the decade of the 1830s, when the territory boasted a population of around 35,000, lists more than twenty newspapers, only two or three of which, like St. Augustine's *Florida Herald* and the *Pensacola Gazette*, were to last for thirty or more years. Mahon accounts for six newspapers in the Florida Territory in 1835 (132).

5. Joe Knetsch, *Florida's Seminole Wars: 1817–1858* The Making of America Series. (Charleston, SC: Arcadia Publishing, 2003), 12, 13; *Fear and Anxiety on the Florida Frontier* (Dade City, FL: Seminole War Foundation, 2008), 227–228. Frank Laumer's account of the Dade Massacre, *Dade's Last Command* (1995) bears an epigraph from Grant Foreman's book, *Indian Removal* (1932): "The war in Florida was conducted largely as a slave-catching enterprise for the benefit of the citizens of Georgia and Florida."

6. Mahon 20.

7. Mahon 134; Charles C. Osborne, *Jubal: The Life and Times of General Jubal A. Early, CSA, Defender of the Lost Cause* (Chapel Hill: Algonquin, 1992) 19.

8. William Bartram, *Travels and Other Writings* (New York: Library of America, 1996), 43, 106.

9. Jacob Rhett Motte, *Journey into Wilderness: An Army Surgeon's Account of Life in Camp and Field during the Creek and Seminole Wars, 1836–1838*, Edited by James F. Sunderman (Gainesville: University Press of Florida, 1953), 192.

10. Augustus Porter Allen, USMA Archives, Box #11.

11. Most of E.J. Steptoe's extant personal correspondence is archived in the Special Collections at the University of Washington. All references to the personal letters pertain to Special Collections, University of Washington Libraries, Accession #4908-0001, Box #1. This letter is Folder #7a.

12. E.J. Steptoe to Nannie Steptoe, Special Collections, University of Washington Libraries, Accession #4908-0001, Box #1, Folder #10.

13. E.J. Steptoe to Kate (Mary Catherine) Steptoe, Special Collections, University of Washington Libraries, Accession #48908-0001, Box #1, Folder #11.

14. E.J. Steptoe to Nannie Steptoe, Special Collections, University of Washington Libraries, Accession #4908-0001, Box #1, Folder #12.

15. See Bernard Mayo, "Henry Clay, Patron and Idol of White Sulphur Springs: His Letters to James Calwell," *Virginia Magazine of History and Biography* 55.4 (October 1947): 301–317. http://www.jstor.org/stable/4245505?seq=15

16. E.J. Steptoe to Dr. William Steptoe, Special Collections, University of Washington Libraries, Accession #4908-0001, Box #1, Folder #18. See also Norbert Hirschhorn, Robert G. Feldman, and Ian A. Greaves, "Abraham Lincoln's Blue Pills," *Perspectives in Biology and Medicine* 44.3 (2001): 315–332.

17. Knetsch, *Florida's Seminole Wars* 88.

18. In a letter to the Adjutant General sent in the spring of 1842, Steptoe indicates he joined "the Florida army" in "the winter of '37" and had not received the full three-month leave normally granted upon graduation from West Point. E.J. Steptoe to Roger Jones, Letters to the Office of the Adjutant General, March 20 1842, M567.

19. Knetsch, *Florida's Seminole Wars* 101.

20. James W. Covington, *The Seminoles of Florida* (Gainesville: University Press of Florida, 1993), 90; Mahon 209. Harney (1800–1889) would command the Second Dragoons in the Mexican War and distinguish himself at Cerro Gordo, where Steptoe was brevetted to major, in mid-April of 1847. Brevetted to brigadier general after that engagement, Harney battled

Notes—Chapter Three

the Sioux in the early wars against the Plains Indians. He took command of the Department of Oregon about the time Steptoe left the Northwest in the spring of 1858. Offered a command by Robert E. Lee during the Civil War, Harney served in administrative positions, retiring in 1863. After the war he was involved in peace negotiations with the Plains tribes.

21. Garrison and Ship Cannons http://www.thepirateking.com/historical/cannon_garrison_and_ship_guns.htm
22. Arthur E. Francke, Jr., *Fort Mellon, 1837-1842: A Microcosm of the Second Seminole War* (Miami: Banyan Books, 1977), 67.
23. Motte 101.
24. Motte 96, 98.
25. Edward C. Coker and Daniel L. Schafer, "A West Point Graduate in the Second Seminole War: William Warren Chapman and the View from Fort Foster," *Florida Historical Quarterly* 68.4 (April 1990): 468.
26. Mahon 225-226.
27. *Florida Herald* http://ufdcweb1.uflib.ufl.edu/ufdc/UFDC.aspx?c=fdnl1
28. Coker and Shafer 467.
29. Mahon 206.
30. Sprague 81.
31. Mahon lists the number of captured at 2,900 with 100 killed (240); Covington puts the number of captured at 2,000 with as many as 400 killed (96); Knetsch in *Florida's Seminole Wars*, indicates that Jesup claimed "2,400 Seminoles and blacks had been removed from Florida, even though the official reports stated 2,104 at the end of 1839" (111).
32. McReynolds 171-173.
33. Peters 170, 173.
34. E.J. Steptoe to Roger Jones, Letters to the Office of the Adjutant General, September 17, 1838, National Archives, M567, #176.
35. Jubal A. Early, "Autobiographical Sketch," *The Memoirs of General Jubal A. Early* (New York: Konecky & Konecky, 1994) n.p.
36. Charles C. Osborne, *Jubal: The Life and Times of General Jubal A. Early, C.S.A., Defender of the Lost Cause* (Chapel Hill: Algonquin, 1992), 20-21.
37. Virginia Historical Society. Richmond, VA. MSS1Ea765670 Steptoe to Early.
38. Motte 165.
39. "Indian River Lagoon." http://en.wikipedia.org/wiki/Indian_River_Lagoon; http://www.floridaoceanographic.org/environ/Indian_River.htm
40. Motte 177.
41. Motte 176.

42. Motte 241.
43. Knetsch, *Fear and Anxiety* 128.
44. Knetsch, *Fear and Anxiety* 129.
45. *Returns from U.S. Military Posts, 1800-1916*. Film #1652, Reel #919.
46. Sprague 98.
47. Mahon 263.
48. E.J. Steptoe to Dr. William Steptoe, Special Collections, University of Washington Libraries, Accession #4908-001, Box #1, Folder #14.
49. Sprague 537. Sprague's appendix lists all of the dead, officers and enlisted men, from both action and disease, during the Second Seminole War, and he provides dates and locations.
50. Mahon 261-263; see also George Walton, *Fearless and Free: The Seminole Indian War, 1835-1842* (Indianapolis: Bobbs-Merrill, 1977), 202-203.
51. Mahon 265.
52. Mahon 276, 278.
53. K. Jack Bauer, *Zachary Taylor: Soldier, Planter, Statesman of the Old Southwest* (Baton Rouge: Louisiana State U, 1985) 94.
54. Knetsch, *Florida's Seminole Wars* 126. The poinsettia was named after Poinsett, who introduced the flower from Mexico, where he served as first U.S. minister.
55. Thomas Sherman, who graduated West Point the year before Steptoe, was promoted to major general during the Civil War, losing his right leg at the Siege of Port Hudson in 1863.
56. On Christmas Eve 1853 Major Taylor was swept overboard in the sinking of the steamer *San Francisco* which was transporting elements of the Third Artillery to California. Steptoe lost uniforms and other personal belongings in that disaster. Dr. Simons was wounded in action at El Molino del Rey before Chapultepec in 1847. Court martialed while on duty at Fort Riley in the Kansas Territory in 1851, he was later reinstated and served with distinction as U.S. Army Surgeon during the Civil War.
57. William T. Sherman, *Memoirs of General William T. Sherman*, 2d ed., Vol. I (New York: D. Appleton, 1904), 19.
58. John F. Marszalek, *Sherman: A Soldier's Passion for Order* (New York: Free Press, 1993), 34.
59. Stephen E. Ambrose, *Duty, Honor, Country: A History of West Point* (Baltimore: Johns Hopkins U, 1966), 156. Marszalek comments on Sherman's literary interests in his biography cited above.

Notes—Chapter Four

60. In a letter dated September 27, 1841, Steptoe mentions having encountered some pieces in *The Southern Literary Messenger* written by his brother William's former schoolmaster, George E. Dabney, who had served as principal of the New London Academy, one of Virginia's earliest secondary schools, beginning in 1837. See Alfred J. Morrison, *The Beginnings of Public Education in Virginia, 1776-1860* (Richmond: Virginia State Board of Education, 1917) 127. By 1841 Dabney was a professor at Washington College. Most early records of the New London Academy were destroyed when Union troops burned down the principal's house during the Civil War.
61. Sherman 19-22.
62. E.J. Steptoe to Roger Jones, Letters to the Office of the Adjutant General, February 17, 1841, May 31, 1841, September 7, 1841, National Archives, M567.
63. Mahon 286.
64. An entry in the *Army and Navy Chronicle*, 13.9 (March 19, 1842) indicates that Steptoe, along with Lieutenants E.O.C. Ord and R.C. Gatlin arrived at Charleston, South Carolina, via steamboat from Pilatka (Palatka), Florida, and Savannah, Georgia, on March 11, 1842: 137.
65. Knetsch, *Fear and Anxiety* 200.
66. E.J. Steptoe to Dr. William Steptoe, Special Collections, University of Washington Libraries, Accession #4908-001, Box #1, Folder #15.
67. Sprague 324.
68. Sherman 24.
69. Sprague 322.
70. Sprague 323. See also Joshua R. Giddings, *Exiles of Florida* (Columbus: Follett, Foster & Co., 1858) 306.
71. Susan A. Miller's *Coacoochee's Bones: A Seminole Saga* (Lawrence: University Press of Kansas, 2003) offers a thorough account of Coacoochee's life. At the end of 1845 he traveled to Texas on a peace mission to the Comanche, but in the summer of 1850 he joined free blacks ("maroons") and members of the Kickapoo tribe in Mexico, where he intended to establish an independent community. He died there of smallpox in January 1857.
72. Knetsch, *Fear and Anxiety* 199.
73. E.J. Steptoe to Dr. William Steptoe, Special Collections, University of Washington Libraries, Accession #4908-001, Box #1, Folder #16.
74. Knetsch, *Fear and Anxiety* 202. See *Returns from U.S. Military Posts, 1800-1916*, Film #1652, Reel #919.
75. Knetsch, *Fear and Anxiety* 203.
76. The Singleton Family Papers: 1759-1905. http://www.lib.unc.edu/mss/inv/s/Singleton_Family.html#d1e507
77. Sprague 556.
78. Mahon 309; Mahon uses figures from Sprague's *Origin, Progress and Conclusion of the Florida War*,.
79. E.J. Steptoe to William Steptoe, Jr., Special Collections, University of Washington Libraries, Accession #4908-001, Box #1, Folder #17.
80. E.J. Steptoe to Roger Jones, Letters to the Office of the Adjutant General, September 17, 1842, National Archives, M567.
81. Manring Archives, typescript of letter to Dr. William Steptoe in private hands dated January 12, 1845, mailed from St. Augustine the next day. EJ reports "My turpentine speculation advances very well" at the end of E.J. Steptoe to Dr. William Steptoe, Special Collections, University of Virginia, Accession #6515, Box #6506, mailed October 10, 1846, preparatory to sailing for Point Isabel, Texas.
82. E.J. Steptoe to Roger Jones, Letters to the Office of the Adjutant General, May 10, 1846, National Archives, M567.
83. E.J. Steptoe to Roger Jones, Letters to the Office of the Adjutant General, July 31, 1846, National Archives, M567.
84. Michael G. Schene, "Not a Shot Fired: Fort Chokonikla and the 'Indian War' of 1849-1850," *Tequesta* 37 (1977): 19-37.
85. Spessard Stone, "Fort Chokonikla." http://freepages.genealogy.rootsweb.ancestry.com/~crackerbarrel/Steptoe.html Getty (1819-1901) graduated in the West Point Class of 1840 and was brevetted to captain during the Mexican War. He rose to the rank of major general during the Civil War where his division led the breakthrough at the Battle of Petersburg and participated in the action leading to Lee's surrender at Appomattox.
86. Spessard Stone, "Billy Bowlegs: Seminole Chief." http://freepages.genealogy.rootsweb.ancestry.com/~crackerbarrel/Bowlegs3.html

Four. In Mexico

1. E.J. Steptoe to Roger Jones, Letters to the Office of the Adjutant General, Main Series (1822-1860). National Archives, M 567, Roll 392.
2. Lucius O'Brien, John T. Metcalfe (USMA 1838), Ripley A. Arnold (USMA 1838), et. Al, "Benny Havens, Oh!" http://www.west-point.

Notes—Chapter Four

org/greimanj/west_point/songs/bennyhavens.htm

3. In 1830 the War Department issued General Order #72, eliminating the whiskey ration and replacing it with a cash stipend. Galen R. Ewing, "'Bug Juice' Use and Abuse: Alcoholism in the Frontier Army" http://www.nps.gov/fosc/learn/education/guard alcoholism.htm

4. David A. Clary, *Eagles and Empire: The United States, Mexico, and the Struggle for a Continent* (New York: Bantam, 2009), 60. I have also consulted Justin H. Smith's two-volume classic, *The War with Mexico* (New York: Macmillan, 1919), K. Jack Bauer's *The Mexican War, 1846-1848* (New York: Macmillan, 1974), Joseph Wheelan's *Invading Mexico: America's Continental Dream and the Mexican War, 1846-1848* (New York: Carroll & Graf, 2007), and with respect to matters concerning combat conditions and statistics and the experiences of soldiers and junior officers, Richard Bruce Winders' *Mr. Polk's Army: The American Military Experience in the Mexican War* (College Station: Texas A&M University Press, 1997). Both Winders and Clary make extensive use of letters and journals of junior officers like George Gordon Meade, P.G.T. Beauregard, and George P. McClellan.

5. Bauer 17.
6. Clary 39.
7. Clary 20.
8. Wheelan 17.
9. Samuel Longfellow, *Life of Henry Wadsworth Longfellow* (Boston: Houghton Mifflin, 1891), 29. Text includes extracts from the journals and correspondence.
10. Ethan Allen Hitchcock, *Fifty Years in Camp and Field: Diary of Ethan Allen Hitchcock*. Edited by W.A. Croffut (New York: Putnam, 1909), 213, 214. Hitchcock (1798-1870), grandson of Revolutionary War General Ethan Allen of the Green Mountain Boys fame, graduated from West Point in 1817 and served with the Third Infantry Regiment in the Second Seminole War. He was brevetted at Contreras and Churubusco to full colonel and to brigadier general at Molino del Rey. As major general he served in administrative capacities during the Civil War.
11. See Francis F. McKinney, *Education in Violence: The Life of George H. Thomas and the History of the Army of the Cumberland* (Detroit: Wayne State University Press, 1961), 28. McKinney records a meeting between Thomas, Ringgold, Steptoe, and other junior officers at Fort McHenry in December 1843.

12. Bauer 57; Wheelan 138; Clary110-111.
13. Bauer 62.
14. Lester R. Dillon, Jr., *American Artillery in the Mexican War, 1846-1847* (Austin, TX: Presidial, 1975), 9-10. Colonel Dillon's small book provides a useful overview, including information on such matters as dimensions of cannon used, range, and purpose.
15. E.J. Steptoe to Ellen Wilkins Tompkins, Tompkins Family, Virginia Historical Society, Mss1. T5996 c 362-365.
16. Tompkins would be involved in iron manufacturing and coal mining until the Civil War erupted, at which time he served as colonel of the 22nd Virginia Infantry Regiment.
17. Unlike most of Steptoe's letters, which are archived in Special Collections at the University of Washington, this letter is included in a volume of Steptoe Family Correspondence at the University of Virginia Special Collections. Most of those letters were written by E.J.'s cousin, John Marshall Steptoe, who served with the Confederate army.
18. Wheelan offers a detailed and vivid account of the action at Monterrey (178-203).
19. Manring Archives, typescript evidently based on handwritten version supplied to B.F. Manring by Nannie Steptoe Eldridge, now in private hands, dated "Tampico Nov. 27" (the year provided by plausible conjecture). Letter is continued on December 2.
20. E.J. Steptoe to Dr. William Steptoe, Special Collections, University of Washington Libraries, Accession #4908-001, Box #1, Folder #19.
21. *Cullum's Register*. http://penelope.uchicago.edu/Thayer/E/Gazetteer/Places/America/United_States/Army/USMA/Cullums_Register/roll/S.html
22. Thomas W. Cutrer, ed., *The Mexican War Diary and Correspondence of George B. McClellan* (Baton Rouge: Louisiana State University Press, 2009), 18.
23. George Gordon Meade, *The Life and Letters of George Gordon Meade* (New York: Scribner's, 1913), 94.
24. Bauer 397; Clary suggests the "total strength of all United States Army forces probably never exceeded 50,000 at any one time" (131).
25. Cutrer 18.
26. Meade 91.
27. Nathaniel Cheairs Hughes, Jr. and Timothy D. Johns, eds., *A Fighter from Way Back: The Mexican War Diary of Lt. Daniel Harvey Hill, 4th Artillery, USA* (Kent, OH: Kent State University Press, 2002), 2, 3.

Notes—Chapter Four

28. Meade 175. In *Mr. Polk's Army* Richard Bruce Winders devotes considerable space to Polk's political generals and offers a table of "Generals of Volunteers, 1846–48," that includes Democrats Robert Patterson, Gideon J. Pillow, John Quitman, James Shields, and future president Franklin Pierce.
29. Meade 102.
30. Meade 194.
31. Meade 175, 177.
32. Meade 177–178.
33. Meade 178.
34. Smith, II 214.
35. E.J. Steptoe to Dr. William Steptoe, Special Collections, University of Washington Libraries, Accession #4908-001, Box #1, Folder #19.
36. Winders 121.
37. Winders 126.
38. Cutrer 65–66. McClellan later refers to Steptoe at the Battle of Cerro Gordo.
39. George Wilkins Kendall, *Dispatches from the Mexican War*, ed. Lawrence Delbert Cress (Norman: University of Oklahoma Press, 1999), 151.
40. Winders 44, 45. Patterson (1792–1881) was unceremoniously relieved of his command of Pennsylvania volunteers early in the Civil War.
41. Robert Anderson, *An Artillery Officer in the Mexican War, 1846-7* (New York: G.P. Putnam's Sons, 1911), 19. Anderson's often lengthy and detailed letters to his wife back in Florida are prefaced by his daughter, Eba Anderson Lawton. He mentions Steptoe several times in passing.
42. Corpus Christi Museum, "Henry Kinney." http://www.ccmuseumedres.com/tour.php?action=details&record=120; Bauer 32, 89.
43. Anderson 13.
44. J. Jacob Oswandel, *Notes of the Mexican War, 1846-1848* (Knoxville: University of Tennessee Press, 2010; originally published in 1885), 29.
45. E.J. Steptoe to Dr. William Steptoe, Special Collections, University of Washington Libraries, Accession #4908-001, Box #1, Folder #20.
46. Oswandel ix. Professor Johnson draws attention to the phrase "gallant little army" in his introduction to the recent reprint of the journal.
47. George Winston Smith and Charles Judah, Eds., *Chronicles of the Gringos: The U.S. Army in the Mexican War, 1846-1848, Accounts of Eyewitnesses & Combatants* (Albuquerque: University of New Mexico press, 1968), 172.
48. E.J. Steptoe to Dr. William Steptoe, Special Collections, University of Washington Libraries, Accession #4908-001, Box #1, Folder #21.
49. Clary 129; Winders 39–40; Bauer 75.
50. Smith, I 361. Discharged from the army at the war's end in 1848, Pillow emerged in 1861 as a brigadier general for the Confederacy. He is often blamed for the defeat at the Battle of Fort Donelson in February 1862 at the hands of a Union general who was a lieutenant during the Mexican War, Ulysses S. Grant.
51. Kendall 427.
52. Cutrer 65.
53. E.J. Steptoe to Dr. William Steptoe, Special Collections, University of Washington Libraries, Accession #4908-001, Box #1, Folder #21.
54. Smith and Judah 174–175.
55. Anderson 18.
56. McClellan 67–68.
57. McClellan 70.
58. McClellan 73.
59. Wheelan xiii–xix; Clary 293.
60. Wheelan xiii.
61. Anderson 74.
62. Bauer 242; his map on page 243 is valuable here, as are his maps throughout.
63. Hill 73.
64. Hill 88.
65. Hill 78.
66. Figures are taken from the *Ordnance Manual of 1841* as cited by Dillon 11–14.
67. Hill 77.
68. Hill 80. Twiggs (1790–1862) served in the War of 1812, the Black Hawk War, and the Seminole Wars. He served briefly as a major general with the Confederacy commanding the Department of Louisiana. He died of pneumonia before the war ended.
69. Hill 82.
70. Bauer 217.
71. Hill 84.
72. Wheelan 316.
73. Bauer 252.
74. Clary 303.
75. Hill 86.
76. Hill 88.
77. E.J. Steptoe to Dr. William Steptoe, Special Collections, University of Washington Libraries, Accession #4908-001, Box #1, Folder #22.
78. Anderson 115.
79. Hill 91.
80. McClellan 121.
81. Clary 311; Bauer 262.

82. Oswandel 56.
83. Hitchcock 250.
84. Oswandel 56.
85. Richard McSherry, *El Puchero, or A Mixed Dish from Mexico* (Philadelphia: Lippincott, 1850), 37, 38. McSherry's reminiscences are organized as 45 letters.
86. Winfield Scott, *Memoirs* (New York: Sheldon, 1864), 445–446.
87. Bauer 265.
88. Bauer 268.
89. Oswandel 118.
90. "The Girl I Left Behind." http://en.wikipedia.org/wiki/The_Girl_I_Left_Behind
91. Allan Peskin, ed., *Volunteers: The Mexican War Journals of Private Richard Coulter and Sergeant Thomas Barclay, Company E, Second Pennsylvania Infantry* (Kent, OH: Kent State University Press, 1991), 86.
92. Smith and Judah 221.
93. Oswandel 87.
94. Hitchcock 257.
95. Bauer 271.
96. Oswandel 87.
97. Kendall 315.
98. McSherry 64.
99. Peskin 180–181.
100. Clary 355; Wheelan 359.
101. Bauer 311 (quoting Lt. Col. Ethan Allen Hitchcock).
102. Anderson 326.
103. McSherry 105.
104. T. Harry Williams, ed., *With Beauregard in Mexico: The Mexican War Reminiscences of P.G.T. Beauregard* (Baton Rouge: Louisiana State University Press, 1965), 74.
105. Williams 5.
106. Williams 96.
107. Dillon 49.
108. Winfield Scott, *Memoirs*, I (New York: Sheldon, 1864), 510.
109. Scott 510, 513.
110. Kendall 410–411.
111. Dillon 58.
112. Hill 125–126.
113. Bauer 321.
114. McSherry 110.
115. McSherry 112, 113.
116. Williams 100.
117. Bauer 331. Lane (1801–1881) served as governor of the Oregon Territory and as senator when Oregon became a state in 1859. A pro-slavery secessionist, he ran for vice president with John C. Breckenridge as a Southern Democrat in 1860.
118. Hill 131.
119. Hill 151.
120. Hill 150.
121. Oswandel 244.
122. "The Mexican-American War and the Media, 1845–1848. http://www.history.vt.edu/MxAmWar/Newspapers/Niles/Nilesk1848.htm#74.004February261848Gen.Winfield
123. NNR 74.017–018.
124. Isaac Ingalls Stevens, *Campaigns of the Rio Grande and Mexico* (New York: D. Appleton, 1851), 107. Stevens (1818–1862) graduated at the top of his West Point class in 1839. As a brigadier general at the Battle of Chantilly on September 1, 1862, he was killed while waving the colors of his old regiment, the 79th New York Volunteers. Leading the Confederate troops that day was fellow West Point graduate (Class of 1846) and Mexican War veteran Stonewall Jackson.
125. Anderson 237.
126. E.J. Steptoe to Roger Jones, Letters to the Office of the Adjutant General, National Archives, M 567, Roll 392.
127. Oswandel 74.
128. E.J. Steptoe to Roger Jones, Letters to the Office of the Adjutant General, National Archives, M 567, Roll 392.
129. E.J. Steptoe to Roger Jones, Letters to the Office of the Adjutant General, National Archives, M 567, Roll 392.
130. "Abstracts of Steptoe Wills & Deeds Recorded in Bedford County, 1848–1895. http://files.usgovarchives.net/va/bedford/slaveabs/ss10005.tx
131. E.J. Steptoe to Roger Jones, Letters to the Office of the Adjutant General, National Archives, M 567, Roll 392.
132. Fort Adams. http://en.wikipedia.org/wiki/Fort_Adams; *Cullum's Register*. http://penelope.uchicago.edu/Thayer/E/Gazetteer/Places/America/United_States/Army/USMA/Cullums_Register/924*.html

Five. The Gunnison Affair

1. *Cullum's Register*, Vol. I, #924: 689. Steptoe received new orders on April 1, 1854 sending him to the western frontier to escort a shipment of horses and mules to Fort Benicia, California; he left Fort Leavenworth in Kansas Territory at the end of May.
2. *New York Times*, Vol. 3, #688, December 1, 1853: 1. Microfilm.
3. H.H. Bancroft, *History of Utah, The Works of Hubert Howe Bancroft*, Vol. 26 (San Francisco: History Company, 1889), 470. See Robert Kent Fielding's *The Unsolicited Chronicler: An Account of the Gunnison Massacre*

Notes—Chapter Five

(Brookline, MA: Paradigm, 1993), which runs more than 470 pages and examines the context in detail. The phrase "unsolicited chronicler" refers to Gunnison, whose 1852 account of the Mormons, presumably intended to be objective, was "unsolicited" and widely resented. Also valuable, particularly for Steptoe's role, is David Henry Miller's unpublished Master of Arts thesis from the University of Utah, "The Impact of the Gunnison Massacre on Mormon-Federal Relations: Edward Jenner Steptoe's Command in Utah Territory, 1854-1855" (June 1968). I am indebted to historian Will Bagley for directing my attention to Josiah Gibbs' account published in the *Utah Historical Quarterly* 1.3 (July 1928) as "Gunnison Massacre—1853—Millard County, Utah—Indian Mareer's Version of the Tragedy—1894": 71-75. Mr. Bagley generously provided me with a copy of pertinent portions of Captain Robert M. Morris's "Journal of an Overland Trip to California and Other Army Assignments, 1849-1853" from the Yale Beinecke Library, WA MSS S-1738, in which Captain Morris indicates that Gunnison suffered "fifteen arrow wounds and had his left arm cut off. His heart was either cut out or eaten out by wolves during the previous night. I am inclined to believe the former" (5).

4. Fielding 149, 151. Beckwith (1818-1881) survived the massacre because his unit was split off from Gunnison's. An 1842 graduate of West Point and a Mexican War veteran, Beckwith served during the Civil War mostly as provost marshal and commissary officer in New Orleans. He was brevetted to brigadier general at the war's end.

5. Fielding 146.

6. Fielding 146, 148. The Pahvants band is variously spelled (Pavants, Parvants); the Utes are also known as Utahs.

7. Fielding 150.

8. Bancroft 471.

9. Robert M. Utley, *Frontiersman in Blue: The United States Army and the Indian, 1848-1865* (New York: Macmillan, 1967), 56; Secretary of War, *Annual Report* (1851): 113.

10. Virginia McConnell Simmons, *The Ute Indians of Utah, Colorado, and New Mexico* (Boulder: University Press of Colorado, 2000), 92. A replica of Fort Utah stands on 120 N 2050 West.

11. Bancroft 472-473.

12. Miller 33-40.

13. Fielding 84.

14. The Maritime Heritage Project. "SS San Francisco." http://www.maritimeheritage.org/ships/sssSanFrancisco.htm; see also, Carl C. Cutler, *Queens of the Western Ocean* (Annapolis, MD: U.S. Naval Institute, 1961), 294 and William Armstrong Fairburn, *Merchant Sail*, ed. Ethel M Richie (Center Lovell, ME: Fairburn Marine Educational Foundation, 1955): III, 1961-1962. See also http://www.sfgenealogy.com/californiabound/cb150.htm for accounts from the *New York Daily Times*, January through February 1854.

15. Fielding 212. Facsimile of Steptoe's orders from the Adjutant General.

16. E.J. Steptoe to Samuel Cooper, Letters to the Office of the Adjutant General, May 29, 1854, National Archives, M567, Roll 505. Allston (1833-1900) graduated from West Point in 1853. A South Carolina native, he served in the Civil War as a colonel in the Fourth Alabama Infantry. After the war he became an Episcopalian clergyman. Mowry (1830-1871) was active in mining and politics in the Arizona Territory. He died in London, England.

17. During the Civil War Ingalls (1818-1893) served as Chief Quartermaster for the Army of the Potomac; in 1882 he was named Quartermaster General of the U.S. Army.

18. "Report of the Trip with Colonel Steptoe from Ft. Leavenworth to Salt Lake, June 1st to August 31st, 1854, and a Trip to California, June 14, 1855. House ex. doc.—[United States], 34th Cong., 1st sess., no. 1; Western Americana, frontier history of the trans-Mississippi West, 1550-1900, reel 567, no. 5840. Pp. 152-168. Cited as "Ingalls." Also available in David A. White's *News of the Plains and Rockies, 1803-1865*, Volume 5 (Spokane, WA: Arthur H. Clark, 1998): 275-302. Cited as "White."

19. Fielding 218.

20. Ingalls 154.

21. E.J. Steptoe to Samuel Cooper, Letters to the Office of the Adjutant General, June 30, 1854, National Archives, M567, Roll 505; White 277.

22. Utley 40-41.

23. William Antes, *Recollections of an Old Soldier* (New Haven: Yale University Press, Beinecke Rare Book and manuscript Library, 18—?) 6. WA MSS S-2898. Available online. The handwritten account concludes with the end of Antes' career in the army in 1867. Antes accompanied Lieutenant Mowry taking the southern route to Fort Tejon, California. Only the first 23 pages concern the Steptoe Expedition to Utah Territory.

24. Antes 7-8.

25. Antes 13. Antes errs later in his account

Notes—Chapter Five

when he claims Lieutenant Mowry acted as judge at the trial of the Gunnison killers and asserts nine were found guilty and hanged "without delay" (20).
26. Ingalls 155.
27. Ingalls 158.
28. White 277.
29. E.J. Steptoe to Samuel Cooper, Letters to the Office of the Adjutant General, August 30, 1854, National Archives, M567, Roll 505.
30. Howard Stansbury, *Exploration of the Valley of the Great Salt Lake* (Washington, DC: Smithsonian Institution, 1988) 131.
31. Fielding 10. Ronald W. Walker, however, maintains the "influential book ... attempted to navigate the usual extremes of the time, Mormon polemics and gentile censure." See "President Young Writes to Jefferson Davis about the Gunnison Massacre Affair," *BYU Studies* 35.1 (1995) 147.
32. John W. Gunnison *The Mormons, or Latter-Day Saints, in the Valley of the Great Salt Lake: A Short History of Their Rise and Progress, Peculiar Doctrines, Present Condition, and Prospects* (Philadelphia: J.B. Lippincott, 1857): 74, 75.
33. Gunnison 80.
34. Gunnison 83–84.
35. Gunnison 141.
36. Gunnison 70.
37. Gunnison 72.
38. Howard Stansbury, *Exploration of the Valley of the Great Salt Lake* (Washington, DC: Smithsonian Institution, 1988) 143. Originally published in 1852 as a congressional document, Stansbury's report, according to Don D. Fowler's introduction to the 1988 reprint, "became immediately popular and was reprinted several times in the following years" (xii).
39. *The Deseret News*, 5.2 (March 21, 1855): [4].
40. "Biography of Col. Steptoe," *New York Evening Post*, Vol. 53, December 20, 1854.
41. Miller 134.
42. Fielding 220.
43. Fielding 221.
44. Sylvester Mowry Letters: Salt Lake City, Utah, to Edward J. Bicknall, Providence, Rhode Island. Manuscript (MS 23526), Church History Library, Salt lake City, UT; see also, Leonard J. Arrington, *Brigham Young: American Moses* (New York: Alfred A. Knopf, 1985): 246. All three letters appear with some deletions in William Mulder and A. Russell Mortensen, Eds., *Among the Mormons: Historic Accounts by Contemporary Observers* (New York: Knopf, 1958) 272–278.

45. Seth Millington Blair, Reminiscences and Journals, 1851–1868. MS 710, Folder 1, LDS Archives. Quoted in Will Bagley, *Blood of the Prophets: Brigham Young and the Massacre at Mountain Meadows* (Norman: University of Oklahoma Press, 2002) 45.
46. Albert Carrington, "Inconsistent Conduct of the United States Toward Her Territories," *The Deseret News* 4.52 (March 8, 1855): [3].
47. Miller 121.
48. Miller 122.
49. Carrington [3].
50. E.J. Steptoe to Samuel Cooper, Letters to the Office of the Adjutant General, September 14, 1854, National Archives, M567, Roll 508.
51. Miller 164.
52. Miller 163.
53. E.J. Steptoe to Samuel Cooper, Letters to the Office of the Adjutant General, October 4, 1854, National Archives, M567, Roll 506.
54. Kinney (1816–1902), born in New York, served seven years on the Iowa Supreme Court before Pierce appointed him Chief Justice in the Utah Territory. He pursued business interests in Salt Lake City.
55. E.J. Steptoe to Samuel Cooper, Letters to the Office of the Adjutant General, November 10, 1854, National Archives, M567, Roll 506.
56. Miller 167.
57. E.J. Steptoe to Samuel Cooper, Letters to the Office of the Adjutant General, November 20, 1854, National Archives, M567, Roll 506.
58. Susa Young Gates and Leah D. Widtsoe, *The Life Story of Brigham Young* (New York: Macmillan, 1930): 169. Gates (one of Young's daughters) and Widtsoe print the entire petition in their biography. See also Norman F. Furniss, *The Mormon Conflict: 1850–1859* (New Haven: Yale University Press, 1960): 43.
59. Miller 123; Arrington 247.
60. Jules Rémy, *A Journey to Great-Salt-Lake City*, Vol. One (London: W. Jeffs, 1861) 190.
61. Hosea Stout, Diary; quoted in Fielding 236.
62. Miller 127.
63. Andrew Love, "Journal," Typescript in Special Collections, Brigham Young University Library, 45.
64. Love 41.
65. E.J. Steptoe to Samuel Cooper, Letters to the Office of the Adjutant General, February 1, 1855, National Archives, M567, Roll 526.
66. E.J. Steptoe to Samuel Cooper, Letters

Notes—Chapter Five

to the Office of the Adjutant General, February 24, 1855, National Archives, M567, Roll 526. An 1841 graduate of West Point, Reynolds (1820–1863) was brevetted to major at the Battle of Buena Vista. He served in the Rogue River War in the Oregon Territory (1856) and on the Utah Expedition in 1858. Leading his troops as major general of Pennsylvania volunteers, he was killed on July 1st at Gettysburg.
67. Fielding 256.
68. Miller 170.
69. Fielding 256.
70. Miller 175.
71. In *The Story of the Mormons: From the Date of Their Origin to the Year 1901* (New York: Macmillan, 1902), journalist William Alexander Linn cites Beadle, but labels C[atherine] Waite's account in *The Mormon Prophet and His Harem*, 5th ed., rev. (Philadelphia: Zeigler , McCurdy, 1867) "circumstantial" (469).
72. J. H. Beadle, *Life in Utah; or, the Mysteries and Crimes of Mormonism* (Philadelphia: National Publishing, 1870) 171, 197. Beadle studied law at the state university of Michigan and practiced for a year in his native Indiana before spending eight years in the West.
73. Miller 176.
74. Love 43.
75. Miller 177.
76. Love 44.
77. Miller 178–180.
78. Love 45.
79. John F. Kinney, Conversation with Governor Brigham Young, July 10, 1855. Federal and Local Government Files, Brigham Young Office Files, 1832–1878, Church History Library, The Church of Jesus Christ of Latter-day Saints, Salt Lake City, UT. I am grateful to reference librarian Marie Erickson for helping me gain access to this conversation as transcribed by David O. Calder, later treasurer of the Utah Territory and managing editor of *The Deseret News*.
80. Waite 39.
81. Waite 40.
82. Norman F. Furniss, *The Mormon Conflict: 1850–1859* (New Haven: Yale, 1960): 54, 232, 248.
83. Fielding 258; Miller 181.
84. Miller 181; Fielding 261.
85. Miller 188.
86. Fielding 267.
87. E.J. Steptoe to Samuel Cooper, Letters to the Office of the Adjutant General, April 15, 1855, National Archives, M567, Roll 527.

88. *New York Daily Times*, March 28, 1855, page 1, microfilm.
89. Ronald W. Walker, "President Young Writes Jefferson Davis about the Gunnison Massacre Affair," *BYU Studies* 35.1 (1995): 146–170.
90. Walker 157.
91. Walker 158.
92. Kurt R. Nelson, *Fighting for Paradise: A Military History of the Pacific Northwest* (Yardley, PA: Westholme, 2007): 134.
93. E.J. Steptoe to Samuel Cooper, Letters to the Office of the Adjutant General, April 25, 1855, National Archives, M567, Roll 527.
94. E.J. Steptoe to William L. Marcy, Special Collections, University of Washington Libraries, Accession #4908-001, Box #1, Folder #23.
95. Fielding 239–240.
96. E.J. Steptoe to Franklin Pierce, Special Collections, University of Washington Libraries, Accession #4908-001, Box #1, Folder #23.
97. Gunnison 155.
98. Gunnison 156, 164.
99. Gunnison 165.
100. Letter to William Bicknall, quoted in Fielding 277.
101. Fielding 276.
102. Fielding 279.
103. Fielding 278, 279 citing one Samuel Hawthornwaite, otherwise not identified; see also William P. MacKinnon, ed., *At Sword's Point, Part One* (Norman, OK: Arthur H. Clark, 2008): 49.
104. Fielding 280.
105. Fielding 290.
106. Lynn R. Bailey, ed., "Lt. Sylvester Mowry's Report on His March in 1855 from Salt Lake City to Fort Tejon," *Arizona and the West* 7.4 (Winter 1965): 338.
107. Bailey 343–344.
108. E.J. Steptoe to Dr. William Steptoe, Special Collections, University of Washington Libraries, Accession #4908-001, Box #1, Folder #24.
109. Ingalls 161.
110. Ingalls 162.
111. Nelson 94.
112. Edward J. Steptoe, Letter of Recommendation for O.P. Rockwell, Special Collections, Brigham Young University Library, Manuscript 3434, Item 11.
113. Rockwell (1813–1878) has been the subject of numerous books, including a four-volume biographical novel, and a few films. The made-for-TV movie, *The Avenging Angel*

(1995) starring James Coburn as Rockwell rates more highly than the 1994 film, *Rockwell*, starring Randy Gleave. There is also a 2010 documentary produced under the aegis of the LDS, *Stories from the Life of Porter Rockwell*.

114. Harold Schindler, *Orrin Porter Rockwell: Man of God, Son of Thunder*, 2nd ed. (Salt Lake City: University of Utah Press, 1983): ix.

115. Ingalls 166.

116. Ingalls 167.

117. Ingalls 167–168.

118. Furniss 67.

119. Will Bagley, *Blood of the Prophets: Brigham Young and the Mountain Meadows Massacre* (Norman: University of Oklahoma Press, 2002) 73.

120. In an essay published in the *Journal of Mormon History* 33.1 (Spring 2007) 121–178, William P. MacKinnon connects the Mountain Meadows Massacre and other atrocities with the Utah Expedition, challenging the "persistent myth" that the confrontation was "bloodless" (122).

121. Information for this section has been drawn largely from books by Walker, Turley, and Leonard and by Furniss, cited above, and from Bancroft's *History of Utah* (543–571).

122. William P. MacKinnon, "Sex, Subalterns, and Steptoe: Army Behavior, Mormon Rage, and Utah War Anxieties," *Utah Historical Quarterly* 76.3 (Summer 2008): 228.

123. Miller 199.

124. Dr. William Steptoe to William Steptoe, Junior, Special Collections, University of Washington Libraries, Accession #4908-001, Box #!, Folder #41.

Six. In the Washington Territory

1. Fort Monroe. http://en.wikipedia.org/wiki/Fort_Monroe

2. E.J. Steptoe to Dr. William Steptoe, October 9, 1855, Special Collections, University of Washington Libraries, Accession #4908-001, Box #1, Folder #25.

3. Philip H. Sheridan, *Indian Fighting in the Fifties in Oregon and Washington Territories* Fairfield, WA: Ye Galleon Press, 1987): 40. Excerpted from *Personal Memoirs*.

4. Peter A. Wallner, *Franklin Pierce: New Hampshire's Favorite Son* (Concord, NH: Plaidswede, 2004): 223–225. Wallner cites letters found in the Pierce Papers. "Prince John" Magurder, as he was sometimes called, graduated West Point in 1830, served in the Second Seminole War, and like Steptoe was brevetted to major and lieutenant colonel at Cerro Gordo and Chapultepec respectively. He served as major general of the Confederacy during the Civil War and later in Mexico under Emperor Maximilian.

5. E.J. Steptoe to Samuel Cooper, Letters to the Office of the Adjutant General, October 11, 1855, National Archives, M567, Roll 527.

6. Lieutenant Lawrence Kip, *The Indian War in the Pacific Northwest* (Lincoln: University of Nebraska Press, 1999): 17. Originally entitled *Army Life on the Pacific* (New York: Redfield, 1859), this edition comes with an introduction by historian Clifford E. Trafzer.

7. Jewel Lansing, *Portland: People, Politics, and Power, 1851–2001* (Corvallis: Oregon State University Press, 2003): 6.

8. William Dietrich, *Northwest Passage: The Great Columbia River* (New York: Simon & Schuster, 1995): 47, 46.

9. Kurt R. Nelson, *Fighting for Paradise: A Military History of the Pacific Northwest* (Yardley, PA: Westholme, 2007): xi.

10. Robert Ignatius Burns, S.J., *The Jesuits and the Indian Wars of the Northwest* (New Haven: Yale University Press, 1966): 63. In addition to this study and to Nelson's book, mentioned above, I have drawn on Frances Fuller Victor's *The Early Indian Wars of Oregon* (Salem: Frank C. Baker, 1894), which deals with Oregon state archival materials, Robert M. Utley's *Frontiersman in Blue* (New York: Macmillan 1967), and Waldo E. Rosebush's *Frontier Steel: The Men and Their Weapons* (Appleton, WA: C.C. Nelson, 1958), published for the Eastern Washington State Historical Society.

11. Carlos A. Schwantes, *The Pacific Northwest: An Interpretive History* (Lincoln: University of Nebraska Press, 1989): 86.

12. Utley 94.

13. Burns 158.

14. Utley 21.

15. Nelson 93.

16. Utley 178.

17. Utley 178.

18. Burns 68–69.

19. Nelson 88. The tribe prefers the medial [a], but the city and county use medial [i], as do many historical citations.

20. Richard D. Scheuerman and Michael O. Finley, *Finding Chief Kamiakin: The Life and Legacy of a Northwest Patriot* (Pullman: Washington State University Press, 2008): 36–37. See also A.J. Splawn's *Ka-mi-akin: The Last

Notes—Chapter Six

Hero of the Yakimas (Portland. OR: Binford & Mort, 1944). Splawn came of age in the Yakama country, where he was a cattleman from the early 1860s until his death in 1917; his accounts are based partly on conversations with tribal leaders, including Lokout.

21. Hazard Stevens, *The Life of Isaac Ingalls Stevens*, II (Boston: Houghton, Mifflin, 1901): 38. Hazard Stevens (1842–1918) was wounded at the Battle of Chantilly (September 1, 1862), where his father, then a Union general, was killed in action. Captain Stevens was awarded the Medal of Honor for gallantry in the Battle of Fort Huger, Virginia, on April 19, 1863. His two-volume biography was published in 1901.

22. Scheuerman and Finley, 19, 20.

23. Scheuerman and Finley 25.

24. B[enjamin] F[ranklin] Manring provides the full text of the controversial treaty in *The Conquest of the Coeur d'Alenes, Spokanes and Palouses* (Spokane: John W. Graham, 1912): 32–42.

25. Manring 32.

26. Scheuerman and Finley 37, 44 and Utley (180n) point out the Klickitat were not represented but Kamiakin was considered "head chief" of that and of other tribes as noted.

27. Utley 187.

28. Nelson 96–97. Haller (1819–1897) participated in the Second Seminole War and served with distinction in the Mexican War. Charged with disloyalty after the Battle of Fredericksburg, Colonel Haller was dismissed from the service in 1863. After the war he became a prominent businessman and industrialist in Seattle. A court of inquiry exonerated him of all charges in 1873.

29. Kip 150–152; Scheuerman and Finley 48–49.

30. Victor 430.

31. Alvin Josephy, Jr., *The Nez Perce Indians and the Opening of the Northwest* (Boston: Houghton Mifflin, 1965, 1997): 359. A Princeton University and Dickinson College graduate, Kelly (1819–1903) practiced law in Pennsylvania before joining in the California gold rush. He built a prosperous law practice in Oregon City and after the Indian wars served in the U.S. Senate and later as Chief Justice of the Oregon Supreme Court.

32. Sheridan 53.

33. *The Journals of the Lewis and Clark Expedition*. http://lewisandclarkjournals.unl.edu/read/?_xmlsrc=1805-10-30.xml&_xslsrc=LCstyles.xsl.

34. Frances Fuller Victor, *The Early Indian Wars of Oregon* (Salem, OR: Frank C. Baker State Printer, 1894): 459.

35. Nelson 122.

36. Victor 461.

37. Sheridan 55.

38. Victor 468.

39. One of the original 1856 blockhouses has been preserved, and the commandant's house and three officers' quarters have been restored. The state park is located about thirty miles southwest of Yakima on the Yakama Reservation. Garnett was killed in action serving as a brigadier general for the Confederacy the first summer of the Civil War.

40. Burns 142.

41. Victor 475.

42. Clifford E. Trafzer and Richard D. Scheuerman, *Renegade Tribe: The Palouse Indians and the Invasion of the Inland Pacific Northwest* (Pullman: Washington State University Press, 1986): 72.

43. Colonel George Wright on the Yakima River, Kittitas Valley, Washington Territory to Major W.W. Mackall, July 18, 1856. 36th Congress, 3rd Session, Senate Executive Documents, Number 5, Volume 2, p. 178.

44. Burns 126.

45. Priscilla Knuth, *"Picturesque" Frontier: The Army's Fort Dalles*, 2nd ed. (Portland: Oregon Historical Society, 1968, 1987): 6.

46. Kip 23.

47. Knuth 11; cited from Mowry's letter to his brother Charles, dated September 16, 1853.

48. Knuth 30, 100n. Before the Civil War, Jordan (1819–1895) was involved in espionage for the South. Promoted to brigadier general after the Battle of Shiloh, he later served under General Beauregard and General Braxton Bragg. In 1869 he commanded the Cuban Liberation Army (known as the Mambi) fighting for independence from Spain.

49. Knuth 45.

50. Kip 24.

51. Knuth 56. The only building to survive is the relatively simple Surgeon's Quarters, now maintained by the Wasco County-The Dalles City Museum Commission.

52. E.J. Steptoe to Dr. William Steptoe, Special Collections, University of Washington Libraries, Accession # 4908-001, Box #1, Folder #26.

53. Quoted in Rosebush 198.

54. Hazard Stevens, *The Life of Isaac Ingalls Stevens*, II (Boston: Houghton Mifflin, 1901): 33.

55. "John E. Wool." http://en.wikipedia.org/wiki/John_E._Wool; see also Burns 129.

Notes—Chapter Six

56. Cited by Hazard Stevens 178–179.
57. Stevens 183.
58. Kent D. Richards, *Isaac I. Stevens: Young Man in a Hurry* (Salt Lake City: Brigham Young University Press, 1979): 298; Nelson, 126.
59. General John Wool, at Benicia, CA, to Colonel L. Thomas, Assistant Adjutant General, Headquarters of the Army, New York City. August 19, 1856. 36th Congress, 3rd Session, Senate Executive Documents, Number 5, Volume 2, page 180.
60. Stevens 206–231; Burns 150, 146.
61. J.S. Whiting, *Forts of the State of Washington*, 2nd ed. (Seattle: self-published, 1951): 117–119.
62. Stevens 207.
63. Richards 303.
64. Rosebush 196; Nelson 127–128.
65. Splawn 80.
66. Utley 198.
67. Stevens 212.
68. Stevens 213.
69. Josephy 373.
70. Stevens 215.
71. Stevens 215–216; Richards 304.
72. Richards 305.
73. Robert H. Ruby and John A Brown, *The Cayuse Indians: Imperial Tribesmen of Old Oregon* (Norman: University of Oklahoma Press, 1972, 2005): 247.
74. Edward J. Steptoe to George Wright, September 18, 1956. 36th Congress, 3rd Session, Senate Executive Documents, Number 5, Volume 2, page 198. Steptoe adds that he thought the Indians regarded them as "sincere and well-meaning friends."
75. Richards 305–306.
76. Splawn 80.
77. Ruby and Brown 249; Splawn 81.
78. Stevens 220; Josephy 375; Ruby and Brown 248; Scheuerman and Finley 65, et al.
79. Stevens 223; Josephy 376; Ruby and Brown 252; Scheuerman and Finley 65, et al. 36th Congress, 3rd Session, Senate Executive Documents, Number 5, Volume 2, page 200.
80. George Wright to W.W. Mackall. October 2, 1856. 36th Congress, 3rd Session, Senate Executive Documents, Number 5, Volume 2, page 197.
81. Eugène de Girardin, "Tour of the Badlands," *Le Tour du Monde* (1864) http://projetgirardin.free.fr/PAGES/BADLANDS5-5.htm See also, Robert A. Bennett, *Walla Walla: Portrait of a Western Town, 1804–1899* (Walla Walla: Pioneer Press, 1980): 41.
82. Returns from U.S. Military Posts, 1800–1916, M-617, Fort Walla Walla, WA, August 1856–May 1867, Reel 1343.
83. Nelson 129.
84. Rosebush 202; Victor 483. See also Nelson 129–130 and Richard 307.
85. Splawn 82.
86. Stevens 226.
87. E.J. Steptoe to Nannie Steptoe, October 27, 1856, Special Collections, University of Washington Libraries, Accession #4908-001, Box #1, Folder #27.
88. William Steptoe, Jr. (1828–1889) served in Company G, "Radford's Rangers" in the Second Virginia Cavalry, raised in Lynchburg by Edward's former West Point classmate, Jubal A. Early. The unit participated in key battles in the east, from First Manassas through Appomattox, including Antietam and Gettysburg. Twice wounded, William was promoted to sergeant major for gallantry and rose to the rank of captain. Colonel Radford's second wife, Frances Callaway Steptoe, was William's first cousin. http://civilwartalk.com/forums/showthread.php?35554-Radford-and-Stuart-or-the-1st-and-2nd-Virginia-Cavalry.
89. E.J. Steptoe to Samuel Cooper, Letters to the Office of the Adjutant General, November 1, 1856, National Archives, M567, Roll 549.
90. E.J. Steptoe to Jefferson Davis, Letters to the Office of the Secretary of War, December 26, 1856, National Archives, M567, Roll 569.
91. E.J. Steptoe, Letter of Introduction for Mis-ta-kai-ya-wa, December 13, 1856, Fort Walla Walla Collection 2/9, Penrose library, Whitman College, Walla Walla, WA.
92. Victor 339.
93. Burns 159. A veteran of the War of 1812, Clarke (d. 1860) was brevetted brigadier general for his action at the Siege of Veracruz in the Mexican War. Like Steptoe, he participated in the Battle of Cerro Gordo and the assault on Chapultepec. Like Wool, he resisted opening the interior Northwest to unmonitored settlement.
94. Nelson 133.
95. Burns 156.
96. Scheuerman and Finley 69.
97. Ruby and Brown 253.
98. William Compton Brown, *The Indian Side of the Story* (Spokane: C.W. Hill, 1961): 181–182. Judge Brown's account is rife with typos and other errors but offers worthwhile insights and speculations on the Steptoe battle and its aftermath. Brown (1869–1963) lived in eastern Washington from 1898 until his death.
99. Burns 194.

100. Guide to the Fort Walla Walla Collection, 1849–1910, Penrose Library, Whitman College, Walla Walla, WA.
101. E.J. Steptoe to Nannie Steptoe, June 1, 1857, Special Collections, University of Washington Libraries, Accession #4908-001, Box #1, Folder #28.
102. John R. Randolph to Dr. William Steptoe, April 8, 1861. Manring Archives, in private hands.
103. E.J. Steptoe to Samuel Cooper, Letters to the Office of the Adjutant General, October 19, 1857, National Archives, M567, Roll 571.
104. Ernest J. Whitaker, "Edward J. Steptoe: Caretaker of the Palouse Hills," *West Pointers and Early Washington*, ed. John A. Hemphill and Robert C. Cumbow (Seattle: West Point Society of Puget Sound, 1992): 170.
105. Burns 161.
106. Burns 164.
107. *Report of the Secretary of War*, 35th Congress, 2nd Session, House Executive Documents #2, Vol. 2, 332. Events pertaining to Steptoe's actions at Fort Walla Walla and to Colonel George Wright's battles following Steptoe's defeat in May of 1858 are recounted in 37 dated documents (pages 330–415); Manring 43. Most of the relevant official correspondence is included accurately in Manring's book, which remains the most immediate available resource. Mackall (1818–1891) graduated eighth in Steptoe's Class of 1837. Wounded in 1839 during the Second Seminole War and again at Chapultepec during the Mexican War, he rose to the rank of brigadier general for the Confederacy.
108. *Report of the Secretary of War* 333; Manring 44.
109. *Report of the Secretary of War* 334; Manring 46–47.
110. *Report of the Secretary of War* 336; Manring 60.
111. *Report of the Secretary of War* 335, 336; Manring 61.

Seven. "Chapter of Accidents"

1. In his study of the Coeur d'Alene (or Schitsu'umsh), *Landscape Traveled by Coyote and Crane* (Seattle: University of Washington Press, 2001), anthropologist Rodney Frey says just 500 warriors were involved (81). Most of those present during the battle, however, indicate around 1,000 with some going as high as 1,600.
2. The Ye Galleon Press edition, published in 1975, appends a biography of Manring, an index, about twenty pages of back matter not found in other versions, and more than two dozen illustrations and maps.
3. *Report of the Secretary of War*, 35th Congress, 2nd Session, House Executive Documents #2, Vol. 2, 338, henceforth referred to as *Report*; Benjamin Franklin Manring, *The Conquest of the Coeur d'Alenes, Spokanes and Palouses* (Spokane: John W. Graham, 1912; reprinted with additions by Ye Galleon Press [Fairfield, WA, 1975]): 61–64. Includes all the relevant correspondence found in *35th Congress, 2nd Session* (1858), Senate Executive Documents 1, Serial 975; also in House Executive Documents 1, Serial 998.
4. *Report* 341; Manring 68–69.
5. A.J. Splawn, *Ka-mi-akin: Last Hero of the Yakimas* (Portland: Oregon Historical Society, 1917; 2nd ed. 1944): 89–90.
6. Then Lieutenant John Mullan's initial investigations for the route date to the winter of 1853–1854. See Louis C. Coleman and Leo Rieman, *Captain John Mullan; His Life Building the Mullan Road* (Montreal, Canada: Payette Radio, 1968) and Keith Petersen, *John Mullan: The Tumultuous Life of a Western Road Builder* (Pullman: Washington State University Press, 2014) 73.
7. E.J. Steptoe to Dr. William Steptoe, April 5, 1858, Special Collections, University of Washington Libraries, Accession #4908-001, Box #1, Folder #29.
8. E.J. Steptoe to Nannie Steptoe, April 5, 1858, Special Collections, University of Washington Libraries, Accession #4908-001, Box #1, Folder #30.
9. Kurt R. Nelson, *Treaties and Treachery: The Northwest Indians' Resistance to Conquest* (Caldwell, ID: Caxton, 2011) 213. See Surgeon John F. Randolph's letter to Dr. William Steptoe, April 18, 1861, in private hands. No solid evidence supports the view that Steptoe was unfit for command in May of 1858.
10. Stella Pickett Hardy, *Colonial Families of the Southern States of America*, 2d ed. (Baltimore: Genealogical Publishing Company, 1968): 487.
11. *Report* 345; Manring 70.
12. Kurt R. Nelson, *Fighting for Paradise: A Military History of the Pacific Northwest* (Yardley, PA: Westholme, 2007): 134.
13. Robert Utley, *Frontiersmen in Blue: The United States Army and the Indian, 1848–1865* (New York: Macmillan, 1967): 19.
14. Returns from U.S. Military Posts, 1800–1916, M-617, Fort Walla Walla, WA, August 1856–May 1867, Reel #1343.

15. Lawrence Kip, *Indian War in the Pacific Northwest: The Journal of Lieutenant Lawrence Kip*, Introduction Clifford E. Trafzer (Lincoln: University of Nebraska Press, 1999) 9. Published in 1859 as *Army Life on the Pacific*. A New Yorker who spent a year at West Point before joining his parents in California in 1854, where his father was Episcopal bishop, Kip (1836–1899) served in the Rogue River War. During the Civil War he served mostly under General Sheridan, being brevetted three times. He resigned in 1867 as brevet lieutenant-colonel.

16. Robert Ignatius Burns, S.J., *The Jesuits and the Indian Wars of the Northwest* (New Haven: Yale University Press, 1966): 207.

17. Report 338; Manring 142.

18. Report 345; Manring 70.

19. Randall A. Johnson, "May 17, 1858: The Ordeal of the Steptoe Command," *Pacific Northwesterner* 17.1 (Winter 1973): 2.

20. Jerome Peltier, *Warbonnets and Epaulets* (Montreal: Payette Radio, 1971): 77.

21. Utley 201, 202.

22. Carl P. Schlicke, *General George Wright: Guardian of the Pacific Coast* (Norman: University of Oklahoma Press, 1988) 147.

23. Clifford E. Trafzer and Richard D. Scheuerman, *Renegade Tribe: The Palouse Indians and the Invasion of the Inland Pacific Northwest* (Pullman: Washington State University Press, 1986): 77.

24. Robert H. Ruby and John A. Brown, *The Spokane Indians: Children of the Sun* (Norman: University of Oklahoma Press, 1970): 109.

25. Burns 202.

26. Burns 202.

27. Manring 73.

28. Report 347; Manring 129.

29. Manring 71.

30. Waldo E. Rosebush, *Frontier Steel: The Men and Their Weapons* (Appleton, WA: C.C. Nelson, 1958): 210. Published for the Eastern Washington State Historical Society. See also Utley 25–26.

31. Rosebush 232, 268–278.

32. Report 348; Manring 132; see also Burns 202.

33. From about 1700 until today, soldiers going into battle carried just a few pounds of ammunition. In the Civil War, the goal was for muzzle-loading infantry to go into battle with 40 rounds apiece (at 11 to 12 shots per pound for 4 pounds). "Spencer Repeating Rifle." http://www.hackman-adams.com/guns/spencermore.htm; "Answering the Call: The Personal Equipment of a Civil War Soldier." https://www.armyheritage.org/education-and-programs/educational-resources/soldier-stories/50-information/soldier-stories/285-civilwarequipment. See also David Cole, *Survey of U.S. Army Uniforms, Weapons and Accoutrements* (2007), page 15. http://www.history.army.mil/html/museums/uniforms/survey_uwa.pdf

34. Manring 72.

35. Rosebush 303.

36. Thomas B. Beall, "Pioneer Reminiscences," *Washington Historical Quarterly* 8.2 (April 1917) 84.

37. Manring 102–103.; Burns 223.

38. Rosebush 231.

39. Utley 27.

40. Cole, page 28. http://www.history.army.mil/html/museums/uniforms/survey_uwa.pdf

41. Report 347; Manring 130.

42. R. Ross Arnold, *Indian Wars of Idaho* (Caldwell, ID: Caxton, 1932): 19.

43. Burns 158.

44. Kriebel 15.

45. Trafzer and Scheuerman 7. Kriebel offers a hypothetical narrative of Coeur d'Alene Indian women harvesting and steaming camas in his monograph (19–21).

46. Report 346; Manring 127.

47. Report 349; Manring 134.

48. Hazard Stevens, *The Life of Isaac Ingalls Stevens*, II (Boston: Houghton Mifflin, 1901): 70–71.

49. Stevens 71.

50. Report 349; Manring 134.

51. Report 346; Manring 127.

52. Including Gregg, Jerome Peltier lists seventeen officers involved in Steptoe's battle and the subsequent expedition conducted by Colonel Wright who rose to the rank of brigadier or major general of Union or Confederate troops by 1865 (325).

53. Manring 76.

54. Manring 281.

55. Mahlon E. Kriebel, *Battle of To-hotsnim-me: The U.S. Army vs. the Coeur d'Alene Indians* (Bloomington, IN: AuthorHouse, rev. 2nd ed. 2012); originally in *Bunchgrass Historian* 34.2&3 (2008). Kriebel does not mention Chief Timothy after he helped Steptoe's troops cross the Snake, page 13.

56. William Compton Brown, *The Indian Side of the Story* (Spokane, WA: C.W. Hill, 1961): 188.

57. Richard D. Scheuerman and Michael O. Finley, *Finding Chief Kamiakin: The Life and Legacy of a Northwest Patriot* (Pullman: Washington State University Press, 2008): 74.

58. Robert Ignatius Burns, S.J., "Pere Joset's Account of the Indian War of 1858," *Pacific Northwest Quarterly* 38.4 (October 1947): 285. See also Burns, *The Jesuits and the Indian Wars*, 205; Trafzer and Scheuerman 77–78.
59. Burns 185.
60. Burns 189.
61. Burns, "Pere Joset's Account" 293.
62. Burns 197.
63. Scheuerman and Finley 74.
64. Burns, "Pere Joset's Account" 294; I've used the modernized version supplied by Scheuerman and Finley, 74.
65. Scheuerman and Finley 74; Burns, "Pere Joset's Account" 294–295.
66. Burns 175.
67. Burns 176.
68. Burns 180; Ruby and Brown 108.
69. Ruby and Brown 110.
70. Scheuerman and Finley 78.
71. Splawn 90.
72. Arnold 37, 44.
73. Johnson 8.
74. Brown 189.
75. Burns 210.
76. Burns 211.
77. Scheuerman and Finley 76–78.
78. Rosebush 232; closely echoed by Helen Addison Howard in "The Steptoe Affair," *Montana: The Magazine of Western History* 19.2 (Spring 1969): 35. (She does not credit Rosebush.).
79. Kip 51.
80. C[harles] S[ydney] Winder, "Captain C.S. Winder's Account of a Battle with the Indians," *Maryland Historical Magazine* 35.1 (Spring 1940): 57.
81. Scheuerman and Finley 76; Burns 211.
82. Manring 82.
83. Rosebush 213.
84. Rosebush 236. See Kriebel's maps with his significant corrections (6, 41).
85. Scheuerman and Finley 76; Rosebush 213. See also Frey 81, who conforms to Scheuerman and Finley.
86. Mahlon Kriebel has meticulously retraced Steptoe's progress following the maps of John Mullan's topographer, Theodore Kolecki. Kriebel's account of the action, enriched by forays into historical fiction is nicely detailed and fleshed out with plausible speculations as to the thoughts and dialogue of the principle persons involved.
87. Manring 83.
88. Rosebush 213.
89. Winder 57.
90. A brochure prepared in 2006 by the Archaeological and Historical Services of Eastern Washington University at Cheney indicates the lake was "likely located" at the "intersection of Cheney Plaza Road and Babb Road."
91. Burns 212.
92. Burns 212–213; Rosebush 217.
93. Burns 222.
94. Burns 215; Burns, "Pere Joset's Account" 295.
95. Nelson 134.
96. Published as Lieutenant John Mullan's *Topographical Memoir of Colonel Wright's Campaign* in Senate Executive Document 32 of the 35th Congress, 2nd Session, Serial 984.
97. Cited in Peltier 103–105; henceforth cited as "Gregg."
98. Rosebush 219.
99. *Report*, Letter from Father Joset to Father Congiato (June 27, 1858), 357; Burns 217; Manring 150.
100. *Report*, Father Joset to Father Congiato, 357; Manring 150.
101. *Report* 357; Manring (Joset's report) 250; Burns 218; Rosebush 220; Kriebel 34. Most commentators recount this episode.
102. Burns 218.
103. Kriebel 34.
104. Burns, "Pere Joset's Account" 296.
105. *Report*, Father Joset to Father Congiato, 358; Manring (Joset's report) 151; Burns 219; Burns, "Pere Joset's Account" 296.
106. Gregg 103.
107. Jack Dozier, "The Coeur d'Alene Indians in the War of 1858," *Idaho Yesterdays* 5.3 (Fall 1961): 26.
108. Burns, "Pere Joset's Account" 296–297; Burns 220–221; Trafzer and Scheuerman 80.
109. Edward J. Kowrach and Thomas E. Connolly, *Saga of the Coeur d'Alene Indians: An Account of Chief Joseph Seltice* (Fairfield, WA: Ye Galleon, 1990): 102. This colorful account by the son of Chief Andrew Seltice (1819–1902), who led the tribe at that time, is often at odds with other historical commentaries.
110. T.C. Elliott, "Steptoe Butte and Steptoe Battle-field," *Washington Historical Quarterly* 18.4 (October 1927): 248. Published as Lieutenant John Mullan's *Topographical Memoir of Colonel Wright's Campaign*.
111. Elliott 249.
112. Burns 221.
113. *Report* 346; Manring 128.
114. Gregg 103.
115. Trafzer and Scheuerman 80.

Notes—Chapter Seven

116. Rosebush 223; Manring 128.
117. Manring 99.
118. Manring 99, 100.
119. *Report* 348; Manring 131.
120. Gregg 104.
121. Manring 103. He indicates the ridgeline runs about three eighths of a mile from base to base. Today a four-acre site in Rosalia is marked by a 25-foot granite obelisk placed by the Daughters of the American Revolution in 1914. Probably none of the fifty or so trees there was standing at the time, but native bunchgrass of various species reached up to three feet in height.
122. Gregg 104.
123. Gregg 104.
124. *Report* 347; Manring 129–130.
125. Manring 129–130; Gregg 104.
126. *Report*, Father Joset to Father Congiato, 359; Manring 154.
127. Manring 107–108.
128. Manring 111; Rosebush 223; Burns 228; Nelson 137.
129. David M. Gregg to B.F. Manring, February 3, 1909. Manring Archives, private collection.
130. *Report* 347;Manring 130.
131. Michael Kenny, Typescript in Fort Walla Walla Collection, Whitman College and Northwest Archives, 2/6. n.p.
132. Manring 113.
133. Rosebush 233; Burns 229; Nelson, *Treaties and Treachery*, 221.
134. Kriebel, 31; Brown 192–193; Peltier 110–111.
135. Kowrach and Connolly 109–112.
136. Frey 81.
137. Brown 195.
138. *Report*, Father Joset to Father Congiato,360; Manring 155; Burns 244.
139. *Report*, Father Joset to Father Congiato, 359; Manring 155.
140. Trafzer and Scheuerman 82.
141. Trafzer and Scheuerman 83.
142. Ball later served with the ill-fated Seventh Cavalry, but only after Custer's defeat, rising to the rank of major by the time of his retirement in 1884. A photograph from Fort Ellis in the Montana Territory dated 1871 shows an erect and bearded no-nonsense Captain Ball among other officers of the post: http://en.wikipedia.org/wiki/File:Soldiers-AtFortEllisMontanaTerritory1871.jpg.
143. Nelson 97.
144. Burns 228.
145. Report 350; Manring 136.
146. Petersen 71.
147. Report 392; Manring 205.
148. Petersen 72.
149. *Report* 348; Manring 132.
150. John Keegan, *The Face of Battle* (New York: Viking, 1976) 107.
151. *New York Herald*, June 28, 1858. Page two of the August 30 edition of the *Herald* had cut the losses to 3 officers and 30 men out of a force reported to be "numbering about sixty." http://fultonhistory.com/Fulton.html
152. California Digital Newspaper Collection (henceforth cited as CDNC), *Sacramento Daily Union* Vol. 15, No. 2240 (June 1, 1858) and Vol. 15, No. 2248 (June 10, 1858); *Daily Alta California* Vol. 10, No. 157 (June 9, 1858).
153. Burns 224; photograph see Manring, facing 88; Manring also prints a photograph of Gaston, facing 104.
154. Gregg 103; also CDNC, *Daily Alta California* (June 9, 1858), *Sacramento Daily Union* (June 10, 1858).
155. CDNC, "Letter from the Dalles: Another Account of Steptoe's Defeat," *Daily Alta California* Vol. 10, No. 161 (June 13, 1858); E.J. Steptoe to Dr. William Steptoe, Special Collections, University of Washington Libraries, Accession # 4908-001, Box #1, Folder #26.
156. "Monthly Record of Current Events," *Harper's New Monthly Magazine* 17.99 (August 1858) 403; 17.100 (September 1858) 545. Henceforth cited as *Harper's*.
157. Kip 24.
158. Kip 25.
159. Kip 31–33.
160. *Harpers* 545.
161. *Report* 392; Manring 205.
162. Keyes (1810–1895), promoted to colonel in May 1861, would be major general after the Battle of Malvern Hill on July 1, 1862. Removed from command after Gettysburg, he retired from the army in May 1864.
163. Petersen 83. Mullan (1830–1909) graduated near the top of his West Point class in 1852. After completion of the wagon road across the Rockies in 1862 he was promoted to captain. He resigned his commission the next year, married, moved to Walla Walla where he dabbled in business, then migrated to California where he became an attorney.
164. An 1841 graduate of West Point, Garnett served in the Second Seminole War and with distinction at Monterrey and Buena Vista during the Mexican War. He supervised construction of Fort Simcoe as Steptoe was building Fort Walla Walla. He was killed while serving as a brigadier general of the Confederacy in the first year of the Civil War.

165. Crook, an 1852 graduate of West Point, served as colonel of Ohio volunteers during the first year of the Civil War. By September 1862 he was a brigadier general, commanding troops at the Battle of Chickamauga and elsewhere. Brevetted major general at the end of the war, Crook was promoted to brigadier in the regular army in 1872. He would become known as the greatest of the Indian fighters, notably for his leadership in the Great Sioux War of 1876–1877. At his death in 1890, he was renowned as a champion of fair treatment for the Indians.

166. E.J. Steptoe to Nannie Steptoe, August 20, 1858, Special Collections, University of Washington Libraries, Accession #4908-1, Box #1, Folder #31.

167. *Report* 386; Manring 188, 190; Peltier 193, 195.

168. Scheuerman and Finley 83.

169. The Battle of Four Lakes Monument, a granite pyramid, was erected in 1935 by the Spokane County Pioneer Society, Medical Lake Commercial Club and Four Lakes Grange. The text claims "700 Army soldiers defeated 5000 allied Indians." http://properties.historicspokane.org/property/?PropertyID=1984.

170. Kip 55.

171. *Report* 388; Manring 193; Peltier 206.

172. Kip 57.

173. *Report* 391; Manring 202–203.

174. Utley indicates the Indians admitted to sixty killed at Four Lakes, but he offers no estimate as to the casualties at Spokane Plains (207).

175. *Report* 395; Manring 213–214.

176. Trafzer and Scheuerman 90.

177. Erasmus D. Keyes, *Fifty Years' Observation of Men and Events Civil and Military* (New York: Charles Scribner's Sons, 1884) 273.

178. *Report* 400; Manring 234.

179. The event is rather sinisterly commemorated in the name of the stream that flows below the city of Spokane, "Hangman Creek," and less darkly but more incongruously in the name of the city-owned golf course that runs along U.S. 195 paralleling the creek—"Qualchan."

180. *Report* 402; Manring 254.

181. *Report* 403–404; Manring 256, 257.

182. Kip 123.

Eight. Last Years

1. Robert Ignatius Burns, S.J., *The Jesuits and the Indian Wars of the Northwest* (New Haven: Yale University Press, 1966): 278, 279.

2. File on Edward J. Steptoe in the Jones Memorial Library in Lynchburg, Virginia.

3. E.J. Steptoe to Samuel Cooper, Letters to the Office of the Adjutant General, December 4, 1858, National Archives, M567, Roll 591.

4. E.J. Steptoe to Samuel Cooper, Letters to the Adjutant General, February 23, 1859, M567, Roll 612.

5. The Miller-Claytor House, built in 1791 for tavern-keeper John Miller, is a modest two-story white frame structure, now located at Riverside Park and listed on the National Register of Historic Places http://www.nps.gov/nr/travel/vamainstreet/mil.htm

6. E.J. Steptoe to Samuel Cooper, Letters to the Adjutant General, April 19, 1859, M567, Roll 612; Randolph's note is appended to Steptoe's letter.

7. E.J. Steptoe to Samuel Cooper, Letters to the Adjutant General, March 17, 1859, M567, Roll 612.

8. E.J. Steptoe to Samuel Cooper, Letters to the Adjutant General, April 19, 1859, M567, Roll 612.

9. Report from St. Louis correspondent dated June 13, 1859, cited in *Sacramento Daily Union*, Vol, 17, #2583, 8 July 1859; however, see also *New York Daily Tribune*, May 25, 1859, where Steptoe, on leave of absence, and the others are said to be traveling as "private individuals" (5). Loring (1818–1886) grew up in St. Augustine and served in the Second Seminole War. He lost his arm at Chapultepec in the Mexican War but went on to serve under Stonewall Jackson and John Bell Hood, rising to the rank of major general. After the war he served as Inspector General for the Khedive of Egypt and wrote a book entitled *A Confederate Soldier in Egypt* (1884).

10. Franklin Pierce, Presidential Papers, Library of Congress Microfilm #263, Series 3, Reel 6. Steptoe's visit to Europe is also mentioned in an item published in the *Richmond Daily Dispatch*.

11. E.J. Steptoe to Nannie Steptoe, August 3, 1859, Special Collections, University of Washington Libraries, Accession #4908-1, Box #1, Folder #32.

12. Clifton Potter and Dorothy Potter, *Lynchburg: A City Set on Seven Hills. The Making of America Series* (Charleston, SC: 2004): 39–40; Philip Lightfoot Scruggs, *The History of Lynchburg, Virginia (1786–1946)* (Lynchburg: J.P. Bell [n.d.—written shortly after World War II but not published until the 1960s]: 2, 18, 52.

13. Barbara Brown Eakley, *The Browns of*

Bedford County (Bowie, MD: Heritage Books, 1998): 9, 49.

14. "Announcement: Complimentary Supper Given to Col. & Mrs. E.J. Steptoe," Jones Memorial Library, Lynchburg, VA (January 30, 1860), Item #2077.

15. E.J. Steptoe to Samuel Cooper, Letters to the Office of the Adjutant General, March 20, 1860, National Archives, M567, Roll 632.

16. E.J. Steptoe to Samuel Cooper, Letters to the Office of the Adjutant General, May 3, 1860, National Archives, M567, Roll 632.

17. Secretary of War at that time was fellow Virginian, John B. Floyd, who resigned on December 29, 1860, nine days after South Carolina seceded.

18. California Digital Newspaper Collection, *Sacramento Daily Union*, October 11, 1860: 6. http://cdnc.ucr.edu/cdnc/cgi-bin/cdnc?a=d&d=SDU19601011.2.4&cl

19. *Richmond Daily Dispatch* http://digitalnewspapers.libraries.psu.edu/Default/Scripting/ArticleWin.asp?From=Archive&Source=Page&Skin=civilwar&BaseHref=PDU/1860/12/31&PageLabelPrint=2&EntityId=Ar00202&DataChunk=Ar00201&ViewMode=GIF

20. "A Gleam of Hope!" *New York Times*, December 31, 1860. http://www.nytimes.com/1860/12/31/news/a-gleam-of-hope.html?scp=43&sq=dec+31+1860&st=p

21. D.H. Hill, "On the Military Spirit and Genius of the Southern People," *Richmond Daily Dispatch*, March 22, 1861. https://civilianwartime.wordpress.com/2011/03/31/%E2%80%9Cmilitary-spirit-and-genius-of-the-south-%E2%80%9D-cw150/.

22. "Notes of the War: Virginia Officers in Lincoln's Army," *Richmond Daily Dispatch*, September 11, 1861. http://dlxs.richmond.edu/cgi/t/text/textidx?c=ddr;cc=ddr;type=simple;rgn=div2;q1=steptoe;view=text;subview=detail;sort=occur;idno=ddr0268.0020.059;node=ddr0268.0020.059%3A9.1

23. Benjamin Franklin Manring, *Conquest of the Coeur d'Alenes, Spokanes & Palouses* (Fairfield, WA: Ye Galleon Press, 1975): 272.

24. E.J. Steptoe to Lorenzo Thomas, Letters to the Office of the Adjutant General, October 10, 1861, M619, Roll 58.

25. Manring 272.

26. Jubal A. Early, *Memoirs* (New York: Konecky & Konecky, 1994) 2.

27. Early 393–394.

28. James I. Robertson, Jr., "Foreword," *The Battle of Lynchburg*, by L. VanLoan Naisawald (Lynchburg: Warwick House, 2004): n.p.

29. Potter and Potter 49.

30. Item #3741, Jones Memorial Library Archives, Lynchburg Virginia.

31. Manring 273.

32. Mary Rosanna Claytor Steptoe (1822–1887). http://www.findagrave.com/cgi-bin/fg.cgi?page=gr&GRid=7546924

33. Many issues of the Lynchburg and Liberty (Bedford) newspapers for April 1865 are missing, and Richmond was under siege. Queries to the Lynchburg Historical Foundation, the Virginia Historical Society, and other quarters have turned up no obituary for Colonel Steptoe. Although it seems unlikely, Steptoe may have remained in hospitals in Philadelphia until the time of his death.

34. That is, "without fear and without reproach," or "fearless and beyond reproach." The phrase refers to the French hero Pierre Terrail LeVieux, Seigneur de Bayard (1473–1524), a cavalryman considered the epitome of chivalry. Known also as "le bon chevalier," he was killed in combat. http://en.wikipedia.org/wiki/Pierre_Terrail,_seigneur_de_Bayard

35. Manring 274.

Epilogue: Legacy

1. Elwood Evans, *History of the Pacific Northwest: Oregon and Washington*, Vol. I (Portland: North Pacific History Co., 1889) 619.

2. Evans 623.

3. Evans 629.

4. Hubert Howe Bancroft, *History of Washington, Idaho, and Montana, 1845–1889*, Vol. XXXI (San Francisco: A.L. Bancroft & Co., 18900) 178–183.

5. Ernest J. Whitaker, "Edward Jevnor Steptoe: Caretaker of the Palouse Hills," *West Pointers and Early Washington*, ed. John A. Hemphill and Robert C. Cumbow (Seattle: West Point Society of Puget Sound, 1992) 180. Whitaker repeats Manring's error with respect to Steptoe's middle name.

6. Whitaker 180; see Manring for Joset's observation, page 155.

7. "History of St. Paul's." http://www.stpaulslynchburg.org/history-of-st-pauls; a copy of Mary Rosanna Claytor Steptoe's will and codicil is item #4037 in the archives of the Jones Memorial Library in Lynchburg, Virginia.

8. Obituary Notice: Mary R. Steptoe, *Lynchburg News*, April 9, 1887, 3. The item erroneously describes her late husband Colonel Edward Steptoe as "an officer in the Confederate army."

9. Maps of the Washington Territory dated 1873 refer to Pyramid Peak, but an 1878 map lists it as "Steptoes Butte." By 1881 the terminal s had been dropped. See Early Washington, Corvallis, OR: Western Guide Publishers, 1974. n.p.

10. "Steptoe Butte State Park." http://www.stateparks.com/steptoe_butte.html

11. B[enjamin] F[ranklin] Manring, *Conquest of the Coeur d'Alenes, Spokanes & Palouses* (Fairfield, WA: Ye Galleon Press, 1975) 20.

12. Manring 19.

13. McCroskey, Virgil Talmadge (1876 1970) http://www.historylink.org/index.cfm?DisplayPage=output.cfm&File_Id=7989

14. The Internet Surname Database: Last Name: Steptoe http://www.surnamedb.com/Surname/Steptoe

15. Walla Walla Chamber of Commerce http://www.wwvchamber.com/index.php?option=com_content&view=article&id=138&Itemid=233

16. Ghost Towns of Nevada http://www.ghosttowns.com/states/nv/steptoecity.htm; http://en.wikipedia.org/wiki/Steptoe_Valley. The *Sacramento Daily Union* Vol 27 #4083, dated April 22, 1864, mentions Steptoe City being laid out in the Steptoe Valley in what was soon to become the 36th state to enter the union.

17. Steptoe, Washington http://en.wikipedia.org/wiki/Steptoe,_Washington

18. Steptoe Village—WSU Housing and Residence Life http://housing.wsu.edu/famgrad/SteptoeVillage

19. Henry Spalding, born 1830, was the son of Presbyterian missionary to the Nez Perce, Henry Harmon Spalding (1803-1874). He resided in Colfax where he served as the town's assessor in the late 1870s.

20. "Steptoe (Tohotonimme) Battlefield," pamphlet prepared by Archaeological and Historical Services, Eastern Washington University, on behalf of the Washington State Parks and Recreation Commission, 2006.

21. Robert M. Lambeth, "Rosalia, WA,"
Spokane Historical, accessed March 2, 2015, http://spokanehistorical.org/items/show/373.

22. Sherman Alexie, *The Lone Ranger and Tonto Fistfight in Heaven* (New York: Grove, 1993) 93. Alexie revisits the horse slaughter movingly in "Horses," from his second book of poems, *Old Shirts & New Skins* (1993).

23. Alexie 101.

24. Alexie 102.

25. Will Henry, *Pillars of the Sky* (New York: Bantam, 1991) xiii.

26. Robert L. Gale, *Will Henry/Clay Fisher (Henry W. Allen)* (Boston: Twayne, 1984) 30.

27. Henry 8.

28. Henry 10.

29. Gale 30–31.

30. Henry 20, 22.

31. Henry 31.

32. Henry 37, 61.

33. Henry 35, 39.

34. Henry 152.

35. Henry 143.

36. Henry 42, 44, 40.

37. *Pillars of the Sky*, Dir. George Marshall, Universal Pictures, 1956 http://www.tcm.com/this-month/article/139135%7C0/Pillars-of-the-Sky.html; http://www.imdb.com/title/tt0049619/

38. Robert Ignatius Burns, S.J., *The Jesuits and the Indian Wars of the Northwest* (New Haven: Yale University Press, 1966): backmatter, n.p.

39. Rodney Frey, *Landscape Traveled by Coyote and Crane: The World of the Schı̨tsu'umsh (Coeur d'Alene Indians)* (Seattle: University of Washington Press, 2001) 81, 84 (photo).

40. Frey 81.

41. Personal email correspondence dated January 15, 2012.

42. Bill London, "The View is a Butte from the Top of Steptoe," *Moscow-Pullman Daily News*, February 11–12, 2012: 4D.

43. Terence L. Day, "Grave Disservice to Col. Steptoe," Letters to the Editor, *Moscow-Pullman Daily News*, February 29, 2012, 7A.

Bibliography

Edward J. Steptoe Correspondence

E.J. Steptoe. Letter of Introduction for Mis-ta-kai-ya-wa, December 13, 1856, Fort Walla Walla Collection 2/9, Penrose library, Whitman College, Walla Walla, WA.

E.J. Steptoe. Letter of Recommendation for O.P. Rockwell, Special Collections, Brigham Young University Library, Manuscript 3434, Item 11.

E.J. Steptoe. Letter to Ellen Wilkins Tompkins. Tompkins Family. Virginia Historical Society, Richmond, VA. Mss1. T5996 c 362–365.

E.J. Steptoe. Letter to Franklin Pierce (June 18, 1860). Franklin Pierce. Presidential Papers, Library of Congress Microfilm #263, Series 3, Reel 6.

E.J. Steptoe. Letter to George Wright, September 18, 1856. 36th Congress, 3rd Session, Senate Executive Documents, Number 5, Volume 2.

E.J. Steptoe. Letter to Jefferson Davis. Letters to the Office of the Secretary of War, December 26, 1856, National Archives, M567.

E.J. Steptoe. Letter to Jubal A. Early. Virginia Historical Society. Richmond, VA. MSS1Ea765670.

E.J. Steptoe. Letters to the Office of the Adjutant General. National Archives. M567. To Roger Jones: September 17, 1838. February 17, 1841. May 31, 1841. September 7, 1841. March 20, 1842, May 10, 1846. July 31, 1846. June 22, 1848. June 23, 1848. August 30, 1848. To Samuel Cooper: May 29, 1854. June 30, 1854. August 30, 1854. September 14, 1854. October 4, 1854. November 10, 1854. November 20, 1854. February 1, 1855. February 24, 1855. April 15, 1855. April 25, 1855. October 11, 1855. November 1, 1856. October 19, 1857. December 4, 1858. February 23, 1859. March 17, 1859. April 19, 1859. March 20, 1860. May 3, 1860. To Lorenzo Thomas: October 10, 1861.

E.J. Steptoe. Special Collection. University of Washington Libraries, Accession #4908-1, Box #1.This File contains 32 letters to family members, the bulk of Edward J. Steptoe's extant personal correspondence. Also included are certificates of his promotions in rank and letters to Secretary of State William L. Marcy and President Franklin Pierce concerning governorship of the Utah Territory in 1855.

E.J. Steptoe to Dr. William Steptoe. Typescript of letter dated January 13, 1845 mailed from St. Augustine, FL, the next day. Manring Archives. In private hands.

E.J. Steptoe to Dr. William Steptoe. Typescript of letter dated November 27, [1846] continued on December 2.from Tampico, Mexico. Manring Archives. In private hands.

E.J. Steptoe to Dr. William Steptoe. October 10, 1846. Special Collections. University of Virginia. Accession #6516. Box #6506. A rare family letter not included in Special Collections at University of Washington.

Other Primary Sources

Abstracts of Steptoe Wills & Deeds Recorded in Bedford County, 1848–1859. http://files.usgwarchives.net/va/bedford/slaveabs/ss100005.tx

Allen, Augustus Porter. USMA Archives. Box #11.

Bibliography

Anderson, Robert. *An Artillery Officer in the Mexican War, 1846–7.* New York: G.P. Putnam's Sons, 1911.
"Announcement: Complimentary Supper Given to Col. & Mrs. E.J. Steptoe" (January 30, 1860). Jones Memorial Library, Lynchburg, VA. Item #2077.
Antes, William. "Recollections of an Old Soldier." New Haven: Yale University Press, Beinecke Rare Book and Manuscript Library, 18—?) 6. WA MSS S-2898. Handwritten account—available online.
Army and Navy Chronicle, 13.9 (March 19, 1842): 137.
Bartram, William. *Travels and Other Writings.* New York: Library of America, 1996.
"Battle of Lake Okeechobee." *Florida Herald.* January 1838. http://ufdcweb1.uflib.ufl.edu/ufdc/UFDC.aspx?c=fdnl_1
Beadle, J[ohn] H[anson]. *Life in Utah; or, the Mysteries and Crimes of Mormonism.* Philadelphia: National Publishing, 1870.
Beall, Thomas B. "Pioneer Reminiscences." *Washington Historical Quarterly* 8.2 (April 1917): 83–90. https://journals.lib.washington.edu/index.php/WHQ/issue/view/567
Beauregard, P[ierre] G[ustave] T[outant]. T. Harry Williams, ed., *With Beauregard in Mexico: The Mexican War Reminiscences of P.G.T. Beauregard.* Ed. by T. Harry Williams. Baton Rouge: Louisiana State University Press, 1965.
"Biography of Col. Steptoe." *New York Evening Post*, Vol. 53, December 20, 1854. Microfilm.
Blair, Seth Millington. "Reminiscences and Journals, 1851–1868." MS 710, Folder 1, LDS Archives.
Cadet Life Before the Civil War. Bulletin #1. West Point: The Library, 1945.
Carrington, Albert. "Inconsistent Conduct of the United States Toward Her Territories." *The Deseret News* 4.52 (March 8, 1855): [3].
"Catalog of the Philanthropic Society." http://docsouth.unc.edu/true/philanthropic/philanthropic.html.
"Colonel Steptoe." *The Deseret News*, 5.2 (March 21, 1855): [4].
Cullum, George W. *Biographical Register of the Officers and Graduates of the United States Military Academy.* "Cullum's Register." Vol. 1, #924, page 689 pertains to E.J. Steptoe. http://penelope.uchicago.edu/Thayer/E/Gazetteer/Places/America/United_States/Army/USMA/Cullums_Register/home.html
Fraser, William. USMA Archives. Box #139.
Gregg, David M. Letter to B.F. Manring dated February 3, 1909. Manring Archives. In private hands. Cited in Peltier, pages 103–105.
Gunnison, John W. *The Mormons, or Latter-Day Saints, in the Valley of the Great Salt Lake: A Short History of Their Rise and Progress, Peculiar Doctrines, Present Condition, and Prospects.* Philadelphia: J.B. Lippincott, 1857. Originally published in 1852.
"Gunnison Massacre." *New York Times*, Vol. 3, #688, December 1, 1853: 1. Microfilm.
Hill. D[aniel] H[arvey]. *A Fighter from Way Back: The Mexican War Diary of Lt. Daniel Harvey Hill, 4th Artillery, USA.* Nathaniel Cheairs Hughes, Jr. and Timothy D. Johns. Kent, OH: Kent State University Press, 2002.
———. "On the Military Spirit and Genius of the Southern People." *Richmond Daily Dispatch*, March 22, 1861. https://civilianwartime.wordpress.com/2011/03/31/%E2%80%9Cmilitary-spirit-and-genius-of-the-south-%E2%80%9D-cw150/
Hitchcock, Ethan Allen. *Fifty Years in Camp and Field: Diary of Ethan Allen Hitchcock.* Edited by W.A. Croffut. New York: Putnam, 1909.
Ingalls, Rufus. "Report of the Trip with Colonel Steptoe from Ft. Leavenworth to Salt Lake, June 1st to August 31st, 1854, and a Trip to California, June 14, 1855. House ex. doc.—[United States], 34th Cong., 1st sess., no. 1; Western Americana, frontier history of the trans-Mississippi West, 1550–1900, reel 567, no. 5840. Pp. 152–168. Also available in David A. White's *News of the Plains and Rockies, 1803–1865*, Volume 5 (Spokane, WA: Arthur H. Clark, 1998): 275–302.
Journals of the Lewis and Clark Expedition. http://lewisandclarkjournals.unl.edu/read/?_xmlsrc=18051030.xml&_xslsrc=LCstyles.xsl
Kendall, George Wilkins. *Dispatches from the Mexican War.* Ed. Lawrence Delbert Cress. Norman: University of Oklahoma Press, 1999.
Kenny, Michael. Typescript in Fort Walla Walla Collection, Whitman College and Northwest Archives, 2/6. n.p.

Bibliography

Kinney, John F. Conversation with Governor Brigham Young, July 10, 1855. Federal and Local Government Files. Brigham Young Office Files, 1832–1878, Church History Library, The Church of Jesus Christ of Latter-day Saints, Salt Lake City This conversation was transcribed by David O. Calder, later treasurer of the Utah Territory and managing editor of *The Deseret News*.

Kip, Lawrence. *The Indian War in the Pacific Northwest*. Lincoln: University of Nebraska Press, 1999. Originally entitled *Army Life on the Pacific*. New York: Redfield, 1859.

Longfellow, Samuel. *Life and Letters of Henry Wadsworth Longfellow*. Boston: Houghton Mifflin, 1891.

Love, Andrew. "Journal." Typescript in Special Collections. Brigham Young University Library.

McClellan, George B. *The Mexican War Diary and Correspondence of George B. McClellan*. Ed. Thomas W. Cutrer. Baton Rouge: Louisiana State University Press, 2009.

McSherry, Richard. *El Puchero, or A Mixed Dish from Mexico*. Philadelphia, Lippincott, 1850.

Meade, George Gordon. *The Life and Letters of George Gordon Meade*. New York: Scribner's, 1913.

"The Mexican-American War and the Media, 1845–1848" http://www.history.vt.edu/MxAmWar/Newspapers/Niles/Nilesk1848.htm#74.004February261848Gen.Winfield

"Monthly Record of Current Events." *Harper's New Monthly Magazine* 17.99 (August 1858) 403; 17.100 (September 1858) 545.

Morris, Robert M. "Journal of an Overland Trip to California and Other Army Assignments, 1849–1853" Yale Beinecke Library, WA MSS S-1738.

Motte, Jacob Rhett. *Journey into the Wilderness*. Gainesville: University Press of Florida, 1953. Journal kept between 1836 and 1838.

Mowry, Sylvester. Letters: from Salt Lake City to Edward J. Bicknall, Providence, Rhode Island. Manuscript (MS 23526), Church History Library, Salt lake City. All three letters appear with some deletions in William Mulder and A. Russell Mortensen, eds., *Among the Mormons: Historic Accounts by Contemporary Observers* (New York: Knopf, 1958): 272–278.

———. Report to *New York Daily Times*, "Interesting from Utah—Trial of the Indian Murders of Captain Gunnison." March 28, 1855, page 1. Microfilm.

Mullan, John. "Lieutenant John Mullan's *Topographical Memoir of Colonel Wright's Campaign*." 35th Congress, 2nd Session. Senate Executive Document 32. Also in T.C. Elliott's "Steptoe Butte and Steptoe Battle-field." *Washington Historical Quarterly* 18.4 (October 1927): 243–353.

Newspaper Reports of Steptoe Disaster. *New York Herald*, June 28, 1858. http://fultonhistory.com/Fulton.html; *Sacramento Daily Union* Vol. 15, No. 2240 (June 1, 1858) and Vol. 15, No. 2248 (June 10, 1858); *Daily Alta California* Vol. 10, No. 157 (June 9, 1858); "Letter from the Dalles: Another Account of Steptoe's Defeat." *Daily Alta California* Vol. 10, No. 161. California Digital Newspaper Collection.

Newspaper Reports of Steptoe's Illness. *Sacramento Daily Union*, October 11, 1860: 6. California Digital Newspaper Collection. http://cdnc.ucr.edu/cdnc/cgi-bin/cdnc?a=d&d=SDU18601011.2.4&cl

Newspaper Report of Steptoe and Virginia's Secession. "Notes of the War: Virginia Officers in Lincoln's Army." *Richmond Daily Dispatch*, September 11, 1861. http://dlxs.richmond.edu/cgi/t/text/textidx?c=ddr;cc=ddr;type=simple;rgn=div2;q1=steptoe;view=text;subview=detail;sort=occur;idno=ddr0268.0020.059;node=ddr0268.0020.059%3A9.1

Newspaper Reports of Steptoe's Visit to Europe. *Sacramento Daily Union*, Vol, 17, #2583, 8 July 1859; *New York Daily Tribune*, May 25, 1859.

Niles Register. NNR 74.017–018.

"Official Account of the Massacre of the United States Troops by the Indians." *New York Spectator*. January 27, 1836. http://www.fultonhistory.com/Fulton.html

Oswandel, J. Jacob. *Notes of the Mexican War, 1846–1848*. Knoxville: University of Tennessee Press, 2010. Originally published in 1885.

Peskin, Allan, ed. *Volunteers: The Mexican War Journals of Private Richard Coulter and Sergeant Thomas Barclay, Company E, Second Pennsylvania Infantry*. Kent, OH: Kent State University Press, 1991.

Pope, John. USMA Archives. Box #268.

Randolph, John R. Letter to Dr. William Steptoe, April 8, 1861. Manring Archives. In private hands.

Register of the Officers and Cadets of the U.S. Military Academy. 1834 and 1837. http://digitallibrary.usma.edu/libmedia/archives/oroc/y1829.pdf

Report of the Secretary of War. 35th Congress, 2nd Session, House Executive Documents #2, Vol. 2. Also 35th Congress, 2nd Session (1858), Senate Executive Documents 1. Events pertaining to Steptoe's actions at Fort Walla Walla and to Colonel George Wright's battles following Steptoe's defeat in May of 1858 are recounted in 37 dated documents (pages 330–415). More significant items are listed in this section under the names of relevant officers.

Returns from U.S. Military Posts, 1800–1916. M617. Fort Pierce, FL. Reel #919. Fort Walla Walla, WA. Reel #1343.

Scarritt, Jeremiah Mason. USMA Archives. Box #286.

Scott, Winfield. *Memoirs.* New York: Sheldon, 1864.

Sheridan, Philip H. *Indian Fighting in the Fifties in Oregon and Washington Territories.* Fairfield, WA: Ye Galleon Press, 1987. Excerpted from *Personal Memoirs* (1888).

Sherman, William T. *Memoirs of General William T. Sherman,* 2d ed., Vol. 1. New York: Appleton, 1904.

Singleton Family Papers: 1759–1905. http://www.lib.unc.edu/mss/inv/s/Singleton_Family.html#d1e507

Smith, George Winston and Charles Judah, eds. *Chronicles of the Gringos: The U.S. Army in the Mexican War, 1846–1848, Accounts of Eyewitnesses & Combatants.* Albuquerque: University of New Mexico Press, 1968.

Sprague, John T. *The Origin, Progress, and Conclusion of the Florida War.* Facsimile ed. of 1848 book. Gainesville: University Press of Florida, 1964.

"SS San Francisco." Accounts from the *New York Times,* January through February 1854. http://www.sfgenealogy.com/californiabound/cb150.htm

Stansbury, Howard. *Exploration of the Valley of the Great Salt Lake.* Washington, D.C.: Smithsonian Institution, 1988. Originally published in 1852.

Steptoe, Mary Claytor (1822–1865). http://www.findagrave.com/cgi-bin/fg.cgi?page=gr&GRid=7546924

_____. Obituary Notice. *Lynchburg News.* April 9, 1887. Jones Memorial Library. Lynchburg, VA.

_____. Will and Codicil. Jones Memorial Library. Lynchburg, VA. Item #4037.

Stevens, Hazard. *The Life of Isaac Ingalls Stevens,* Vol. II. Boston: Houghton, Mifflin, 1901.

Stevens, Isaac Ingalls. *Campaigns of the Rio Grande and Mexico.* New York: D. Appleton, 1851.

Stout, Hosea. *On the Mormon Frontier: The Diary of Hosea Stout, 1844–1889.* Ed. by Juanita Brooks. Salt Lake City: University of Utah Press, 2009.

The Virginian. December 21, 1826. April 6, 1827. November 5, 1827. Microfilm. Jones Memorial Library. Lynchburg, Virginia.

Waite, C[atherine]. *The Mormon Prophet and His Harem,* 5th ed., rev. Philadelphia: Zeigler, McCurdy, 1867.

Winder, C[harles] S[ydney]. "Captain C.S. Winder's Account of a Battle with the Indians." *Maryland Historical Magazine* 35.1 (Spring 1940): 56–59.

Wool, John. General John Wool, at Benicia, CA, to Colonel L. Thomas, Assistant Adjutant General, Headquarters of the Army, New York City. August 19, 1856. 36th Congress, 3rd Session, Senate Executive Documents, Number 5, Volume 2.

Wright, George. Colonel George Wright on the Yakima River, Kittitas Valley, Washington Territory to Major W.W. Mackall, July 18, 1856. 36th Congress, 3rd Session, Senate Executive Documents, Number 5, Volume 2. Also October 2, 1856.

Secondary Sources

Abbot, John L., "Presentation of the Portrait of James Steptoe to the Circuit Court of Bedford County." October 13, 1953: 13. Manuscript in Jones Memorial Library, Lynchburg, VA.

Alexie, Sherman. *The Lone Ranger and Tonto Fistfight in Heaven.* New York: Grove, 1993.

_____. *Old Shirts & New Skins.* Los Angeles: American Indian Studies, 1993.

Ambrose, Stephen E. *Duty, Honor, Country: A History of West Point.* Baltimore: Johns Hopkins, 1966, 1999.

Arnold, Matthew. "Literature and Science." *Norton Anthology of English Literature: The Victorian Age,* 8th ed. New York: Norton, 2005. 1415–1427.

Bibliography

Arnold, R. Ross. *Indian Wars of Idaho.* Caldwell, ID: Caxton, 1932.
Arrington, Leonard J. *Brigham Young: American Moses.* New York: Alfred A. Knopf, 1985.
Bagley, Will. *Blood of the Prophets: Brigham Young and the Massacre at Mountain Meadows.* Norman: University of Oklahoma Press, 2002.
Bailey, Lynn R., ed. "Lt. Sylvester Mowry's Report on His March in 1855 from Salt Lake City to Fort Tejon." *Arizona and the West* 7.4 (Winter 1965): 329–346.
Bancroft, H[ubert] H[owe]. *History of Utah, The Works of Hubert Howe Bancroft,* Vol. 26. San Francisco: History Company, 1889.
Bauer, K. Jack. *The Mexican War, 1846–1848.* New York: Macmillan, 1974.
———. *Zachary Taylor: Soldier, Planter, Statesman of the Old Southwest.* Baton Rouge: Louisiana State University Press, 1985.
Bear, James A. and Lucia Stanton, eds. *Jefferson Memorandum Books,* Vol. 1. Princeton: Princeton University Press, 1997.
Bennett, Robert A. *Walla Walla: Portrait of a Western Town, 1804–1899.* Walla Walla: Pioneer Press, 1980.
Boyd, Julian P., ed. *The Papers of Thomas Jefferson,* Vol. 6. Princeton: Princeton University Press, 1952.
Boyd, Mark F. "Florida Aflame: The Background and Onset of the Seminole War, 1835." *Florida Historical Quarterly* 30.1 (July 1951): 1–115. Available as monograph.
Brown, William Compton. *The Indian Side of the Story.* Spokane: C.W. Hill, 1961.
Burns, Robert Ignatius, S.J. *The Jesuits and the Indian Wars of the Northwest.* New Haven: Yale University Press, 1966.
———. "Pere Joset's Account of the Indian War of 1858." *Pacific Northwest Quarterly* 38.4 (October 1947): 285–314.
Chambers, S. Allen, Jr. *Poplar Forest and Thomas Jefferson.* Little Compton, RI: Fort Church, 1993.
Clarke, William. *The Boy's Own Book of Games.* Bedford, MA: Applewood Books, 1996. Originally published in 1829.
Clary, David A. *Eagles and Empire: The United States, Mexico, and the Struggle for a Continent.* New York: Bantam, 2009.
Coker, Edward C. and Daniel L. Schafer. "A West Point Graduate in the Second Seminole War: William Warren Chapman and the View from Fort Foster." *Florida Historical Quarterly* 68.4 (April 1990): 447–475.
Coleman, Louis C. and Leo Rieman, *Captain John Mullan; His Life Building the Mullan Road* Montreal, Canada: Payette Radio, 1968.
Collier, Edna Jones. "The Old Virginia Gentleman." *American Monthly Magazine* 38.1 (January 1911): 1.
Covington, James W. *The Seminoles of Florida.* Gainesville: University Press of Florida, 1993.
Coxe, John Redman, ed. "Medical Commencement." *Philadelphia Medical Museum,* Vol. 4, Medical and Philosophical Register: lix.
Crackel, Theodore. *The Illustrated History of West Point.* New York: Harry N. Abrams, 1991.
Cutler, Carl C. *Queens of the Western Ocean.* Annapolis, MD: U.S. Naval Institute, 1961.
Day, Terence. "Grave Disservice to Col. Steptoe." Letters to the Editor, *Moscow-Pullman Daily News,* February 29, 2012, 7A.
Dietrich, William. *Northwest Passage: The Great Columbia River.* New York: Simon & Schuster, 1995.
Dillon, Lester R., Jr. *American Artillery in the Mexican War, 1846–1847.* Austin, TX: Presidial, 1975.
Dilts, James D. *The Great Road: The Building of the Baltimore and Ohio, the Nation's First Railroad, 1823–1853.* Stanford: Stanford University Press, 1993.
Dozier, Jack. "The Coeur d'Alene Indians in the War of 1858." *Idaho Yesterdays* 5.3 (Fall 1961): 22–32.
Eakley, Barbara Brown. *The Browns of Bedford County, Virginia, 1748–1840.* Bowie, MD: Heritage Books, 1998.
Early, Jubal A. *Memoirs.* New York: Konecky & Konecky, 1994.
Early Washington. Corvallis, OR: Western Guide Publishers, 1974. n.p.
Evans, Elwood. *History of the Pacific Northwest: Oregon and Washington,* Vol. I. Portland: North Pacific History Co., 1889.

Fairburn, William Armstrong. *Merchant Sail*. Ed. Ethel M Richie. Center Lovell, ME: Fairburn Marine Educational Foundation, 1955.
Fielding, Robert Kent. *The Unsolicited Chronicler: An Account of the Gunnison Massacre*. Brookline, MA: Paradigm, 1993.
Fleming, Thomas J. *West Point: The Men and Times of the United States Military Academy*. New York: William Morrow, 1969.
Foote Shelby. *The Civil War, A Narrative: Red River to Appomattox*. New York: Random House, 1974.
Francke, Arthur E., Jr. *Fort Mellon, 1837–1842: A Microcosm of the Second Seminole War*. Miami: Banyan Books, 1977. Booklet format.
Frey, Rodney. *Landscape Traveled by Coyote and Crane*. Seattle: University of Washington Press, 2001. Study of the Coeur d'Alene (or Schitsu'umsh).
Furniss, Norman F. *The Mormon Conflict: 1850–1859*. New Haven: Yale University Press, 1960.
Gale, Robert L. *Will Henry/Clay Fisher (Henry W. Allen)*. Boston: Twayne, 1984.
Gates, Susa Young and Leah D. Widtsoe. *The Life Story of Brigham Young*. New York: Macmillan, 1930.
Gibbs, Josiah. "Gunnison Massacre—1853—Millard County, Utah—Indian Mareer's Version of the Tragedy—1894." *Utah Historical Quarterly* 1.3 (July 1928): 71–75.
Giddings, Joshua R. *Exiles of Florida*. Columbus, OH: Follett, Foster & Co., 1858.
Green, Constance McLaughlin. *Washington: Village and Capital, 1800–1878*. Princeton: Princeton University Press, 1962.
Greenberg, Kenneth S., ed. *Nat Turner: A Slave Rebellion in History and Memory*. New York: Oxford, 2003.
Guide to the Fort Walla Walla Collection, 1849–1910, Penrose Library, Whitman College, Walla Walla, WA.
Hardy, Stella Pickett. *Colonial Families of the Southern States of America: A History and Genealogy of Colonial Families Who Settled in the Colonies Prior to the Revolution*, 2d ed. Baltimore: Genealogical Publishing, 1958.
Henry, Will. *Pillars of the Sky*. New York: Bantam, 1991.
Hirschhorn, Norbert and Robert G. Feldman and Ian A. Greaves. "Abraham Lincoln's Blue Pills." *Perspectives in Biology and Medicine* 44.3 (2002): 315–332.
Howard, Helen Addison. "The Steptoe Affair." *Montana: The Magazine of Western History* 19.2 (Spring 1969): 28–36.
Howe, Henry. *Historical Collections of Virginia*. Charleston, SC: Babcock, 1845.
Johnson, Randall. "May 17, 1858: The Ordeal of the Steptoe Command." *Pacific Northwesterner* 17.1 (Winter 1973). 35 pages. http://www.historylink.org/index.cfm?DisplayPage=output.cfm&file_id=8123
Josephy, Alvin, Jr. *The Nez Perce Indians and the Opening of the Northwest*. Boston: Houghton Mifflin, 1965, 1997.
Keegan, John. *The Face of Battle*. New York: Viking, 1976.
Keyes, Erasmus D. *Fifty Years' Observation of Men and Events Civil and Military*. New York: Charles Scribner's Sons, 1884.
Knetsch, Joe. *Fear and Anxiety on the Florida Frontier*. Dade City, FL: Seminole Wars Foundation, 2015.
_____. *Florida's Seminole Wars 1817–1858*. The Making of America Series. Charleston, SC: Arcadia, 2003.
Knuth, Priscilla. Knuth, *"Picturesque" Frontier: The Army's Fort Dalles*, 2d ed. Portland: Oregon Historical Society, 1968, 1987.
Kowrach, Edward J. and Thomas E. Connolly. *Saga of the Coeur d'Alene Indians: An Account of Chief Joseph Seltice*. Fairfield, WA: Ye Galleon, 1990.
Kriebel, Mahlon E. *Battle of To-hots-nim-me: The U.S. Army vs. the Coeur d'Alene Indians*. Bloomington, IN: AuthorHouse, rev. 2d ed. 2012. Originally in *Bunchgrass Historian* 34.2&3 (2008).
Lansing, Jewel. *Portland: People, Politics, and Power, 1851–2001*. Corvallis: Oregon State University Press, 2003.
Laumer, Frank. *Dade's Last Command*. Gainesville: University Press of Florida, 1995.
Lindermann, Erika. "Overview: 1830–1839." In Snider, *True and Candid Compositions*. See Online Sources.

_____. "The School Day and the School Year." In Snider, *True and candid Compositions*. See Online Sources.
Linn, William Alexander. *The Story of the Mormons: From the Date of Their Origin to the Year 1901*. New York: Macmillan, 1902.
Lloyd, Richard B. and Bernard K. Murdy. *Lynchburg: A Pictorial History*. Virginia Beach: Donning, 1975.
London, Bill. "The View is a Butte from the Top of Steptoe." *Moscow-Pullman Daily News*, February 11–12, 2012: 4D.
MacKinnon, William, ed. *At Sword's Point, Part One: A Documentary History of the Utah War to 1858*. Norman, OK: Arthur H. Clark, 2008.
_____. "'Lonely Bones': Leadership and Utah War Violence." *Journal of Mormon History* 33.1 (Spring 2007): 121–178.
_____. "Sex, Subalterns, and Steptoe: Army Behavior, Mormon Rage, and Utah War Anxieties." *Utah Historical Quarterly* 76.3 (Summer 2008): 227–246.
Mahon, John K. *History of the Second Seminole War*, rev. ed. Gainesville: University Press of Florida, 1992.
Manring, B[enjamin] F[ranklin]. *The Conquest of the Coeur d'Alenes, Spokanes and Palouses*. Spokane, WA: John W. Graham, 1912. See also the Ye Galleon edition, Fairfield, WA, 1975, for useful appendices.
Marszalek, John F. *Sherman: A Soldier's Passion for Order*. New York: Free Press, 1993.
Martin, Ann Smart. *Buying into the World of Goods: Early Consumers in Backcountry Virginia*. Baltimore: Johns Hopkins, 2008.
Martin, Joseph. *A New and Comprehensive Gazetteer of Virginia and the District of Columbia*. Charlottesville: Moseley & Tompkins, 1835.
Mayo, Bernard. "Henry Clay, Patron and Idol of White Sulphur Springs: His Letters to James Calwell." *Virginia Magazine of History and Biography* 55.4 (October 1947): 301–317.
McKinney, Francis F. *Education in Violence: The Life of George H. Thomas and the History of the Army of the Cumberland*. Detroit: Wayne State University Press, 1961.
McReynolds, Edwin C. *The Seminoles*. Norman: University of Oklahoma Press, 1972.
Meacham, Jon. *American Lion: Andrew Jackson and the White House*. New York: Random House, 2008.
Miller, David Henry. Unpublished Master of Arts thesis from the University of Utah, "The Impact of the Gunnison Massacre on Mormon-Federal Relations: Edward Jenner Steptoe's Command in Utah Territory, 1854–1855" (June 1968).
Miller, Susan A. *Coacoochee's Bones: A Seminole Saga*. Lawrence: University Press of Kansas, 2003.
Morrison, Alfred J. *The Beginnings of Public Education in Virginia, 1776–1860*. Richmond: Virginia State Board of Education, 1917.
Morrison, James L., Jr. *"The Best School in the World": West Point, the Pre-Civil War Years, 1833–1866*. Kent, OH: Kent State University Press, 1986.
Nelson, Kurt R. *Fighting for Paradise: A Military History of the Pacific Northwest*. Yardley, PA: Westholme, 2007.
_____. *Treaties and Treachery: The Northwest Indians' Resistance to Conquest*. Caldwell, ID: Caxton, 2011.
Osborne, Charles C. *Jubal: The Life and Times of General Jubal A. Early, CSA, Defender of the Lost Cause*. Chapel Hill: Algonquin, 1992.
Passonneau, Joseph R. *Washington through Two Centuries*. New York: Monacelli, 2004.
Peltier, Jerome. *Warbonnets and Epaulets*. Montreal: Payette Radio, 1971.
Peters, Virginia Bergman. *The Florida Wars*. Brooklyn: Shoe String, 1979.
Petersen, Keith. *John Mullan: The Tumultuous Life of a Western Road Builder*. Pullman: Washington State University Press, 2014.
Potter, Clifton, and Potter, Dorothy. *Lynchburg: A City Set on Seven Hills*. The Makers of America Series. Charleston, SC: Arcadia, 2004.
_____, and _____. *Lynchburg: "The Most Interesting Spot."* Lynchburg, VA: Beric, 1985.
Potter, Dorothy, and Potter, Clifton. *Lynchburg 1757–2007*. Images of America Series. Charleston, SC: Arcadia, 2007.
Read, Deborah Imogene. *New London Today and Yesterday*. Lynchburg, VA: J.P. Bell, 1950.
Rémy, Jules. *A Journey to Great-Salt-Lake City*, Vol. One. London: W. Jeffs, 1861.

Richards, Kent D. *Isaac I. Stevens: Young Man in a Hurry.* Salt Lake City: Brigham Young University Press, 1979.
Robertson, James I., Jr. "Foreword." *The Battle of Lynchburg.* By L. VanLoan Naisawald. Lynchburg: Warwick House, 2004: n.p.
Rosebush, Waldo E. *Frontier Steel: The Men and Their Weapons.* Appleton, WA: C.C. Nelson, 1958.
Ruby, Robert H. and John A Brown, *The Cayuse Indians: Imperial Tribesmen of Old Oregon.* Norman: University of Oklahoma Press, 1972, 2005.
Schene, Michael G. "Not a Shot Fired: Fort Chokonikla and the 'Indian War' of 1849–1850." *Tequesta* 37 (1977): 19–37.
Scheuerman, Richard D. and Michael O. Finley. *Finding Chief Kamiakin: The Life and Legacy of a Northwest Patriot.* Pullman: Washington State University Press, 2008.
Schindler, Harold. *Orrin Porter Rockwell: Man of God, Son of Thunder*, 2d ed. Salt Lake City: University of Utah Press, 1983.
Schlicke, Carl P. *General George Wright: Guardian of the Pacific Coast.* Norman: University of Oklahoma Press, 1988.
Schwantes, Carlos A. *The Pacific Northwest: An Interpretive History.* Lincoln: University of Nebraska Press, 1989.
Scruggs, Philip Lightfoot. *The History of Lynchburg, Virginia (1786–1946).* Lynchburg: J.P. Bell, 1975.
Simmons, Virginia McConnell. *The Ute Indians of Utah, Colorado, and New Mexico.* Boulder: University Press of Colorado, 2000.
Smith, Justin H. *The War with Mexico.* New York: Macmillan, 1919.
Snider, William D. *Light on the Hill: A History of the University of North Carolina at Chapel Hill.* Chapel Hill: University of North Carolina, 1992.
Splawn, A. J. *Ka-mi-akin: The Last Hero of the Yakimas.* Portland, OR: Binford & Mort, 1944.
Steptoe City, NV. *Sacramento Daily Union* Vol 27 #4083, April 22, 1864. California Digital Newspaper Collection.
"Steptoe (Tohotonimme) Battlefield." Archaeological and Historical Services, Eastern Washington University, on behalf of the Washington State Parks and Recreation Commission, 2006. Pamphlet.
Trafzer, Clifford E. and Richard D. Scheuerman. *Renegade Tribe: The Palouse Indians and the Invasion of the Inland Pacific Northwest* Pullman: Washington State University Press, 1986.
Utley, Robert M. *Frontiersman in Blue: The United States Army and the Indian, 1848–1865.* New York: Macmillan, 1967.
Victor, Frances Fuller. *The Early Indian Wars of Oregon.* Salem, OR: Frank C. Baker, 1894.
Walker, Ronald W. "President Young Writes to Jefferson Davis about the Gunnison Massacre Affair." *BYU Studies* 35.1 (1995): 146–170.
Wallner, Peter A. *Franklin Pierce: New Hampshire's Favorite Son.* Concord, NH: Plaidswede, 2004.
Walton, George. *Fearless and Free: The Seminole Indian War, 1835–1842.* Indianapolis: Bobbs-Merrill, 1977.
Wheelan, Joseph. *Invading Mexico: America's Continental Dream and the Mexican War, 1846–1848.* New York: Carroll & Graf, 2007.
Whitaker, Ernest J. "Edward Jevnor Steptoe: Caretaker of the Palouse Hills." *West Pointers and Early Washington*, ed. John A. Hemphill and Robert C. Cumbow. Seattle: West Point Society of Puget Sound, 1992. 167–180. Erroneous middle name follows B.F. Manring.
Whiting, J.S. *Forts of the State of Washington*, 2d ed. Seattle: self-published, 1951.
Wiltse, Charles M. *John C. Calhoun: Nullifier, 1829–1839.* Indianapolis: Bobbs-Merrill, 1949.
Winders, Richard Bruce. *Mr. Polk's Army: The American Military Experience in the Mexican War.* College Station: Texas A&M University Press, 1997.

Online Sources

"Answering the Call: The Personal Equipment of a Civil War Soldier." https://www.armyheritage.org/education-and-programs/educational-resources/soldier-stories/50-information/soldier-stories/285-civilwarequipment

Bibliography

"Battle of Four Lakes Monument. "http://properties.historicspokane.org/property/?Property-ID=1984
Captain Edward Ball. Photograph (1871). http://en.wikipedia.org/wiki/File:SoldiersAtFort EllisMontanaTerritory1871.jpg
"Chesterfield Railroad." http://en.wikipedia.org/wiki/Chesterfield_Railroad
Cole, David. "Survey of U.S. Army Uniforms, Weapons and Accoutrements" (2007). http://www.history.army.mil/html/museums/uniforms/survey_uwa.pdf
Ewing, Galen R. "'Bug Juice' Use and Abuse: Alcoholism in the Frontier Army." http://www.nps.gov/fosc/learn/education/guardalcoholism.htm
"Federal Hill." http://www.dhr.virginia.gov/registers/Counties/Campbell/015-0003_Federal_Hill_1982_Final_Nomination.pdf
"Fort Adams." http://en.wikipedia.org/wiki/Fort_Adams
"Fort Monroe." http://en.wikipedia.org/wiki/Fort_Monroe
"Garrison and Ship Cannons." http://www.thepirateking.com/historical/cannon_garrison_and_ship_guns.html
Girardin, Eugène de. "Tour of the Badlands." Le Tour du Monde (1864) http://projetgirardin.free.fr/PAGES/BADLANDS5-5.
"The Girl I Left Behind." http://en.wikipedia.org/wiki/The_Girl_I_Left_Behind
"A Gleam of Hope!" *New York Times*, December 31, 1860. http://www.nytimes.com/1860/12/31/news/a-gleam-of hope.html?scp=43&sq=dec+31+1860&st=p
"Henry Kinney." Corpus Christi Museum. http://www.ccmuseumedres.com/tour.php?action=details&record=120
"History of St. Paul's" (Lynchburg, VA). http://www.stpaulslynchburg.org/history-of-st-pauls
"Indian River Lagoon." http://en.wikipedia.org/wiki/Indian_River_Lagoon; http://www.florida oceanographic.org/environ/Indian_River.htm
"Ivy Cliff." http://www.historicivycliff.com/Home_Page.php
"John E. Wool." http://en.wikipedia.org/wiki/John_E._Wool
"McCroskey, Virgil Talmadge (1876–1970)." http://www.historylink.org/index.cfm?DisplayPage=output.cfm&File_Id=7989
Miller-Claytor House. http://www.nps.gov/nr/travel/vamainstreet/mil.htm
"Natural Bridge, Virginia." http://en.wikipediaiki/Natural_Bridge_%28Virginia%29
O'Brien, Lucius and John T. Metcalf and Ripley A. Arnold, et al. Lyrics to "Benny Havens, Oh!" http://www.west-point.org/greimanj/west_point/songs/bennyhavens.html
"Peaks of the Otter." http://en.wikipedia.org/wik/Peaks¬of_Otter
Pillars of the Sky (film). Dir. George Marshall, Universal Pictures, 1956. http://www.tcm.com/this-month/article/139135%7C0/Pillars-of-the-Sky.html; http://www.imdb.com/title/tt00 49619/
"Point of Honor." http://www.pointofhonor.org/history/index.php
Powell, William S. "Carolina—A Brief History." http://www.unc.edu/about/history.html
"Qualchan Golf Course." http://properties.historicspokane.org/property/?PropertyID=1984
"Rosalia, Washington." By. Robert M. Lambeth. http://spokanehistorical.org/items/show/373.
"Seigneur de Bayard (1473–1524)." http://en.wikipedia.org/wiki/Pierre_Terrail,_seigneur_de_ Bayard
"Seizure of the Forts at Charleston." *Richmond Daily Dispatch*. http://digitalnewspapers.libraries. psu.edu/Default/Scripting/ArticleWin.asp?From=Archive&Source=Page&Skin=civil war&BaseHref=PDU/1860/12/31&PageLabelPrint=2&EntityId=Ar00202&DataChunk=Ar 00201&ViewMode=GIF
Shedden, David. "Florida Journalism History Project," http://uflib.ufl.edu/fljhist/full.html.
Snider, William D. *True and Candid Compositions: The Lives and Writings of Antebellum Students at the University of North Carolina.* http://docsouth.unc.edu/true/chapter/chp02-ol/chp02-01,html
"Spencer Repeating Rifle." http://www.hackman-adams.com/guns/spencermore.htm
"SS San Francisco." The Maritime Heritage Project. http://www.maritimeheritage.org/ships/ss SanFrancisco.htm
"Steptoe." The Internet Surname Database: Last Name: Steptoe. http://www.surnamedb.com/Surname/Steptoe
"Steptoe Butte State Park." http://www.stateparks.com/steptoe_butte.html

"Steptoe Portrait Returns to Courthouse." http://www.bedfordbulleton.com/content/steptoe-portrait-returns-courthouse

"Steptoe Family." http://www.familytreemaker.genealogy.com/users/r/i/t/Donna-L-Ritter/Gen

"Steptoe Valley." Ghost Towns of Nevada. http://www.ghosttowns.com/states/nv/steptoecity.htm; http://en.wikipedia.org/wiki/Steptoe_Valley

"Steptoe Village." WSU Housing and Residence Life. http://housing.wsu.edu/famgrad/Steptoe Village

"Steptoe, Washington." http://en.wikipedia.org/wiki/Steptoe,_Washington

Stone, Spessard. "Billy Bowlegs: Seminole Chief." http://freepages.genealogy.rootsweb.ancestry.com/~crackerbarrel/Bowlegs3.html

_____. "Fort Chokonikla." http://freepages.genealogy.rootsweb.ancestry.com/~crackerbarrel/Steptoe.html

"Visitor Guide." *Thomas Jefferson's Poplar Forest*. See http://www.poplarforest.org/retreat/landrest

"Walla Walla Chamber of Commerce." http://www.wwvchamber.com/index.php?option=com_content&view=article&id=138&Itemid=233

Index

abolition 18, 21, 31–32, 37, 61, 65, 112, 121, 182
Adams, Pres. John Quincy 16, 21
Adams, Norman 197
Adjutant General, Office of 3, 51, 56, 59, 61, 62, 64, 90, 94–97, 102, 105–106, 109–111, 115, 116, 121–122, 130, 134, 137, 140, 143, 148, 156, 175–177, 180, 182, 185, 205*n*
African Americans 17, 46, 50, 200
Ahtanum Creek (WA) 125–126
Alabama 3, 40, 46, 51, 86
CSS *Alabama* 86
Alamo 32, 43, 65, 66
Albany, NY 33
Alexander, Col. Edward 118
Alexander the Great 89
Alexandria, VA 20
Alexie, Sherman 192–193
Alleatsokee (Halpatiokee) River (FL) 58
Alleghany Springs, VA 181
Allen, Augustus Porter 43
Allen, Ethan 208*n*
Alligator see Halpatter
Allston, Col. Benjamin (CSA) 96, 106, 122, 211*n*
Alpowa Creek (WA) 156
Alpowa Summit 156
American Board of Commissioners for Foreign Missions 87
Ampudia, Gen. Pedro de 68–69
Alta California 64–66
Ambrose, Stephen 23, 36
Anaya, Pedro María de 75–76
Anderson, Maj. Robert 73–74, 77, 79, 85, 89, 181, 184, 209*n*
Angell, Truman O. 93
Anglo-Saxon 73, 84, 191
Ansara, Michael 196
Antes, Pvt. William 97, 211*n*
Anti-Jacksonian 21

Antigua River (Río Antiqua) 81
Apache Indians 142
Apalachicola River 41
Appomattox, VA 3, 19, 187, 207*n*
Arab 74, 115
Archer, Sen. William S. 57
Arista, Gen. Mariano 66–67
Arkansas 24, 44, 50, 57, 118, 164
Armistead, Gen. Walker K. 54, 56
Army Life on the Pacific 122
Army of Northern Virginia 29
Army of the North (Mexican) 67
Army of the Potomac 28, 70, 142, 211*n*
Army of the Tennessee 28
Arnold, Benedict 25
Arnold, Matthew 23
Arnold, R. Ross 147, 156, 160
Arpeika (Sam Jones) 46, 63
Ashlock, Mr. & Mrs. 55
Asia 89
Aston pistol, Model 1842, .54 caliber 155
Astor House 61
Atalaya Hill (Mexico) 80, 81
Atlantic Ocean 31, 52, 132
Austria 61, 181
Austro-Sardinian War 4, 181
The Avenging Angel (film) 213*n*
Aztec Club 120
Aztecs 83

Babbitt, Almon 108
Bacchus 110
Bagley, Will 118, 210–211*n*
Ball, Sgt. Edward 169–170, 171, 193–194, 197, 220*n*
Baltimore & Ohio (B&O) Railroad 15, 20, 33, 34
Bancroft, H[ubert] H[owe] 92, 189
Bannock Indians 148
Baptist 14

Index

Barclay, Sgt. Thomas 82–84, 89, 210n
Bartow, FL 63
Bartram, William 42
Basinger, 1st Lt. William E. 39
Battle Days, Battle Days Museum (WA) 192
Battle of Antietam 70, 216n
Battle of Bear Paw 196
Battle of Bethel Church 184
Battle of Buena Vista 69, 78, 87, 88, 213n, 220n
Battle of Cascades (Cascade Locks) 2, 133; see also Cascades
Battle of Cedar Mountain 142
Battle of Cerro Gordo 2, 79–82, 205n, 209n, 216n
Battle of Chantilly 209n
Battle of Chapultepec 2, 62, 71, 82, 85–87, 124, 142, 206n, 214n, 216n, 217n, 221n
Battle of Chickamauga 221n
Battle of Churubusco 82, 84, 85, 142, 208n
Battle of Contreras 82, 83, 84, 85, 208n
Battle of Corrick's Ford 179
Battle of First Manassas 216n
Battle of Four Lakes 146, 147, 163, 171, 174, 175, 192, 197, 221n
Battle of Fort Huger 215n
Battle of Fredericksburg 185, 215n
Battle of Gaines Mill 185
Battle of Gettysburg 28, 70, 86, 204n, 213n, 216n, 220n
Battle of Glorieta Pass 28
Battle of Grande Ronde 134
Battle of Guilford Courthouse 10
Battle of Lake Okeechobee 49–50, 66
Battle of Lockahatchee (Loxahatchee) 51, 67
Battle of Lynchburg 4, 186–187
Battle of Malvern Hill 220n
Battle of Molino del Rey 85, 89, 206n, 208n
Battle of Monterrey 68, 70, 71, 88, 208n, 220n
Battle of New Orleans 12
Battle of Palo Alto 66–67, 70
Battle of Petersburg 207n
Battle of Pine Creek see Battle of Tohotsnimme
Battle of Plattsburg 23
Battle (Siege) of Port Hudson 206n
Battle of Resaca de la Palma 67
Battle of San Jacinto 43–44, 65
Battle of Santo de Rosales 142, 146
Battle of Shiloh 118, 126, 215n
Battle of Solferino 181
Battle of Spokane Plains 147, 174–176, 192, 221n
Battle of Spotsylvania Court House 61
Battle of the Little Bighorn 171

Battle of Tohotsnimme (also Tohotonimme) 3, 142, 146–178
The Battle of To-hots-nim-me 146, 197
Battle of Williamsburg 142
Bauer, K. Jack 65, 78, 209n
Beacon Rock (WA) 123
Beadle, J[ohn] H[anson] 107, 213n
Beall, Thomas B. 146, 151, 154–155, 158, 164
Bean, George Washington 107
Bear River (UT) 96, 116
Beauregard, Gen. Pierre Gustave Toutant (CSA) 2, 29, 78, 81, 85, 87, 184, 208n, 210n, 215n
Beckwith, Lt. Edward G. 93, 211n
Bedford, VA see Liberty
Bedford Alum Springs Tavern 11
Bedford Bulletin 9
Bedford County 7–9, 11, 17, 32, 41, 180
Beehive House (UT) 100
Bell, Sen. John 183
Belton, Capt. Francis S. 40
Benicia, CA (Fort Benicia, Benicia Barracks, Benecia Arsenal) 95, 99, 101, 111, 114–116, 120, 145, 148, 191, 210n
Bennett, Robert A. 152
Benny Havens tavern and song 24, 26, 29, 37, 64, 207–208n
Bibb, Sen. George M. 21, 203n
Bicknall, Edward 101, 102, 106, 212n
Big Elk (Ute chief) 94
Big Otter River (VA) 11, 12
Billy Bowlegs see Holata Micco
Bitterroot Mountains 177
Black Creek (FL) 49
Black Hawk War 46, 209n
Blackfeet 159
Blair, Helen 49
Blair, Seth Millington 102
Blue as the Lake: A Personal Geography 200
Blue Mountains (OR) 137, 191
Blue Ridge Mountains (VA) 11, 13, 149
Blue River, Big and Little (NE) 96
Boise, ID 122
Bolon, Andrew Jackson 125–127, 136
Bombastes Furioso 16
Bond, Ward 195
Book of Mormon 93
Boone, Daniel 74
Boston, MA 35, 37
Boston Advertiser 83
Bottom, Hildie 5, 38
Bouchey, Willis 195
Bradford Storehouse 129
Bradner, Chuck 5
Bragg, Gen. Braxton (CSA) 2, 28, 43, 78, 215n
Brazos Island, Brazos Santiago 62
Breckenridge, Sen John C. 183

Index

Bridal Veil Falls (OR) 123
Britain, British 9, 12, 16, 20, 22, 25, 55, 59, 82, 114
Broken Arrow 196
Brooklyn, NY 200
Brown, Ann "Nancy" *see* Steptoe, Ann "Nancy" Brown
Brown, B.W. 129
Brown, Lt. H. 90
Brown, Capt. Henry (E.J.'s maternal grandfather) 7, 10, 12, 25, 27, 32, 182, 201n, 204n
Brown, J. Ross (Indian agent) 144
Brown, John (abolitionist) 112, 121, 182, 216n, 218n, 219n, 220n
Brown, John A. (historian) 136, 147, 153, 160, 169
Brown, John Thompson (E.J.'s uncle) 10, 12, 20
Brown, John Thompson II (E.J.'s cousin) 10
Brown, Samuel Thompson (E.J.'s uncle) 10
Brown, William Compton (historian) 141, 147, 158, 160, 169, 216n, 218n
Brownsville, TX 66
Brulé Lakota (Sioux) 97
Buchanan, Pres. James 112, 115, 118, 121
Buffalo, NY 53
Bunker Hill monument 35
Burns, Robert Ignatius, S.J. 4, 123, 124, 130, 134, 141, 144, 147, 152, 154, 156, 158–160, 162, 164–166, 169, 171, 172, 179, 197
Butler, Gen. Benjamin 120, 184
Butler, Gen. William 88
Byron, Lord George Gordon 68

Cabell, Dr. George 15
Calder, David O. 213n
Calhoun, Sen. John 11, 21–22, 203n
California 64–66, 67, 69, 91, 93–96, 98–99, 101, 105, 109, 110–111, 115, 116, 118, 120, 123, 144, 148, 151, 171–172, 179, 191, 193, 206n, 210n, 211n, 215n, 218n, 220n
Call, Bishop Anson 93, 94
Call, Gen. Richard 46
Callaway-Steptoe Cemetery 187
Caloosahatchee River (FL) 52, 54
Camel Corps 116
Camp Cooper (NE) 96
Camp Drum (OR) 130
"Camptown Races" 98
Canada 43, 59, 196
Canis, George F. 158
Cape Hatteras, NC 95
Carrington, Albert 102
Carson Valley (NV) 116
Cascade Mountains 138, 141
Cascades Indians 129
Cascades Massacre 129, 168
Cascades of the Columbia, WA 120, 123, 128, 129, 133, 168
Cass, Lewis 22
Castilian 83, 89
Castillo de San Marcos, FL *see* Fort Marion
Castle of Chapultepec 85
Cataldo Mission (ID) 159
Catlin, George 24
Cayuse Indians 87–88, 1243, 125, 126, 128, 133–137, 148, 153
Cayuse War 88, 123–124
Cedar City, UT 101
Cedar Grove 7, 10, 183
Cerro Gordo *see* Battle of Cerro Gordo
Chalk Creek (UT) 93
Chandler, Jeff 195
Chapel Hill, NC 17–18, 37, 45, 59
Chaplin, Charlie 196
Chaplin, Sydney 196
Chapman, Capt. William Warren 49–50
Chapultepec *see* Battle of Chapultepec
Charleston, SC 40, 41, 59, 90, 180, 184, 207n
Charlotte Harbor, Port Charlotte, FL 52
Charlottesville, VA 12
Cheney, WA 197
Chenowith 129
Cherokees 46
Cherry Creek (NV) 191
Chesterfield railroad (VA) 33
Childs, Gen. Thomas 56, 58, 87
Christianity 13, 18, 35, 113, 194–196
Christmas 49, 50, 66, 88, 95, 106, 137, 140, 149, 183, 206n
Christoff, Suzanne 5
Christy, Howard 94
Churubusco River (Mexico) 84
Civil War 1, 2, 3, 17, 21, 26, 30, 43, 55, 61, 82, 86, 92, 108, 116, 120, 128, 142, 154, 155, 171, 179, 186, 195, 203n, 204n, 206n, 207n, 208n, 209n, 211n, 214n, 215n, 218n, 220n, 221n
Clark, George Rogers 8
Clark, Ransom 39–40
Clarke, Gen. Newman S. 141, 142, 144–145, 216n
Clarke, William 202n
Clarkston, WA 157
Clary, David A. 65, 208n
Clay, Sen. Henry 11, 21, 45, 58, 59, 205n
Claytor, Samuel Leftwich 182
Clinch, Gen. Duncan L. 40, 41, 46
Coa Hadjo 47
Coacoochee (WildCat) 1, 41, 46, 47, 50, 52–53, 54, 56–57, 207n
Coburn, James 214n
Cochise 196
Coe, L.W. 129

Index

Coeur d'Alene, ID 159
Coeur d'Alene Indians 3, 38, 141, 146–148, 152–154, 158–160, 162–169, 175–177, 189–190, 192, 197–198, 199, 217*n*, 218*n*, 219*n*
Coeur d'Alene Lake 159, 177
Coeur d'Alene mission 147
Coeur d'Alene Reservation 192
Coeur d'Alene River 159
Cole, David 155
Colestah 177
Colfax, WA 141, 148, 150–151, 158, 192, 223*n*
Collado Beach (Mexico) 77
Colonial Families of the Southern States of America 14
Colt revolver 154–155
Colt Third Model Dragoon .44 caliber revolver 197
Columbia Gorge 123
Columbia River 122–123, 128, 130–132, 135, 138, 141, 149
Colville, WA 1, 132, 136, 144, 147–148, 150, 153, 157–158, 162, 194
Colville Indians 177
Colville Reservation 177
Comanche Indians 207*n*
Compromise of 1850 21
Compromise Tariff 21
Confederacy 2, 4, 17, 28, 29, 31, 36, 43, 71, 85, 86, 118, 126, 139, 143, 154, 155, 179, 184, 185, 186, 195, m209*n*, 210*n*, 214*n*, 215*n*, 217*n*, 218*n*, 220*n*, 221*n*, 222*n*
Congiato, Father Nicholas, S.J. 147
Congress 13, 19, 20, 21, 33, 44, 47, 53, 57, m64, 65, 75, 80, 108, 123, 127, 140, 141, 150, 194, 212*n*, 215*n*, 216*n*, 217*n*, 219*n*
Connecticut 25
Connolly, Charles E. 147
Conquering Bear (Lakota chief) 97
Conquest of the Coeur d'Alenes, Spokanes, and Palouses 3, 38, 146, 201*n*, 204*n*, 217*n*
Conrad, Charles M. 94
Constitutional Union Party 183
Cooper, James Fenimore 15
Cooper, Col. Samuel 95–96, 98, 103–104, 106, 110–111, 115, 121, 140, 180, 182, 183, 185
Corps of Engineers *see* Engineering
Corpus, Christi, TX 66, 74
Correa de la Serra, Abbé Joseph 13
Cortez, Hernando 83
Creeks 40, 46
Crimean War 114
Crockett, Davy 66
Crook, Gen. George 174, 197, 221*n*
Crown Point (OR) 123
Cuauhtémoc 83
Cuban Liberation Army (Mambi) 215*n*

Cullum, Gen. George Washington 26–27
Cullum's Register 69, 203*n*, 208*n*, 210*n*
Cumming, Alfred 115, 118
Custer, Gen. George A. 171, 200, 220*n*

Dabney, George E. 207*n*
Dade, Maj. Francis L.; Dade Massacre 32, 39–43, 46, 56, 62, 168, 171, 205*n*
Dahmen, Theresa 5
The Daily Alta California 172
The Daily Picayune 73, m75, 85
Dan River (VA) 16
Danites 117
Dartmouth College 203*n*
Daughters of the American Revolution 192, 198, 220*n*
Davis, James A. "Cashup" 191
Davis, Jefferson 101, 110, 140, 154, 212*n*, 213*n*, 216*n*
Day, Terence L. 200
"The Day of the Comet and the Retreat of Steptoe" (TV documentary) 197
Democratic Party 44, 58, 59, 118, 121, 132, 183, 209*n*, 210*n*
DeMoy, Pvt. Victor C. 155
Dent, Capt. Frederick T. 142, 162
Department of War 105
DeRussy, Maj. René 23, 28
Deseret, State of 98
The Deseret News 102, 114
Dickinson College 215*n*
Dietrich, William 122
Dillon, Lester R. 86
Dillon, Mary *see* Steptoe, Mary Dillon
Dr. Rush's Anti-Dyspeptic or Sour Stomach Pills 16
Donation Land Claim Act 140
Donegana Hotel 184
Doughface 110
Douglas, Stephen A. 132, 150
Dow, Lorenzo 14
Downing, Andrew Jackson 131
Dozier, Jack 147, 166
Dutton, William 26, 36
Duval, Thomas J. 16

Early, Gen. Jubal A. (CSA) 2, 4, 29, 30, 34, 37, 43, 51, 185–187, 204*n*, 205*n*, 206*n*, 216*n*, 222*n*
The Early Indian Wars of Oregon 128
Eastern Washington State Historical Society 199
Eastern Washington University 197, 219*n*, 223*n*
Eccles, Catherine T. 190
L'École Polytechnique
Eden, Eden-like 72, 90

Index 239

Edinburgh Review 34
Egan Mountains (NV) 191
Egypt 84, 221*n*
8th US Infantry 56
Eldridge, Maj. John Wesley (CSA) 31, 139
Eldridge, Nannie Steptoe (EJ's half-sister) 2, 9, 18, 31, 38, 44, 45, 119, 138–139, 142–143, 146, 149–150, 174, 180, 181–182, 185, 201*n*, 204*n*, 208*n*
Elliott, T.C. 147
El Telégrafo (hill) 81
Elysium 42, 48
Emerald Isle 86
Encero 81
Engineering 22, 23, 26, 29, 30, 31, 34–35, 70, 72, 78, 85, 89, 92, 100, 166, 203*n*
England 34, 58, 211*n*
English 5, 14, 18, 41, 55, 131, 146, 191, 196, 200
Enquist, Jeff 5
Enquist, Col. Robert 5
Episcopalian 3, 14, 33, 37, 101, 150, 187, 190, 211*n*, 218*n*
Erebus 125
"An Essay on Man" 26
Europe 4, 30, 59, 181, 184–185, 221*n*
Evans, Elwood 189
Everett, Edward 35, 203*n*
Everglades 52, 54, 58

The Face of Battle 171
Farías, Valentín Gómez 75
Favorite, T.J. 192
Federal Hill 7, 10, 11, 201*n*
Fielding, Robert Kent 4, 93, 101, 105, 107–109, 115
5th [actually 4th] US Infantry 40
Fighting for Paradise 123, 147
Fillmore, Pres. Millard 88
Fillmore, UT 4, 92–93, 103–106
Finding Chief Kamiakin 147
Finley, Michael O. 147, 158, 160, 163
1st Pennsylvania Volunteers 74
First Seminole War 40, 41
1st US Artillery 49, 86
1st US Dragoons 142, 151, 164, 166, 172, 176, 180
1st Virginia Artillery 10
Flathead Indians, Kutenai 153, 172, 177
Fleming, Thomas J. 23, 25, 26, 34, 203*n*, 204*n*
Florida, Florida Territory 2, 4, 12, 17, 19, 25, 32, 34, 36, 37, 39–63, 64, 67, 68, 69, 70, 73, 74, 79, 80, 89, 91, 97, 103, 150, 183, 190, 204*n*, 205*n*, 206*n*, 207*n*, 209*n*
Florida Herald 50
Florida Historical Society 4

Florida Institute of Technology 4
Floyd, John B. 222*n*
Force Bill 21–22
Foreman, Grant 205*n*
Forest Depot VA 5, 7, 11, 180, 181, 183; *see also* New London
Fort Adams (RI) 63, 91, 210*n*
Fort Ann (FL) 55
Fort Arnold (NY) 25
Fort Benicia, Benicia Barracks *see* Benicia, CA
Fort Benton (MT) 148
Fort Boise (ID) 148
Fort Bridger (UT) 118
Fort Brooke (FL) 39, 40, 46, 49, 50, 57, 62, 63, 74
Fort Chokonikla (FL) 63
Fort Clinton (NY) 25
Fort Colville (WA) 125; *see also* Colville
Fort Dalles (OR) 122, 123, 125–131, 136–137, 145, 148, 171, 173
Fort Ellis (MT) 220*n*
Fort Erie (Canada) 40
Fort Foster (FL) 49
Fort Frazer (FL) 63
Fort Gardner (FL) 63
Fort Hall (ID) 145, 148
Fort Jones (CA) 151
Fort Kearny (NE) 96–97
Fort King (FL) 39
Fort Lane (OR) 116
Fort Laramie (WY) 97
Fort Leavenworth (KS) 95–97, 101, 118, 122, 210*n*
Fort Marion (FL, Castillo de San Marcos) 47–48, 62, 69, 79
Fort McHenry (MD) 61, 64, 69, 89, 208*n*
Fort Mellon (FL) 42, 46–49, 51
Fort Mellon, 1837–1842 48
Fort Monroe (AV, "Old Point Comfort") 58, 64, 90, 120
Fort Moultrie (SC) 41, 47, 62, 67, 69, 180
Fort Na-Chess 130
Fort Nez Perce, Old Fort Walla Walla (Hudson's Bay) 123, 130–132
Fort Payne (AL) 3
Fort Pierce (FL) 2, 4, 41, 43, 30–56, 58, 85, 186
Fort Pike (LA) 50
Fort Putnam (NY) 25
Fort Rains (WA) 129
Fort Riley (KS) 206*n*
Fort Simcoe (WA) 130, 173–174, 179, 220*n*
Fort Steilacoom (WA) 128–129
Fort Steptoe (WA) 134
Fort Stevens (DC) 186
Fort Sumter (SC) 2, 85, 181, 184

Index

Fort Taylor (WA) 174
Fort Tejon (CA) 111, 211*n*
Fort Texas (TX) 66
Fort Utah (UT) 94, 211*n*
Fort Vancouver, Vancouver Barracks (WA) 122, 123, 128–130, 135, 143, 157, 173
Fort Walla Walla 5, 12, 18, 63, 88, 118, 119, 120–145, 146, 148–156, 162–163, 165, 169–170, 172–175, 178, 180, 191, 217*n*, 221*n*
Fort Walla Walla Museum 5
Fort Wood (NY) 91, 92
44th Virginia Infantry 185
Foster, Stephen Collins 98
4th Alabama Infantry 211*n*
4th Illinois Volunteers 82
Fourth of July 89
4th US Artillery 71, 78
4th US Infantry 126, 142, 151, 173
Fowler, Don D. 211*n*
France 22, 37, 83, 114, 155, 160, 181, 222*n*
Franciscan 48, 84
Francke, Arthur E., Jr. 48
Franklin Hotel 15
Fraser, William D. 26, 27, 29–30
Free-soilers, Free-staters 121
Frey, Rodney 169, 197–199, 217*n*
From Behind the Veil: A Study of Afro-American Narrative 200
"Frontier Fury" 193
Frontier Steel 147, 163
Frontiersmen in Blue 147
Furniss, Norman F. 108

Gaines, Gen. Edmund 46
Gale, Robert L. 194
Garfield, WA 146
Garita de Niño Perdido 85–86
Garita de San Cosme 86
Garnett, Gen. Robert S. (CSA) 130, 174, 179, 215*n*, 220*n*
Gaston, Judge William 18, 203*n*
Gaston, Lt. William 18, 142, 160, 164, 166–168, 177–178, 194
Gatlin, Lt. R. C. 207*n*
General George Wright: Guardian of the Pacific Coast 147
Georgia 2, 40, 42, 46, 61, 69, 205*n*, 207*n*
Germany 16, 97, 131, 149, 191
Getty, Capt. George W. 63, 207*n*
Ghirardelli 116
Gibbon, Edward 34
Gibbs, George 130
Gibbs, Josiah 211*n*
Gilmer, Francis Walker 13
Girardin, Eugène de 137
"The Girl I Left Behind Me" 82
Gladwell, Elizabeth 9

Gleave, Randy 214*n*
Goliad, TX 65, 66
Grande Ronde, River (OR) 134, 137
Grant, Gen. Ulysses S. 86, 122, 142, 209*n*
Grattan, Lt. John Lawrence; Grattan Massacre 97, 168, 171
Great American Desert 44
The Great Outbreak 124
Great Salt Lake, Valley of the Great Salt Lake 83, 97–99, 111, 212*n*
Great Salt Lake City *see* Salt Lake City
Great Sioux War 221*n*
Greece 18, 23, 89
Green Mountain Boys 208*n*
Green River (WY) 96, 98, 128
Green River Indians 128
Greene, Gen. Nathaniel 10
Gregg, Gen. David McMurtrie 142, 146, 157, 164–168, 172, 176, 180, 189
Grier, Gen. William N. 142, 162, 176–177
Guadalupe Hidalgo 87
Gulf of Mexico 43, 52, 68
Gunnison, Capt. John; Gunnison Massacre 1, 28, 34, 92–119, 168, 171, 210*n*, 211*n*, 212*n*, 213*n*

"Hail, Columbia" 77
Halifax County (VA) 4
Haller, Maj. Granville 125–127, 171, 189, 215*n*
Halpatter (Alligator) 41, 46, 50
Hampton, VA 58, 184
Hampton Roads, VA 120
Hangman, Latah Creek 166, 221*n*
Hardee, Gen. William, Jr. (CSA) 2, 155
Harney, Gen. William S. 46, 54, 79, 80, 205*n*
Harpers Ferry, VA (WV) 33, 81, 182
Harper's New Monthly Magazine 172–173, 174
Harris, Lt. Joseph W. 50
Harrison, Pres. William Henry ("Old Tippecanoe") 55, 57
Haulover Canal (FL) 55
Havana, Cuba 182
Havens, Benny *see* Benny Havens tavern and song
Heintzelman, Samuel Peter 30
Henderson, Bvt. 2nd Lt. Richard 39–40
Hengen, Nona 197
Henry, Patrick 11
Henry, Will (Henry Wilson Allen) 193–195
Hernandez, Gen. Joseph 46–47
Hetzel, Abner 24, 25
Hill, Gen. D[aniel] H[arvey] (CSA) 4, 71, 77–79, 86–88, 184, 187
Hillsborough River 39, 49
Historical Collections of Virginia 8
History of England 34

History of the Pacific Northwest: Oregon and Washington 189
History of the United States 34
History of Utah 92
History of Washington, Idaho, and Montana 190
Hitchcock, Col. Ethan Allen 66, 81, 83, 208*n*
Holata Micco (Billy Bowlegs) 63
Hollman, Joseph 107–108, 109
Hollywood, CA 195
A Home Elsewhere: Reading African American Classics in the Age of Obama 200
Homestead Act 140
Hominy Hall (also Homany, Nominy) 9
Hook, Johnny 11–12
Hooker, Gen. Joseph 2, 28, 29, 34
Hote or Holata Emathla (Jumper) 41, 46, 50
Houston, Sam 33
Howard, Helen Addison 147
Howard, Gen. Oliver O. 196
Howe, Henry 25, 40
Huamantla, Mexico 87
Hudson River (NY) 25, 40
Hudson's Bay Company 122, 130, 132
Humboldt River (NV) 111, 116
Hume, David 34
Hunter, Gen. David A. 186–187
Huntington, Dimick 93
Hyde, Orson 100

Idaho 123, 135, 145, 147, 192
Idaho Yesterdays 147
Illinois 8, 17, 26, 30, 46, 82, 108
Indian Queen Hotel (Jess Brown's Indian Queen) 20
Indian River Lagoon (FL) 51, 52
The Indian Side of the Story 147, 216*n*
Indian Wars of Idaho 147, 156
Indies 76
Ingalls, Gen. Rufus 96–98, 115–118, 122, 211*n*
Ingossomen Creek (WA) 146, 163, 166
Iowa 212*n*
Ireland 73, 82, 195, 196
Israel 93, 107
Italy 181
Ivy Cliff 7, 10, 12, 202*n*

Jackson, Pres. Andrew 3, 11, 16, 20–21, 22, 29, 40, 41, 44, 70, 125, 203*n*
Jackson, Gen. Thomas "Stonewall" (CSA) 3, 86, 142, 210*n*, 221*n*
Jalapa 79–83, 89, 90
James, Wiley 16
James River (VA) 8, 14, 15, 25, 186
Jefferson, Pres. Thomas 2, 7–9, 11–13, 14, 22, 32, 187, 201*n*, 202*n*
Jefferson's Memorandum Book 8

Jenner, Edward 9–10
Jesuits 123, 141, 147, 175
The Jesuits and the Indian Wars of the Northwest 123, 147
Jesup, Gen. Thomas Sidney 46–50, 52, 54, 131, 206*n*
Joaquín de Herrera, José 66
John Calhoun Smith Memorial Fund 4
John Jumper 63
Johnson, Randall A. 147, 160
Johnson, Timothy D. 74
Johnston, Gen. Albert Sidney (CSA) 118
Johnston, Gen. Joseph E. (CSA) 86
Joint Base Leis-McChord (WA) 5
Jones, Gen. Roger 51, 90, 295*n*
Jones Memorial Library (Lynchburg, VA) 5, 13
Jordan, Gen. Thomas (CSA) 131, 215*n*
Joseph, OR 195
Josephy, Alvin 127, 135
Joset, Father Joseph, S.J. 141, 147, 154, 158–159, 164–166, 168–169, 171, 190, 195
Judd, Lt. 74
Jumper *see* Hote or Holata Emathla
Jupiter Inlet (FL) 51, 55

Kalispel, Pend Oreille Indians 153, 176, 189
Ka-mi-akin: Last Hero of the Yakimas 147
Kamiakin 124–130, 135–138, 141, 148, 158, 160–162, 172, 174–177, 189, 192, 194–196, 215*n*
Kanawha Canal (VA) 186
Kanosh 103–108, 110
Kansas, Kansas Territory 44, 95, 112, 121, 206*n*, 210*n*
Kansas City, MO 193
Kansas-Nebraska Act 112, 121
Kaskaskia, IL 26
Keais, Bvt. 2nd Lt. John 39–40
Kearny, Gen. Stephen 69, 96
Keegan, John 171
Kelly, Col. James K. 127, 215*n*
Kelly, Sgt. Matthew 129
Kendall, George Wilkins 73, 75, 83, 85, 89
Kenny, Sgt. Michael 168
Kentucky 21, 22, 58, 98, 203*n*
Kettle Indians 152
Key, Francis Scott 61
Keyes, Gen. Erasmus D. 174–175, 177, 220*n*
Khedive of Egypt 221*n*
KHQ television 197
Kickapoo Indians 207*n*
Kimball, Heber C. 102, 114
King Philip 46–48, 51
Kinney, Col. Henry 74
Kinney, John F. 103, 105–111, 114, 212*n*, 213*n*
Kinney's Post 66, 74

Index

Kip, Lt. Col. Lawrence 4, 122, 130–131, 151, 162, 173–176, 218n
kipuka 191
Kissimmee, FL 63
Kittitas (Upper Yakama) Indians 125
Klamath Indians 123
Klickitat Indians 123, 125, 126, 128, 215n
Knetsch, Joe 41, 52, 54, 56, 57, 58, 63, 206n
Knuth, Priscilla 131
Koledki, Theodore 219n
Kotzebue, August von 16
Kowrach, Edward J. 147
Kriebel, Mahlon E. 3, 4, 146, 147, 156, 158, 162–165, 169, 197, 218n, 219n
Kumpaskat, Jean Pierre 165
Kutenai Indians, Flathead 153, 172

La Grande, OR 134
Lake Monroe (FL) 47, 49
Lake Okeechobee (FL) 52, 56
Lakeland, FL 63
Laman 93
Lamebull, Shawn 199
Lane, Gen. Joseph 87, 88, 210n
Lansing, Jewel 122
La Piedad, Mexico 85
Laqunda (Lake) Hotel, Mexico City 88
Lassen Meadows (CA) 116
The Last of the Mohicans 15
Latah Creek *see* Hangman Creek
Latin 14, 18, 23
Latin America 13
Latter Day Saints, Church of Jesus Christ of 83, 98, 100, 104, 113, 119
Latter Day Saints Church History Library 5, 17, 213n
Laumer, Frank 205n
Lawyer (Nez Perce) 136, 144
Leatherstocking Tales 15
Lee, Gen. Robert E. (CSA) 3, 19, 30, 38, 78, 81, 84, 120, 186, 187, 206n, 207n
"The Leg I Left Behind Me" 82
Lester, Melvin 5
Levi 165
Levi Strauss 116
Lewis & Clark Expedition 12, 122–123, 128, 135, 159
Leyden, Anne 5, 200
Liberty, VA (now Bedford) 1, 7, 9, 11, 13, 17, 187, 222n
Library of Congress 47, 80, 197, 221n
Lichtenberger, Randy 5
Life in Utah; or, the Mysteries and Crimes of Mormonism 107
Lincoln, Pres. Abraham 46, 150, 183–184, 186, 204n
Lindermann, Erika 18

Lobos Island (Mexico) 74, 75–76
Lokout 136, 215n
London 181, 211n
London, Bill 200
The Lone Ranger and Tonto Fistfight in Heaven 192
Longhorne, Col, J.M. 182
Longfellow, Henry Wadsworth 65, 77
Longstreet, Gen. James (CSA) 86
Loring, Gen. William W. 181, 221n
Los Angeles, CA 111
Lost Cause 187
Louisiana 28, 71, 209n
Louisiana Purchase 13
Love, Andrew 106, 107–108
Lucifer 102
Lynch, Col. Charles 14
Lynch, John 14
Lynchburg, VA 1, 2, 3, 4, 5, 7–19, 25, 36–38, 45, 48, 51, 91, 180, 182–183, 186–187, 190, 194, 200, 202n
Lynchburg College 17, 182
Lynchburg Historical Foundation 222n
Lynchburg Daily Virginian see *The Virginian*
Lynch's Law 14

Machiavelli, Niccolò 190
Mackall, Gen. W[illiam] W[hann] (CSA) 130, 144–145, 148, 150, 153, 156–157, 171, 173, 217n
MacKinnon, William P. 119, 214n
Macomb, Gen. Alexander 52
Madison College 182
Magruder, Gen. John Bankhead 120–121, 184, 214n
Mahan, Dennis Hart 23
Mahon, John K. 39, 41, 50, 53, 54, 56, 205m, 206n
Maine 21, 36, 59
Malone, Dorothy 195
Manifest Destiny 1, 77, 189
Manring, B[enjamin] F[ranklin] 3, 4, 13, 17, 38, 146, 147, 154–155, 157–159, 163, 167–168, 181, 185, 187–188, 190–191, 201n, 204n, 207n, 208n, 217n, 220n
Marcy, William L. 102, 111–112
Marshall, George 195
Marszalek, John F. 55
Martin, Ann Smart 8–9
Martin, Joseph 14, 15
Marvin, Lee 195
Maryland, Marylander 142
USS *Massachusetts* 74
Matamoros, Mexico 66, 68, 71
Matanzas River 48
Matthews, Greg 5
Matthews, Prof. Lycurgus G. 182

Index 243

Maximilian, Emperor of Mexico 214n
McClellan, Gen. George B. 69–71, 73, 75, 76–78, 80, 125, 208n, 209n
McCroskey, Virgil T. 191
McCulloch, Capt. Ben 69
McDowell, Gen. Irvin 2
McFarland, Earl A. 4
McFarland, George 4
McFarland, Mary Maxine Stullenburger 4
McFarland, Tom 4
McReynolds, Edwin C. 50
McSherry, Richards 81, 83, 85–87, 210n
Meade, Gen. George 43, 70–72, 208n
Melkapsi 165
Mellon, Capt. Charles 48
Memphis, TN 139
Merritt Island, FL 55
Methodism 7, 14, 182
Mexican War 1, 19, 56, 64–91, 92, 96, 99, 100, 120, 124, 142, 150, 154, 174, 179, 184, 185, 186, 1887, 205n, 207n, 209n, 210n, 211n, 215n, m216n, 217n, 220n, 221n
Mexico 2, 11, 13, 32, 43–44, 51, 60, 62, 64–92, 103, 120, 134, 150, 181, 183, 184, 206n, 207n, 214n
Mexico City 3, 65, 69, 74, 75, 81, 82, 85, 87–90, 120, 123
Miami River (FL) 53
Micanopy 41, 46, 47
Miccosukees 40, 41, 56
Michigan 24, 25, 36, 213n
Mill Creek (WA) 134–135, 137, 152
Miller, David Henry 4, 101–109, 119, 211n
Miller, John 221n
Miller, Susan A. 207n
Miller-Clayton House 221n
Minorcan 48, 55
Mississippi 81, 154, 184, 203n
Mississippi, Yager rifle, Model 1841, .54 caliber 154
Missouri 21, 116, 142, 193
Missouri Compromise 21, 121
Missouri River 149
Mis-ta-kai-ya-wa 140
Mobile, AL 40
Mohawk and Hudson Railroad (NY) 33
Molino del Rey 85, 89, 206n, 208n
Monroe, Pres. James 13
Monroe Doctrine 13
Montana 147, 159, 177, 190, 196, 220n
Montana: The Magazine of Western History 147
Monterey, CA 67, 186
Monterrey, Mexico 68, 70, 71, 88, 186
Montezuma, "Halls of Montezuma" 83, 88
Monticello 7, 12
Montreal 184, 185

Morales, Gen. Juan 78
Mormonism 1, 3, 17, 83, 92–120, 121, 144–145, 148, 194, 211n, 212n, 213n, 214n
The Mormons or Latter-Day Saints 98, 117
The Morning Oregonian 192
Morris, Capt. Robert M. 92–93, 211n
Morrison, Alfred J. 207n
Morrison, James L., Jr. 23, 25, 33–35, 203n, 204n
Moscow-Pullman Daily News 200
Mosquito Lagoon (FL) 51
Motte, Jacob Rhett 42–43, 48–49, 51–52, 205n
Mountain Meadows Massacre 118–119
Mowry, Lt. Sylvester 96, 101–102, 106–111, 114–115, 117–118, 122, 130, 211n, 212n
Mudge, 2nd Lt. Robert R. 39–40
Mufaro's Beautiful Daughters 200
Mullan, Capt. John 153, 163, 166, 171, 174–175, 197, 219n, 220n
Mullan Road 149, 174, 195, 217n
Muscogee (Lower Creek) 41
Musketoon *see* Springfield Model 1847
"My Old Kentucky Home" 98

Naches River (WA) 130
Napoleon 30
Napoleon 34
Napoleon III 181
Nashville Convention 11
Nat Turner's Rebellion 17
National Archives 3, 4
National Bank 58
National Bridge (Puente Nacional) 81
National Road (Camino Real) 80–81
Native American 15, 125, 140, 196
Natural Bridge (VA) 13
Nauvoo, IL 17
Nauvoo Legion 118
Nebraska, Nebraska Territory 44, 96, 109, 112, 121
Negro Fort 41
Negroes 11, 16, 41, 50
Nelson, Kurt R. 4, 116, 123–124, 129, 147, 164
Nephi, UT 94, 103, 106, 107, 110
Nesmith, Col. James W. 126, 144
Nevada 111, 116, 191
New Bedford, MA 14
New London, VA 5, 7, 10–12, 13, 15, 17–19, 20, 37, 38, 67, 187
New London Academy 3, 7, 10, 15, 183, 207n
New Mexico, New Mexico Territory 66, 96, 109, 142
New Orleans, LA 12, 40, 50, 72, 73, 85, 89, 183, 211n
New Smyrna Beach, FL 51
New Year 50, 69, 90, 106, 145, 184

Index

New York 17, 23, 25, 32, 33, 53, 131, 182, 212*n*, 218*n*
New York City 3, 4, 33, 35, 59, 61, 91, 92, 94, 134, 144, 179, 180, 181, 182, 202*n*, 210*n*, 216*n*
New York Daily Times, *New York Times* 92, 109, 184, 210*n*, 211*n*, 213*n*, 222*n*
New York Daily Tribune 221*n*
New York Evening Post 100, 212*n*
New York Herald 172, 220*n*
New York Spectator 40, 205*n*
Newport, RI 91
Nez Perce Dick 137
Nez Perce Indians 125, 133, 135–137, 151–153, 156–159, 162, 165, 168–170, 172, 175, 190, 193–194, 196, 223*n*
Nez Perce Reservation 196
Niagara Falls, NY 181–182
Nicholas Nickleby 55
Niles Register 89
9th US Infantry 111, 112, 142, 151, 162, 164
Niños Héroes 86
Nisqually Indians 128
North Carolina 17–18
Northern Pacific Railroad 141, 153
Northern Paiute 148
Northern Plateau Indians 1, 13, 18, 124, 125, 160, 169, 173, 176, 179, 180, 187, 190, 197
Northwest Passage: The Great Columbia River 122–123
Norvell House 182
Nueces River (Mexico) 66
Nullification Crisis 21

Oakesdale, WA 159
Oblate order 125
Ocala, FL 39
Ocklawaha River (FL) 53
Ogden River (UT) 116
"Oh! Susannah" 98
Ohio 2
Ohio River 33
Oklahoma, Oklahoma Territory 44, 51
Old Chief Joseph 196
"Old Folks at Home" 98
Old High German 191
Oliver Twist 55
Olympia, WA 189
Ontario 43
Orange & Alexandria Railroad 182
Ord, Gen. Edward O.C. 43, 53
Ordway, Sgt. John 128
Oregon, Oregon Territory 13, 59, 116, 120, 122–130, 133, 134, 140, 147, 150, 174, 179, 180, 181, 189, 195, 196, 206*n*, 210*n*, 213*n*
Oregon City, OR 122, 215*n*
Oregon Territorial Volunteers 129

Oregon Trail 87
The Oregonian, *The Morning Oregonian* 171–172, 192
Orizaba, Mount 77, 89
Osceola 41, 46, 47
Oswandel, Pvt. Jacob 74–75, 77, 80–83, 88, 89, 90
Ottoman Empire 114
Owhi 125, 130, 160, 177

Pacific Northwest, Inland Pacific Northwest 132, 141, 147
Pacific Northwest Quarterly 158
The Pacific Northwesterner 147
Pacific Ocean 95, 116, 122, 130, 132, 143, 180
Pahvant Utes, Pah=Utahs 93, 94, 103, 104, 106, 109, 110, 115, 211*n*
"Painting in the Details" (DVD) 197
Paixhan guns 78
Paiutes (Pi=utes) 94, 104, 118, 144
Palatka, FL 53, 207*n*
Palouse country, hills, plain, region 1, 5, 156, 167, 172, 177, 192, 196
Palouse Indians 123–125, 128, 130, 136–137, 141, 148, 151–154, 156–162, 164–169, 174–177, 189–190, 194, 197
Palouse River (WA) 141, 148, 150, 162, 164
Panama, Isthmus of Panama 120, 122, 179, 180
Pandosy, Father 126
Panic of 1837 18, 21, 34, 35, 44, 45, 53, 58
Parades de Arrillaga, Mariano 66
Paris 30, 203*n*
Parsons, VA (WV) 179
Partch, Greg 4, 38
Paschal Stellam 165
Pataha Creek (WA) 156
Patterson, Gen. Robert 70–73, 78, 80, 88–89, 209*n*
Paulus, Michael J., Jr. 5
Pawnee Indians 97
Payne, Capt. George S. 63
Payne, James 5
Paynes Creek Historic State Park (FL) 63
Peace River (Pease Creek, FL) 52, 63
Peaks of Otter (VA) 13
Peltier, Jerome 147, m153, 218*n*
Peña y Peña, Manuel de la 75–76
Pennsylvania 20, 22, 24, 30, 32, 73, 74, 82, 84, 121, 142, 172, 180, 182, 203*n*, 209*n*, 210*n*, 213*n*, 215*n*
Peopeo Moxmox 127
Persia 89
Petersen, Keith 171, 220*n*
Philadelphia, PA 42, 49, 59, 76, 98, 185, 200, 201*n*, 204*n*, 222*n*
Philip of Macedonia 89
Pickett, Gen. George (CSA) 86

Index

Pickett, Stella Hardy 14
Picolata, FL 49
Piedmont 181
Pierce, Col. B[enjamin] K[endrick] 50
Pierce, Pres. Franklin 1–3, 83, 99, 101–102, 107, 111–113, 116, 117, 120–121, 124, 132, 139, 181, 188, 209*n*, 212*n*, 213*n*
Pillars of the Sky 193–195
Pillars of the Sky (film) 195–197
Pillow, Gen. Gideon J. 75, 81, 88, 209*n*
Pizarro; or, The Death of Rolla 16
Plains Indians 97, 128, 206*n*
Platte River (NE) 96–97
Plecker, A.H. 38
Plummer, ID 199
Pocatello, ID 145, 148
Poe, Edgar Allan 24, 34, 55
Poinsett, Joel 54, 206*n*
Point of Honor (VA) 15
Poland 61
Polatkin 160, 177
Polk, Pres. James K. 59, 63–66, 70, 71, 73, 75, 84, 88, 209*n*
Ponce de Leon Inlet 51
Pontiac 124
Poole, Lt. Benjamin 51
Pope, Alexander 26
Pope, Gen. John 26, 27
Poplar Forest (VA) 2, 9, 11, 12
Popocatepetl, Mount 89
Port (Point) Isabel, TX 66, 68, 207*n*
Portland, OR 120
Portugal 13
Potomac River 20, 186
Potter, Clifton 14
Potter, Dorothy 14
The Prairie 15
Presbyterian 14, 18, 187
Presbyterian Cemetery 187
Princeton University 10, 215*n*
Protestantism 159
Providence, RI 101
Provo, UT 94
Provo River 101
Prussia 61, 197
Puebla, Mexico 83, 87, 88
Puente Nacional, Mexico 81
Puget Sound (WA) 124, 128
Pullman, WA 192
Pyramid Peak, Steptoe Butte (WA) 151, 190, 199, 223*n*

Quaker 14
Qualchan 125, 136, 160, 166, 177, 193, 221*n*
Quebec 43
Quiltenenock 136
Quitman, Gen. John A. 81, 83–84, 88, 209*n*

Radford, Col. Richard Carlton 185
Radford's Rangers 185, 216*n*
Rains, Gen. Gabriel (CSA) 126–127
Ramsay, David 34
Randolph, John F. 137, 143, 150, 167, 180–181, 194, 217*n*
Rea, Gen. Joaquín 87
Red Sweet Springs 36, 45, 59, 91, 182
Red Wolf 156–157
Red Wolf's Crossing 156–157
Register of Officers and Cadets 29
Rember, Bill 5
Renegade Tribe: The Palouse Indians and the Invasion of the Pacific Northwest 147
Republican Party 121, 183
Republic of Texas *see* Texas
Revolutionary War 2, 8, 10, 11, 25, 100, 208*n*
Reynolds, Gen. John F. 107, 213*n*
Rhodes, William Barnes 16, 36
Richards, Kent D. 134, 136
Richmond, VA 5, 38, 181, 184, 186, 187, 222*n*
Richmond Daily Dispatch 181
Ringgold, Maj. Samuel 67, 208*n*
Rio Grande, Río Bravo 65–66
Roanoke, VA 181
Rock Lake (WA) 177
Rockwell, Orrin Porter 117, 213*n*–214*n*
Rocky Mountains 135, 149, 189, 220*n*
Rogue River (OR) 116, 124, 125
Rogue River Indians 127
Rogue River Wars 124, 213*n*, 218*n*
Rosalia, WA 1, 146, 158, 159, 161–162, 170, 192, 194, 196, 197, 198, 220*n*
Rose, Lucy Steptoe (EJ's half-sister) 143
Rosebush, Waldo E. 4, 134–135, 147, 154–155, 160, 162–164, 167–168
Ruby, Robert H. 136, 147, 153, 160
Rush Valley (UT) 98, 103, 114
Russell, Capt. Samuel L. 53
Russia 61, 114, 203*n*

Sacramento Daily Union 172, 183–184
Sacred Heart Mission *see* Cataldo
Sacrificios Island 77
The Saga of the Coeur d'Alene Indians 147
Sahaptin 126, 128, 159
St. Augustine, FL 3, 40, 47–50, 53–57, 62, 79, 205*n*, 207*n*, 221*n*
St. Francis Barracks (FL) 48, 62
St. Joe River (ID) 159
St. John River (FL) 42–43, 47–49
St. Joseph's Mission 125
St. Louis, MO 92, 120
St. Lucie River (FL) 50, 58
St. Paul's Episcopal Church (VA) 190
Salish 128, 136, 159
Salmon River (ID) 145

Index

Salt lake City, UT 1, 4, 5, 93–95, 97–103, 105, 111, 115–117, 120, 130, 191, 212*n*
Salt Lake Reporter 107
Salt Lake Tribune 117
San Agustín, Mexico 84
San Antonio, Mexico 85
San Francisco, CA 65, 116–117, 130, 144, 156, 173, 179, 180
San Francisco (steamship) 95, 142, 206*n*
San Francisco Herald 179
San Joaquin River (CA) 111
San Juan de Ulúa 77, 79
Sanders Creek (WA) 163
Sandy River (WY) 96
Sanford, FL 42
Santa Anna, Gen. Antonio López de 44, 65, 69, 75, 78, 80–84, 87
Sardinia 181
Savannah, GA 56, 61, 69, 207*n*
Scarritt, Jeremiah Mason 30, 39–40
Schenectady, NY 33
Scheuerman, Richard D. 147, 153, 156, 158, 160, 163, 167, 169, 215*n*
Schindler, Harold 117, 214*n*
Schlicke, Carl P. 147, 153
School, Louis 131
Scotland 41
Scott, Beverly R. 16
Scott, Sir Walter 34, 55
Scott, Gen. Winfield ("Old Fuss and Feathers") 46, 59, 65, 69, 71, 72, 74–75, 77–85, 87–88, 155, 171, 172, 184
Seattle, WA 122, 177
Sebastian 169
Second Italian War of Independence 181
Secretary of State 22, 58, 102, 111, 112
Secretary of War 22, 54, 94, 101, 110, 138, 140, 171, 183, 222*n*
Sedgwick, Gen. John 28–29
2nd Pennsylvania Infantry 82, 210*n*
Second Seminole War 2, 4, 12, 17, 19, 32, 37, 39–63, 64, 67, 68, 70, 92, 100, 150, 185, 204*n*, 205*n*
2nd US Dragoons 54
2nd US Infantry 53, 116
2nd Virginia Cavalry 36, 185, 216*n*
Seltice, Andrew 169, 219*n*
Seltice, Joseph 169, 219*n*
Seminoles 1, 2, 4, 32, 39–63, 97, 140, 186, 190
The Seminoles 50
Semmes, Adm. Raphael (CSA) 86
Senate (US) 3, 11, 20, 21, 22, 101, 132, 138, 215*n*, 216*n*, 217*n*, 219*n*
7th US Cavalry 196, 220*n*
79th New York Volunteers 82
Sevier Desert (UT) 93
Sevier River (UT) 93, 105

Sgalgalt 160, 164
Sharps Model m1853 .52 caliber carbine 154, 155, 179
Shaw, Col. Benjamin F. 133–134, 136–137
Shedden, David 205*n*
Shell Creek (NV) 191
Shelton, Robert S. 14
Shenandoah River (VA) 81
Shenandoah Valley (VA) 149, 186
Sheridan, Gen. Philip 2, 30, 120, 128–129, 214*n*, 218*n*
Sheridan, Richard Brinsley 16
Sherman, Gen. Thomas W. 43, 78, 206*n*
Sherman, Gen. William T. 2, 3, 30, 43, 54–55, 56–57, 85, 206*n*
Shoshones 94
Sibley, Gen. Henry H. (CSA) 28, 29
Siege of Vera Cruz *see* Vera Cruz
Sierra Madres 79
Silé, Sila, Seelah (WA) 165
Simcoe Creek (WA) 125
Simons, James 54, 85, 206*n*
Singleton, Matthew 59
Singleton, Richard 59
Sinkiuse Indians, Ile des Pierres 136
Sioux Indians 97, 206*n*, 221*n*
Sklassams Creek *see* Steptoe Creek
Skloom 130
slavery 8–12, 17, 18, 21, 31–32, 37, 40–41, 48, 61, 65, 90, 99, 112, 121, 131, 132, 172, 182, 200, 201*n*, 203*n*, 205*n*, 210*n*
Slidell, John 66
Smith, Joseph, Jr. 17, 114, 117
Smith, Justin H. 72, 75
Smithsonian Institute 20, 120
Smoke Signals 192
Snake Indians (Bannock, Northern Paiute, Shoshone) 148
Snake River (ID) 5, 148, 156–157, 162–164, 168, 173, 192
Snoqualmie Indians 123
Sohon, Gustav 161, 170, 197
South Carolina 21, 42, 67, 69, 180, 181, 183, 184, 207*n*, 211*n*, 222*n*
South Pass (WY) 98
Southern Democrats 183
Southern Literary Messenger 24
Spain 13, 40, 41, 42, 48, 65, 68, 77, 83, 87, 215*n*
Spalding, Rev. Henry Harmon 158, 223*n*
Spalding, Henry Hart 192, 223*n*
Die Spanier in Peru 16
Spence, Rick 4
Spinosa, Gen. 87
Splawn, A.J. 135–136, 138, 147–148, 160, 215*n*
Spokane, WA 122, 144, 146, 148, 175, 177, 192, 197, 221*n*
Spokane County 192; Pioneer Society 221*n*

Index

Spokane Garry 159–160, 176
Spokane Indians 128, 138, 148, 152–154, 158–160, 162–164, 169, 175–177, 189–190, 192
The Spokane Indians: Children of the Sun 147, 160
Spokane Plains 156, 163
Spokane River 125, 163, 166, 177
Sprague, John T. 50, 56–57, 60, 205n, 206n
Springfield Model 1847 musketoon 62, 154–155, 179, 197
Springfield Model 1855 rifle-musket 155, 175
Spur Award (Best novel of the American West) 193
Squaw Creek (WA) 163
Stansbury, Maj. Howard 98, 100, 117, 212n
The Star-Spangled Banner 61
Statue of Liberty 91, 94
steptoe (etymology) 191
steptoe (geology) 191
Steptoe, Ann "Nancy" Brown (EJ's mother) 9–10, 18
Steptoe, Charles Yancey (EJ's cousin) 185
Steptoe, Edmund Dillon (EJ's cousin) 10, 37
Steptoe, Frances (Fanny) Callaway (EJ's cousin) 185, 216n
Steptoe, George (EJ's uncle, father's twin) 9, 13, 15
Steptoe, George, Jr. (EJ's cousin) 13, 15
Steptoe, Col. James (EJ's great grandfather) 9
Steptoe, James Calaway (also Calloway) (EJ's uncle) 9,, 10, 30, 37
Steptoe, James "Jemmy" (EJ's paternal grandfather) 7–12, 32, 201n
Steptoe, Javaka 200
Steptoe, John 200
Steptoe, John Marshall (EJ's cousin, George's son) 9, 208n
Steptoe, Dr. John R. (EJ's half-brother, Jack) 9, 32, 37, 45, 60, 68, 150
Steptoe, Mary Catherine (EJ's half-sister, Kate) 10, 38, 45
Steptoe, Mary Dillon (EJ's stepmother) 10, 27
Steptoe, Mary Rosanna Claytor (EJ's wife) 38, 180, 182, 183, 185, 190, 222n
Steptoe, Michele 200
Steptoe, Dr. Patrick (EJ's half-brother) 9, 60, 150
Steptoe, Prof. Robert 200
Steptoe, Robert M., Jr. (Thomas Steptoe's great-great grandson) 5
Steptoe, Rosanna Eliza (EJ's daughter) 184, 187
Steptoe, Dr. Thomas Eskridge (EJ's half-brother) 5, 200, 201n
Steptoe, Dr. William (EJ's father) 7–19, 20, 27–28, 30–32, 35–36, 60–61, 119, 143
Steptoe, William, Jr. (EJ's half-brother) 11, 31, 32, 36, 37, 38, 44, 60–61, 68, 119, 139, 143, 150, 185, 190, 216n
Steptoe and Johnson (law firm) 200
Steptoe Battlefield 192
Steptoe Butte 147, 151, 190–192, 199, 200, 223n
Steptoe Canyon 157
Steptoe City (NV) 191, 223n
Steptoe County (WA) 192
Steptoe Creek (WA) 157, 192
Steptoe Grange (WA) 192
Steptoe Lodge #24 (NV) 191
Steptoe Valley (NV) 191
Steptoe Valley Mining & Smelter Company (NV) 191
Steptoe Village 192
Steptoe, WA 192
Steptoeville, WA 144, 191
Stevens, Hazard 125, 133–136, 215n
Stevens, Gov. Isaac Ingalls 2, 89, 124–127, 132–141, 144, 153, 157, 194, 197, 210n
Stories from the Life of Porter Rockwell (film) 214n
Stout, Hosea 106
Sullivan's Island (SC) 180
Superintendent of Indian Affairs 116, 124, 126, 144, 174
Survey of U.S. Army Uniforms, Weapon and Accoutrements 155
Suwanee River (FL) 54
Sweetwater River (WY) 96, 97
Switzerland 141
Symonds, Lt. 95
Syrian 196

Tacoma, WA 122
Tales of the Grotesque and Arabesque 55
Tallahassee, FL 39, 41, 53
Tampa, FL 39, 56
Tampa Bay 50, 62
Tampico, Mexico 68–76, 90, 208n
Tanner, Madlyn 5
Tanner, Stephen 5
Taos, NM 142
Tariff of Abominations 21
Tariff of 1832 21
Taylor, Capt. Francis 84–86, 206n
Taylor, Lt. George 54, 58
Taylor, Capt. Oliver Hazard Perry 142, 145, 148, 164, 166–168, 172, 174, 177–178, 194
Taylor, Pres. Zachary ("Old Rough and Ready") 46, 49–50, 52, 54, 58, 65–71, 78, 88
Tecumseh 124
El Telégrafo (hill) 81
Tennessee 28, 66, 75, 139, 183, 185
10th US Infantry 184–185
Texas 32, 33, 44, 45, 62, 64, 65, 66, 69, 73, 74, 207n

Index

Texas Rangers 69, 73–74
Thatcher, Daniel A. 25
Thayer, Gen. Sylvanus 22–23, 28, 29, 55, 203*n*, 210*n*
Third Seminole War 47, 63
3rd US Artillery 40, 43, 54, 56, 58, 60, 62, 67, 70, 73, 79, 90, 95, 111, 116, 142, 174, 206*n*
30th Virginia Volunteers 185
Thomas, Gen. George H. 43, 60, 208*n*
Thomas, Jesse 5
Thomas, John 40
Thomas, Gen. Lorenzo 134
Thoreau, Henry David 65–66, 77
Tiffany (Toppe), Georgia 4
Tilcoax 141, 148, 158–160, 164–165, 174–177, 197
Tillamook Indians 123
Timothy (Tammutsa) 148, 156–159, 162, 168–170, 189, 190, 193–196, 218*n*
To Follow a Flag 193
tobacco 1, 10, 12, 14–15, 17, 180, 182
Tohotsnimme *see* Battle of Tohotsnimme
Tohotsnimme Creek 151, 164, 167, 169, 170
Toluca, Mexico 90
Tompkins, Capt. Charles Quarles 67–68, 208*n*
Tompkins, Ellen Wilkins 67–68
Toppenish Creek (WA) 126
Tories, Tory 14
Touchet River (WA) 156, 174
Trafzer, Clifford E. 147, 153, 156, 167, 169, 214*n*
Trail of Tears 3, 51
Travels Through North & South Carolina, Georgia, East & West Florida ("Bartram's Travels") 42
Treaties and Treachery 147
Treaty of Guadalupe-Hidalgo 88
Treaty of Payne's Landing 41
"The Trial of Thomas Builds-the-Fire" 192–193
Trist, Nicholas 84
Tucannon River (WA) 156, 174, 177
Turner, Nat 17
Tuspan (Tuxpan), Mexico 73
22nd Virginia Infantry 208*n*
Twiggs, Gen. David E. 63, 70, 78, 80, 85, 209*n*
Tyler, Pres. John 55, 57, 58, 64–65

Umatilla Indians 123, 125, 128, 134–136, 140
Union Flat Creek (WA) 157
Union Gazette (Lynchburg, VA) 15
Union Restaurant (Tampico, Mexico) 73
Union (Tabernacle, Temple) Square (Salt Lake City) 97

Uniontown, PA 182
United States 1, 5, 14, 22, 32, 34, 47, 48, 50, 59, 64, 65, 68–69, 71, 84, 88, 89, 105, 108, 130, 132, 179, 181, 205*n*, 208*n*
United States Hotel (Tampico, Mexico) 73
United States Military Academy (see West Point)
Universal International 195
University of Idaho 4, 5
University of Mexico 87
University of North Carolina 17, 59
University of Pennsylvania 10
University of Washington 2
US 195 192
Utah, Utah Territory 1, 3, 4, 5, 17, 83, 92–120, 121–122, 131, 144, 145, 148, 150, 188, 211*n*, 212*n*, 213*n*
Utah Expedition 119, 213*n*, 214*n*
Utah Historical Quarterly 94, 98
Utah Historical Society 99, 104
Utah Lake 93
Utah War, Mormon War 112, 116, 118, 119, 144, 148, 214*n*
Utahs *see* Pahvant Utes
Utley, Robert M. 4, 96, 124, 125, 135, 147, 151, 153, 155, 215*n*, 221*n*

Van Buren, Pres. Martin 32, 35, 44, 45
Vancouver, WA 4
Van Horne, Maj. Jefferson 50
Vera Cruz, Veracruz, Siege of Vera Cruz (Mexico) 3, 60, 68, 69, 71–81, 88–90, 142, 216*n*
Vermont 100
Viceroyalty of New Spain 13
Victor 165, 166
Victor, Francis Fuller 128–130, 147, 158, 214*n*
Victoria 43
Vincent 154, 159–160, 162, 164–165, 169
Virginia 1, 2, 5, 7–19, 20, 23, 29–31, 33, 36, 38, 41, 44, 48, 51, 53, 55, 57, 58, 64, 67, 72, 80, 90, 91, 120, 132, 143, 149–150, 155, 167, 179–188, 194, 195, 200, 207*n*, 215*n*
Virginia Historical Society 222*n*
Virginia House of Burgesses 8
Virginia House of Delegates 10
Virginia Military Institute 186
Virginia Peninsula 184
The Virginian (*Lynchburg Daily Virginian*) 14–17, 187
Voltaire 84

Waiilatpu mission (OR) 123, 138
Waite, Catherine 107, 108, 112
Wa-kara (Walker, Pahvant chief) 94, 103–104, 105

Index

Walker, Dale L. 193–194
Walker War 94, 103, 104
Wall, Lt. William 51
Walla Walla, WA 1, 2, 4, 87, 197, 220*n*
Walla Walla Councils 125, 133–138, 170, 173
Walla Walla Indians 189
Walla Walla: Portrait of a Western Town, 1804–1899 152
Walla Walla River, valley 130, 131, 132, 137, 138, 149, 156
Walla Walla State Penitentiary 193
Wallowa Mountains (OR) 196
War of 1812 22, 23, 40, 46, 51, 56, 209*n*, 216*n*
The War with Mexico 72
Warbonnets and Epaulettes 147
Wasatch Range (UT) 98
Wasco County–Dalles City Museum Commission (OR) 215*n*
Washington, Washington Territory 1, 2, 3, 4, 5, 12, 18–19, 62, 87, 89, 118, 120–145, 146–178, 184, 189–192, 196–200, 201*n*, 223*n*
Washington College (Washington and Lee University) 186, 207*n*
Washington, DC 2, 4, 11, 19, 20–21, 25, 37, 59, 72, 105, 120, 121–122, 141, 180, 185, 186
The Washington Historian 158
Washington Historical Quarterly 147
Washington Route 193 157
Washington State Parks 190–191
Washington State University 192, 199, 200
Wawawai Road 157
Wayles, John 12
Weber River (UT) 98, 116
Webster, Sen. Daniel 11, 21, 58
Weippe Prairie (ID) 135
Wells Fargo 116
West Point (United States Military Academy) 1, 2, 4, 5, 10, 11, 17–19, 20–38, 39, 43, 55, 59–62, 64, 67, 69–71, 78, 83, 85, 86, 89, 92, 96, 99, 100, 122, 124, 128, 130, 142, 167, 174, 179, 184, 185, 190, 194–195, 204*n*, 205*n*, 206*n*, 207*n*, 208*n*, 210*n*, 211*n*, 213*n*, 214*n*, 216*n*, 218*n*, 220*n*, 221*n*
West Point Hotel 24
West Virginia 36, 44, 179
Westmoreland County (VA) 9
Wheeling, VA (WV) 33
Whelan, Joseph 65, 76–77, 78, 208*n*
Whidden, Dempsey 63

Whigs 21, 55, 57, 58, 65, 88, 121, 183, 186
Whitaker, Ernest J. 190
White, David A. 98
White House 20, 55, 69, 102, 120, 121, 203*n*, 211*n*, 217*n*
White Sulphur Springs 36, 44, 45, 48, 51, 59, 91, 182, 205*n*
Whitman, Dr. Marcus 87, 123
Whitman, Narcissa 87, 123
Whitman College (WA) 5
Whitman County (WA) 192
Whitman County Historical Society 3
Whitman Massacre 88, 123, 132
Wilkins, Sen. William 22, 203*n*
Willamette River (OR) 122
William and Mary College 2, 7
Williams, J. Gary 5
Williams, Sgt. William C. 166
Williamsburg, VA 7
Wilmington, NC 184
Winder, Capt. Charles S. 142,, 162–165, 167–168
Winders, Robert 73, 208*n*, 209*n*
Withlacoochee River, Cove of (FL) 46, 56
Wool, Gen. John 69, 124, 127–128, 132–135, 138, 140–141, 144, 216*n*
Wordsworth, William 123
Worth, Gen. William Jenkins 56, 58–60, 70, 77, 83–85, 88
Wright, Col. George 121, 122–123, 128–131, 133–138, 146–147, 151, 153, 155, 161, 171, 173–177, 179, 187, 190, 192, 197, 217*n*

Yakima, WA 125, 130, 215*n*
Yakima Indians 124–130, 133–136, 138, 141, 148, 153, 160, 161, 171, 174, 175, 177, 189, 199, 215*n*
Yakima Indian Agency 130
Yakama Indian Reservation 215*n*
Yakima River (WA) 130, 215*n*
Yakima War 126, 161
"Yankee Doodle" 77
Yankees 21, 81, 89
Ye Galleon Press 158
Young, Brigham 1, 2, 5, 17, 83, 93–94, 100–101, 105–109, 111–112, 114, 117–119, 213*n*
Young Chief Joseph 196
Yuchi Billy 48

Zane Grey's Western Magazine 193